Josh G.

Josh O.

Software Specification Methods

Software Specification Methods

Edited by
Henri Habrias
Marc Frappier

First published in Great Britain and the United States in 2006 by ISTE Ltd

ISTE Ltd
6 Fitzroy Square
London W1T 5DX
UK

ISTE USA
4308 Patrice Road
Newport Beach, CA 92663
USA

www.iste.co.uk

Library of Congress Cataloging-in-Publication Data

Software specification methods / edited by Henri Habrias, Marc Frappier.
p. cm.
Includes index.
ISBN-13: 978-1-905209-34-7
ISBN-10: 1-905209-34-7
1. Formal methods (Computer science) 2. Computer software--Specifications. I. Habrias, Henri. II. Frappier, Marc, 1965-
QA76.9.F67S64 2006
004'.01'51--dc22

2006009290

British Library Cataloguing-in-Publication Data
A CIP record for this book is available from the British Library
ISBN 10: 1-905209-34-7
ISBN 13: 978-1-905209-34-7

Printed and bound in Great Britain by Antony Rowe Ltd, Chippenham, Wiltshire.

To Jean-Raymond Abrial,

for his dedication to moving formal methods
from an academic dream to an industrial reality

To Jean-Raymond Abrial

Preface

Objectives of this book

This book is an introduction to a set of software specification methods. Its targeted audience are readers who do not wish to read pages of definitions in order to understand the basics of a method. The *same case study* is used to introduce each method, following a rigorously uniform presentation format. Special care has been devoted to ensure that specifications do not deviate from the case study text. As much as the method allows, what is specified is what appears in the case study text. The benefits are twofold. First, the reader can easily switch from one method to another, using his knowledge of the case study as a leverage to understand a new method. Second, it becomes easier to compare methods, because the same behavior is specified in each case.

Each method presentation follows the same pattern. The concepts are progressively introduced when they are needed. To illustrate the specification process, questions that the specifier should raise during the analysis of the case study are stated. Answers are provided as if they were given by an imaginary client. The question/answer process guides the derivation of the specification. Interestingly, the questions raised depend on the method, which is illustrative of the differences between them. When a question is raised in one method and not in another, the reader has an issue to resolve: does the other method allow this question? If so, what should the answer be? As such, this book is a trigger to stimulate the reader's curiosity about specification methods; it does not intend to provide all the answers. More elaborate materials are referenced in each chapter for a deeper coverage.

Some definitions

A specification *method* is a sequence of activities leading to the development of a product, called a specification. A method should provide enough guidance on how to conduct the activities and on how to evaluate the quality of the final product. A *specification* is a precise description, written in some notation (language), of the client's requirements. A notation is said to be *formal* if it has a formal syntax and formal semantics. A notation is said to be *semi-formal* if it only has a formal syntax.

Several characteristics of a system can be specified. One may distinguish between functional requirements, efficiency requirements and implementation requirements. Functional requirements address the input-output behavior of a system. Efficiency requirements address the execution time of a system. The client may be interested in specifying a time bound for obtaining a response from the system. Some authors argue[1] that a specification without time bounds is not an effective specification: indeed, strictly speaking, if the specification does not include a time bound, the implementation may take an arbitrary duration to provide a response. It is impossible to distinguish between an infinite loop and a program that takes an arbitrary time to respond. Implementation requirements address issues like the programming language to use, the software components to reuse, the targeted hardware platform, the operating systems. The methods described in this book address functional requirements.

Specifications as contracts

A specification constitutes a *contract* between the client and the specifier. As such, the client must be able to understand the specification, in order to validate it. Typically, clients are not sufficiently versed in specialized notations to understand a specification. There are several ways to circumvent this lack of familiarity. The least is to rephrase the specification in the client's natural language, avoiding ambiguities as much as possible. If the specification is executable, scenarios can be tested with the client. The use of examples and counter-examples is a good technique to ensure that the client and the specifier understand each other.

The specification is also a contract between the specifier and the implementor. Of course, it is expected that the implementor understands the notation used for the specification. The implementor may not be familiar at all with the client's requirements and his application domain. The natural langage description provided to the client is also essential to the implementor, because it justifies and explains the specification. It allows the implementor to map specification concepts to application domain concepts. The textual description is to a specification what explanations are to formulas in mathematics.

Risks of not using specifications

Developing a software system without a specification is a random process. The implementation is doomed to be modified, sometimes forever, because it never precisely matches the client's needs. The goal of a specification is to capture the client's requirements in a concise, clear, unambiguous manner to minimize the risks of failure in the development process. It is much cheaper to change a specification than to change an implementation.

Additionally, the specification must leave as much freedom as possible to the implementor, in order to find the best implementation in terms of development cost, effi-

[1] Hehner E.C.R. (1993) *A Practical Theory of Programming*. Springer-Verlag

ciency, usability and maintainability. Abstraction is a good mechanism to support implementation freedom. For instance, if a sort function must be specified, the specifier need not to specify that a particular sort algorithm should be used. The implementor is free to pick any sorting algorithm like quicksort or bubblesort. Non-determinism is another good mechanism to provide more freedom for the implementation. For instance, one may specify a function that changes a dollar for a set of coins by just stating that the sum of the coins is equal to one dollar. The specification need not to prescribe how the set of coins is selected. During the implementation, an algorithm that minimizes the number of coins may be used, or one that gets rid of five-cent coins first, in order to minimize the weight of the coins in the machine (just for the sake of the argument).

Even when the implementation is finished, the specification is very useful. Conducting maintenance without a specification is a risky, expensive business. To modify a program, one must first know what it does.

Validation of a specification

A fundamental issue is to make sure that the specification "matches" the client's needs. This activity is called *validation*. Note that we use the verb "match" instead of a stronger verb like "prove", or "demonstrate", in the definition of the validation concept. By its very nature, a specification cannot be "proved" to match the client's requirements. If such a proof existed, then it would require another description of the requirements. If such a description is available, then *it is* a specification.

A specification is the starting point of the development process. It has the same status as axioms of a mathematical theory. They are assumed to be right. Of course, one can prove that a specification is *consistent* (i.e., that it does not include a contradiction), just as one can prove that the axioms of a theory are consistent. But this is a different issue from validation.

Validation consists essentially of stating *properties* about the specification, and proving that the specification satisfies these properties. Properties describe usage scenarios at various levels of abstraction. They can refer to concrete sequences of events, or they can be general statements about the safety or the liveness of the system.

The more properties are stated, the more the confidence in the specification validity is increased. Properties are like theorems of a theory: they must follow from the specification. In summary, validation is an empirical process; a specification is deemed valid until one finds a desired property that is not satisfied.

Satisfaction of a specification

It must be possible to demonstrate that the implementation *satisfies* the specification. A first approach is to progressively *refine* the specification until an implementation is reached. If it is possible mathematically to prove that each refinement satisfies the specification, we say that the development process is *formal*. Another approach is to test the implementation. *Test cases* are derived from the specification. The results obtained by running the implementation for these test cases are compared with the results prescribed by the specification. Such a development process is said to be *informal*. For most practical applications, it is not feasible to exhaustively test a system.

From a theoretical viewpoint, proving the correctness of an implementation is more appropriate than testing it. From a practical viewpoint, testing is easier to achieve. Since Gödel and Turing, we know the strengths and the limitations of formal development processes. For more than 30 years now, computer scientists have investigated the application of mathematics to the development of software systems, with the ultimate goal of developing techniques to prove that an implementation satisfies a specification. Progress has been made, but much remains to be done.

Tools

A semi-formal notation may be supported by tools like editors and syntax checkers. A formal notation, thanks to its formal semantics, may also be supported by interpreters, theorem provers, model checkers and test case generators. Support for informal notations is limited to general purpose editors using templates for documents.

Structure of the book

This book is divided in four parts. The first part includes state-based specification methods. In these methods, the description of the system behavior is centered around the notion of state transition. The operations (also called functions) of the system are specified by describing how their execution change the state of the system.

The second part is dedicated to event-based methods. An event is a message that is exchanged between the environment and the system. Event-based methods describe which events can occur and in what order. Some of these methods are related to state-based specifications, as they also describe state transitions. Others use process algebras or traces to describe the possible sequences of events.

The third part includes methods based on three quite different paradigms. The first method uses an algebraic approach. The system is described using sorts, operations and equations. Abstract data types are classical examples of algebraic specifications. The second method is based on higher-order logic and typed lambda calculus. Operations are defined as functions on the system state. The last two are based on Petri nets. A Petri net is a graph with two kinds of vertices: places and transitions. Tokens are assigned to places. The behavior of the system is represented by the movement of tokens between places using transitions.

To help the reader in understanding and comparing the methods, the last part provides a qualitative comparison of the methods based on a number of attributes such as paradigm, formality, provability, verification and graphical representation. It also includes a glossary of the most important concepts used in the chapters, providing a definition of their contextual usage.

Summary of changes in the second edition

The first edition of this book was published by Springer-Verlag London in 2001. This new edition welcomes six new chapters: four new methods (ASM, Event B, TLA+, and UML-Z), the comparison and the glossary. Finally, existing chapters have been revised to adjust their contents to reflect recent developments.

The case study

The next sections reproduce the text of the case study that was submitted to authors and the guidelines for preparing their specifications. The case study seems very simple the first time through. When reading the various solutions, one quickly finds that its detailed analysis is surprisingly stimulating.

The text of the case study

1. The subject is to invoice orders.
2. To invoice is to change the state of an order (to change it from the state "pending" to "invoiced").
3. On an order, we have one and one only reference to an ordered product of a certain quantity. The quantity can be different to other orders.
4. The same reference can be ordered on several different orders.
5. The state of the order will be changed into "invoiced" if the ordered quantity is either less or equal to the quantity which is in stock according to the reference of the ordered product.
6. You have to consider the two following cases:
   (a) Case 1
   All the ordered references are references in stock. The stock or the set of the orders may vary:

   - due to the entry of new orders or cancelled orders;
   - due to having a new entry of quantities of products in stock at the warehouse.

   However, we do not have to take these entries into account. This means that you will not receive two entry flows (orders, entries in stock). The stock and the set of orders are always given to you in a up-to-date state.
   (b) Case 2
   You do have to take into account the entries of:

   - new orders;
   - cancellations of orders;
   - entries of quantities in the stock.

The guidelines for preparing specifications

Perhaps you will consider that the case study text is incomplete or ambiguous. One goal of this exercise is to know what questions are raised by each method.

You may propose different solutions (expressing consistent requirements) and you will explain how your method(s) have brought you to propose these solutions.

The questions that you had to deal with in order to solve the case study should be stated according to the following guidelines:

- Questions must be on the problem domain. They are directed to the user. They must be specific.
- Questions are better answered by several answers (options); pick one answer to continue the analysis.
- Show what verifications your method has allowed you to do (e.g., detection of inconsistencies in the answers that you have chosen).

Finally, do not extend the domain. For example, do not specify stock management (e.g., when to restock, following what minimum quantity, etc.), do not add new information such as category of customer, category of product, payment modality, bank account, etc.

Warning

This book illustrates some specification methods using a single case study. Although it is an excellent approach, from a pedagogical viewpoint, to provide an overview and a basic comparison of methods, the reader should not conclude that it is sufficient to evaluate and select specification methods. Each method has it strengths and weaknesses. A single case study cannot claim to properly represent all of them.

Wishing to contribute?

We would like this project to continue to evolve. If you wish to solve this case study using your favorite method, please check the book's web page at:

`http://www.dmi.usherb.ca/~spec`

Your contribution and comments are welcome. The case study, guidelines, new solutions, comments about solutions and additional materials about specification methods will be available at this address.

Acknowledgements

This book is part of a long story. In 1994, Henri Habrias proposed to the community of software engineering the Invoicing case study. The first solution, with *SA/RT* and *SCCS*, was submitted by Andy Galloway (University of York, UK) and distributed to the participants of the École d'été *CEA-EDF-INRIA* in June 1995. Three years later, an International Workshop on Comparing Systems Specification Techniques, titled *"What questions are prompted by one's particular method of specification?"* was co-organized in Nantes by M. Allemand, C. Attiogbé and H. Habrias in March 1998[2].

This book was developed and refined in a collaborative effort. Each contributor has reviewed chapters of other contributors. Their mutual suggestions and comments have significantly enriched the final version of this book. Andy Galloway and Steve Dunne kindly reviewed several chapters. Panawe Batanado provided precious help for typesetting of the final version, enjoying the intricate pleasure of LaTeX. We are grateful to all these people.

Marc Frappier
Henri Habrias
Sherbrooke and Nantes
March 2006

[2]M. Allemand, C. Attiogbé and H. Habrias, editors, (Invoice'98) International Workshop on *Comparing Systems Specification Techniques — What Questions are Prompted by One's Particular Method of Specification?*, Nantes, France, 26-27 March 1998, ISBN 2-906082-29-5.

Contents

List of Contributors

- **Nuno Amálio**
  University of York
  Department of Computer Science
  York, YO10 5DD
  UK

- **Hubert Baumeister**
  Institut für Informatik
  Ludwig-Maximilians-
  Universität München
  Oettingenstr. 67
  80538 München
  Germany

- **Didier Bert**
  CNRS, Laboratoire
  Logiciels-Systèmes-Réseaux
  BP 72
  38402 Saint-Martin d'Hères
  France

- **Egon Börger**
  Università di Pisa
  Dipartimento di Informatica
  56127 Pisa
  Italy

- **Jonathan P. Bowen**
  London South Bank University
  Institute for Computing Research
  Faculty of BCIM, Borough Road
  London SE1 0AA
  UK

- **Dominique Cansell**
  Université de Metz
  LORIA
  57045 Metz
  France

- **Annie Choquet-Geniet**
  ENSMA et Université de Poitiers
  Laboratoire d'Informatique Scientifique
  et Industrielle
  Futuroscope
  France

- **Hassan Diab**
  Université de Sherbrooke
  Département d'informatique
  Sherbrooke, Québec, J1K 2R1
  Canada

- **Marc Frappier**
  Université de Sherbrooke
  Département d'informatique
  Sherbrooke, Québec, J1K 2R1
  Canada

- **Angelo Gargantini**
  Università di Bergamo
  Dipartimento di Ingegneria
  gestionale e dell'informazione
  viale Marconi 5
  24044 Dalmine (BG)
  Italy

• **Frédéric Gervais**
CEDRIC, CNAM-IIE
18 Allée Jean Rostand
91025 Evry Cedex
France
and
Université de Sherbrooke
Département d'informatique
Sherbrooke, Québec, J1K 2R1
Canada

• **Henri Habrias**
Université de Nantes
Laboratoire d'Informatique de
Nantes Atlantique (LINA)
2, rue de la Houssinière
B.P. 92208
44322 Nantes Cédex 3
France

• **Régine Laleau**
Université de Paris 12
Laboratoire LACL
IUT Fontainebleau
Route forestiere Hurtault
77300 Fontainebleau
France

• **Eric Lallet**
Institut National des Telecoms
Département Logiciels-Réseaux
91011 Evry
France

• **Leslie Lamport**
Microsoft Research
1065 La Avenida
Mountain View, California 94043
U.S.A.

• **Amel Mammar**
Université du Luxembourg, SE2C
6 rue Richard Courdenhove-Kalergi
1359 Luxembourg-Kirchberg
Luxembourg

• **Dominique Méry**
Université Henri Poincaré Nancy 1
LORIA
54506 Vandoeuvre-lès-Nancy
France

• **Jean-François Monin**
Université Joseph Fourier Grenoble 1
Verimag
2 avenue de Vignate
38610 Gières
France

• **Laurence Pierre**
Université de Nice
Département d'informatique
Parc Valrose
06108 Nice cedex 2
France

• **Pascal Poizat**
Université d'Évry Val d'Essonne
LaMI UMR 8042 CNRS
Genopole, Tour Évry 2
523 place des terrasses de l'Agora
91000 Évry
France

• **Fiona Polack**
University of York
Department of Computer Science
York, YO10 5DD
UK

• **Jean-Luc Raffy**
Institut National des Telecoms
Département Logiciels-Réseaux
91011 Evry
France

• **Elvinia Riccobene**
Università di Milano
Dipartimento di Tecnologie
dell'Informazione
via Bramante 65
26013 Crema (CR)
Italy

- **Pascal Richard**
  Laboratoire d'Informatique
  Scientifique et Industrielle
  ENSMA et Université de Poitiers
  France
- **Richard St-Denis**
  Université de Sherbrooke
  Département d'informatique
  Sherbrooke, Québec, J1K 2R1
  Canada
- **Christophe Sibertin-Blanc**
  Université Toulouse 1
  Sciences Sociales
  Institut de Recherche en Informatique
  Place A. France
  31042 Toulouse Cedex
  France
- **Mihaela Sighireanu**
  Université de Paris 7
  LIAFA
  2 Place Jussieu
  75251 Paris
  France
- **Jane Sinclair**
  University of Warwick
  Department of Computer Science
  Coventry, CV4 7AL
  UK
- **Susan Stepney**
  University of York
  Department of Computer Science
  York, YO10 5DD
  UK
- **Kenneth J. Turner**
  University of Stirling
  Computing Science and Mathematics
  Stirling, FK9 4LA
  UK

Part I

State-Based Approaches

Chapter 1

Z

Jonathan P. BOWEN

Oui, l'oeuvre sort plus belle
D'une forme au travail
Rebelle,
Vers, marbre, onyx, émail.

[Yes, the work comes out more beautiful from a material that resists the process, verse, marble, onyx, or enamel.]

– Théophile Gautier (1811–1872) *L'Art*

1.1 Overview of the Z notation

Z (pronounced 'zed') is a formal specification notation based on set theory and first order predicate logic. The mathematical notation is supported by a library of operators known as the 'Z toolkit', which is largely formally defined within the Z notation itself [ISO 02, SPI 01]. The operators have a large number of algebraic laws which aid in the reasoning about Z specification. As well as the mathematical notation, there is a '*schema*' notation to aid in the structuring of the mathematics for large specification by packaging the mathematical notation into boxes that may be used and combined subsequently.

There are many Z textbooks, some of which are available online (see for example, [BOW 03, JAC 97, LIG 00, WOO 96]). A widely used reference book is also accessible online [SPI 01]. Z has subsequently undergone a lengthy international ISO standardization process culminating in 2002 [ISO 02], which could help in the development of further tools to support the notation. In particular, an open source *Community Z Tools* (CZT) initiative is underway, based around XML [MAL 05]. Z has been extended in a number of ways, especially with object-orienting features (e.g.,

Object-Z [SMI 00]). The theoretical basis of Z has been explored extensively (e.g., see [HEN 03]). A range of case studies and a Z glossary may be found in [BOW 03].

1.1.1 The process of producing a Z specification

Z is typically used in a modelling style [BOW 04] in which an *abstract state* is included, containing enough information to describe changes in state that may be performed by a number of *operations* on the system. Each of the operations defines a *relation* between a *before* and *after* version of the state. The state may contain *invariants* which are predicates relating the various components in the abstract state which should always apply regardless of the current state of the system.

An *initial state* is defined as a special case of the more general abstract state, with the addition of extra constraining predicates. The description of the system is then modeled by this initial state, followed by an arbitrary interleaving of the operations in any order, only limited by any *preconditions* imposed by individual operations.

Often operations are designed to be *total* (i.e., with a precondition of *true*) so that they can be applied in any situation. This is especially useful in maintenance of the implemented operations (which could typically be procedure calls, for example) since preconditions are not explicitly obvious in a program implementation and a maintainer unaware of such restrictions may be tempted to use the operation in an inappropriate situation.

In the case of Z, a good place to start the specification is by positing a possible abstract state to model the system. Inevitably this will have to be changed in the course of producing the rest of the specification (except in trivial cases), but that is part of the learning process by which knowledge and understanding of the system is gained.

Next, some operations which may be performed on the system should be considered. Initially only the result of successful operations which perform the desired result with no problems should be formulated. The abstract state should be modified as required if some important aspect cannot be adequately modeled without it, always checking for the possible effect on other operations.

As the specification evolves, given sets and useful axiomatic or generic definitions can be assumed, then formally defined and added at the beginning of the specification. Errors reports in the case of unsuccessful operations should be considered and added. Some of these will normally be common across several operations in a specification of any size.

In practical specifications, it will be found that parts of the specification are repeated across groups of operations. It is often worthwhile factoring out these parts, presenting and explaining their purpose once, and then using them subsequently. This will considerably reduce the size of most large specifications and make their assimilation easier for the reader.

Total operations are normally formulated typically as a disjunction of the successful and, if required, a number of error cases. An appropriate error indication, normally as some form of output, is normally included depending on the requirements.

Finally (perhaps surprisingly) the initial state should be considered as a special case of the abstract state. Often the contents of much of the state are most easily considered to be empty or to have some fixed value at the start of the life of the system, but may be more loosely specified if the exact value is unimportant.

During the production of the specification, questions will inevitably be raised. These should be discussed within the design team, with other colleagues, or with the customer as appropriate, normally in that order, to resolve the issues. In the next section of this chapter, a Z specification is presented with some of these questions interspersed with the formal Z specification. Informal description of the formal specification is also included. This should be designed to reinforce the concepts presented in the Z specification, especially in relating it to the real world.

In a finished and polished Z specification, the informal annotation should normally be about the same length as the formal description. As a rule of thumb, it is a good idea to attempt to describe each line of predicate in Z schema boxes with a matching sentence of text written in a natural style. Ideally the informal part of the specification should be meaningful on its own, even if the formal part is removed. In fact this could be useful if the description is to be presented to a customer who may be unable to assimilate the Z specification itself.

1.2 Analysis and specification of case 1

Most specifications, formal or otherwise, are presented as a *fait accompli* after the specification has been produced, normally with no hint as to how the specification has been produced. There is some guidance on the use of formal methods in general, but in the case of specific notations, even most textbooks tend to concentrate on finished specifications rather than the progress of specifications from initial concept (requirements) to completion.

In practice, the *process* of producing the specification can be as important as or even more important than the specification itself. The knowledge gained by the specifier in preparation before consideration of implementation details can be invaluable in resolving errors before the detailed design and subsequent stages, making them much cheaper to correct. In this section we consider typical questions posed during the specification process when using the Z notation for the first case study.

Question 1: What *given sets* are needed for the specification?

Answer: Z, as a typed language, provides the facility of including a number of distinct sets (called '*given sets*' or '*basic types*') for subsequent use in a specification. The sets are potentially infinite unless limited to being finite later in the specification. The set of integers, $\mathbb{Z}$, is available in all Z specifications as part of the standard mathematical 'toolkit' library. Other given sets are normally discovered as a Z specification is formulated. Here, we define sets of order identifiers and products which can potentially be held in stock:

$[OrderId, Product]$

The exact nature of the elements of these set is unimportant to the specification and is thus not elaborated further. An implementor would chose a specific representation for them in due course.

Question 2: What states can orders have?

Answer: The requirements mention two states, 'pending' and 'invoiced'.

We define a set *OrderState* with just two elements in it to model the states of *pending* and *invoiced* which an order can take as it progresses:

$$OrderState ::= pending \mid invoiced$$

Here, *OrderState* is defined as a given set, but is limited to having two distinct elements, *pending* and *invoiced*, representing different possible states. Further states could be added later if that proves to be necessary.

Question 3: What *abstract state* is needed to model the system?

Answer: In Z, operations normally act on an abstract state, relating a *before state* to an *after state*. We need to model the state products in stock and orders including their invoicing status.

The quantity of each of the products in stock needs to be recorded, so a bag (also known as multiset) can be used to model this in a *vertical schema* called *Stock*:

```
┌─ Stock ──────────────────────────
│ stock : bag Product
└──────────────────────────────────
```

This includes a single *state component*, a bag called *stock* drawn from the set of bag *Product*. In Z, as with many programming languages, the ':' in declarations can be read as 'is a member of' like '∈' in predicates. Note that Z is case sensitive and many Z specifications use this in standard ways to help the reader. For example, here lower case names are used for state components and names starting with an upper case letter are used for given sets and schema names.

In the Z toolkit, the set of bags is defined as: $\mathrm{bag}\, X == X \pfun \mathbb{N}_1$, the set of partial functions between some set X and the strictly positive integers (greater than zero). This creates a record of the number of products in stock in the *Stock* schema above. For example, if *nuts* and *bolts* are valid products, then $stock = \{nuts \mapsto 5, bolts \mapsto 6\}$ would indicate that there are 5 *nuts* and 6 *bolts* in stock. $a \mapsto b$ is a graphic *maplet* notation used in Z to indicate the *Cartesian product* pair (a, b).

Question 4: Is it really required that an order be limited to a single type of product and an associated quantity or would a set of these be preferable?

Answer: The informal requirements indicate this, but it might be considered over-restrictive. A user may wish to order several types of product at once and this should be discussed with the customer. Here, we assume that the customer decides to allow orders of one *or more* products for extra flexibility, but not empty orders (i.e., an order for no products).

Since *stock* is defined as a bag of products, it is convenient to define an order as a bag of products too. However, whereas the stock may be completely empty, an order must consist of one (or more) products:

$$Order == \{order : \text{bag}\, Product \mid order \neq \varnothing\}$$

In the above, *Order* is defined using an *abbreviation definition* ('==') and *set comprehension* ('$\{\ldots \mid \ldots\}$'). Subsequently, any use of *Order* is the equivalent of using the right hand side of this definition directly. This is useful for expressions that are reused a number of times during a specification. The properties of the expression can be introduced in one place informally; the expression can be given a name formally and then used later as required. The constraint predicated after the '|' in the set comprehension above (which can be read as 'such that') normally limits the declaration(s) in some way (here to being non-empty).

The predicate constraint $order \neq \varnothing$ could also have been equivalently written as $\#order > 0$ or $\#order \geq 1$ where '#' indicates the cardinality (size) of a set. If it was decided that only a single product is to be allowed, we could write $\#order = 1$. This would allow us to easily change the specification subsequently if the customer changes his/her mind. We could even allow empty orders ($Order == \text{bag}\, Product$). The rest of the specification can be left the same, whichever of these choices are made.

Continuing with the definition of the abstract model, the status of orders can be modeled as a function from an identifying *OrderId* to their state (*pending* or *invoiced*). State components *orderStatus* and *orders* are packaged into an *OrderInvoices* schema with appropriate *type* information:

OrderInvoices

$orders : OrderId \rightarrow\!\!\!\!\!+ Order$

$orderStatus : OrderId \rightarrow\!\!\!\!\!+ OrderState$

$\text{dom}\, orders = \text{dom}\, orderStatus$

Here, *orderStatus* and *orders* are *partial functions* from the set *OrderId*. The functions are partial (i.e., their domains do not necessary cover the whole of the *OrderId* set in this case) since only valid orders are mapped in this way.

All orders have a status associated with them. This type of general information that must apply at all times (whatever the specific state of the system at any given time) is presented as a state *invariant* predicate in most Z specifications (e.g., $\text{dom}\, orders = \text{dom}\, orderStatus$ above, constraining the domains of both functions to always be the same).

Question 5: Should order identifiers be unique for the entire lifetime of the system?

Answer: We could decide that new identifiers must never have been used previously or that they just need to be unique at any given time. The state specification so far assumes the former, which is easiest. However, if the latter is required, we must augment the state with further information on fresh new references that can be issued at any particular time.

The schemas *Stock* and *OrderInvoices* can be combined in a new *State* schema using *schema inclusion*, together with a further state component *newids*. The inclusion of *Stock* and *OrderInvoices* means all the declarations and associated predicates are available.

$$
\begin{array}{|l}
\textit{State} \\
\hline
\textit{Stock} \\
\textit{OrderInvoices} \\
\textit{newids} : \mathbb{P}\,\textit{OrderId} \\
\hline
\operatorname{dom} \textit{orders} \cap \textit{newids} = \varnothing \\
\hline
\end{array}
$$

Question 6: What initial state is required for the system?

Answer: The requirements do not make this clear; if not defined in Z, the system could start in any valid state that satisfies any state invariants. Typically, many state components are most usefully initialized to empty sets or some predetermined value. For example:

$$
\begin{array}{|l}
\textit{InitState} \\
\hline
\textit{State}' \\
\hline
\textit{stock}' = \varnothing \\
\textit{orders}' = \varnothing \\
\textit{newids}' = \textit{OrderId} \\
\hline
\end{array}
$$

The decoration '′' added to the *State* schema included above percolates through to all the state components declared in the schema ($\textit{stock}'$, etc.). Note that all the predicates are combined using conjunction by default. The predicate $\textit{orderStatus}' = \varnothing$ is implied because of the state invariant $\operatorname{dom} \textit{orders}' = \operatorname{dom} \textit{orderStatus}'$ from the $\textit{OrderInvoices}'$ schema and hence can be omitted. All possible identifiers are available for use initially.

Question 7: Are there any constraints that apply for all operations on the system?

Answer: If so, they may be specified using the 'Δ' convention of Z:

$$\begin{array}{l} \_\Delta State\_\_\_ \\ State \\ State' \\ \hline newids' = newids \setminus \operatorname{dom} orders' \end{array}$$

Here, an undashed *before state* (*State*) and a matching dashed *after state* (*State'*) are included.

If any new identifiers are used for orders (and hence their status), these are no longer available for use by any subsequent operation. Thus they are removed from the set of new identifiers. Any operation including $\Delta State$ need not explicitly consider the value of *newids'* since it will automatically be handled by the predicate in the schema above.

A change of state is specified using the $\Delta State$ schema convention. This defines a 'before' state *State* (which includes the four state component *stock*, *orderStatus*, *orders* and *newids* in this case) and an 'after' state *Invoices'* which includes matching dashed state component (*stock'*, etc.).

Question 8: What operations are required?

Answer: Only a single operation to invoice an order seems to be required since many aspects do not have to be taken into account.

Question 9: What inputs and/or outputs are needed by the operation?

Answer: An input *id*? is required to specify which invoice is to be updated. Note that in Z, a trailing '?' indicates an input and a trailing '!' indicates an output by convention.

Question 10: What *preconditions* apply?

Answer: In Z, preconditions are predicates in operations that apply only to before states and inputs. Preconditions may be calculated by existentially quantifying the after states and outputs, and then simplifying the resulting predicate. See below for an example.

For an order to be successfully invoiced, there must be enough stock available to fulfill the order and the status must be pending. These are *preconditions* that must be satisfied to change the order state to *invoiced*.

Question 11: What is the effect of the operation?

Answer: The effect of the operation is a relation between the before state and inputs with the after state and outputs, proving a *postcondition* for the operation. Often, although not always, this can be specified *explicitly* (e.g., in the form $stock' = \ldots$, etc. for all after state components and outputs). Indeed, checking for predicates in this form is a useful check to ensure that no important postconditions have been omitted. The lack of a predicate in this form for a particular after state component or output is not necessarily an indication of an error in the specification, but it is all too easy to omit a predicate of the form $x' = x$ when no change of state is required.

All this information discussed above is included formally in an *InvoiceOrder* operation as follows:

InvoiceOrder

$\Delta State$
$id? : OrderId$

$orders(id?) \sqsubseteq stock$
$orderStatus(id?) = pending$
$stock' = stock ⩁ orders(id?)$
$orders' = orders$
$orderStatus' = orderStatus \oplus \{id? \mapsto invoiced\}$

$\sqsubseteq$ is the sub-bag relational operator from the Z toolkit. As used in the schema above, this ensures a precondition that there are enough quantities of the required product(s) in stock. For example, $\{nuts \mapsto 3\} \sqsubseteq \{nuts \mapsto 5, bolts \mapsto 6\}$ is *true*.

Another precondition is that the status of the order must be *pending*. If the preconditions are satisfied, the required product quantities are removed from the available stock using the bag difference operator ('⩁', cf. the set difference operator '\' for sets). Here, for example, $\{nuts \mapsto 5, bolts \mapsto 6\} ⩁ \{nuts \mapsto 3\}$ would result in $\{nuts \mapsto 2, bolts \mapsto 6\}$.

The precondition $id? \in \operatorname{dom} orders$ could be included if an explicit check for $id?$ being a valid existing order identifier is required. This is also equivalent to $id? \in \operatorname{dom} orderStatus$ due to the invariant $\operatorname{dom} orders = \operatorname{dom} orderStatus$. However, this precondition is implied by both the preconditions included in the *InvoiceOrder* implicitly since $id?$ is applied to *orders* and *orderStatus* using *function application*; this is only valid if $id?$ (in this case) is in the domain of the function. Here, we decide to omit an explicit check for simplicity of presentation. However, consideration of this precondition as a separate case could affect the errors conditions returned by the complete operation (see later) and this should be discussed with the customer.

The orders themselves are unaffected by the operation above, as specified by $orders' = orders$. The order status is updated to *invoiced* using the *overriding* operator ('$\oplus$') from the Z toolkit. This operator is commonly used in Z specifications to update a small part of state components that are binary relations (often functions) in Z operation schema. Here, the state of the maplet $id? \mapsto pending$ is replaced by a new maplet $id? \mapsto invoiced$, leaving the status of all other orders unchanged.

Question 12: What about error conditions?

Answer: Normally successful operations, where the preconditions are satisfied and the operation does what is required, are considered first in Z. The precondition can be calculated and the error condition(s) must have a precondition which handle the negation of this to eventually produce a *total operation* with a precondition of *true* (i.e., it can be invoked safely at any time) by combining the successful and error cases using disjunction.

Question 13: Are *error reports* required?

Answer: Nothing is said in the requirements, but most customers would wish to know if an operation was successful or not once it has been undertaken. They will probably wish to know the nature of the error as well if more than one error is possible in a particular operation. Thus, we define a set of possible reports from operations:

$$Report ::= OK \mid order\_not\_pending \mid not\_enough\_stock \mid no\_more\_ids$$

If further error reports prove necessary (e.g., if the system is upgraded later), they could be added to *Report* above as required subsequently. Above we define all error reports used in this chapter.

For successful operations, a suitable report is normally required to inform the user. Since this is a standard feature of successful operations, this can be separated out in a separate schema production an output report *rep*!:

```
┌─ Success ─────────────────────
│ rep! : Report
├───────────────
│ rep! = OK
└───────────────────────────────
```

Question 14: What if the order state is not pending?

Answer: For error cases where the precondition does not hold, it is normal to assume that the state is not to change. We define an error schema with a precondition that is the negation of one of the preconditions in the *InvoiceOrder* schema:

```
┌─ InvoiceError ────────────────
│ ΞState
│ id? : OrderId
│ rep! : Report
├───────────────
│ orderStatus(id?) ≠ pending
│ rep! = order_not_pending
└───────────────────────────────
```

$\Xi State$ ensures that all the dashed state components in the after state are the same as the matching undashed state components in the before state; in this case, $stock' = stock \wedge \ldots$ Thus, the entire state afterwards is the same as the state before in the case of the error above.

Question 15: What if not enough stock is available for the order?

Answer: Here, we return an alternative error report so the user can detect which error has occurred:

$$
\begin{array}{|l}
\hline
\textit{StockError} \\
\hline
\Xi State \\
id? : OrderId \\
rep! : Report \\
\hline
\neg\ orders(id?) \sqsubseteq stock \\
rep! = not\_enough\_stock \\
\hline
\end{array}
$$

Question 16: Should either error take priority if they both occur?

Answer: If so, an extra predicate giving the negation of the other error's precondition will be needed in one or other error schema above. If not, perhaps because the customer has no preference, this can be left non-deterministic. The decision can then be made by the implementor, depending on which is easiest, most efficient, etc., in the final design. It is good practice to leave design decisions to after the specification stage if they are not important at this point to give the design team as much freedom as possible in the implementation.

An error schema covering the case of $id? \notin \mathrm{dom}\, orders$ explicitly (i.e., the specified *id*? is not a valid order in the system) could also be added if required by the customer, but we have omitted this case here for brevity. Instead one or other of the two errors that are included may be returned (non-deterministically) in this case.

A total operation for ordering where the precondition is *true* can now be specified:

$$
\begin{array}{l}
InvoiceOrderOp == \\
\qquad (InvoiceOrder \wedge Success) \vee InvoiceError \vee StockError
\end{array}
$$

The above is a *horizontal schema* definition for a new schema *InvoiceOrderOp* in terms of a number of existing schemas. These are combined using schema operators, namely schema conjunction ('$\wedge$') and disjunction ('$\vee$'), based on the matching logical connectives. Both operators merge the state components of the schemas involved. Any components with the same name must be type-compatible (and are normally declared in an identical manner to avoid confusion). The predicates in the schemas involved are combined using logical conjunction or disjunction respectively.

Schema conjunction is normally used when building up a larger specification from smaller specification parts. Schema disjunction is normally used when specifying choice between two or more alternatives, typically successful and error operations. Normally any preconditions are disjoint to avoid any unexpected consequences. In a total operation, the disjunction of all the preconditions of the schema being combined is *true*.

If we do not have to take new orders, cancellations and additions to the stock into account, no other operations are required. However, the precondition of the *InvoiceOrder* operation schema is such that the invoice must already be *pending* and there must be enough stock available to fulfill the order. Other operations are needed to make these true. Here, we could assume that an arbitrary operation $\Delta State$ can be invoked at any time before *InvoiceOrderOp* operations.

In Z, exactly which schemas represent the abstract state, initial state and allowed operations is normally left informal and is just indicated in the accompanying text. There is no syntactic feature to distinguish these in Z, although some tools (e.g., the ZANS animator) have hidden directives to indicate these if required. In this particular example, the allowed operations is an area that would certainly need further discussion with the customer to avoid any misunderstanding.

1.3 Analysis and specification of case 2

Question 17: What extra operations are needed?

Answer: Assuming that case 2 is an extension of case 1, three further operations are indicated from the requirements to handle new orders, cancellation of orders and entries of quantities in the stock. However, these are not elaborated further.

Question 18: What inputs/outputs, preconditions and postconditions need to be included for an operation to handle new orders?

Answer: An order must be provided as an input and a valid fresh identifier is output by the operation. A new order leaves the stock unchanged, but updates the orders and their status appropriately.

NewOrder

$\Delta State$
$order? : Order$
$id! : OrderId$

$id! \in newids$
$stock' = stock$
$orders' = orders \cup \{id! \mapsto order?\}$
$orderStatus' = orderStatus \cup \{id! \mapsto pending\}$

Note that *id*! is not explicitly set and can be any convenient new identifier. Here, we assume that the status of the new order is *pending*; this should be discussed with the customer to check that this is what is actually required.

Question 19: When cancelling an order, is information concerning the order to be retained by the system?

Answer: We could either remove all information associated with the order from the system completely, or retain this information for possible future use. Here, we assume that the information is no longer required, which is the simplest option, but this should be discussed with the customer. Perhaps some sort of auditing will be required of the system, including cancelled orders.

Question 20: What inputs/outputs, preconditions and postconditions are required for an operation to handle cancellations of orders?

Answer: Cancelling an order completely removes an existing order (determined by a valid order identifier input *id*?) from the system:

$$
\begin{array}{|l}
\hline
\textit{CancelOrder} \\
\Delta \textit{State} \\
\textit{id}? : \textit{OrderId} \\
\hline
\textit{orderStatus}(\textit{id}?) = \textit{pending} \\
\textit{stock}' = \textit{stock} \\
\textit{orders}' = \{\textit{id}?\} \lhd \textit{orders} \\
\textit{orderStatus}' = \{\textit{id}?\} \lhd \textit{orderStatus} \\
\hline
\end{array}
$$

The Z toolkit domain anti-restriction operator '$\lhd$' used above removes part of a relation (often a function) where the domain overlaps with a specified set. In the above example, a single element is removed in each case. We have assumed that the status of the order to be cancelled is *pending* as opposed to *invoiced* since this avoids problems of re-adding stock; this should be discussed with the customer. As for the *InvoiceOrder* operation previously, $id? \in \mathrm{dom}\, orders$ is implied.

Note that cancelled order identifiers can in fact be inferred as $OrderId \setminus (newsids \cup \mathrm{dom}\, orders)$ given the operation above. This could be useful if further requirements are added in the future.

Question 21: Is the finiteness of stock quantities (or any other state component for that matter) important?

Answer: Here, natural numbers have been used for stock quantities and these are potentially infinite and hence of unbounded size in any corresponding implementation. Practical implementations will require some limit on the maximum size of stock, often determined by the system's computer architecture. If this is to be modeled in the specification, additional preconditions and error schemas will be required. In the specification below we assume no such requirements, but finiteness of state components is something that should always be discussed with the customer in practice.

Question 22: What inputs/outputs, preconditions and postconditions are required for an operation to handle entries of quantities in the stock?

Answer: Entering new stock can be effected using bag union:

$$
\begin{array}{|l}
\textit{EnterStock} \\
\hline
\Delta State \\
newstock? : \mathrm{bag}\,Product \\
\hline
stock' = stock \uplus newstock? \\
orders' = orders \\
orderStatus' = orderStatus \\
\hline
\end{array}
$$

The bag union operator ('$\uplus$') takes two bags and forms a new bag consisting of the sums of matching elements in these two bags (or just the elements in cases where there is no match). For example, $\{nuts \mapsto 5, bolts \mapsto 6\} \uplus \{nuts \mapsto 3, washers \mapsto 1\}$ would result in $\{nuts \mapsto 8, bolts \mapsto 6, washers \mapsto 1\}$.

Here, we assume that there is no limit on the amount of stock that can be held; in practice there may be a limit; this should be discussed with the customer and added as a precondition if appropriate.

Question 23: Are error reports required and to what level of detail?

Answer: Most customers will want operations to report errors and take appropriate action in these cases (typically although not always leaving the system state unchanged). The error report could simply be some status value or further information could be useful. Details of error handling are often omitted or glossed over in requirements documents, but should be discussed in detail with the customer before implementation. Producing a Z specification and calculating preconditions of successful operation is a good way to determine what errors are relevant to each operation. In case 2, the following additional error reports are needed.

In the *NewOrder* operation $id! \in newids$ implies that $newids \neq \varnothing$. This is an example of an *implicit precondition* (i.e., a precondition that is not explicitly stated). Such preconditions can be found by formally calculating the precondition. This involves existentially quantifying the after states and outputs:

$$
\begin{array}{l}
\exists\, State'; id! : OrderId \bullet \\
\quad newids' = newids \setminus \mathrm{dom}\, orders' \land \\
\quad id! \in newids \land \\
\quad stock' = stock \land \\
\quad orders' = orders \cup \{id! \mapsto order?\} \land \\
\quad orderStatus' = orderStatus \cup \{id! \mapsto pending\}
\end{array}
$$

The *one-point rule* allows existentially quantified variables that occur once in the form '$x = \ldots$' to be eliminated, giving:

$\exists id! : OrderId \bullet id! \in newids$

Since for an element to be a member of a set, the set must be non-empty, this simplifies to:

$newids \neq \varnothing$

Because of this implicit precondition, the (perhaps unlikely) event of running out of new identifiers needs to be handled:

```
┌─ IdError ──────────────────────────────
│ ΞState
│ rep! : Report
├──────────────
│ newids = ∅
│ rep! = no_more_ids
└────────────────────────────────────────
```

Notice that the value of *id*! is not explicitly defined in the case of an error and thus could take on any value.

The total operations with appropriate reports can now be specified:

$NewOrderOp == (NewOrder \land Success) \lor IdError$
$CancelOrderOp == (CancelOrder \land Success) \lor InvoiceError$
$EnterStockOp == (EnterStock \land Success)$

Question 24: Are further operations such as status operations required?

Answer: It is often useful to have operations which return part of the state while leaving the system state unchanged. Once an abstract state for the modelling of the system has been formulated, this can be inspected and potentially useful status operations can be suggested to the customer. In this case, the state components comprise of *orderStatus*, *stock* and *orders*, and information on any of these could be returned.

1.4 Validation of the specification

There are a number of checks that are worth performing on a Z specification once a draft has been formulated to reduce the number of errors it contains. For example:

- Check that the change of state for all components of the abstract state has been considered in every operation. It is easy to forget some parts of the state, in which case the meaning of the specification is that the after state for that component is totally unrelated to the before state and thus may take on any arbitrary value in an implementation. This is rarely what the customer wants in practice.

- Check that preconditions of successful and error parts of operations are disjoint in general. Otherwise there may be incompatibilities or potentially even a *false* specification otherwise.
- Check that preconditions of total operations are *true*. If they are not, there some cases that are not specified and which may be problematic in the implementation or subsequent maintenance.
- Check the specification type-checks using a mechanical type-checker. If the specification is not type-correct it is meaningless in a formal sense, although of course it can still impart some useful information to a human reader. A number of both free and commercial Z type-checkers have been produced (e.g., CADiZ, Formaliser, *f*UZZ and ZTC). It is recommended that all but the most trivial Z specifications should be mechanically type-checked. The Z text presented in this chapter has been type-checked using the *f*UZZ and ZTC tools.
- Attempt validation proofs to check the specification behaves as expected. If provable, these help in confirming the correct understanding and intuition of the specification; if they turn out to be false this may indicate a problem in the specification, or at least in the understanding of it. Mechanical tool support for proofs in Z, such as Z/EVES, is available, but takes a significant amount of skill to use effectively.
- Animate the specification (e.g., using the ZANS animator associated with the ZTC type-checker). This can be useful to check the specification acts as expected, but will typically only work for 'explicit' and finite cases where the after state and output are defined explicitly and deterministically in terms of the before state and inputs. Normally a specification will need some adaptation to allow it to be animated. Nevertheless, this may prove to be a useful exercise in the removal of errors from the original specification. Indeed, ZANS reports whether operations are *explicit* (i.e., all the after state components and outputs are deterministically defined in terms of the before state components and inputs) and this is itself useful information for checking a specification.

  An alternative approach is to rapid-prototype the specification in a high-level programming paradigm, such as a logic or functional programming language. Prolog is a popular choice for rapid-prototyping Z specifications.

Note that a Z specification cannot be *verified* formally in general since there is (normally) no other mathematical description to verify it against. Typically, requirements used to produce a formal specification are informal (e.g., natural language, diagrams, etc.), and this is certainly true in this case.

However, it is possible to *validate* a Z specification by posing challenge hypotheses that are believed (and hoped) to be true for the intuition of the developer. Proving these to be true increases the confidence in the correctness of the specification (i.e., that the specification is what is required).

Checks on the consistency of the specification can also be formally undertaken as proofs. For example, the existence of an initial state for the entire system, or a post-state for each operation, can be checked. In general it is considered desirable in Z to specify total operations where the precondition is *true* (as demonstrated earlier in this chapter). The precondition for each operation can be formally calculated to check this (as done earlier for the *NewOrder* operation in section 1.3).

Animation (attempting to execute the specification directly) or rapid-prototyping (producing an executable version of the specification with minimal development using a very high-level programming language, e.g., in the form of a logic program or a functional program) are additional approaches that help in the validation of the specification.

1.5 The natural language description of the specifications

The Z-style of specification dictates that the natural language description should accompany the formal Z text. This is what has been done in sections 1.2 and 1.3 although extra didactic material has also been included.

Typically, the informal description is of approximately the same length as the formal description, and certainly this is a good guideline to follow. It is a good aim to describe the system being specified in a form such that removal of the formal text would still render an understandable informal document. Often it is found that producing a formal Z document results in a better, clearer, less ambiguous informal description of the system as well (e.g., for inclusion in a manual or for presentation to a customer).

1.6 Conclusion

Z is mainly used at the specification level. Some data and operation refinement towards an implementation is possible in Z [DER 01], but at some point a jump to code must be made, typically informally. A program is considered correct with respect to a Z specification operation if it can be run in more situations (the precondition is more relaxed) or if it is more deterministic (the postcondition is more strict). However, many Z operations already have a precondition of *true* (i.e., the operation is 'total' and can be used in any situation) and are often 'explicit' (i.e., the operation is deterministic). In the operations specified in this chapter, total operations have been provided. Most of the operations are explicit apart from the allocation of identifiers for new orders.

If an operation is invoked in a state where it is not defined, then anything can happen. It is typically not desirable, and is the reason why total operations are normally specified.

If significant formal development is required, it is normally better to use a notation designed for this, such as the Abstract Machine Notation (AMN) of the B-Method. However, many systems can cost-effectively benefit from formal specification alone, to help in avoiding the introduction of errors at the specification stage. In this case, Z is a very appropriate general purpose formal specification to use. Normally, formal *development* is much more expensive than formal *specification* and may only be worthwhile in very high-integrity systems [BOW 99].

The Z specification in this chapter was originally produced in less than a day. Problems, inconsistencies and misunderstandings have been resolved by the author alone on an ad hoc basis. A number of specific questions have been raised explicitly and possible different specifications presented. The next step in practice would be to discuss these with the customer to solve the issues; however, this has not yet been done. Thus the case study specification as presented is a specification in the course of construction and perhaps has added interest for that reason.

For further online information on Z maintained by the author, see:

`http://vl.zuser.org/`

Bibliography

[BOW 03] Bowen J.P. *Formal Specification and Documentation Using Z: A Case Study Approach*, 2003. Originally published by International Thomson Computer Press, London, 1996. URL: `http://www.zuser.org/zbook/`

[BOW 99] Bowen J.P., Hinchey M.G. *High-Integrity System Specification and Design*. Formal Approaches to Computing and Information Technology series (FACIT). Springer-Verlag, London, 1999. URL: `http://vl.fmnet.info/hissd/`

[BOW 04] Bowen J.P., Hinchey M.G. Formal models. In: Tucker, Jr. A.B. (ed.) *Computer Science Handbook*, 2nd edition. Chapman & Hall / CRC, ACM, Chapter 106, 106-1–106-25, 2004.

[DER 01] Derrick J., Boiten E.A. *Refinement in Z and Object-Z*. Formal Approaches to Computing and Information Technology series (FACIT). Springer-Verlag, London, 2001

[HEN 03] Henson M.C., Reeves S., Bowen J.P. Z logic and its consequences. *CAI: Computing and Informatics*, 22(4):381–415, 2003

[ISO 02] ISO/IEC *Information Technology – Z Formal Specification Notation – Syntax, Type System and Semantics*, ISO/IEC 13568:2002

[JAC 97] Jacky J. *The Way of Z: Practical Programming with Formal Methods*. Cambridge University Press, Cambridge, 1997. URL: `http://staff.washington.edu/~jon/z-book/`

[LIG 00] Lightfoot D. *Formal Specification Using Z*, 2nd edition. Palgrave, Basingstoke, 2000

[MAL 05] Malik P., Utting M. CZT: A framework for Z tools. In Treharne H., King S., Henson M., Schneider S. (eds.) *ZB 2005: Formal Specification and Development in Z and B*. Lecture Notes in Computer Science, volume 3455, 65–84. Springer-Verlag, Berlin, 2005

[SMI 00] Smith, G. *The Object-Z Specification Language*. Advances in Formal Methods series. Kluwer Academic Publishers, 2000. URL: `http://www.itee.uq.edu.au/~smith/objectz.html`

[SPI 01] Spivey J.M. *The Z Notation: A Reference Manual*, 2nd edition, 2001. Originally published by Prentice Hall International Series in Computer Science, London, 1992. URL: `http://spivey.oriel.ox.ac.uk/~mike/zrm/`

[WOO 96] Woodcock J.C.P., Davies J. *Using Z: Specification, Proof and Refinement*. Prentice Hall International Series in Computer Science, London, 1996. URL: `http://www.usingz.com/`

Chapter 2

SAZ

Fiona POLACK

2.1 Overview of the SAZ method

SAZ [MAN 95, POL 93] is an integrated method developed at the University of York[1]. The method takes a diagram-and-text specification and develops a formal description of (Z) state and operations. SAZ was originally developed [POL 94] for use with SSADM version 4, and has been shown to raise issues which are not traditionally apparent in systems analysis and design [PAR 95].

SAZ and SSADM

SSADM version 4 [CCT 90, GOO 95] and its subsequent variants form the UK *de facto* standard for information systems development. The method is best suited to complex, multi-analyst projects. However, the philosophy of SSADM version 4 is adaptation, and it is thus possible to apply selected parts of the method to much smaller information systems, such as these case studies. SSADM version 4 provides a development structure, and suggested diagram-and-text techniques.

SAZ uses SSADM Requirements Specification (RS). This is derived from a Requirements Analysis (RA) which extracts and clarifies requirements using high-level data and functional models. RS specifies an abstract system to meet the requirements using data, dynamic and functional models. SSADM includes minimal cross-checking among its models; constraints (dynamic and static) are not routinely recorded.

The first task of the developer is to determine which parts of the method are appropriate for a project. The RA techniques used on the case studies comprise an

[1] The project, which was carried out at the Department of Computer Science, University of York, 1990-94, was supported by the UK Science and Engineering Research Council under grants GR/F98529 and GR/J81655.

entity-relationship diagram with simple documentation and a logical data flow diagram (DFD). Using the SSADM RS techniques, the data model is then validated against the scope of the system. The data flow diagram is reworked to *function definitions*. These, rather than the DFDs, are the specification of system processing. Function definitions are text descriptions of the processing required of the system, and are derived by identifying system events and tracing their effects through the DFD. SSADM advises that the results are referred to client users, who may combine, divide or replicate the functions. The RS also considers the dynamics of each entity, using entity life histories (ELHs).

The case studies use the notations suggested (but not mandated) by SSADM version 4. The specifications are developed sequentially through the chapter.

SAZ and Z

This chapter uses a conventional Z approach[2] and Z notations defined in the draft standard [TOY 99]. Data types (for attribute domains) are defined as Z given sets, enumerated types and schemas. Schemas define the types of entities, sets of instances, and relationships. Z processing is defined on the combined state schema. Z specifications of SSADM function definitions are completed using schema calculus [WOO 89].

2.2 Analysis and specification of case 1

The SSADM **RA** is expressed as a high level data model and a data flow model.

Question 1: What entities and relationships can be identified?

Answer: The case study refers to orders and quantities ordered from stock. These are modelled as order and product entities. It is assumed that orders have customers. Each instance of product must be related to one or more instances of order, whilst each instance of order must be related to exactly one product.

Question 2: How are customer and order instances related?

Answer: Customers could be either tightly bound to orders or allowed to exist independently. The former is assumed here.

These features are modelled in Figure 2.1. In the diagram, boxes represent entity types; lines represent relationships between the entities. The diagram states that an instance of order must be related to one customer and one product; an instance of customer must be related to one or more orders; an instance of product may be related to some orders.

[2]SAZ Z style has varied over the years. The Z in this case study is close to the original SAZ approach [POL 94], which is less elegant than later work. Presentation follows the style of [BAR 94]. The Z in this chapter has been type-checked and set using the CADi$\mathbb{Z}$ tool, available by ftp, see http://www-users.cs.york.ac.uk/~ian/cadiz/.

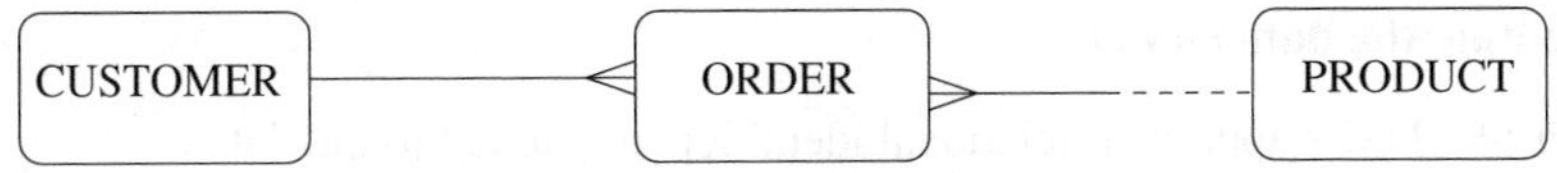

Figure 2.1: SSADM-style Logical Data Model

Question 3: What information does the system hold on these entities?

Answer: It is stated that orders are for quantities of a product, and that products have a stock level. No other data is within the scope of the system.

Question 4: How is it known that an order has been invoiced?

Answer: It is stated that the status of orders changes from *pending* to *invoiced.*

The SSADM data dictionary which accompanies the data model would comprise dozens of forms, at too low a level of abstraction. Here, the attributes of each entity in Figure 2.1 are summarised as a simple table:

ORDER	quantity, status
PRODUCT	stock level

Question 5: What processes, data stores and external entities exist?

Answer: There is only an order-processing process. This interacts with stored orders and stock levels. Although external entities must be involved in triggering this processing, these are outside the case study scope.

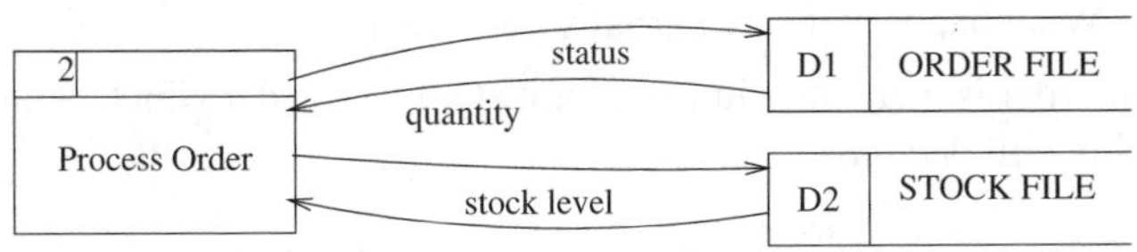

Figure 2.2: DFD using SSADM logical DFD notations

Figure 2.2 shows the single process, *Process Order*. The arrows are data flows to and from the data stores, *Order File* and *Stock File*. Additional documentation is not included, since the explanation is the case study text.

In SSADM RA, data stores on DFDs correspond to one or more entities from the data model. This is a non-rigorous matching, in which some entities or attributes may be present in more than one data store. Here, the order file comprises the order and customer entities; the stock file is the product entity.

The **RS** comprises a data model and a SSADM function definition. There is no significant dynamic component to the system.

Extending the data model

Using SSADM's approach, relational identifiers are added to the data model created in the RA.

Question 6: Are there any unique identifiers inherent in the system?

Answer: None is described.

Conventionally, identifiers are either an existing (set of) attribute(s) which must have a unique value for any tuple, or an attribute added to act as a surrogate key. The latter is used, since the data specification is abstract, and there are no grounds for assessing the properties of potential tuples. The surrogate attributes are named with the entity name followed by *Id*.

Function definitions

There is one function definition, corresponding to the process in Figure 2.2.

Question 7: Are all orders processed as soon as they are received?

Answer: Yes. The set of orders is always up-to-date.

Question 8: How are orders validated and processed?

Answer: Implicitly, the order must be for an existing product. The detail of the processing algorithm is not relevant at this level of abstraction. This is represented as an atomic (i.e., indivisible) process which, when there is sufficient stock, reduces the quantity in stock and sets the status of the order to *invoiced*.

Question 9: What happens to any partially met orders?

Answer: An order is met either in full or not at all. An order which cannot be met is explicitly still *pending*.

The SSADM-style function definition is expressed as follows.

> **Function Definition 1: Process Order** Order processing involves checking the stock level of the ordered product. The order status is set to *invoiced* if it can be met from stock and to *pending* otherwise. The stock level is reduced by the ordered amount.

2.2.1 Z specification

The Z state

SAZ defines data types, entity types, entity sets and then the full state, including relationship representations.

Question 10: What are the domains (sets of permitted values) of the quantity and stock level attributes?

Answer: The domains need to be numeric.

The most general solution would be to use real numbers which could represent volumes of a product. However, the less-general integer (whole number) type is used here, since this is the only built-in type in Z. It is assumed that stock level is at least 0 (i.e., the domain is natural numbers), that quantity at least 1, and that the domains have the same upper limit.

The Z defines domains by defining two subsets of natural numbers. This captures the required minima and imposes an arbitrary upper limit, *MAX*:

$$MAX : \mathbb{N}_1$$
$$STOCK\_LEVEL == 0 \mathrel{..} MAX$$
$$QUANTITY == 1 \mathrel{..} MAX$$

The domain of the *status* attribute is defined explicitly by enumeration:

$$STATUS ::= pending \mid invoiced$$

The entity identifiers (Question 6) are defined as Z given sets since their details are irrelevant at this level of specification:

$$[CUSTOMER\_ID, ORDER\_ID, PRODUCT\_ID]$$

The set of customers is simply a set of identifiers:

$$CUSTOMER\_SET == [customers : \mathbb{F}\, CUSTOMER\_ID]$$

The other entity type definitions use Z schemas to declare the attributes and domains, and then define sets of instances using partial functions from identifiers to the entity type (presented in horizontal format to save space):

$$ORDER == [quantity : QUANTITY; status : STATUS]$$

$$ORDER\_SET == [orders : ORDER\_ID \pfun ORDER]$$

$$PRODUCT == [stockLevel : STOCK\_LEVEL]$$

$$PRODUCT\_SET == [products : PRODUCT\_ID \pfun PRODUCT]$$

Question 11: Can a customer place more than one order for the same product?

Answer: The case study is not explicit about customers. The SSADM data model is not capable of expressing such structural constraints. The options are that multiple orders for the same product are permitted or multiple orders are not permitted. The former is selected here since it is a more abstract solution.

The complete state schema includes the three entity set definitions, and adds Z declarations expressing the relationships in Figure 2.1. The predicates express each entity's participation in the relationships: mandatory relationships are represented by equality, optional relationships by set inclusion.

$$
\begin{array}{l}
\textit{STATE} \\
\hline
\textit{CUSTOMER\_SET};\ \textit{ORDER\_SET};\ \textit{PRODUCT\_SET} \\
\textit{orderCustomerRel} : \textit{ORDER\_ID} \nrightarrow \textit{CUSTOMER\_ID} \\
\textit{orderProductRel} : \textit{ORDER\_ID} \nrightarrow \textit{PRODUCT\_ID} \\
\hline
\mathrm{dom}\,\textit{orderCustomerRel} = \mathrm{dom}\,\textit{orderProductRel} = \mathrm{dom}\,\textit{orders} \\
\mathrm{ran}\,\textit{orderCustomerRel} = \textit{customers} \\
\mathrm{ran}\,\textit{orderProductRel} \subseteq \mathrm{dom}\,\textit{products}
\end{array}
$$

The Z processing

The Z models the semantics of the SSADM function definition, above (see Question 8). There is no consideration of how orders arrive.

Following common Z practice, SAZ defines the processing schemas and corresponding error schemas. These do not update the state, but output explanatory messages. Conventional Z style uses an output message for each possible outcome. The following message type is defined here:

$$
\begin{array}{l}
\textit{PROCESS\_MESSAGE} ::= \textit{stockTooLow} \mid \textit{alreadyProcessed} \mid \textit{orderNotThere} \\
\qquad \mid \textit{unknownProcessError} \mid \textit{processedOK}
\end{array}
$$

The processing input is an order identifier, and its output is the appropriate message. The predicates specify the operation preconditions (Question 8), that the order exists, that it is in the *pending* state, and that there is sufficient stock of the ordered product. The operation postcondition, also expressed as a predicate, updates the state of the order and the level of stock for the ordered product. Other state elements are unchanged.

$$
\begin{array}{|l}
\hline
\textit{PROCESS\_ORDER} \\
\Delta STATE; \Xi CUSTOMER\_SET \\
ordId? : ORDER\_ID \\
processingMessage! : PROCESS\_MESSAGE \\
\hline
ordId? \in \operatorname{dom} orders \land (orders\ ordId?).status = pending \\
(products(orderProductRel\ ordId?)).stockLevel \geq \\
\quad (orders\ ordId?).quantity \\
(orders'\ ordId?).status = invoiced \\
(products(orderProductRel'\ ordId?)).stockLevel = \\
\quad (products(orderProductRel\ ordId?)).stockLevel - \\
\quad (orders'\ ordId?).quantity \\
\operatorname{dom} products' = \operatorname{dom} products \\
orderProductRel' = orderProductRel \\
orderCustomerRel' = orderCustomerRel \\
processingMessage! = processedOK \\
\hline
\end{array}
$$

The Z error schema specifies that the state does not change. Its predicates comprise the negations of the precondition predicates in the above schema, each of which returns an appropriate error message.

$$
\begin{array}{|l}
\hline
\textit{PROCESS\_ORDER\_ERR} \\
\Xi STATE \\
ordId? : ORDER\_ID \\
processingMessage! : PROCESS\_MESSAGE \\
\hline
processingMessage! = \\
\quad (\text{if } ordId? \notin \operatorname{dom} orders \text{ then } orderNotThere \\
\quad \text{else}(\text{if}(orders\ ordId?).status \neq pending \\
\qquad \text{then } alreadyProcessed \\
\quad \text{else}(\text{if}(products(orderProductRel\ ordId?)).stockLevel < \\
\qquad\quad (orders\ ordId?).quantity \text{ then } stockTooLow \\
\quad \text{else } unknownProcessError))) \\
\hline
\end{array}
$$

The specification is completed using a schema calculus disjunction:

$$ProcessFunction == PROCESS\_ORDER \lor PROCESS\_ORDER\_ERR$$

2.3 Analysis and specification of case 2

The case study defines a single state space. Thus, the data model and Z state are not changed for case 2.

RA modifications

The processing, and thus the DFD (Figure 2.3), must express the receipt and cancellation of orders and the arrival of new stock. The notation is as for Figure 2.2, except that data store D1 appears twice, to facilitate drawing. The duplication is indicated by the added bar at the left of the data store boxes.

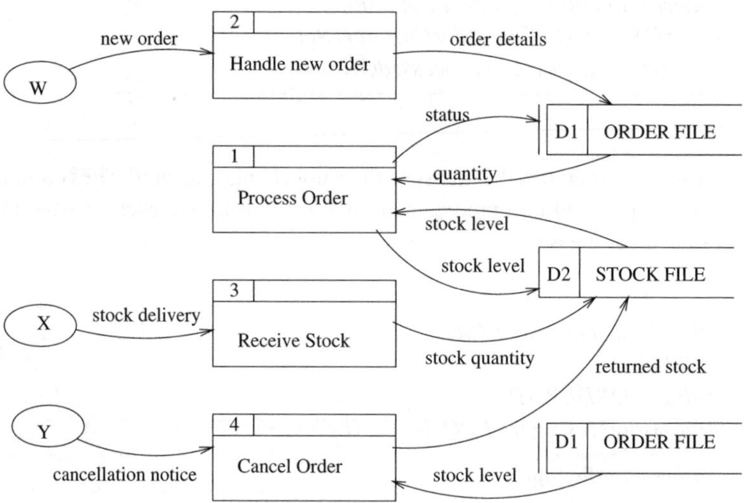

Figure 2.3: Extended DFD, SSADM logical DFD notations

The SSADM DFD notation does not allow hanging data flows. Data flowing in and out of the system requires terminal external entities (ellipses). Since the case study has no information on the interaction of the system and its environment, these are given arbitrary identifiers.

Question 12: What happens when stock is received?

Answer: As a result of receipt of stock, the status of one or more orders for the product may be changed to *invoiced*. This requires *pending* orders for this product to be re-processed. The case study gives no information about how this occurs, and at this level of abstraction, none is assumed.

RS modifications

The function definitions extend that presented for Case 1. The RS incorporates system dynamics for each entity in Figure 2.1, expressed in text (for Customer and Product) or as an entity life history (ELH, Figure 2.4).

Question 13: How does the client envisage the processing being allocated to SSADM function definitions, in order to support the users' roles?

Answer: The case study provides no information on the client's business. Options are to keep separate order receipt, order processing, order cancellation and stock receipt, or to give some combined function definitions. Here, order processing is combined with each of the other three separate function definitions.

> **Function Definition 1: Receive Order**
> Order is entered in the system (DFD process 2). It is processed immediately. If it can be met from stock (quantity $\leq$ stock), its status is set to *invoiced* and the level of stock reduced by the ordered amount; otherwise it is set to *pending* (DFD process 1).

Question 14: When can an order be cancelled?

Answer: The case study provides no information. Options are to restrict cancellation to *pending* orders, to impose some cut-off, or to permit any order to be cancelled. The latter is chosen since this is the most general solution.

Question 15: What happens when an order is cancelled?

Answer: The case study provides no information. Options, given that it has been decided to accept cancellations at any stage, are to delete or retain the record of the cancelled order. The latter would require an attribute to indicate that an order had been cancelled. The former option is chosen here. If an order is in the *invoiced* state, then the amount of stock assigned to it is added to the stock for that product. The system treats this in the same way as the receipt of new stock (see Question 12).

> **Function Definition 2: Cancel Order**
> An order is cancelled and any stock allocated to it is reinstated to the product (DFD process 4). Any *pending* order which can be met from any returned stock has its status set to *invoiced* (DFD process 1). This is repeated until the stock or the *pending* orders for that product are exhausted. The cancelled order is deleted.

> **Function Definition 3: Receive Stock**
> When stock is received for a product known to the system, the amount of stock received is added to the product's current stock level (DFD process 3). Any pending order which can be met is processed (DFD process 1). This is repeated until the stock or the *pending* orders for that product are exhausted.

Dynamic model

The set of events affecting the system is incomplete.

Question 16: How are products created and deleted?

Answer: The set of known products could be the set of products ever ordered, a set of products defined by the company, or a set of products currently in stock. Here it is assumed that there is a set of products defined by the company. The events announcing the introduction or removal of a product are outside the scope of the case study. It is assumed that deliveries of stock (and orders) are accepted only for known products.

Between the notification of creation and deletion, the dynamics of a product is a continuous cycle of stock changes.

Question 17: How are customers created and deleted?

Answer: Every order must have a customer, so an order for an unknown customer might either be rejected or trigger creation of a new customer instance. The latter is chosen here. No other way of creating a customer instance is specified. The deletion of a customer might occur on request or when the last order for that customer is deleted. Deletion on request could entail removal of linked order records, or require that all orders for that customer had already been deleted. Here, the specification assumes that the customer is deleted when their last order is deleted.

The dynamics of customer are simply a creation event and a deletion event.

The order dynamics are expressed in an ELH. This notation is hard to use well, and thus hard to validate. Cross-referencing to other models is implicit. However, the permitted processing sequences are critical to the success of the specification. The event effects are the leaf (larger text) boxes, read left-to-right. The children of a node (box) may be in sequence (unannotated), groups of options (each with *o* in one corner), or repeated zero or more times (each with * in one corner).

The expressed dynamics complement the function definitions, and are derived from Questions 8, 9, 14 and 16.

The reading of Figure 2.4 is that an order instance is created by an event called here *Order Received*. It is then processed. The first processing event may occur zero, one or many times because there is *insufficient stock*. Eventually, the iterations cease. There are two possible event effects which cause this. The first, presumed to be consequent on the receipt of stock, is *Invoice order*, with its side effect *reduce stock*. The alternative is a null event, a diagrammatic ruse to model the fact that a pending order may be susceptible to other events without being invoiced.

The final set of effects on an order instance are due to *deletion* events. Two effects are modelled here, and others may exist. These are options, indicating that the effect of deletion is determined by the status of the order instance. The deletion of a pending order is different to that of an order to which stock has been assigned.

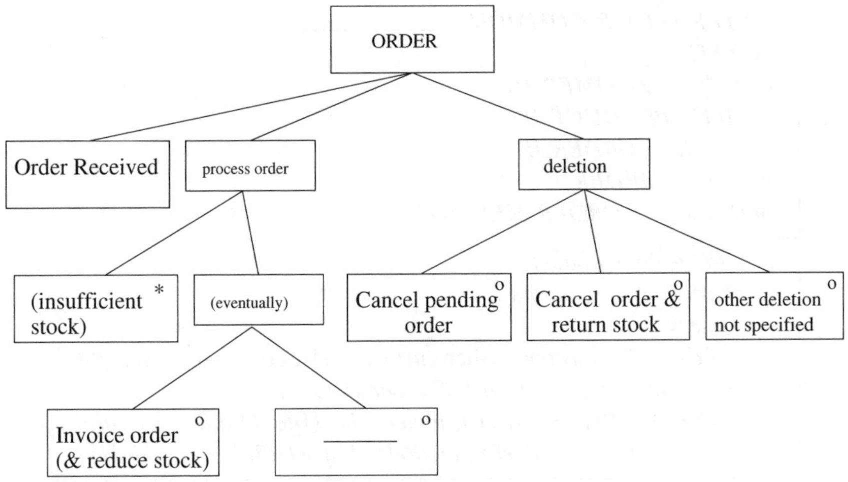

Figure 2.4: Entity life history of order

A full interpretation of the effects of events on the system requires that the ELH is read in parallel with the function definitions derived by the RS, above. Thus, function definition 1 explains (implicitly) that the effect labelled *(insufficient stock)* sets or retains the order status *pending*, whilst that headed *Invoice order* occurs if an order can be met, and sets the order status to *invoiced*). Details of deletion effects are in function definition 2, above.

The Z processing

Each SSADM function definition results in a schema calculus expression, which is constructed from schemas specifying the relevant processing for each part of the state.

The **receipt of an order** (function definition 1) is specified in four parts. The first defines the elements common to the receipt of all orders. The specification requires an output message of the type:

$$ORDER\_MESSAGE ::= unknownProductOrdered \mid orderIdExists \mid \\ unknownOrderError \mid orderProcessed \mid orderPending$$

The inputs are identifiers of an order, a customer and a product, and an instance of order. The product identifier must already exist, but the order identifier must not. The remaining predicates formalise the text of function definition 1.

$$
\begin{array}{|l}
\hline
\textit{ENTER\_ORDER\_COMMON} \\
\Delta STATE \\
custId? : CUSTOMER\_ID \\
prodId? : PRODUCT\_ID \\
newOrdId? : ORDER\_ID \\
newOrd? : ORDER \\
ordMessage! : ORDER\_MESSAGE \\
\hline
prodId? \in \operatorname{dom} products \\
newOrdId? \notin \operatorname{dom} orders \\
customers' = \\
\quad \text{if } custId? \in customers \text{ then } customers \text{ else } customers \cup \{custId?\} \\
orders' = orders \cup \{(newOrdId? \mapsto newOrd?)\} \\
orderCustomerRel' = orderCustomerRel \cup \{(newOrdId? \mapsto custId?)\} \\
orderProductRel' = orderProductRel \cup \{(newOrdId? \mapsto prodId?)\} \\
\hline
\end{array}
$$

The additional processing of a pending order simply adds it to the state.

$$
\begin{array}{|l}
\hline
\textit{ENTER\_PENDING} \\
ENTER\_ORDER\_COMMON \\
\hline
newOrd?.quantity > (products\ prodId?).stockLevel \Rightarrow \\
\quad newOrd?.status = pending \\
products' = products \\
ordMessage! = orderPending \\
\hline
\end{array}
$$

For an order which can be met from stock, the definition is as follows.

$$
\begin{array}{|l}
\hline
\textit{ENTER\_INVOICED} \\
ENTER\_ORDER\_COMMON \\
\hline
newOrd?.quantity \leq (products\ prodId?).stockLevel \Rightarrow \\
\quad newOrd?.status = invoiced \\
\{prodId?\} \lhd products' = \{prodId?\} \lhd products \\
(products'\ prodId?).stockLevel = \\
\quad (products(prodId?)).stockLevel - newOrd?.quantity \\
ordMessage! = orderProcessed \\
\hline
\end{array}
$$

The error schema negates the outstanding preconditions from each schema.

$$
\begin{array}{|l}
\hline
\textit{ENTER\_ERR} \\
\Xi \textit{STATE} \\
\textit{newOrdId?} : \textit{ORDER\_ID} \\
\textit{prodId?} : \textit{PRODUCT\_ID} \\
\textit{orderMessage!} : \textit{ORDER\_MESSAGE} \\
\hline
\textit{orderMessage!} = \text{if } \textit{prodId?} \notin \text{dom } \textit{products} \\
\qquad\qquad \text{then } \textit{unknownProductOrdered} \\
\qquad \text{else if } \textit{newOrdId?} \in \text{dom } \textit{orders} \\
\qquad\qquad \text{then } \textit{orderIdExists} \\
\qquad \text{else } \textit{unknownOrderError} \\
\hline
\end{array}
$$

The full definition is a schema calculus disjunction, as before:

$$
\begin{array}{l}
\textit{receiveOrderFunction} == \\
\qquad \textit{ENTER\_PENDING} \lor \textit{ENTER\_INVOICED} \lor \textit{ENTER\_ERR}
\end{array}
$$

The Z definition of the **cancellation of an order** (function definition 2) expresses the *cascade delete* required to enforce the mandatory relationships in Figure 2.1 (see Question 2). The full specification is split in to logical components, and again requires a message type:

$$
\begin{array}{l}
\textit{CANCEL\_MESSAGE} ::= \textit{cancelledPending} \mid \textit{cancelledInvoiced} \mid \\
\qquad \textit{orderNotFound}
\end{array}
$$

The input is an order identifier, which must exist in the set of known orders.

$$
\begin{array}{|l}
\hline
\textit{CANCEL\_ORDER\_COMMON} \\
\Delta \textit{STATE} \\
\textit{ordId?} : \textit{ORDER\_ID} \\
\textit{cancelMessage!} : \textit{CANCEL\_MESSAGE} \\
\hline
\textit{ordId?} \in \text{dom } \textit{orders} \\
\textit{orders}' = \{\textit{ordId?}\} \ntriangleleft \textit{orders} \\
\textit{orderProductRel}' = \{\textit{ordId?}\} \ntriangleleft \textit{orderProductRel} \\
\textit{orderCustomerRel}' = \{\textit{ordId?}\} \ntriangleleft \textit{orderCustomerRel} \\
\textit{customers}' = (\text{if } \{\textit{ordId?}\} \lhd \textit{orderCustomerRel} = \varnothing \\
\qquad \text{then } \textit{customers} \setminus \{\textit{orderCustomerRel ordId?}\} \text{ else } \textit{customers}) \\
\hline
\end{array}
$$

Cancellation of pending orders is a simple deletion. Its additional predicates are *(orders ordId?).status = pending*, *products' = products*, and *cancelMessage! = cancelledPending*. When an invoiced order is cancelled, its stock is returned. The schema outputs the product identifier for later use[3].

[3]Details of *CANCEL_ORDER_PENDING* and *CANCEL_ORDER_ERROR* schemas are not shown.

$$
\begin{array}{|l}
\hline
\textit{CANCEL\_ORDER\_INVOICED} \\
\hline
\textit{CANCEL\_ORDER\_COMMON} \\
\textit{prodId}! : \textit{PRODUCT\_ID} \\
\hline
(\textit{orders ordId}?).\textit{status} = \textit{invoiced} \\
(\textit{products}(\textit{orderProductRel ordId}?)).\textit{stockLevel} + \\
\quad (\textit{orders ordId}?).\textit{quantity} \leq \textit{MAX} \\
\{(\textit{orderProductRel ordId}?)\} \lhd \textit{products}' = \\
\quad \{(\textit{orderProductRel ordId}?)\} \lhd \textit{products} \\
(\textit{products}'(\textit{orderProductRel ordId}?)).\textit{stockLevel} = \\
\quad (\textit{products}(\textit{orderProductRel ordId}?)).\textit{stockLevel} + \\
\qquad (\textit{orders ordId}?).\textit{quantity} \\
\textit{prodId}! = (\textit{orderProductRel ordId}?) \\
\textit{cancelMessage}! = \textit{cancelledInvoiced} \\
\hline
\end{array}
$$

Cancellation of an order releases stock, which can be used to re-process orders. This is specified in two parts, and requires a further output message type:

$$\textit{IP\_MESSAGE} ::= \textit{furtherOrdsProcessed} \mid \textit{noFurtherOrdsProcessed}$$

A summation operator is defined as a function from a set of numbers to a single number; the details are not relevant at this level of abstraction:

$$\textit{sumOf} : \mathbb{F}\,\mathbb{N}_1 \rightarrow \mathbb{N}_1$$

The re-processing first selects a set of *pending* orders which could be met from the product stock. This is an arbitrary set such that no further order could be met. This level of abstraction is not concerned with optimising or otherwise rationalising the set of orders selected (Question 12).

$$
\begin{array}{|l}
\hline
\textit{SELECT\_INVOICEABLE\_ORDERS} \\
\hline
\Delta \textit{STATE} \\
\textit{prodId}?, \textit{prodId}! : \textit{PRODUCT\_ID} \\
\textit{invoiceableSet}! : \mathbb{F}\,\textit{ORDER\_ID} \\
\hline
\textit{invoiceableSet}! = \\
\quad \{\textit{os} : \textit{orderProductRel}^{\sim} (\!| \{\textit{prodId}?\} |\!) \mid \\
\qquad (\textit{orders os}).\textit{status} = \textit{pending} \wedge \\
\qquad \textit{sumOf}\{\textit{ord} : \textit{orders} (\!| \{\textit{os}\} |\!) \bullet \textit{ord.quantity}\} \leq \\
\qquad\quad (\textit{products prodId}?).\textit{stockLevel}\} \\
\textit{prodId}! = \textit{prodId}? \\
\hline
\end{array}
$$

The selection predicate produces a set of invoiceable orders which correspond to the product identifier. This uses the relational image of the product identifier over the relationship function, $\textit{orderProductRel}^{\sim} (\!| (\{\textit{prodId}?\}) |\!)$. All members of the set have *pending* status and the sum of quantities of the included orders is less than the stock level of the product.

The selected set of orders is input to the second part of the definition. Unless the set is empty (i.e., there are no invoiceable orders), the status of each order is set to *invoiced* and the stock level of the product reduced by the sum of the ordered quantities.

$$
\begin{array}{l}
\textit{INVOICE\_PENDING\_ORDERS} \\
\hline
\Delta STATE \\
prodId? : PRODUCT\_ID \\
invoiceableSet? : \mathbb{F}\, ORDER\_ID \\
ipMessage! : IP\_MESSAGE \\
\hline
orderCustomerRel' = orderCustomerRel \\
orderProductRel' = orderProductRel \\
customers' = customers \\
invoiceableSet? \neq \varnothing \Rightarrow \\
\quad (\forall os : invoiceableSet? \bullet \\
\qquad (orders'\ os).status = invoiced \wedge \\
\qquad invoiceableSet? \lhd orders' = invoiceableSet? \lhd orders) \wedge \\
\quad (products'\ prodId?).stockLevel = (products\ prodId?).stockLevel - \\
\qquad sumOf\{ord : orders(\!|\ invoiceableSet?\ |\!) \bullet ord.quantity\} \wedge \\
\quad (\{prodId?\} \lhd products' = \{prodId?\} \lhd products \wedge \\
\quad ipMessage! = furtherOrdsProcessed) \\
invoiceableSet? = \varnothing \Rightarrow orders' = orders \ \wedge \\
\quad products' = products \ \wedge \\
\quad ipMessage! = noFurtherOrdsProcessed
\end{array}
$$

The predicates of this schema define the after state of products and orders. The predicates specifying the unchanged parts of the system use domain subtraction to extract the unchanged order and product instances, for example $\{prodId?\} \lhd products'$.

The formal definition of function definition 2 is expressed in two steps, using schema calculus pipes, $\gg$, which link the output of the first schema to the inputs of the second:

$$
\begin{array}{l}
WHOLE\_INVOICE\_PENDING\_ORDERS == \\
\quad SELECT\_INVOICEABLE\_ORDERS \\
\quad \gg \\
\quad INVOICE\_PENDING\_ORDERS
\end{array}
$$

$$
\begin{array}{l}
cancellationFunction == \\
\quad CANCEL\_ORDER\_PENDING \vee \\
\quad CANCEL\_ORDER\_ERROR \vee \\
\quad (CANCEL\_ORDER\_INVOICED \gg \\
\qquad WHOLE\_INVOICE\_PENDING\_ORDERS)
\end{array}
$$

The Z specification of function definition 3, **handle stock receipt** requires a further message type:

$$STOCK\_MESSAGE ::= productNotInCatalogue \mid tooMuchStock \mid stockDeliveryOK \mid unknownDeliveryError$$

The schema outputs the product identifier, *prodId!*, to facilitate subsequent order processing. The predicates check that the upper limit of the stock level domain wont be exceeded, add the new stock amount, and leave all other parts of the state explicitly unchanged.

RECEIVE_STOCK

$$\Delta STATE$$
$$prodId?, prodId! : PRODUCT\_ID$$
$$amount? : \mathbb{N}_1$$
$$stockMessage! : STOCK\_MESSAGE$$

$$prodId? \in \operatorname{dom} products$$
$$(products\ prodId?).stockLevel + amount? \leq MAX$$
$$(products'\ prodId?).stockLevel = (products\ prodId?).stockLevel + amount?$$
$$customers' = customers \land orders' = orders$$
$$orderProductRel' = orderProductRel$$
$$orderCustomerRel' = orderCustomerRel$$
$$stockMessage! = stockDeliveryOK$$

The error schema is again a simple negation of preconditions.

RECEIVE_STOCK_ERR

$$\Xi STATE$$
$$prodId? : PRODUCT\_ID$$
$$amount? : \mathbb{N}_1$$
$$stockMessage! : STOCK\_MESSAGE$$

$$stockMessage! = \text{if } prodId? \notin \operatorname{dom} products \text{ then } productNotInCatalogue \text{ else if } (products\ prodId?).stockLevel + amount? > MAX \text{ then } tooMuchStock \text{ else } unknownDeliveryError$$

The full definition uses the schema composite defined for cancellation:

$$stockReceiptFunction == (RECEIVE\_STOCK \gg WHOLE\_INVOICE\_PENDING\_ORDERS) \lor RECEIVE\_STOCK\_ERR$$

2.4 Natural language description of the specifications

2.4.1 Case 1

The system has a data structure comprising customers, orders and products. An order must relate to a customer and a product. Only products exist independently in the system.

Customer details are not defined at this level. Orders have status (pending or invoiced) and quantity (a whole number between 1 and some arbitrary upper limit), whilst products have stock level (a whole number between 0 and some arbitrary upper limit).

There is one process in the system. This compares the quantity attribute of a *pending* order to the stock level of the related product. If the order can be met, then the status is set to *invoiced* and the stock level is reduced by the ordered quantity. No other state elements are changed. A message reports the success of the process. The process fails if the order is not in the system, it is not in the *pending* state, or there is not enough stock for the product. The failed process outputs an explanatory message but makes no change to the system state.

2.4.2 Case 2

The data structure is the same as for case 1.

The system processing comprises three function definitions: the receipt of an order, the cancellation of an order, and the receipt of stock.

The receipt of an order adds the order instance, and its links to a customer and a product instance, to the system state, on the conditions that the order identifier does not already exist in the system and the ordered product is known to the system. An order from a customer not known to the system causes the creation of a new customer instance. The processing of an order is an integral part of its receipt. This compares the ordered quantity to the stock level of the ordered product. If the order can be met, then the status is set to *invoiced* and the stock level is reduced by the ordered quantity. Otherwise the status is set to *pending* and the product state is unchanged. Explanatory messages are output.

The cancellation of an order and the receipt of stock use a common sub-process which selects an arbitrary set of *pending* orders that could be met from the stock level of the relevant product. If there are some such orders, those in the selected set have their status set to *invoiced*; the product stock level is reduced by the sum of the ordered quantities of the selected orders.

Cancellation of orders can occur at any time. This removes the order instance and its relationships. Any order in the system can be cancelled. If the order is the only one for its customer, then the customer instance is removed, otherwise the state of customer is unchanged. If the order to be cancelled is in the *pending* state, no other changes occur. If it is in the *invoiced* state, then the stock for the related product is increased by the ordered quantity and the common sub-process is triggered. Messages are output indicating what the process achieved.

When stock is received for a known product, the received quantity is added to the stock level of the product, on condition that maximum amount is not exceeded. The common sub-process is triggered. Messages are output indicating what the process achieved.

In all the function definitions, the specification explicitly does not update the state whenever the processing is invalid (i.e., the operation preconditions are not met by the system and/or the process inputs). Each failure outputs an explanatory message.

2.5 Conclusions

The SAZ method is applicable to abstract system specification. Lower level design or implementation issues such as the sequencing of components within atomic processes or selection algorithms are not in the scope of the method. The analysis and specification of the invoicing case study using SAZ demonstrates the complementarity of the formal and structured notations. SAZ provides a more complete specification than either of its components, and a more coherent method than exists for the Z notation.

SAZ addresses the problem of ill-defined model overlap, characteristic of all structured methods, by representing the models in one (Z) notation. The processing is expressed (and type-checked) in terms of the formal system state, and the complete specification could be subjected to formal proofs of consistency.

In SAZ, each model (data model, functional model, dynamic model, Z model) is a view of the system providing its own insights about the system. SAZ can thus exploit the complementary strengths of the techniques. However, the lack of formally-demonstrated equivalences among the models introduces a new case of the general failure of structured methods to adequately consider model overlap.

Model and process documentation is a common failing of development methods. SAZ addresses the weak SSADM model documentation, using Z to clarify data domains, constraints and operation details at an appropriate level of abstraction. However, none of the component techniques includes rigorous documentation of inherent assumptions. These include presumptions in the definition of the *SumOf* operator in the Z processing (case 2), the sources and sinks of data crossing the system boundary in the DFDs (cases 1 and 2), and the uniqueness requirement on entity identifiers.

Bibliography

[BAR 94] Barden R., Stepney S., Cooper D. *Z In Practice*. BCS Practitioner Series. Prentice-Hall, New York, 1994

[CCT 90] CCTA *SSADM Version 4 Reference Manual*. NCC Blackwell Ltd, Oxford, 1990

[GOO 95] Goodland M., Slater C. *SSADM Version 4. A Practical Approach*. McGraw-Hill, London, 1995

[MAN 95] Mander K.C., Polack F. Rigorous specification using structured systems analysis and Z. *Information and Software Technology*, 37(5):285–291, 1995

[PAR 95] Parker H.E.D., Polack F., Mander K.C. Trial of SAZ: Reflections on the Use of an Integrated Specification Method. In H. Habrias, ed, *Z Twenty Years On: What Is Its Future?, Nantes, France, October 1995*. IRIN, University of Nantes, 1995

[POL 93] Polack F., Whiston M., Mander K.C. The SAZ project: Integrating SSADM and Z. In J.C.P. Woodcock and P.G. Larsen, eds, *FME'93: Industrial Strength Formal Methods at Odense, Denmark, April 1993*, volume 670 of *LNCS*, pages 541–557. Springer-Verlag, Heidelberg, 1993

[POL 94] Polack F., Whiston M., Mander K.C. The SAZ method version 1.1. Technical Report YCS207, University of York, 1994

[TOY 99] Toyn I. Z notation – final committee draft. Technical report, ISO, Project No JTC1.33.45, 1999 Available from `http://www-users.cs.york.ac.uk/~ian/zstan/CD.html`

[WOO 89] Woodcock J.C.P. Structuring specifications in Z. *Software Engineering Journal*, 4(1):51–65, 1989

Chapter 3

B

Hassan DIAB and Marc FRAPPIER

3.1 Overview of the B notation

The B notation [ABR 96] was developed by Jean-Raymond Abrial. It supports a large segment of the development life cycle, from specification to implementation. The B notation is formal: it has an axiomatic semantics based on the weakest-precondition calculus of Dijkstra [DIJ 76]. Abrial has significantly extended the initial set of Dijkstra's guarded commands, proposing a complete specification and design notation scalable to large system development. Some of these extensions are inspired from the work of the programming research group at Oxford (e.g., [MOR 90]). The B notation is closely related to the Z notation and the VDM notation (Abrial was a strong contributor to the development of Z).

The basic building block of B specifications is the notion of an *abstract machine*. Such a construct serves to encapsulate suitable (set-theoretic) *state variables*, the values of which must always satisfy its *invariant* (stated as a predicate). The behavioral aspects are specified in terms of an *initialisation*, and a set of *operations* that may be used to access or modify this abstract state.

One distinctive characteristic of the B method is that every such specification is validated by means of (automatically generated) *proof obligations*. At the level of an abstract machine, the main proofs ensure that its initialisation *establishes* the specified invariant, and that this is then *preserved* by any calls to its associated operations (see section 3.4).

Both the initialisation and each individual operation are defined using *generalised substitutions*. Such substitutions are similar to conventional 'assignment statements', but with a well-defined (mathematical) semantics. They identify which variables are modified, without mentioning those that are not. The generalisation proposed by Abrial allows the definition of non-deterministic specifications, guarded specifications and *miraculous* specifications. For some initial state, a miraculous specification may terminate in a state which satisfy any predicate, including **false**. Obviously, a miraculous specification is not implementable.

Large machines are constructed using smaller machines through various machine access relations. A machine may *include*, *use*, *see*, *import* or *extend* other machines. Each access relation imposes constraints on the access, from the referencing machine, to the various parts of the referenced machine. Encapsulation is supported by allowing the modification of the state variables only through the operations of a machine; on the other hand, a state variable may be read by the referencing machines in some of the access relations. Other details on the B notation will be provided as the case study specifications are presented.

There are two commercially available case tools that support the B notation: Atelier B [STE] and the B tool [BCO]. They both provide syntax checkers, theorem provers and document management facilities. For this case study, we used Atelier B.

3.2 Analysis and specification of case 1

There are several ways of tackling a specification problem with the B notation. In this chapter, we start by identifying the operations required from the system according to the user requirements; operations provide the inputs, the outputs and the relationship between. Alternative approaches [ABR 96] begin with the identification of the state variables and their invariant.

3.2.1 Identifying operations

The first question one should ask to conduct the analysis is:

Question 1: What operations are required from the system?

Answer: The only operation required is **invoice_orders**.

The next question is:

Question 2: What are the input parameters of this operation?

Answer: The user requirements provides that orders are invoiced according to the state of the stock. There are two options:

1. invoice all pending orders;
2. invoice a subset of the pending orders.

We select option 2. Therefore, a set of orders is an input parameter of the operation.

This choice raises another question:

Question 3: In what sequence should the orders of this set be processed?

Answer: The processing sequence is important, because it may affect the ability to invoice a particular order. For instance, assume that two orders reference the same product and that there is enough stock for only one of them. Depending on the sequence in which these orders are processed, one order will be invoiced and the other will remain in the pending state, since there is not enough stock left after invoicing the first order. There are three options:

1. non-deterministically select a sequence in the set of orders;
2. accept as input a sequence of orders instead of a set of orders;
3. accept as input a single order.

We select option 3, because of its simplicity. Hence, we assume that the operation takes one order in parameter instead of a set of orders; the user has to invoke the operation once for each order, thereby specifying his preferred sequence of processing for orders.

Note that it is possible in B to specify non-deterministic operations; hence, either option in the answer above can be chosen. However, specifying the invoicing of a sequence of orders is more difficult (significantly) than specifying the invoicing of a single order. This fact may seem surprising, because a natural reflex would be to specify the invoicing of a sequence of orders by a loop over the sequence elements and invoicing them one by one. However, loop statements and sequential composition (";") are not allowed at the specification level in B. They are only allowed in implementations.

Question 4: How does the user specify the order?

Answer: There are two options:

1. submit as input a complete order with all its product references;
2. submit as input the order number.

We select option 2 since it is the most practical solution from a user perspective.

Question 5: How does the user specify the stock?

Answer: We assume that the stock is not an input parameter. Rather, the operation uses the current status of the stock, which means that the stock is accessed through state variables.

Question 6: Does the operation have output parameters?

Answer: We assume that the operation has a single output, a response code, indicating if the order was successfully invoiced.

3.2.2 Defining the state space

Before proceeding with the definition of the operation body, we must define the state space of the specification. We mentioned previously that the main building block of a B specification is the machine construct. The next decision to take is to determine how many machines are required. This is an internal issue which does not involve the user. For the sake of reusability and maintainability, it is desirable to define highly cohesive machines. An appropriate solution is to create two machines, *Product1* and *Invoicing1*. We first provide the definition of the *Invoicing1* machine. The first clause provides the machine name.

MACHINE

Invoicing1

The next clause defines the sets which are used as types for state variables and operation parameters. We may ask the following questions to the user.

Question 7: What are the possible values for the order number, the product number, the ordered quantity, the order status and the output message?

Answer: The user requirements are not specific about the type of these elements. We choose to defer the definition of a type for an order number and a product number. We assume that the ordered quantity is a natural number. An order status is either *Order_pending* or *Order_invoiced*. An output message is either *Updated* or *Not_updated*.

In B, we may defer the actual definition of types to implementation. In the SETS clause given in the sequel, we define the possible values for the status of an order and the output messages. The specification of the possible values for order are deferred to implementation. The **INVARIANT** clause will assign a type to each state variable.

Question 8: How many products does an order reference?

Answer: The user requirements are rather ambiguous about this issue. For the following statement of the user requirements:

> "On an order, we have one and only one reference to an ordered product of a certain quantity. The quantity can be different to other orders."

we see two interpretations:

1. an order contains exactly one product reference;
2. an order may contain several product references, but each product is referenced only once per order.

We select option 2. In the sequel, the word *item* denotes the reference of a product on an order.

The next clause defines the sets of machine *Invoicing1*.

SETS

$ORDER$;
$STATUS = \{ Order\_pending, Order\_invoiced \}$;
$RESPONSE = \{Updated, Not\_updated\}$

The set *ORDER* contains the set of valid order numbers. The definition of the elements of set *ORDER* is deferred to the implementation of this machine. The other sets, *STATUS* and *RESPONSE*, are defined by enumeration. The former represents the possible values for the status of an order while the latter represents possible outputs for operation **invoice_order**. The sets of a **SETS** clause are assumed to be finite and non-empty.

The next clause, **INCLUDES**, provides that machine *Invoicing1* has direct read access to the state variables of machine *Product1*, and that it may invoke *Product1* operations to modify *Product1* state variables. The definition of machine *Product1* is given in section 3.2.4.

INCLUDES

Product1

The **INCLUDES** relationship is transitive for variables: if some machine *M* includes machine *Invoicing1*, it can access state variables of *Product1*. The include relationship is *not* transitive for operations. Clause **PROMOTES** *op_name* may be used in machine *Invoicing1* to state that operation *op_name* from machine *Product1* is also an operation of machine *Invoicing1*.

The state of machine *Invoicing1* is defined using four variables given in the clause **VARIABLES**. Each variable is given a type in the clause **INVARIANT**. It represents a possible formalisation of the answers to Question 7 and Question 8.

VARIABLES

order, status, item, ordered_qty

INVARIANT

$order \subseteq ORDER \land$
$status \in order \rightarrow STATUS \land$
$item \in order \leftrightarrow product \land$
$ordered\_qty \in item \rightarrow \mathbf{NAT}$

Variable *order* contains the set of order numbers currently in the system. It is a subset of set *ORDER* (the set of all valid order numbers, as mentioned earlier). Variable *status* is a total function ($\rightarrow$) from *order* to *STATUS*; it provides the status of an order.

Variable *item* is a relation ($\leftrightarrow$) between *order* and *product*. Variable *product* is defined in machine *Product1*, which will be described in section 3.2.4. Variable *ordered_qty* provides the ordered quantity of an item.

If the reader is accustomed to the formal notation for relational database specification, he might find the following alternative state space definition more natural.

VARIABLES

order, item

INVARIANT

$order \subseteq ORDER \times STATUS \wedge$
$item \subseteq ORDER \times PRODUCT \times \mathbf{NAT}$

These definitions provide that *order* and *item* are relations. In B, one must use projection functions $\mathbf{prj}_1$ or $\mathbf{prj}_2$ to access a particular *coordinate* (i.e., an *attribute* in relational database terminology) of a tuple of a Cartesian product. That makes specifications less explicit, which is thus harder to read and understand. Moreover, the integrity constraints that the order number is unique (primary key) and that a couple order number and product is also unique are already catered for in the first definition. Consequently, the first definition of the state space is preferred.

The **INITIALISATION** clause defines the initial state of the *Invoicing1* machine.

INITIALISATION

$order := \varnothing \;||$
$status := \varnothing \;||$
$item := \varnothing \;||$
$ordered\_qty := \varnothing$

Each variable is assigned a value using an *elementary substitution*. An elementary substitution is of the form $v := t$, where v is a state variable or an operation output parameter, and t is a term. An elementary substitution behaves like an assignment statement: after the execution, the new value of v is t; the other variables of the machine are not modified; the state variables in t refer to the value before the execution. In this case, we have chosen to initialise each variable to empty. In B, a function is represented by a set of pairs (i.e., a deterministic binary relation). The operation "||" denotes the simultaneous execution of all the elementary substitutions.

3.2.3 Defining the behavior of the invoicing operation

We may now define the body of operation **invoice_order**. The following questions are raised.

Question 9: What are the necessary conditions to invoice an order?

Answer: According to the user requirements, the system can invoice an order if:

1. its status is pending;
2. it contains at least one product reference;
3. there is enough stock for each product reference of the order.

Question 10: What is the result of the operation if the previous conditions are satisfied?

Answer: According to the user requirements, we have:

1. the status is set to invoiced;
2. the items of the order are removed from the stock.

In addition, we assume that the output message "*Updated*" is issued.

Question 11: What is the result of the operation if the previous conditions are not satisfied?

Answer: We assume that:

1. the system state is unchanged;
2. the output message "*Not_updated*" is issued.

We provide below the specification of the operation according to these answers.

OPERATIONS

$response \leftarrow \mathbf{invoice\_order}(oo) \triangleq$

$$
\begin{array}{l}
\textbf{PRE} \\
\quad oo \in ORDER \\
\textbf{THEN} \\
\quad \textbf{IF} \\
\qquad status(oo) = Order\_pending \wedge \\
\qquad oo \in \mathbf{dom}(item) \wedge \\
\qquad \forall pp.(\, pp \in product \ \ \wedge \ \ (oo \mapsto pp) \in item \\
\qquad\qquad \Rightarrow \\
\qquad\qquad ordered\_qty(oo \mapsto pp) \leq quantity\_in\_stock(pp)) \\
\quad \textbf{THEN} \\
\qquad \mathbf{status}(oo) := Order\_invoiced \ || \\
\qquad \mathbf{decrease\_stock}(\\
\qquad\quad \lambda pp.(\, pp \in product \ \ \wedge \ \ (oo \mapsto pp) \in item \\
\qquad\qquad\quad | \\
\qquad\qquad\quad ordered\_qty(oo \mapsto pp))) \ || \\
\qquad response := Updated
\end{array}
$$

```
        ELSE
            response := Not_updated
        END
    END
```

The operation has an input parameter, *oo*, and an output parameter, *response*. Parameter *response* is set to *Updated* if the order was successfully invoiced, otherwise it is set to *Not_updated*.

To write a complex operation that modifies several variables, elementary substitutions are combined using compound substitutions. The main substitution of operation **invoice_order** is a *precondition* substitution of the form **PRE** p **THEN** S **END**, where p is a predicate and S is a substitution. This construct means that the substitution (corresponding to S) is only well-defined when p holds – which gives rise to a (static) proof obligation in the context of each separate call (as opposed to a 'run-time' test). A minimal precondition for an operation must specify at least the 'types' of its input parameters, if any, but as shown in the sequel, additional constraints may be introduced as well.

The **THEN** part of the precondition substitution is expressed as a *conditional* substitution of the form **IF** p **THEN** S_1 **ELSE** S_2 **END**, where p is a predicate, and S_1 and S_2 are substitutions. Such a construct has the same meaning as in conventional programming language. The condition of the **IF** contains three conjuncts which refer to the three conditions raised in the answer of Question 9. Two variables of machine *Product1* are referenced: *product*, which denotes the set of product numbers currently in the system; *quantity_in_stock*, which denotes the number of product units in inventory for a product number.

The **THEN** part of the **IF** contains a multiple substitution of the form $S||T$. Substitutions S and T are executed simultaneously. Note that the first elementary substitution is of the form $f(xx) := t$; it is an abbreviation of the substitution $f := f \mathbin{\lhd\!\!+} \{(xx, t)\}$, where $\mathbin{\lhd\!\!+}$ is the override operation for relations (recall that a function is represented by a deterministic binary relation). Operator $\mathbin{\lhd\!\!+}$ is defined as follows using operators $\lhd$ (domain restriction), $\mathbin{\lhd\!\!-}$ (domain subtraction), and $\mapsto$ (pair construction). Let r and s be relations and A be a set; we have

$$A \lhd r \triangleq \{x, y \mid x \mapsto y \in r \wedge x \in A\}$$

$$A \mathbin{\lhd\!\!-} r \triangleq (\mathbf{dom}(r) - A) \lhd r$$

$$r \mathbin{\lhd\!\!+} s \triangleq (\mathbf{dom}(s) \mathbin{\lhd\!\!-} r) \cup s\ .$$

The next substitution of the **THEN** clause is a call to operation **decrease_stock** of machine *Product1*. This operation accepts one parameter, a partial function f from *product* to **NAT**, and reduces the stock of $f(pp)$ units for each product pp in the domain of f. The argument provided in the operation call is a function defined using a lambda abstraction $\lambda x.(p \mid e)$. It denotes a function f whose domain is the set of x such that p holds and the image of x is given by expression e.

3.2.4 The Product1 machine

The *Invoicing1* machine includes the *Product1* machine. Its definition is given below:

MACHINE

Product1

SETS

PRODUCT

VARIABLES

product, *quantity_in_stock*

INVARIANT

$product \subseteq PRODUCT \wedge$
$quantity\_in\_stock \in product \rightarrow \mathbf{NAT}$

INITIALISATION

$product := \varnothing \;||$
$quantity\_in\_stock := \varnothing$

The *Product1* machine would be better encapsulated if we had defined an operation to access the quantity in stock. However, it would be useless in this case to define such an operation, because the B notation does not enable a call to an operation in the predicate accessing the quantity in stock in operation **invoice_order**. The encapsulation mechanism of B may seem weaker than those typically found in an object-oriented programming language, where it is possible to prevent an external access to class variables. However, encapsulation is fostered at a different level of abstraction in B. A machine may be refined and implemented using machines with completely different state variables, as long as they preserve the signature of the operations and their observable behavior. A machine M is refined by a machine N, noted $M \sqsubseteq N$, if and only if, for any sequence of operation calls where machine M terminates, machine N also terminates and delivers a result that machine M can deliver. Hence, machine N refines machine M by possibly extending the set of call sequences where M terminates and by possibly reducing the non-determinacy of M.

Machine *Product1* has only one operation, **decrease_stock**, which is invoked from machine *Invoicing1* when an order is invoiced, or when product units are removed from the inventory.

OPERATIONS

decrease_stock(*prod_qty*) $\triangleq$

$$
\begin{array}{l}
\textbf{PRE} \\
\quad prod\_qty \in product \rightarrow\!\!\!\!\!+ \ \textbf{NAT} \wedge \\
\quad \lambda\, xx.(\, xx \in \textbf{dom}(prod\_qty) \mid quantity\_in\_stock(xx) - prod\_qty(xx)) \\
\qquad \in product \rightarrow\!\!\!\!\!+ \ \textbf{NAT} \\
\textbf{THEN} \\
\quad quantity\_in\_stock := quantity\_in\_stock \mathbin{\lhd\!\!\!+} \\
\qquad \lambda\, xx.(\, xx \in \textbf{dom}(prod\_qty) \mid quantity\_in\_stock(xx) - prod\_qty(xx)) \\
\textbf{END}
\end{array}
$$

Operation **decrease_stock** has one input parameter, *prod_qty*. The first conjunct of the precondition provides that this parameter is a partial function ($\rightarrow\!\!\!\!\!+$) from *product* to the set of natural numbers. For each product *pp* in the domain of function *prod_qty*, the operation must reduce the quantity in stock by *prod_qty*(*pp*) units. The override of the quantity in stock is carried out with a function defined by a lambda abstraction.

To preserve the invariant of machine *Product1*, which provides that the quantity in stock is a natural number, we must verify in the precondition of **decrease_stock** that there are enough units in inventory for each product in the domain of function *prod_qty*. When an operation defined using a **PRE** *p* **THEN** *S* **END** is called, it is the responsibility of the caller to ensure that the operation is invoked in a state where *p* is satisfied. Otherwise, the operation call *may* abort (it *may* terminate because the implementation of an operation is allowed to weaken the precondition defined in the abstract machine). To prove that an operation *op* preserves the invariant, it is also necessary to prove that the precondition of each operation called by *op* is satisfied.

Note that we could have specified this conjunct in an **IF** substitution within the **THEN** part of the **PRE** substitution. In that case, the substitution would terminate normally without modifying the inventory if there was not enough stock. It would then be natural to add an output parameter to the operation indicating if the inventory has been successfully modified, like we did for operation **invoice_order**.

Several specification styles may be used in B. A typical B specification is structured into 'layers' of machines. An interface layer defines the interaction with the environment using input-output operations. This layer reads inputs from the environment, validates them, calls appropriate operations of machines from an object layer to compute the responses (outputs) and to update the state of the objects, and writes the responses to the environment.

Our specification of the invoicing case study does not include an interface layer. We only specify machines of the object layer. Moreover, our specifications are incomplete, as they do not contain all the operations that would be expected for a complete system. For instance, we have omitted an operation to add a product to the set of products (variable *product*). The next chapter also presents a B specification, which is derived from a UML object model. Its object layer is more structured than the one presented in this chapter.

3.3 Analysis and specification of case 2

Case 2 is an extension of case 1. We have defined new machines, *Product2* and *Invoicing2*, which have the same state space (state variables and invariant) as the machines in case 1, but we have added to these machines operations to increase stock and to manage orders. In the sequel, we identify the operations and provide their specifications.

3.3.1 Identifying operations

Question 12: What are the operations required?

Answer: Considering the user requirements of case 2, we have identified the following operations in addition to the operations of case 1:

- **increase_stock**, which is the inverse of the **decrease_stock** operation; it takes a set of items and increases the quantity in stock for these items;
- **create_order**, which creates an order;
- **add_item**, which adds an item to an order;
- **cancel_order** and **cancel_item**, which are the inverse of the previous two operations. We assume that these operations only modify pending orders; invoiced orders cannot be modified.

No other operation is needed, considering the given requirements. Note that there is no operation to create a new product or to delete a product from the stock.

3.3.2 The Product2 machine

Operation **decrease_stock** is the same as in machine *Product1*; hence we omit its definition. Operation **increase_stock** is similar to **decrease_stock**. Its definition is given below:

increase_stock(*prod_qty*) $\triangleq$

PRE
$prod\_qty \in product \nrightarrow \mathbf{NAT} \wedge$
$\lambda\, xx.(\, xx \in \mathbf{dom}(prod\_qty) \mid quantity\_in\_stock(xx) + prod\_qty(xx))$
$\in product \nrightarrow \mathbf{NAT}$
THEN
$quantity\_in\_stock := quantity\_in\_stock \mathbin{\lhd\!\!\!-}$
$\lambda\, xx.(\, xx \in \mathbf{dom}(prod\_qty) \mid$

```
            quantity_in_stock(xx) + prod_qty(xx))
    END
```

3.3.3 The Invoicing2 machine

Operation **invoice_order** is the same as in *Invoicing1*; we omit its specification. Operation **create_order** uses a non-deterministic substitution, the unbounded choice (clause **ANY-WHERE-THEN-END**), to pick a value for local variable *oo* that satisfies the condition $oo \in ORDER - order$. This order number is then used to create a new order whose status is pending. The definition of this operation is given below:

```
OPERATIONS

response ← create_order ≜

    IF
        order ≠ ORDER
    THEN
        ANY  oo WHERE
            oo ∈ ORDER − order
        THEN
            order := order ∪ { oo } ||
            status(oo) := Order_pending ||
            response := Updated
        END
    ELSE
        response := Not_updated
    END
```

The next operation adds an item to an order. It updates the state if and only if the order status is pending and if the product of the item is not already referenced on the order. Its definition is very similar to operation **create_order**.

```
response ← add_item(oo, pp, qq) ≜

    PRE
        oo ∈ ORDER ∧
        pp ∈ PRODUCT ∧
        qq ∈ NAT
    THEN
        IF
            oo ∈ order ∧
            status(oo) = Order_pending ∧
            pp ∈ product ∧
            (oo,pp) ∉ item
```

```
        THEN
            item := item ∪ {oo ↦ pp} ||
            ordered_qty(oo ↦ pp) := qq ||
            response := Updated
        ELSE
            response := Not_updated
        END
    END
```

The next operation, **cancel_order**, removes a pending order from the set of orders. It must update all variables related, by the invariant, to the set *order* and the relation *item*.

```
response ← cancel_order(oo) ≜

    PRE
        oo ∈ ORDER
    THEN
        IF
            oo ∈ order ∧
            status(oo) = Order_pending
        THEN
            order := order − {oo} ||
            item := {oo} ⩤ item ||
            ordered_qty := ({oo} ⩤ item) ◁ ordered_qty ||
            status := {oo} ⩤ status ||
            response := Updated
        ELSE
            response := Not_updated
        END
    END
```

Operation **cancel_item** is very similar to operation **cancel_order**.

```
response ← cancel_item(oo, pp) ≜

    PRE
        oo ∈ ORDER ∧
        pp ∈ PRODUCT
    THEN
        IF
            oo ∈ order ∧
            status(oo) = Order_pending ∧
            pp ∈ product ∧
            (oo,pp) ∈ item
```

THEN
item := *item* − {*oo* ↦ *pp*} ||
ordered_qty := {*oo* ↦ *pp*} ⩤ *ordered_qty* ||
response := *Updated*
ELSE
response := *Not_updated*
END
END

3.4 Validation of the specification

We have mentioned previously that operations must preserve the invariant. The B method defines proof obligations for each operation and for initialisation substitutions. Discharging these proof obligations provides a form of specification validation. As an example, the following predicate is part of a proof obligation (a simplified version) for operation **create_order**:

$$
\begin{array}{ll}
(1) & order \subseteq ORDER \wedge \\
(2) & order \neq ORDER \wedge oo \in ORDER \wedge oo \notin order \\
 & \Rightarrow \\
(3) & order \cup \{oo\} \subseteq ORDER
\end{array}
$$

This predicate provides that when the invariant holds (1) and when the conditions of the **PRE** and **ANY** clauses hold (2), the substitution applied to the invariant must also hold (3). In other words, after adding *oo* to *order*, *order* must still be a subset of *ORDER*.

We have used Atelier B to generate all the proof obligations and to conduct the proofs. Its theorem prover has automatically discharged all proof obligations except one – which was very easy to prove in interactive mode. Interactive proofs may represent a fair challenge. When the prover fails to find a proof, one must determine whether there is something wrong in the specification or if the prover is simply unable to find a proof. When the specification seems correct, one must build a proof in interactive mode. This task requires a good knowledge of the proof rules used by the prover and the different ways of applying them. It is sometimes necessary to rewrite specifications in a different manner to obtain proof obligations which are easier to discharge with the theorem prover. Difficult proof obligations are usually good hints that the specification needs to be rewritten in a simpler manner.

Table 3.1 provides a summary of the proof obligation statistics.

We have found one defect in our specification with the theorem prover. In the precondition of operation **increase_stock**, we had forgotten to check that, for each product, the number of product units plus the quantity in stock did not exceed **MAXINT**. We found several defects with the type checker of Atelier B. Before using the prover, we conducted several inspections and walkthroughs of the specification which allowed us to find various defects.

Machine	Proof Obligations	Automatic Proofs	Interactive Proofs
Product1	5	5	0
Invoicing1	7	7	0
Product2	7	7	0
Invoicing2	22	21	1
Total	41	40	1

Table 3.1: Proof obligation statistics

3.5 The natural language description of the specifications

3.5.1 Case 1

An order has a number, a status and items. The status may be *Order_pending* or *Order_invoiced*. An item is reference to a product in an order. Each item has an ordered quantity given by a natural number. Among the items of a given order, there must not be two references to the same product. The stock consists of a set of products. A quantity in stock, given as a natural number, is associated to each product.

The system provides an operation, **invoice_order**, which accepts an order number as input, and produces an information message as output. This operation behaves as follows. If the order status is *Order_pending*, if it has at least one item, and if, for each item, the ordered quantity is greater or equal to the quantity in stock, then the order status is changed to *Order_invoiced*, the quantity in stock for each product referenced in an item is decreased by the ordered quantity, and the information message is set to *Updated*; otherwise, the order and the stock are left unchanged, and the information message is set to *Not_updated*.

To invoice a set of orders, the user must invoke operation **invoice_order** once for each order, in the sequence he prefers. There is no concurrency in the system: it is assumed that operations are invoked in sequence.

3.5.2 Case 2

It is an extension of case 1. The definitions of orders and stock are the same as in case 1. New operations are provided. Operation **create_order** creates an order with an empty set of items. The order must not *exist* in the system, that is, it has never been created, or it has been created then deleted. Operation **add_item** adds an item to an order. The product reference must not exist in the order. Operation **cancel_order** and **cancel_item** are the inverses of operations **create_order** and **add_item**, respectively. These last three operations update the system state only if the order status is *Order_pending*; invoiced orders cannot be modified.

3.6 Conclusion

The elicitation of the invoicing user requirements using B leads us to a more precise statement of the expected system functions. We had to specify the inputs, the outputs, the state space and the relation between them. The fact that we have used a formal language does not prevent us from creating incorrect description of the user requirements; it only allows us to make precise statements which can then be systematically validated to determine if they are appropriate.

Mathematics provided a common language for resolving arguments and discussions between the authors during the validation. This is a significant improvement over classical informal methods like structured analysis [YOU 89] or object-oriented analysis [BOO 94]. The precise semantics of the B notation and its powerful data abstractions like sets, functions and relations allowed us to identify exactly what information the system could convey and the exact behavior of the operations transforming this information. Using mathematics and the B notation helped dispel ambiguities and misunderstandings in matching the user requirements with the specification. The B notation, as described in [ABR 96], does not make it possible to model concurrency or dynamic constraints. We refer the reader to [BUT 96] for a treatment of concurrency and [ABR 98] for the specification of dynamic constraints.

Readability is one of the weaknesses of a formal notation like B. It comprises a large array of symbols, some of which are not common in ordinary mathematics. Moreover, the "structure" of a state space is not as easy to grasp in a B specification as it is in a graphical notation such as an entity-relationship (E-R) model. For instance, consider an order and an item. In an E-R model, they would be represented as two entities with a relationship between them. The attributes would be listed on each entity. The same information in a B specification is given in a flat list of predicates. It takes more time to get a good mental representation of the information structure in a B specification than with a graphical E-R model.

Acknowledgements

The authors would like to thank Henri Habrias and Pierre Levasseur for useful suggestions on improvements to the specification.

Bibliography

[ABR 96] Abrial J.-R. *The B-Book*. Cambridge University Press, 1996

[ABR 98] Abrial J.-R., Mussat L. "Introducing Dynamic Constraints in B". in Bert D. (Ed.) *B'99: Recent Advances in the Development and Use of the B Method*. LNCS 1393, Springer-Verlag, 83–128, 1998

[BOO 94] Booch. G. *Object-Oriented Analysis and Design with Applications*. 2nd edition, Benjamin-Cummings, 1994

[BUT 96] Butler M., Waldén M. "Distributed System Development in B". in Habrias H. (Ed). *First Conference on the B Method*. Institut de Recherche en Informatique de Nantes, Nantes, France, 155–168, 1996

[BCO] B-Core Limited: Oxford, UK, `http://www.b-core.com`

[DIJ 76] Dijkstra E.W. *A Discipline of Programming*. Prentice Hall, 1976

[MOR 90] Morgan C. *Programming from Specifications*. Prentice Hall, 1990

[STE] Stéria Méditerranée: Aix-en-Provence, France, `http://www.atelierb.societe.com`

[YOU 89] Yourdon E. *Modern Structured Analysis*. Yourdon Press, 1989

Chapter 4

From UML Diagrams to B Specifications

Régine LALEAU and Amel MAMMAR

4.1 Overview of the method

To add formality to information systems (IS) development, we have developed the IS-UML method that produces the B specifications [ABR 96] of a system described by a subset of UML diagrams endowed with an IS semantics [LAL 00a, LAL 01, LAL 02]. This method is supported by a tool [LAL 00b, MAM 05] and consists of these main phases:

1. expressing the static structure and the basic operations of a system using a class diagram extended with IS features such as static constraints;
2. generating a B specification from the previous class diagram;
3. describing the functionalities of the system using IS specialized state and collaboration diagrams. We call these functionalities *transactions*;
4. translating the graphical representation of the functionalities into B specifications;
5. proving the consistency of the model, by discharging the consistency proofs derived by the B prover (here, Atelier B).

Let us note that a tool, called UB2SQL, that automates both the generation of B specifications from UML diagrams and its validation has been developed [MAM 05]. In this chapter, we illustrate this method throughout the proposed case study.

4.1.1 Summary of the B method

Introduced by J. R. Abrial [ABR 96], B is a formal method for the development of safe projects. In B, specifications are organized in abstract machines. Each machine encapsulates state variables on which operations are expressed. The set of the possible states of the system are described using an invariant, which is a predicate in a simplified version of the ZF-set theory, enriched with many relational operators. It is possible to declare given sets in machines by giving their name without further details. This allows the actual definition of types to be deferred to implementation.

Operations are specified in the Generalized Substitution Language which is a generalization of the Dijkstra's guarded command notation. A substitution is like an assignment statement. It allows us to identify which variables are modified by the operation, while avoiding mentioning those that are not. The B notations relevant for the understanding of the chapter are either presented in the chapter [DIA 06] or explained in the course of the chapter when necessary.

In B, large machines are constructed using smaller machines through various access links. A machine Ma that uses another machine Mb (link **USES**) can read the variables of Mb but not modify them. A machine Ma may include another machine Mb (link **INCLUDES**): the variables of Mb can be read in Ma but modified only by using the operations of Mb.

To establish the correctness of a B specification, proof obligations are generated. Proof obligations ensure that each operation maintains the invariant. To carry out these proofs, AtelierB [CLE 03] includes two complementary provers. The first one is an automatic prover implementing a decision procedure based on a set of backward deduction and rewriting rules. The second prover allows user to enter into a dialogue with the automatic prover by defining his own deduction and/or rewriting rules that help the prover find the right way to discharge the proofs.

4.1.2 Data specification

For the static aspect, we use class diagrams with the semantics of ER diagrams [ELM 04].

4.1.2.1 Class diagram

The *class* concept is used to structure the knowledge about objects existing in a system: a class assembles the objects sharing common characteristics. An object represents an instance of a class. An *attribute* is defined by its name and has a type that determines the set of its possible values.

Links between objects may be defined. In our model, a link concerns exactly two objects and may have attributes. A type of link is called an *association*. For a given association, a link is completely identified by the two objects it connects. An association is characterized by its name and multiplicity constraints with values *"1"*, *"1..n"*, *"0..1"* or *"0..n"* (minimum and maximum numbers of links for each object). We have chosen the graphical notation of the UML language since it is widely used in the software engineering domain.

4.1.2.2 B representation

A machine is associated with each class. Each class is modeled by the set of all the possible instances and a variable representing the set of existing instances. We call such a variable a *class variable*. Each attribute of a class A is modeled by a relation defined from the class variable, assigned to A, to the attribute type. This machine contains also the basic operations (create, delete, change of attribute values, etc.). Each association is modeled by a variable which is a relation defined between the two class variables corresponding to the classes involved by the association. Depending on the multiplicities of an association (respectively an attribute), additional constraints may be added.

The machine which contains an association variable is determined according to association characteristics. Roughly speaking, if operations are defined on an association, a new machine is created, otherwise the association variable is defined in one of the two class machines.

4.1.3 Transaction specification

Transactions are defined by users to specify IS functionalities. A transaction can access and modify data. It is executed atomically and must preserve the integrity constraints of the IS. In IS-UML, transactions are expressed using either UML state and collaboration diagrams or stereotyped classes that extend the initial class diagram of the system.

4.1.3.1 State and collaboration diagrams

A state diagram is a graph whose nodes are states and whose directed arcs are transitions that may be labeled with event names. It is defined in order to describe the dynamic behavior of each object of a class or an association class. Definitions of the basic concepts of state diagrams are given following the standard UML notations for which we have defined a specific semantics dedicated to the database domain.

In a state diagram, an object may change its state in response to an event. Events may have parameters (graphically represented in parentheses after the event name). A *state* is an abstraction of the value of some attributes and links of an object.

A *transition* allows an object to move from a receiving state to a target state when an event occurs. A transition may be subjected to a *condition*, graphically represented in brackets, called a *guard*. An event may be associated with a transition. A transition is fired if and only if its possible event, if any, occurs and its guard is fulfilled. An *action* labeling a transition is executed when the related transition is fired.

We assume that an event can only appear if it can trigger at least one transition. This means that the user has to verify this condition before transmitting the event. The alternative would be to take into account in the state diagrams all the possible cases (with regard to error handling) and ensure that for each event there is at least one transition whose guard is satisfied. The disadvantage is that diagrams quickly become unreadable.

A *state diagram* relates events and states and concerns a single class or association class. All the transitions leaving a state must correspond either to different events or, if there are several transitions associated with the same event, they must be guarded. Moreover, we impose that all the guards must be disjoint. Thus, it is a deterministic system. We consider there is no possible parallelism in the event handling.

To describe more elaborate transactions that may involve several classes and/or associations, we use collaboration diagrams. A collaboration diagram shows how the effect of a transaction is decomposed into internal messages sent to each class or association. In our context, three kinds of actor are used to represent a collaboration diagram. The $Environment$ actor represents the external environment in which the system evolves and from which it receives external messages corresponding to the transactions. We call these messages *triggering messages*. Each triggering message is received by a special actor of the system called a *manager*. A specific *manager* gathers all the transactions related to the same business sub-system. Such actors are responsible for defining the effects of triggering messages by sending appropriate internal messages to different classes and associations that themselves denote the main actors of the underlying application. The managers are also responsible for creating new objects required by the related transaction. Each internal message sent to a class (respectively an association class) must either correspond to a basic operation or an event of the state diagram of the related class (respectively association class).

Both internal and triggering messages may have parameters graphically represented in parentheses after the message name. They may also be guarded. The guard of a triggering message specifies conditions that must be satisfied at the reception of the message, whereas the guard of an internal message states conditions to be verified for sending the message. If the guard of an internal message is not satisfied, the message is skipped.

The annotations on both state and collaboration diagrams use B expressions generated from the class diagram. For example, actions are calls to basic operations and guards specified on transitions are boolean expressions involving B variables.

4.1.3.2 State and collaboration diagrams translation

Each state diagram of a class (respectively an association class) is translated into a B machine that includes the machine corresponding to the related class (respectively association class). Each state is specified by a predicate and each event is translated into a B operation that formally specifies the effect on the system data of the related event. In [LAL 02, LAL 00b], we have defined translation rules which allow us to generate the global structure of the operation. Its body consists of calls to basic operations that correspond to the actions described in state diagrams. We have also defined a formal approach that helps us identify the parameters and preconditions (typing of the current object and parameters). Furthermore, additional proof obligations are raised on the generated operations. These proof obligations ensure that the execution of each action, specified on a transition, makes an object move from the source state of the transition into its target state.

All the triggering messages of a collaboration diagram arriving at the same manager are translated into a single B machine associated with this manager. This machine includes either the machines associated with the classes and associations or those translating their state diagrams. Each triggering message is translated into a B operation that formally specifies the effect of the message on the system data. In [LAL 02, LAL 00b], we have defined translation rules which allow us to generate the operation translating a collaboration diagram. Each collaboration diagram is translated into a B operation whose body consists in creating the relevant new objects and then calling operations that correspond to the specified internal messages. The precondition of these operations and the conditions that the created objects must satisfy are inferred from the way these parameters are used in the operation calls. From a practical point of view, it consists in replacing, in the preconditions of the called operations, each formal parameter with its corresponding actual parameter. More details can be found in [MAM 05].

4.1.3.3 Extended class diagram

There are some transactions that cannot be specified by state and collaboration diagrams, such as transactions that return values. We propose to extend the class diagram by using the UML concept of stereotype to manage such transactions. We define two kinds of stereotyped class. An *EntityControl* class is linked to one class. It allows control of access to the basic operations of the class. A *TransactionControl* class effectively describes the transactions related to the same business sub-system. It can be linked to *EntityControl* classes and/or directly to classes. The links that relate *Control* classes and classes are described using UML dependency links with stereotypes: $\ll op \gg$ represents calls to operations of the target class; $\ll var \gg$ represents read-only use of variables of the target class.

Obviously, there are links between on one hand *EntityControl* classes and state diagrams and on the other hand *TransactionControl* classes and collaboration diagrams. Consequently, operations described by a state diagram associated to a class C and those described by the *EntityControl* class of class C are translated into the same B machine. With each manager defined in collaboration diagrams, we associate a *TransactionControl* class.

4.1.3.4 Architecture of the obtained B specification

A B specification generated from UML diagrams is structured in three levels. The first level contains the translation of the classes and associations together with their basic operations. The second level is composed of machines corresponding to the translation of the events of the state diagrams or the operations of *EntityControl* classes. Finally in the last level, we find the operations translating the transactions described with collaboration diagrams or *TransactionControl* classes. Each level is linked to its sub-level by **INCLUDES** or **USES** links.

4.2 Specification of case 1

4.2.1 The class diagram and its B representation

In order to build the class diagram, the first question that is raised is:

Question 1: What are the classes, associations, attributes required from the system?

Answer: We consider the following sentences of the case study:

1. "On an order, we consider one and only one reference to an ordered quantity of a certain product. The quantity may be different from other orders". So we define:
   - two classes Order and Product;
   - an association Reference between these two classes. The sentence is ambiguous: either we consider that an order can contain more than one product but all the ordered products of a given order are different, or we consider that an order can make reference to one and only one product. We have chosen the latter interpretation. Thus, the multiplicity constraint for Order is *"1"*;
   - an attribute OrderedQty. As the multiplicity constraint for Order is *"1"*, this attribute is defined in Order rather than in the association Reference.
2. "To invoice is to change the state of an order (to change it from the state pending to invoiced)": we need to know the state of an order so we define an attribute Status for Order.
3. "The same reference may be ordered on several different orders": the multiplicity constraint of Product with respect to Reference is *"0..n"*.
4. "... if the ordered quantity is either less or equal to the quantity which is in stock according to the reference of the ordered product": we define an attribute StockQty for Product, that gives the quantity in stock for each product.

Question 2: What are the types of the attributes?

Answer: The type of Status is obviously the set {pending, invoiced}. No precision is given in the description of the case study. We assume that an order quantity and a stock quantity are natural numbers.

Thus we obtain the class diagram illustrated in Figure 4.1.
By applying the rules described in section 4.1.2.2, we obtain:

- An abstract machine Product for the class Product which comprises the set of existing products and the variable representing the attribute StockQty.

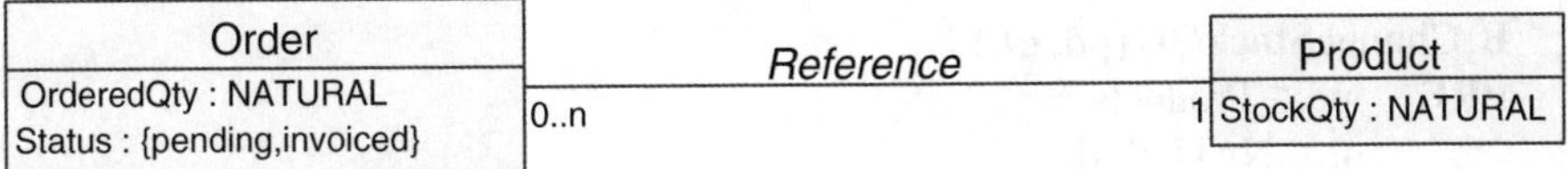

Figure 4.1: The class diagram of case 1

MACHINE	Product
SETS	PRODUCTS
VARIABLES	Products, StockQty
INVARIANT	Products $\subseteq$ PRODUCTS $\wedge$ StockQty $\in$ Products $\rightarrow$ NATURAL
INITIALISATION	Products, StockQty := $\emptyset, \emptyset$

- An abstract machine Order for the class Order which comprises the set of existing orders, the variables representing the attributes OrderedQty and Status. In order to determine in which machine the association Reference is defined, the following question is raised:

  Question 3: Is it possible to change the product referenced by an order?

  Answer: We assume it is not possible. So the variable which represents the association is defined in the machine Order.

  A **USES** link from Order to Product is created in order to be able to refer to the variable Products in the invariant defining the association Reference.

MACHINE	Order
USES	Product
SETS	ORDERS ; STATE = {pending, invoiced}
VARIABLES	Orders, Status, Reference, OrderedQty
INVARIANT	Orders $\subseteq$ ORDERS $\wedge$ Status $\in$ Orders $\rightarrow$ STATE $\wedge$ Reference $\in$ Orders $\rightarrow$ Products $\wedge$ OrderedQty $\in$ Orders $\rightarrow$ NATURAL
INITIALISATION	Orders, Status, Reference, OrderedQty := $\emptyset, \emptyset, \emptyset, \emptyset$

The basic operations (creation, deletion, update of attributes) of the machines Product and Order are automatically generated. Below are presented the operations relevant for the chapter. In Product, we consider only the basic operation B_ChangeStockQty that updates the quantity in stock of a given product.

B_ChangeStockQty(pd, qt) $\triangleq$
PRE pd $\in$ Products $\wedge$
qt $\in$ NATURAL
THEN StockQty(pd) := qt
END

In Order, we consider only the basic operations:

- B_ChangeStatus that modifies the state of an order.

B_ChangeStatus(ord,new_state) $\triangleq$
PRE ord $\in$ Orders $\wedge$ new_state $\in$ STATE
THEN Status(ord) := new_state
END

- B_AddOrder that adds a new order.

B_AddOrder(ord, pd, qt, state) $\triangleq$
PRE ord $\in$ ORDERS $-$ Orders $\wedge$
pd $\in$ Products $\wedge$
qt $\in$ NATURAL $\wedge$
state $\in$ STATE
THEN Orders := Orders $\cup$ $\{$ord$\}$ $\|$
Reference := Reference $\cup$ $\{$ord $\mapsto$ pd$\}$ $\|$
OrderedQty := OrderedQty $\cup$ $\{$ord $\mapsto$ qt$\}$ $\|$
Status := Status $\cup$ $\{$ord $\mapsto$ state$\}$
END

- B_RemoveOrder that deletes an order.

B_RemoveOrder(ord) $\triangleq$
PRE ord $\in$ Orders
THEN Orders := Orders $-$ $\{$ord$\}$ $\|$
Status := $\{$ord$\}$ $\lhd\!\!-$ Status $\|$
Reference := $\{$ord$\}$ $\lhd\!\!-$ Reference $\|$
OrderedQty := $\{$ord$\}$ $\lhd\!\!-$ OrderedQty
END

4.2.2 Transaction specification

We need to identify the different input messages that trigger the transactions.

Question 4: What are the input messages that may occur in the system?

Answer: The only input message is Invoicing orders.

Question 5: What are the parameters of this message?

Answer: No details are given in the description of the case study, two options may be considered:

1. invoicing a set of orders;
2. invoicing a single order.

We select option 2.

Question 6: How this order is chosen?

Answer: Again, two options may be considered:

1. the order is determined by the system (for example according to its receipt date);
2. the order is chosen by the user.

We select option 2, option 1 will be considered in case 2; thus an order is a parameter of the message Invoicing.

Question 7: Is it possible to invoice any order?

Answer: There are two conditions. The status of an invoicing order must be "pending" and there must be enough stock for the ordered product.

Question 8: What are the effects of the message on the system data?

Answer: According to the user requirements, we have:

(i) the corresponding order is invoiced and its status is set to "invoiced";
(ii) the quantity in stock of the ordered product is reduced.

This transaction is very simple, we just need a collaboration diagram to specify it (Figure 4.2). The guard of the input message Invoicing corresponds to the two conditions needed to invoice an order. The effect of the transaction consists in calling the two basic operations B_ChangeStatus of Order and B_ChangeStockQty of Product.

By applying the rules described in section 4.1.3.2, we define a machine OrderManagement, which includes the two basic machines Order and Product, and contains the operation Invoicing corresponding to the transaction of case 1.

```
MACHINE       OrderManagement
INCLUDES      Product, Order
OPERATIONS
 Invoicing(ord) ≙ ...
END
```

Figure 4.3 provides the specification architecture.

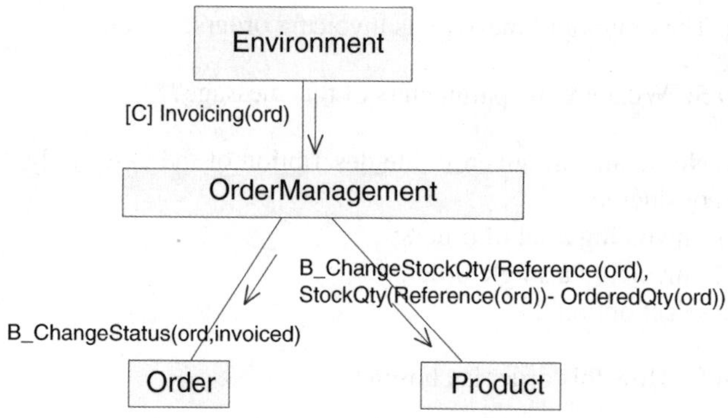

Figure 4.2: The collaboration diagram of case 1

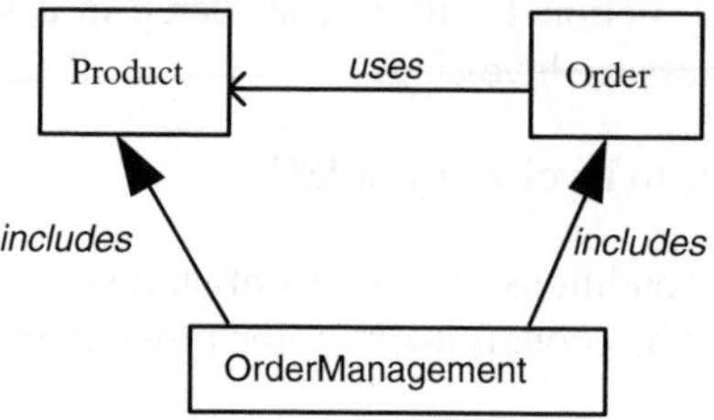

Figure 4.3: The B specification architecture of case 1

Question 9: What is the body of the operation Invoicing?

Answer: It is automatically generated from the collaboration diagram, and consists of two operation calls: one is B_ChangeStatus in order to set the status of the pending order to "invoiced" and the other is B_ChangeStockQty in order to decrease the quantity in stock of the ordered product.

```
Invoicing(ord) ≙
PRE
   ord ∈ Orders ∧
   StockQty(Reference(ord))-OrderedQty(ord) ∈ NATURAL ∧
   Status(ord) = pending ∧ OrderedQty(ord)≤ StockQty(Reference(ord))
THEN
   B_ChangeStatus(ord,invoiced)||
   B_ChangeStockQty(Reference(ord),
                    StockQty(Reference(ord))-OrderedQty(ord))
END
```

The precondition of this operation contains four conjuncts. The first two are derived from the preconditions of the called operations. They are obtained by replacing, in the preconditions of the called operations, the formal parameters by the actual ones. The last two conjuncts correspond to the guard of the triggering message.

4.3 Specification of case 2

The class diagram and thus the generated B specification are the same for the two cases.

4.3.1 Transactions specification

Question 10: What are the input messages?

Answer: According to the requirements, we have defined four messages:

- CreateOr which triggers the creation of a new order for a given product and a given quantity;
- AddStock which triggers a stock increase for a given product;
- CancelOr which cancels an existing order;
- InvoiceAnyOr which triggers the invoicing of an order.

4.3.1.1 Transaction CreateOr

The effect of this transaction is to add a new order in the system. The status of this created order depends on the quantity available in stock of the ordered product. If there is enough quantity, the order is invoiced and the quantity in stock is decreased, otherwise the ordered is pending. Figure 4.4 depicts the collaboration diagram that describes this transaction.

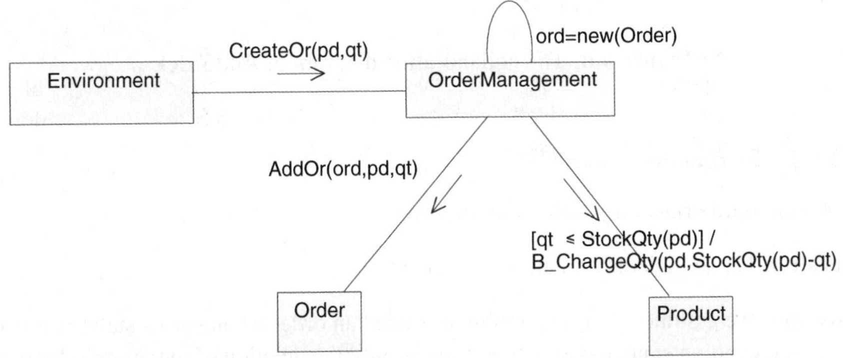

Figure 4.4: The collaboration diagram of CreateOr

The AddOr message is captured in the state diagram of Order shown in Figure 4.5.

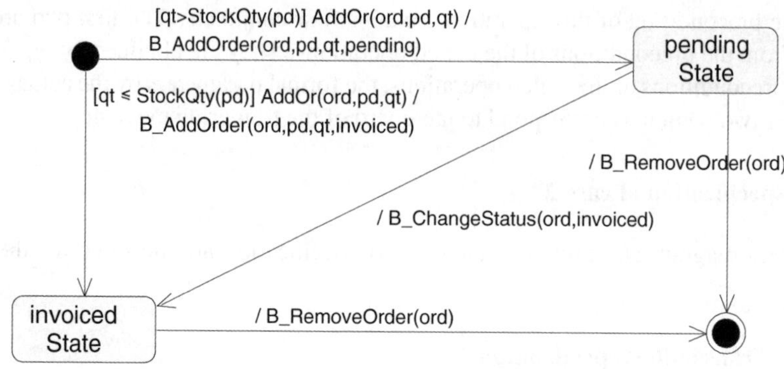

Figure 4.5: The state diagram of Order

4.3.1.2 **Transaction** AddStock

The effect of this transaction is to increase a given quantity of a given product. This transaction corresponds exactly to the call to the basic operation B_ChangeStockQty. Figure 4.6 depicts the collaboration diagram representing this transaction.

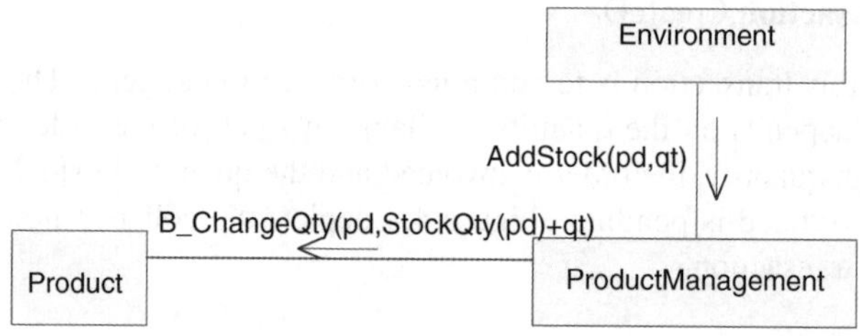

Figure 4.6: The collaboration diagram of AddStock

4.3.1.3 **Transaction** CancelOr

This transaction raises the following question.

Question 11: Which orders can be canceled?

Answer: We assume that it is possible to cancel an order whatever its state: if it is in the pending state, the message triggers only the deletion of the order, otherwise the message triggers in addition the increase of the quantity in stock of the product referenced by the canceled order. This increase corresponds to the quantity previously ordered.

Figure 4.7 depicts the collaboration diagram that describes this transaction.

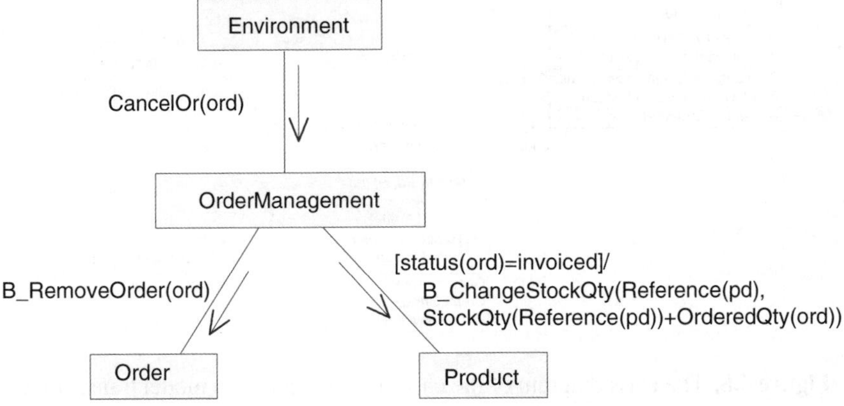

Figure 4.7: The collaboration diagram of CancelOr

4.3.1.4 Transaction InvoiceAnyOrder

This transaction raises the following question.

Question 12: When is an order invoiced?

Answer: There are two options:
1. at any time, by the user;
2. when the order is created if there is enough stock for the ordered product.

The second option corresponds to the message CreateOr. The first option raises another question.

Question 13: What order is chosen to be invoiced?

Answer: Again there are two options as in case 1 and we select the first one. We decide to take an arbitrary pending order such that there is enough product in stock to invoice it. At this level of design, we do not need to specify how the order is chosen. The transaction needs only a return parameter to inform the user about the chosen order.

As this transaction needs to return a value, it is specified in the *TransactionControl* class associated with the manager OrderManagement. Figure 4.8 shows the initial class diagram extended by the control classes Order_Control, OrderManagement and ProductManagement.

Order_Control contains the operations generated from the state diagram of the class Order. Similarly, a *TransactionControl* class is associated with each manager of the collaboration diagrams. The operation InvoiceAnyOrder has been added to the class OrderManagement. Its body is described directly in B. The following section gives the B formal specification corresponding to the extended class diagram.

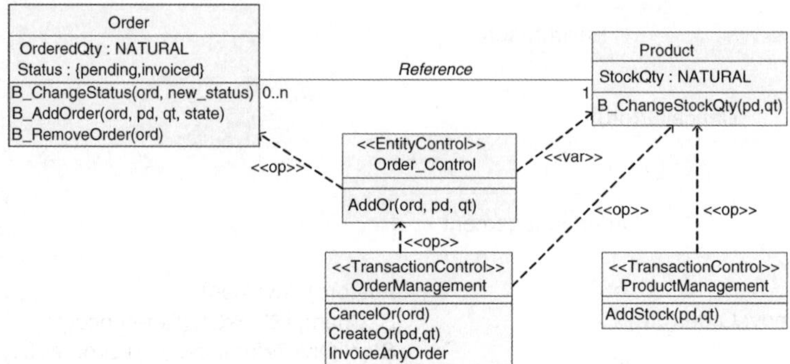

Figure 4.8: The class diagram of the case study extended to model transactions

4.3.2 The formal specification

The architecture of the specification generated for case 2 is shown in Figure 4.9. It is composed of three levels described hereafter:

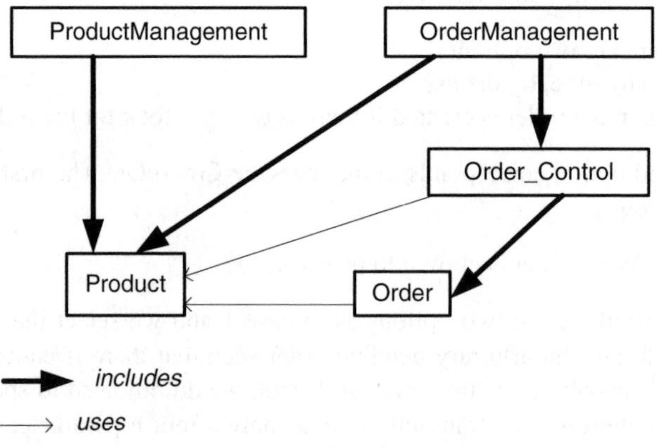

Figure 4.9: The specification architecture of case 2

1. The first level contains the basic machines generated from the class diagram, that is, the machines Product and Order which are the same as in case 1.
2. The second level contains the machine Order_Control generated from the state diagram of the class Order. It includes Order and uses Product. Order_Control specifies the operation AddOr that corresponds to the event of the same name.

```
MACHINE       Order_Control
INCLUDES      Order
USES          Product
PROMOTES  B_ChangeStatus, B_RemoveOrder
DEFINITIONS
   Initial(ord) ≜ ord ∈ ORDERS − Orders;
   Pending (ord) ≜ Status(ord)=pending;
   Invoiced (ord) ≜ Status(ord)=invoiced;
   Final(ord) ≜ ord ∈ ORDERS − Orders
OPERATIONS
AddOr(ord, pd, qt) ≜
PRE    ord ∈ ORDERS − Orders ∧ pd ∈ Products ∧ qt ∈ NATURAL ∧
       Initial(ord) ∧
       ((qt > StockQty(pd)) or (qt ≤ StockQty(pd)))
THEN
       SELECT qt > StockQty(pd)
          THEN B_AddOrder(ord, pd, qt,pending)
       WHEN qt ≤ StockQty(pd)
          THEN B_AddOrder(ord, pd, qt, invoiced)
       END
END
END
```

Let us give some explanations about how the machine Order_Control is constructed. First the states of the state diagram are expressed as **DEFINITIONS**. Each basic operation appearing as an internal message in a collaboration diagram must be promoted to make it visible from another machine that might include the machine Order_Control. In our case, for instance, we have to promote the two basic operations B_ChangeStatus and B_RemoveOrder. The operation AddOr is the translation of the event with the same name in the state diagram. According to the semantics of events we have chosen (see section 4.1.3.1), the straightforward translation into B is a preconditioned substitution. The precondition is composed of a set of conjuncts. The first three conjuncts concern the typing of the input parameters of the event. They are obtained by substituting, in the preconditions of the called operations, the formal parameters with the actual ones. The fourth predicate corresponds to the predicate of the source state of the event. The last predicate denotes the disjunction of the guards of the different transitions associated with the event. The **THEN** part of the preconditioned substitution is expressed as a **SELECT** substitution, which corresponds roughly to a **CASE** statement. Each part of the **SELECT** corresponds to a transition fired by the event AddOr according to the related guard and contains a call to the basic operation associated with the transition.

3. The third level is composed of the machines OrderManagement and Product-

Management. OrderManagement (respectively ProductManagement) contains all the operations derived from the collaboration diagrams whose triggering message arrives at OrderManagement (respectively ProductManagement). These machines are specified as follows:

```
MACHINE       ProductManagement
INCLUDES      Product
OPERATIONS
AddStock(pd, qt) ≜
PRE   pd ∈ Products ∧
      qt ∈ NATURAL ∧
      StockQty(pd) + qt ∈ NATURAL
THEN
      B_ChangeStockQty(pd,StockQty(pd)+qt)
END
END
```

```
MACHINE       OrderManagement
INCLUDES      Order_Control, Product
OPERATIONS
CreateOr(pd, qt) ≜
PRE   pd ∈ Products ∧
      qt ∈ NATURAL ∧
      ∃ ord.( ord ∈ ORDERS-Orders)∧
      qt ≤ StockQty(pd) ⇒ StockQty(pd) − qt ∈ NATURAL
THEN
      ANY ord WHERE ord ∈ ORDERS-orders THEN
            AddOr(ord, pd,qt)||
            IF qt ≤ StockQty(pd)
            THEN B_ChangeStockQty(pd, StockQty(pd)-qt)
            END
      END
END;
CancelOr(ord) ≜
PRE   ord ∈ Orders ∧
      Status(ord) = invoiced ⇒
          StockQty(Reference(ord))+
                          OrderedQty(ord) ∈ NATURAL
THEN
      B_RemoveOrder(ord)||
      IF Status(ord) = invoiced
```

```
        THEN B_ChangeStockQty(Reference(ord),
                        StockQty(Reference(ord))+OrderedQty(ord))
        END
END;
invoicedOr ⟵ InvoiceAnyOrder ≜
PRE  ∃ oo · (oo ∈ Status⁻¹[{pending}] ∧
                StockQty(Reference(oo)) ≥ OrderedQty(oo)) ∧
        ∀oo.(oo ∈ Status⁻¹[{pending}]∧
             StockQty(Reference(oo)) ≥ OrderedQty(oo) ⇒
        StockQty(Reference(oo)) − OrderedQty(oo) ∈ NATURAL)
THEN ANY ord WHERE ord ∈ Status⁻¹[{pending}] ∧
                StockQty(Reference(ord)) ≥ OrderedQty(ord)
        THEN
                B_ChangeStatus(ord,invoiced) ||
                B_ChangeStockQty(Reference(ord),
                        StockQty(Reference(ord))- OrderedQty(ord))||
                invoicedOr := ord
        END
END
END
```

Let us detail how we obtain an operation (for example CreateOr):

- its name and parameters are those of the triggering message CreateOr of the corresponding collaboration diagram (Figure 4.4);
- its body is constructed in three steps. Firstly, each internal message gives a B substitution. If the message is guarded, then the B substitution denotes an **IF** substitution whose condition corresponds to the guard of the related message. Secondly, these substitutions are put in parallel. Finally, this parallel substitution is enclosed in an unbounded choice (**ANY** substitution) that translates the action of creating the new object *ord*;
- its precondition is composed of four conjuncts. The first two conjuncts concern the typing of the input parameters. The third conjunct is a necessary and sufficient condition that ensures the feasibility of the **ANY** substitution. Finally, the last conjunct is automatically generated from preconditions of the called operations to ensure that they will be satisfied when they are actually executed. In this particular case, we subscribe such conjuncts in italic since they are always true, and hence they can be removed. From a proof point of view, keeping such conjuncts may facilitate the proof process. In fact, for operation $AddStock$, for instance, removing predicate ($P_1 \triangleq StockQty(pd) + qt \in NATURAL$) obliges the prover to establish two additional proofs that were obvious in the presence of P_1.

4.4 Validation

In order to establish the correctness of a B specification, the B method defines proof obligations that ensure that the invariant is satisfiable and that the operations maintain it. Furthermore, we generate a new proof for each transition of a state diagram. This proof allows us to check that the execution of the action associated with the transition makes the predicate of the target state satisfied.

All the abstract machines presented in this chapter have been proved using AtelierB (release 3.6) from Clearsy [CLE 03]. Table 4.1 presents for each machine:

- the number of generated proof obligations;
- the number of proofs automatically discharged by AtelierB;
- the number of proofs that have been interactively proved;
- the last column shows that all the interactive proofs have been solved.

Machine	Proof Obligations	Automatic Proofs	Interactive Proofs	% Proved
Product	7	7(100%)	0 (0%)	100%
Order	23	22 (96%)	1 (4%)	100%
OrderManagement (case 1)	9	9 (100%)	0 (0%)	100%
Order_Control	19	19 (100%)	0 (0%)	100%
OrderManagement (case 2)	40	40 (100%)	0 (0%)	100%
ProductManagement	5	5 (100%)	0 (0%)	100%
Total	103	102 (99%)	1 (1%)	100%

Table 4.1: Summary of the proofs

The only proof that the automatic prover of AtelierB fails to discharge is related to the relational operator domain substraction ($\lhd$) used in B_RemoveOrder on the variable Status whose codomain denotes an enumerated given set. This is not due to lack of rules in the prover, but the prover fails to find the right sequence of rules that must be applied to discharge such proofs. Nevertheless, they can be automatically discharged by defining additional tactics following the approach we have developed in [MAM 03]. Let us note that all the proofs of the operations translating state and collaboration diagrams have been automatically discharged. This is not surprising; in fact these operations have been specified by taking the preconditions of the called operations into account.

4.5 The natural-language description of the specifications

4.5.1 Case 1

An order has only one product reference, an ordered quantity which is a natural number and a status which specifies whether it is a pending or an invoiced order. A product may be ordered by several orders. For each product, a quantity in stock is defined. It is a natural number.

There is one input message Invoicing which takes an order as input. It can occur only if there is enough stock for the ordered product and if the order status is Pending. This message triggers an operation whose effects are to: change the order status to Invoiced and decrease the quantity in stock of the relevant product of the ordered quantity.

4.5.2 Case 2

The definitions of order and product are the same as in case 1. The following input messages are defined:

- Create an order: the message may occur only if the product exists in the system and if the system can accept new orders. It triggers an operation which creates a new order for a product and a given quantity. If there is enough stock for the relevant product, then the order status is Invoiced and the quantity in stock is decreased. Otherwise, the order status is Pending.
- Increase the quantity in stock for a given product.
- Cancel an order: we assume that it is possible to cancel an order in either state. If it is in the Pending state, the message only triggers the deletion of the order, otherwise it triggers in addition the increase of the quantity in stock of the product referenced by the canceled order. This increase corresponds to the quantity previously ordered.
- Invoice an order: the message may occur only if there is at least one pending order with an ordered quantity less than or equal to the quantity in stock of the ordered product. In this case, the status of the chosen order becomes invoiced, and the quantity in stock of the ordered product is decreased by the ordered quantity. The order is non-deterministically chosen from the set of pending orders for which there is enough quantity in stock.

4.6 Conclusion

In this chapter, we have shown the usefulness of combining graphical notations (UML) with formal methods (B). The use of UML allows us to rapidly obtain an intuitive and synthetic overview of the two studies, while the use of the B method provides automatic tools to check and validate the generated specification. From this first view, the derivation of a B formal specification has raised new questions. The direct writing of a B specification would perhaps have raised the same questions, but without that intuitive view which is so useful for end-users. Thus, the UML-B combination appears to be fruitful, by taking advantage of the benefits of both methods. In [FAC 00], we already undertook a similar experiment with OMT notations, and our conclusion is as follows. Despite the graphical advantages of OMT, the expressivity of its behavioral diagrams are rather reduced; they are not appropriate for the descriptions of the different aspects of database applications. More details about these limits can be found in [FAC 00].

From the property verification point of view, in a system two kinds of property may be modeled:

- operational (or functional) properties that describe a system in a "passive" way by giving its data (or entities) and the global operations that act upon them;
- behavioral properties such as temporal properties (how long does it take to invoice an order?), liveness properties (a pending order eventually becomes invoiced) or concurrency control, that is, managing simultaneous events (new orders, stock entries ... that simultaneously occur in the system).

In B, the first set of properties may be directly verified thanks to the B model itself. Conversely, behavioral properties are more difficult to verify, even if they could be expressed in B but in a somewhat artificial manner. Note that "dynamic invariants" [ABR 98] proposed by J.R. Abrial tackles some of these problems.

However, this combination raises some problems, especially for the dynamic aspects:

- the semantics of state diagrams is not always clear: for instance is it possible to have an event when no condition is true? And if it is, how is such an event handled? In this chapter, we have assumed that such a case is not possible: the diagrams provide preconditions (thus proof obligations to the events). But another possible interpretation would consider the diagrams as being incomplete (not giving the error cases);
- in UML, there is no notation to precisely describe the creation of new objects. For that, we have been obliged to introduce a new notation on collaboration diagrams by attaching this action to a specific manager;
- lastly, it turns out that state and collaboration diagrams are not sufficient to describe database transactions with return values. To overcome this limitation, we have extended class diagrams by stereotyped classes in which these transactions are directly specified with B notations.

In addition to its property verification purpose, the translation of UML diagrams into B notations offers a formal framework for the generation of safe implementations. In [MAM 02, MAM 06], we have shown how it is possible to derive a trustworthy relational database implementation using the B refinement technique.

Bibliography

[ABR 96] ABRIAL J. R., *The B-Book: Assigning Programs to Meanings*, Press Syndicate of the University of Cambridge, 1996.

[ABR 98] ABRIAL J.-R. M. L., "Introducing Dynamic Constraints in B", in *B'98: 2nd International B Conference*, LNCS 1393, Springer-Verlag, April 1998.

[CLE 03] CLEARSY, "AtelierB: Manuel de Référence", 2003, available at http://www.atelierb.societe.com.

[DIA 06] DIAB H., FRAPPIER M., "B: a model-based method using generalised substitutions", in in FRAPPIER M., HABRIAS H., Eds., *Software Specification Methods: An Overview Using a Case Study*, Hermes Science Publishing Ltd, London, 2006.

[ELM 04] ELMASRI R., NAVATHE S. B., *Fundamentals of Database Systems*, Addison-Wesley, 4th edition, 2004.

[FAC 00] FACON P., LALEAU R., NGUYEN H. P., "From OMT Diagrams to B Specifications", in FRAPPIER M., HABRIAS H., Eds., *Software Specification Methods: An Overview Using a Case Study*, Springer, FACIT series, 2000.

[LAL 00a] LALEAU R., "On the Interest of Combining UML with the B Formal Method for the Specification of Database Applications.", in *ICEIS2000: 2nd International Conference on Enterprise Information Systems*, July 2000.

[LAL 00b] LALEAU R., MAMMAR A., "An Overview of a Method and its Support Tool for Generating B Specifications from UML Notations", in *ASE '00: Proceedings of the Fifteenth IEEE International Conference on Automated Software Engineering*, IEEE Computer Society, September 2000.

[LAL 01] LALEAU R., POLACK F., "Specification of Integrity-Preserving Operations in Information Systems by Using a Formal UML-Based Language", *Information and Software Technology*, vol. 43, p. 693-704, 2001.

[LAL 02] LALEAU R., "Conception et Développement Formels d'Applications Bases de Données", Habilitation thesis, CEDRIC Laboratory, December 2002, available at http://www.univ-paris12.fr/lacl/laleau/.

[MAM 02] MAMMAR A., "Un Environnement Formel pour le Développement d'Applications Bases de Données", PhD thesis, CEDRIC Laboratory, November 2002, available at http://cedric.cnam.fr/.

[MAM 03] MAMMAR A., LALEAU R., "Design of an Automatic Prover Dedicated to the Refinement of Database Applications", in *FME2003: Formal Methods*, LNCS 2805, Springer-Verlag, September 2003.

[MAM 05] MAMMAR A., LALEAU R., "UB2SQL: A Tool For Building Database Applications using UML and the B Formal Method", Technical Report, University of Luxembourg, 2005, available at http://se2c.uni.lu/users/AM.

[MAM 06] MAMMAR A., LALEAU R., "From a B Formal Specification to an Executable Code: Application to the Relational Database Domain", *Information and Software Technology Journal*, vol. 48(4), p. 253-279, 2006.

Chapter 5

UML+Z: Augmenting UML with Z

Nuno AMÁLIO, Fiona POLACK, and Susan STEPNEY

5.1 Overview of *UML + Z*

UML + Z is a framework for building, analysing and refining models of software systems based on the UML and the formal specification language Z. It is, in fact, an instance of an approach to build rigorous engineering frameworks for model-driven development based on templates, which we call *CiTRUS* [AMA 06]. *UML + Z* is targeted at developers who have minimal knowledge of Z, but are familiar with UML-based modeling. *UML + Z* models comprise class, state and object UML diagrams, which are represented in a common Z model (the semantic domain) in Figure 5.1; the Z model gives the precise meaning of the diagrams. The framework tries to minimise exposure to the Z model, with UML diagrams acting like a graphical interface for the formality (Z) that lies underneath, but this is not always possible and one Z expert is required in the development to describe system properties that are not expressible diagrammatically (mainly operations and constraints).

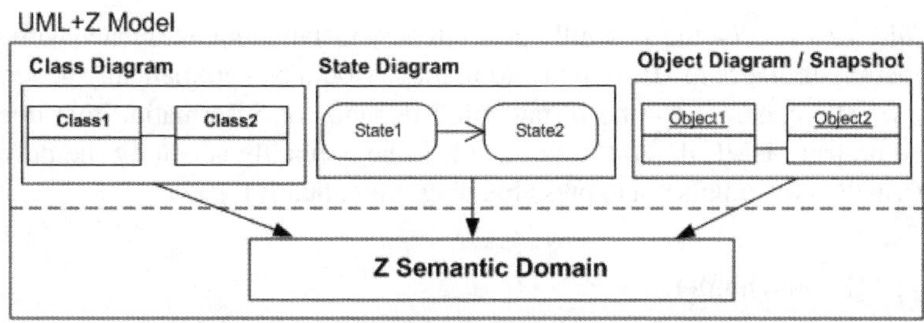

Figure 5.1: Models in the *UML + Z* framework

A crucial component of *UML* + *Z* is a catalogue of *templates* and *meta-theorems*. Templates are generic representations of sentences of some formal language, which, when instantiated, yield actual language sentences. To express templates, we have developed the formal template language (FTL), which enables an approach to proof with template representations of Z (*meta-proof*). This enables the representation of structural Z patterns as templates (e.g. the structure of a Z operation), but also reasoning with these template representation to establish *meta-theorems* (e.g. calculate a precondition). Every sentence of the Z model in *UML*+*Z* is generated by instantiating one of the templates, and meta-theorems can be used to simplify, and in some cases fully discharge, proofs associated with the Z model.

The modeling and analysis process with *UML* + *Z* begins with the drawing of UML class and state diagrams. These diagrams are then used to instantiate templates from the catalogue to generate the Z model. The developer then adds operations and system constraints that are not expressed diagrammatically to the Z model. The Z specification is then checked for consistency using the meta-theorems of the *UML*+*Z* catalogue and a Z theorem prover. Finally, there is a process of model analysis, where the developer draws snapshots to validate the model; these snapshots are represented in Z and the analysis is assisted by the Z/Eves theorem prover. Usually, the analysis phase of the process results in changes to the diagrams or the portion of the Z model not expressed diagrammatically.

Currently, the process of instantiating templates is manual. The templates from the catalogue are manually selected and instantiated with names from the diagrams. The reasoning with templates is also based on manual instantiation, but it is assisted by Z proof tools such as Z/Eves [SAA 97].

5.2 Analysis and specification of case 1

We start by modeling the static and behavioral aspects of the system with UML class and state diagrams. Then we discuss the Z model that is generated from the diagrams by instantiating templates. Finally, the *UML* + *Z* model is consistency-checked and analysed.

The following terminology is used to refer to the Z generated from templates:

- *fully generated* – the Z is fully generated by instantiating templates with information of diagrams. If we had a tool, the Z would be automatically generated;
- *partially generated* – the instantiation depends on information that does not come from UML diagrams, but needs to be explicitly added by the developer (usually constraints not expressible diagrammatically).

5.2.1 UML class model

A UML class diagram describes *classes* and their relationships. At the abstract level, a class diagram captures the main entities (or concepts) of a system and the structural relationship that exists between them. A class denotes a set of objects (individuals) that share certain *attributes* and *operations*.

Question 1: What data does the system manage? What are the main entities of the system and what are the relationships among them?

Answer: The case study states that the system is about invoicing orders that are placed for products. We model *order* and *product* as two UML classes and relate them with an association.

Question 2: Are there limits on the number of products that an order can reference? How many orders can reference the same product?

Answer: The case study makes clear that each order references precisely one product, but a product can be referenced by many orders. We assume that there are products that are not referenced by orders. We represent this information in the multiplicity of the association between *Order* and *Product*: *Order* references *one* product, but a product may be referenced by *many* orders.

Question 3: What information should the system hold for products and orders?

Answer: The case study states that orders can be for different quantities of the same reference; we represent the ordered *quantity* as an attribute of the class *Order*. The case study also refers to quantities of products available in stock. We model the *stock* quantity as an attribute of class *Product*.

Question 4: Do we know what type of information these quantities hold? Are products whole things (eg. books or parts) or continuous amounts (eg. water or cloth)? Can there be negative stock?

Answer: The case study does not fully answer these questions. We assume that the attributes are of the same type, since the things being ordered are from the stock of a product. We know that a mathematical ordering on the type is required (since stock may be less than or equal to the ordered quantity). So, based on our intuitive notion of quantity, we assume that the attributes *quantity* and *stock* are natural numbers (we do not allow negative stock).

These features are modeled in a UML class diagram in Figure 5.2. This says that there are two classes, *Order* and *Product*, each representing a set of objects (the orders and products of the system). Each *Order* object has a *quantity* attribute, referring to the ordered quantity of a product, and each *Product* object has a *stock* attribute, recording how much of the product is available in stock. *Order* and *Product* are related through an association, which says that each order refers to exactly one product, and that each product may be referred by many orders.

5.2.2 UML state models

UML state diagrams describe the permitted state transitions of the objects of a class. Here we draw the UML state diagram of class *Order*.

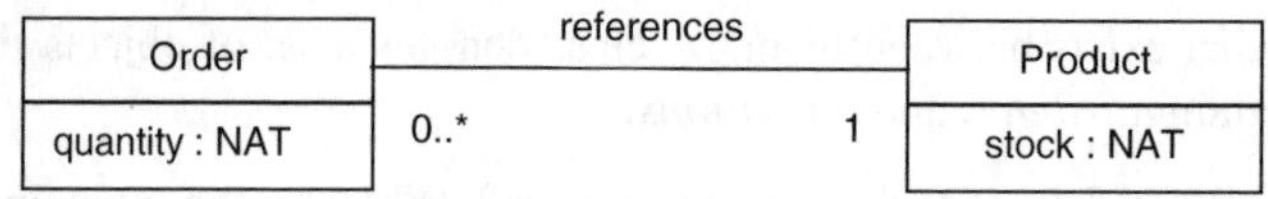

Figure 5.2: Initial version of the high-level UML class diagram

Question 5: What happens when a product is ordered? What happens to an order?

Answer: The case study says that an order can be *invoiced*, and that this changes the state of an order from *pending* to *invoiced*. Invoicing only occurs if the ordered quantity is either less than or equal to the quantity that is in stock. We assume that all new orders have the state, *pending*. When invoiced, the order changes from the state *pending* into the state *invoiced*. This is captured in the state diagram of Figure 5.3. Note that the constraint *orders are invoiced only if there is enough stock to fulfill the order* (ordered $quantity \leq stock$ quantity) is not expressed here as a guard of the state transition. This because that constraint involves the state of a *Product* object and here we are restricted to state constraints expressible in terms of the state of *Order*.

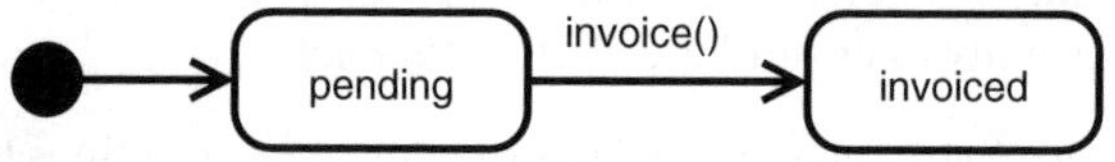

Figure 5.3: The state diagram of *Order*

5.2.3 The Z model

The Z model resulting from the UML class and state diagrams above is *fully generated*. It enables formal consistency-checking and validation of the whole $UML + Z$ model. The Z model follows a structuring to specify object-oriented (OO) systems in Z, which uses *views* to separate the description of the different aspects of a system (see [AMA 05] for full details); there are five views, namely, structural, intensional, extensional, relational and global. In the following, the fully generated Z model is presented for each view.

The Z model follows certain naming conventions. The names of operations that perform a change of state include the symbol Δ. The names of extensional view definitions are prefixed by $\mathbb{S}$, and the ones of the relational view by $\mathbb{A}$.

5.2.3.1 Structural view

The *structural* view defines the set of all classes of a model as atoms, and assigns to each class a set of objects: the set of all possible objects of the class.

The Z toolkit of $UML + Z$ defines the set of all objects (OBJ) and asserts that this set is non-empty:

$$[OBJ] \qquad\qquad OBJ \neq \varnothing$$

The set $CLASS$ defines the set of all classes of a model and the function $\mathbb{O}$ gives all the possible objects of a class. As we do not have *subclassing* (inheritance) in our model the sets of objects of each class are mutually disjoint:

$$CLASS ::= OrderCl \mid ProductCl$$

$$\begin{array}{|l} \mathbb{O} : CLASS \rightarrow \mathbb{P}_1\, OBJ \\ \hline \text{disjoint}\, CLASS \lhd \mathbb{O} \end{array}$$

5.2.3.2 Intensional view

The intensional view describes the intensional meaning of a class, that is: the properties shared by all its objects. This amounts to defining: (a) the state space of objects, which includes the definition of class attributes; (b) the initialisation of state; and (c) the operations of the objects of the class.

The class *Order* requires a type representing the set of all states of the state diagram:

$$ORDERST ::= pending \mid invoiced$$

The state space comprises *state*, which records the current state of an *Order* as defined in the state diagram, and *quantity*, which is defined in the class diagram:

$$\begin{array}{|l} \multicolumn{1}{l}{\underline{\ Order\ }} \\ state : ORDERST \\ quantity : \mathbb{N} \\ \hline \end{array}$$

$$\begin{array}{|l} \multicolumn{1}{l}{\underline{\ OrderInit\ }} \\ Order' \\ quantity? : \mathbb{N} \\ \hline state' = pending \\ quantity' = quantity? \\ \hline \end{array}$$

The invoice operation captures the state transition from *pending* to *invoiced*, as described in the state diagram:

$$\begin{array}{|l} \multicolumn{1}{l}{\underline{\ Order_{\Delta}Invoice\ }} \\ \Delta Order \\ \hline state = pending \land state' = invoiced \land quantity' = quantity \\ \hline \end{array}$$

The intension of *Product* is defined as described in the class diagram in Figure 5.2:

$$\begin{array}{|l} \multicolumn{1}{l}{\underline{\ Product\ }} \\ stock : \mathbb{N} \\ \hline \end{array}$$

$$\begin{array}{|l} \multicolumn{1}{l}{\underline{\ ProductInit\ }} \\ Product' \\ \hline stock' = 0 \\ \hline \end{array}$$

5.2.3.3 Extensional view

The extensional view describes the extensional meaning of classes, that is, the set of all existing objects of a class. Like intensions, class extensions comprise a state space, an initialisation and operations. A class extension is defined by using Z *promotion* [WOO 96, STE 03], a structuring technique for constructing aggregate (or whole-part) structures. Promotion is used whenever there is a component that comprises independent parts, with their own state. In this case, the state of a class extension is defined as an aggregate structure comprising all its existing objects (each an instance of a class intension): the class extension *promotes* its intension.

The state space of all class extensions is defined by instantiating the $\mathbb{S}\mathrm{Class}$ *generic* schema of the framework's Z toolkit. This generic introduces the parameters *OSET* and *OSTATE*, which are to be substituted by the set of all objects of the specific class and the intensional state space of the class (as defined above). The schema component *objs* represents the set of existing objects of the class and, *objSt* is a function that gives the current state of one object:

$$\mathbb{S}\mathrm{Class}\,[OSET, OSTATE]$$
$$objs : \mathbb{P}\, OSET$$
$$objSt : OSET \nrightarrow OSTATE$$
$$\mathrm{dom}\, objSt = objs$$

The extension of *Order* instantiates the class generic. The components of the generic are renamed to avoid name clashes when all the extensional schemas are put together to make the system schema (see below). The initialisation sets the schema components to the empty set: in the initial state there no orders:

$$\mathbb{S}Order == \mathbb{S}\mathrm{Class}[\mathbb{O}OrderCl, Order][orders/objs, orderSt/objSt]$$
$$\mathbb{S}OrderInit == [\ \mathbb{S}Order\,' \mid orders' = \varnothing \wedge orderSt' = \varnothing\ ]$$

Operations defined using promotion require an auxiliary schema that specify the *frame* of the operation: the aggregate components that are to change as a result of the operation and those that should remain unaltered. There are different kinds of promotion frames (see [AMA 05, WOO 96, STE 03] for details). To create a new *Order* object, we need a frame specifying the addition of a new object to the class extension (names of promotion frames are preceeded by Φ):

$$\Phi\mathbb{S}OrderNew$$
$$\Delta\mathbb{S}Order\ ;\ Order\,'$$
$$oOrder! : \mathbb{O}OrderCl$$
$$oOrder! \in \mathbb{O}OrderCl \setminus orders$$
$$orders' = orders \cup \{oOrder!\}$$
$$orderSt' = orderSt \cup \{oOrder! \mapsto \theta Order'\}$$

The Z operator θ captures a schema binding: an assignment of values to the schema's variables. The frame says that the newly created object (*oOrder*!) will be mapped to some state, which is defined in the initialisation being promoted. The actual operation to create a new *Order* object uses the framing schema:

$$\mathbb{S}_{\Delta}OrderNew == \exists\ Order\,' \bullet \Phi\mathbb{S}OrderNew \wedge OrderInit$$

The binding ($\theta Order'$) of the frame is specified in *OrderInit*.

The update frame specifies a state transition of a single *Order* object:

$$\begin{array}{l}
\Phi\mathbb{S}OrderUpdate \\
\hline
\Delta\mathbb{S}Order\ ;\ \Delta Order \\
oOrder? : \mathbb{O}OrderCl \\
\hline
oOrder? \in orders \\
\theta Order = orderSt\ oOrder? \\
orders' = orders \\
orderSt' = orderSt \oplus \{oOrder? \mapsto \theta Order'\}
\end{array}$$

The extension operation to invoice an *Order* uses the update frame:

$$\mathbb{S}_{\Delta}OrderInvoice == \exists\ \Delta Order \bullet \Phi\mathbb{S}OrderUpdate \wedge Order_{\Delta}Invoice$$

The extension of *Product* is similarly defined.

5.2.3.4 Relational view

The relational view defines the associations between classes. Associations are represented as a relation in Z, and denote a set of object tuples (the objects being related).

The state of the association *References* is defined as a mathematical relation between the set of all objects of the class *ORder* and that of *Product*. The initialisation sets all tuples to empty: in the initial state there are no objects and no links between them:

$$\mathbb{A}References == [\ references : \mathbb{O}OrderCl \leftrightarrow \mathbb{O}ProductCl\ ]$$
$$\mathbb{A}ReferencesInit == [\ \mathbb{A}References\,' \mid references' = \varnothing\ ]$$

5.2.3.5 Global view

This view looks at the system from a global viewpoint. It represents the system structure as a composition of local structures (classes and associations), and constraints that can only be expressed in the context of the system as a whole.

The multiplicity of associations is a constraint that cannot be expressed in the relational view. These constraints affect the existing objects of the associated classes, defined in the class extension. The schema *Link*$\mathbb{A}$*References* expresses the multiplicity constraint of the association *References* using the generic $\mathrm{Rel}_{*,1}$ from the Z toolkit of *UML* + *Z*; this says that *references* (a relation) is constrained to be a total function, from the set of existing orders to the set of existing products:

$$\mathrm{Rel}_{*,1}[X, Y] == X \rightarrow Y$$

```
┌─ LinkAReferences ────────────────────
│ SOrder; SProduct; AReferences
├──────────────
│ references ∈ Rel*,1[orders, products]
└──────────────────────────────────────
```

The system schema includes all component schemas and the association constraint:

```
┌─ System ─────────────────────────────
│ SOrder; SProduct; AReferences
├──────────────
│ LinkAReferences
└──────────────────────────────────────
```

The initialisation of the system is the initialisation of the system's components:

$$SysInit == System' \wedge \mathbb{S}OrderInit \wedge \mathbb{S}ProductInit \wedge \mathbb{A}ReferencesInit$$

5.2.4 Checking model consistency

Question 6: Is the model internally consistent?

Answer: The Z model is type-correct (checked with Z-Eves). But a model can be type-correct and still be inconsistent. The consistency of Z models is demonstrated by proving certain conjectures. Z conjectures have the form $\vdash ?\ P$, where P is a well-formed Z predicate, which is said to be proved under the statements of the specification; when P is true, the conjecture establishes a theorem of the specification.

To demonstrate the consistency of state space descriptions, one is required to prove initialisation conjectures, to show that there is at least one valid instance of the state space description satisfying its initialisation (an existence proof). For example, the initialisation conjecture for *Order* (intensional view, above) is: $\vdash ?\ \exists\, OrderInit \bullet \mathrm{true}$.

We prove initialisation conjectures for the various system components and the whole system:

- the initialisation conjectures of class intensions are simplified by appeal to *UML*+ *Z* meta-theorems, and they are then automatically proved in Z/Eves;
- the initialisation conjectures of class extensions, associations and system are *true by construction*, by appeal to meta-theorems of *UML* + *Z*.

5.2.5 Validating the model

Question 7: How can we be confident that the model expresses the intent of our customer?

Answer: We need to check the model against the requirements of the system. A model may be consistent and still not meet the system requirements. We have developed a technique, based on Catalysis snapshots [D'S 99] and formal proof, to validate the models of our framework [AMA 04]; this validation is assisted by Z/Eves.

Catalysis snapshots are UML object diagrams. These diagram are instances of class diagrams, describing the objects of a system and the way they are linked among each other at a point in time. The use of diagrams helps to involve the customer of the system in model validation, by drawing diagrams that illustrate the system's requirements.

Question 8: Obviously, we can't validate everything, but how would we know that an order really can only reference one product? Does the system accept a situation where two products are linked to one order?

Answer: The snapshot in Figure 5.4 is used to validate this requirement. It shows a state that should not be accepted by the model of the system: an order that refers to two products.

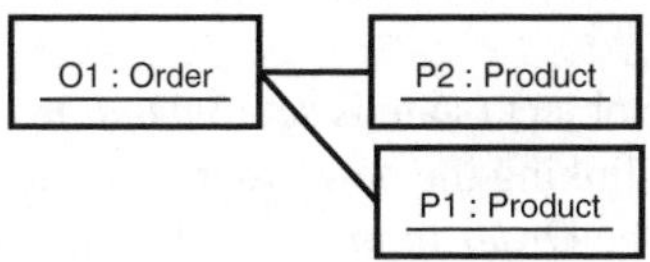

Figure 5.4: A snapshot showing an Order associated with two products

The Z representation of this snapshot is fully generated by template instantiation:

$$\begin{array}{|l}
\textit{StSnap}1 \\
\hline
\textit{System} \\
\hline
\textit{orders} = \{\textit{oO}1\} \land \textit{orderSt} = \{\textit{oO}1 \mapsto \textit{O}1\} \\
\textit{products} = \{\textit{oPX}, \textit{oPY}\} \land \textit{productSt} = \{\textit{oPX} \mapsto \textit{PX}, \textit{oPY} \mapsto \textit{PY}\} \\
\textit{references} = \{\textit{oO}1 \mapsto \textit{oPX}, \textit{oO}1 \mapsto \textit{oPY}\}
\end{array}$$

(Some definitions are omitted, such as names and states of objects.)

The state described by the snapshot should not be accepted by the system, thus we prove the conjecture (the negation of the positive case):

$$\vdash ?\ \neg\ (\exists\ \textit{StSnap}1 \bullet \text{true})$$

This conjecture is provable in Z/Eves, which means that the state described by the snapshot is not valid in the model of the system.

5.3 Analysis and specification of case 2

The second case study does not change the state space, but it adds external behavior, and modifies internal behavior. Case 2 requires that the system provide the following operations:

- entries of new orders;
- cancellation of orders;
- entries of quantities in the stock.

For each of these operations in turn, we discuss its specification, then review its verification and validation. The existing generated Z model is unchanged.

5.3.1 Entries of new orders

Question 9: What must the system do when an order is received? What are the changes to the system?

Answer: ¿From the case study we deduce that the system creates the order and associates it to the ordered product. Then, if there is enough stock, the order is set to *invoiced*, otherwise it is set to *pending*. This involves the following component operations:

1. create an *Order* object (state is set to *pending*);
2. create the tuple linking the new order with the ordered product;
3. set the state of the *Order* to *invoiced* if there is enough stock.

First, we specify component operations individually, and then their composition. The first and third operations have already been specified for *Order* ($\mathbb{S}_{\Delta}OrderNew$ and $\mathbb{S}_{\Delta}OrderInvoice$, above). The second operation is defined in the relational view (*fully generated*):

$$
\begin{array}{|l}
\mathbb{A}_{\Delta}ReferencesAdd \\
\hline
\Delta\ \mathbb{A}References \\
oOrder? : \mathbb{O}OrderCl \\
oProduct? : \mathbb{O}ProductCl \\
\hline
references' = references \cup \{oOrder? \mapsto oProduct?\}
\end{array}
$$

The system operation is defined as the composition of the component operations. This is *partially generated*. To simplify matters, the operation specification is divided in two parts: (a) create the object and tuple in the association references; (b) set the order to invoiced if there is sufficient stock. The two parts are then combined using the schema composition operator ($\fatsemi$) [WOO 96], which means that part (a) is followed by part (b).

In part (a), we start by defining the frame of the operation, which makes explicit what is to change and what is to remain unchanged. The name of system operation frames are prefixed by Ψ (by analogy to Φ promotion frames), and are formed by conjoining Δ *System* with the Ξ (nothing changes) of every system component whose state is to remain unchanged. In the system operation to create new orders, the $\mathbb{S}$*Product* component should remain unchanged (there are no changes to products):

$$\Psi NewOrder_a == \Delta System \wedge \Xi \mathbb{S}Product$$

The system operation is specified as the conjunction of the frame and the component operations; the renaming is needed so that elements of the schemas correctly communicate across the composition:

$$\begin{aligned} & SysNewOrder_a == \Psi NewOrder_a \\ & \quad \wedge \mathbb{S}_\Delta OrderNew \wedge \mathbb{A}_\Delta ReferencesAdd[oOrder!/oOrder?] \end{aligned}$$

In part (b), we need a schema stating the condition on the state transition *pending* to *invoiced*, which says that an order may change to *invoiced* only if the ordered quantity is less than or equal to the stock for the ordered product:

$$\begin{array}{|l} \textit{CondStockIsAvailable} \\ \hline \mathbb{S}Product \\ oProduct? : \mathbb{O}ProductCl \\ quantity? : \mathbb{N} \\ \hline oProduct? \in products \wedge quantity? \leq (productSt\ oProduct?).stock \\ \hline \end{array}$$

The frame of part (b) says that only the *Order* component may change. The actual operation says that if there is enough stock to fulfill the order then it should be invoiced, otherwise there is no change in the system:

$$\begin{aligned} & \Psi NewOrder_b == \Delta System \wedge \Xi \mathbb{S}Product \wedge \Xi \mathbb{A}References \\ & SysNewOrder_b == \Psi NewOrder_b \\ & \quad \wedge CondStockIsAvailable \wedge \mathbb{S}_\Delta OrderInvoice[oOrder!/oOrder?] \\ & \quad \vee \neg\ CondStockIsAvailable \wedge \Xi System \end{aligned}$$

Finally, the two parts are put together to make the system operation:

$$SysNewOrder == SysNewOrder_a \fatsemi SysNewOrder_b$$

Question 10: Is the operation consistent? What is its precondition?

Answer: The precondition of a Z operation describes the sets of states for which the outcome of the operation is properly defined. An operation is consistent (or satisfiable) if its precondition is not *false*. The precondition of the new operation is:

$$\mathbb{O}OrderCl \setminus orders \neq \varnothing \land oProduct? \in products$$

This precondition is not *false*. It states that the system has capacity for another *Order* object and that the ordered product is an existing product. This is exactly what we expect the precondition to be.

Question 11: Can we examine the model with a snapshot for the case that there is enough stock to fulfill an order?

Answer: We can write snapshots that describe state transitions. These snapshots are divided in two parts: the system state before an operation, and the state of the system after the operation.

Figure 5.5 shows a before state at the top (there is one product *PX*); the values of all the attributes are shown in the object boxes. The required after state of the first running of the operation is in the middle – there is now one order for *PX*. Order *O1* is for a *quantity* less than product *PX*'s quantity of *stock*, so the *state* of *O1* is *invoiced*. This is also the before state for another running of the operation, which adds *O2*, another order whose *quantity* is less than product *PX*'s quantity of *stock*, so its *state* is also *invoiced*.

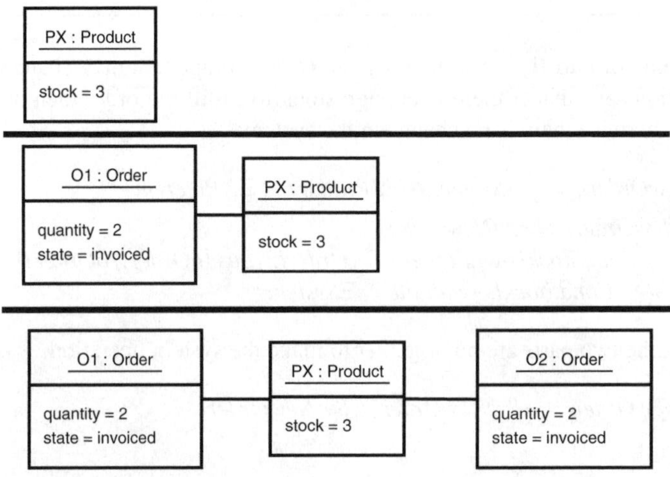

Figure 5.5: *SysNewOrder* snapshot: request for a product with enough stock

To check the validity of the operation snapshot, we represent the states in Z and we prove conjectures that perform three types of checks. The first checks that (a) the before-state is a valid system state and (b) it satisfies the operation precondition, an existence proof. The second checks that the after-state is a valid system state. The third checks that the operation satisfies the constraints described by the snapshot. These conjecture are captured by templates (see [AMA 06, AMA 04] for full details).

The conjectures for the snapshot in Figure 5.5 are all provable by Z/Eves.

Question 12: But how can we keep placing orders against product *PX*? Why is the stock not running out?

Answer: Here, the visualisation highlights a problem with the model. The case study does not say anything about what happens to *stock* when an order is performed. We assume that the stock is subtracted the ordered *quantity* each time.

Question 13: What do we need to do to the models?

Answer: First, we change the snapshot to describe what we want the system to do. Figure 5.6 shows the snapshot for the corrected second running of the operation: now the ordered amount is subtracted from the stock.

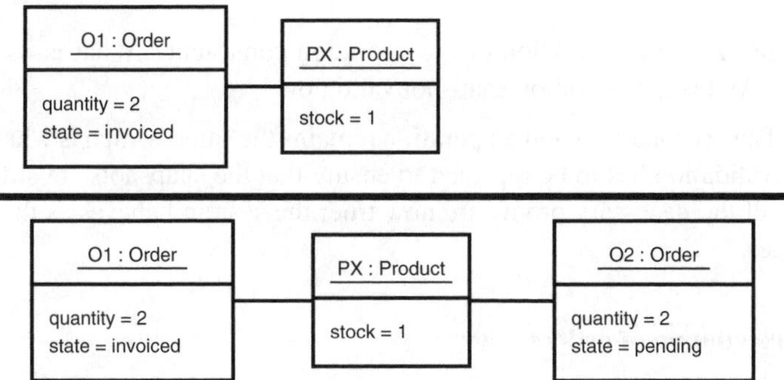

Figure 5.6: Revised *SysNewOrder* snapshot with deletion of quantity from stock

As expected, this snapshot fails to validate. The first two checks (above) are still true, since the before and after states are valid states of the system, and the before state is a valid precondition state for the operation. The third conjecture, which looks at whether the operation actually changes the before state into the after state, is false (its negation is *true*) – the operation does not perform the required transition. The Z operation specification needs to be corrected so that stock subtraction is performed.

We specify an operation in the intension of *Product* to subtract an input quantity (*quantity*?) from the product *stock*:

$$\begin{array}{|l}
\hline
Product_{\Delta}StockSubtract \\
\Delta Product \\
quantity? : \mathbb{N} \\
\hline
stock' = stock - quantity? \\
\hline
\end{array}$$

As before, the operation is promoted in the extensional view (*fully generated*):

$$\mathbb{S}_{\Delta}ProductStockSubtract == \exists\ \Delta Product \bullet \\ \quad \Phi\mathbb{S}ProductUpdate \wedge Product_{\Delta}StockSubtract$$

The original *SysNewOrder* has two components: the creation, then the invoicing. The stock change only applies to orders that can be invoiced. The calculated precondition of the new operation now captures the precondition previously expressed in the schema *CondStockIsAvailable*, so this is no longer required. The new version is:

$$\Psi NewOrder_b == \Delta System \wedge \Xi\mathbb{A}References$$
$$SysNewOrder_b == \Psi NewOrder_b \\ \quad \wedge\ \mathbb{S}_{\Delta}OrderInvoice[oOrder!/oOrder?] \wedge \mathbb{S}_{\Delta}ProductStockSubtract \\ \quad \vee \neg \text{ pre } \mathbb{S}_{\Delta}ProductStockSubtract \wedge \Xi System$$
$$SysNewOrder == SysNewOrder_a \mathbin{;} SysNewOrder_b$$

Question 14: Is the new version of the operation consistent? What is its precondition? And is the operation snapshot valid now?

Answer: The precondition of the operation remains the same, which is what we want. The validation has to be repeated to ensure that the snapshots are still valid. In fact all the necessary proofs are now true; the system behaves as the customer wishes.

5.3.2 Cancellation of orders

Question 15: What happens when an order is cancelled? Is the data relating to the cancelled order retained in the system?

Answer: The case study just says that orders may be cancelled. We assume that cancelled orders are deleted from the system. (The alternative, recording cancelled orders, would require the addition of a *cancelled* state to the state diagram of *Order*.)

Question 16: Can an invoiced order be cancelled?

Answer: The case study is not clear on restrictions on cancellation. Here, we assume that only *pending* orders can be cancelled. (The cancelling of *invoiced* orders would require that the ordered quantity be placed back into the stock.)

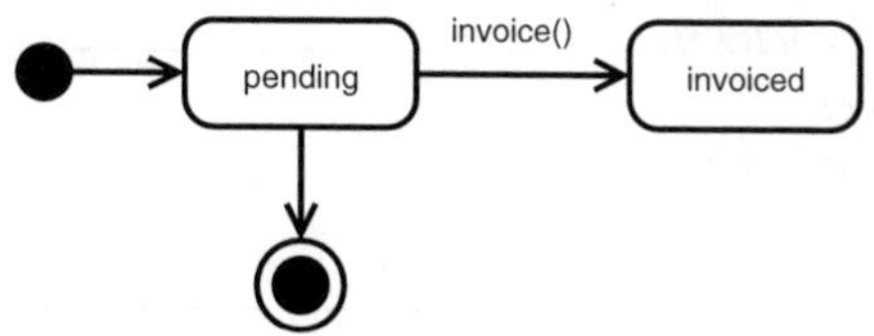

Figure 5.7: The updated state diagram of *Order*

To express cancellation we need to change the state diagram of *Order*, by adding an arrow from the state *pending* to the terminal state (Figure 5.7). This means that the object is deleted only when in the *pending* state.

This new arrow requires that more Z is *fully generated* from templates. In the intension of *Order*, finalisation captures the fact that *Order* objects may be deleted only if in the *pending* state:

$$OrderFin == [\, Order \mid state = pending \,]$$

The finalisation is then promoted in the extensional view. The delete promotion frame for *Order* removes an object from the class extension:

$$\begin{array}{l}
\Phi\mathbb{S}OrderDelete \\
\hline
\Delta\mathbb{S}Order \\
Order \\
oOrder? : \mathbb{O}OrderCl \\
\hline
oOrder? \in orders \\
\theta Order = orderSt\ oOrder? \\
orders' = orders \setminus \{oOrder?\} \\
orderSt' = \{oOrder?\} \ntriangleleft orderSt
\end{array}$$

The operation that deletes *Order* objects uses the frame to promote the finalisation:

$$\mathbb{S}_{\Delta}OrderDelete == \exists\, Order \bullet \Phi\mathbb{S}OrderDelete \land OrderDelCond$$

Question 17: What must the system do when an order is received? What are the changes to the system?

Answer: ¿From the case study and our assumptions, we deduce that the system must delete the *Order* object and its tuple in the association *References*. This involves two component operations: deletion of the order object (above) and deletion of tuple; both are *fully generated*.

The association operation deletes the tuple from the association, given an *Order* object as input:

$$\begin{array}{|l}
\hline
\mathbb{A}_{\Delta}ReferencesDelOrder \\
\Delta\ \mathbb{A}References \\
oOrder? : \mathbb{O}OrderCl \\
\hline
references' = \{oOrder?\} \lhd references \\
\hline
\end{array}$$

The system operation to cancel orders conjoins its frame with the component operations:

$$\Psi CancelOrder == \Delta System \land \Xi \mathbb{S}Product$$
$$SysCancelOrder == \Psi CancelOrder \land \mathbb{S}_{\Delta}OrderDelete \land \mathbb{A}_{\Delta}ReferencesDelOrder$$

Question 18: Is the operation consistent? What is its precondition?

Answer: The precondition predicate (calculated with Z/Eves) is:

$$oOrder? \in orders \land (orderSt\ oOrder?).state = pending$$

The operation is satisfiable, its precondition requires that the order to be cancelled is an existing order and that its *state* is *pending*, as expected.

Question 19: Does the order cancellation operation do what we expect?

Answer: Yes. The operation has been validated. We do not show the validation snapshots here, but we tested the case where the order to delete is *pending* (conjectures were all true) and the case where the order to delete is *invoiced* (one conjecture was false, as expected).

5.3.3 Entries of quantities into stock

Question 20: What is an "entry of quantities in the stock"? Does the required operation have to (a) just add stock, as in stock delivery or return; (b) also subtract stock, as in stock decay or wastage; or (c) accommodate arbitrary re-setting of the stock, as in stock-taking?

Answer: The case study does not elaborate on the meaning of stock entry. We assume that it adds an input quantity to the *stock* attribute.

The modeler needs to specify an operation to add stock, on the intension of *Product*. The operation receives a quantity of stock as input and adds this quantity to the existing stock:

$$\begin{array}{|l}
\hline
Product_{\Delta}StockAdd \\
\Delta Product \\
nStock? : \mathbb{N} \\
\hline
stock' = stock + nStock? \\
\hline
\end{array}$$

This operation is promoted in the extension of *Product* (fully generated):

$$\mathbb{S}_{\Delta}ProductStockAdd == \exists\ \Delta Product \bullet$$
$$\Phi\mathbb{S}ProductUpdate \land Product_{\Delta}StockAdd$$

The system operation simply puts the promoted operation into the context of the system:

$$\Psi AddStock == \Delta System \land \Xi\mathbb{S}Order \land \Xi\mathbb{A}References$$
$$SysAddStock == \Psi AddStock \land \mathbb{S}_{\Delta}ProductStockAdd$$

Question 21: Is the operation consistent? What is its precondition?

Answer: The precondition (calculated in Z/Eves) is:

$$oProduct? \in products$$

The operation is consistent, its precondition requires that the product to which stock is to be added is an existing product.

Question 22: Can we validate this operation with a snapshot?

Answer: We draw a snapshot illustrating the addition of stock to a product (Figure 5.8). A quantity of eight is added to the *stock* of *PY*, but there is an order *pending* with a *quantity* of three. This snapshot is valid in our model (conjectures proved in Z/Eves), but this poses a question.

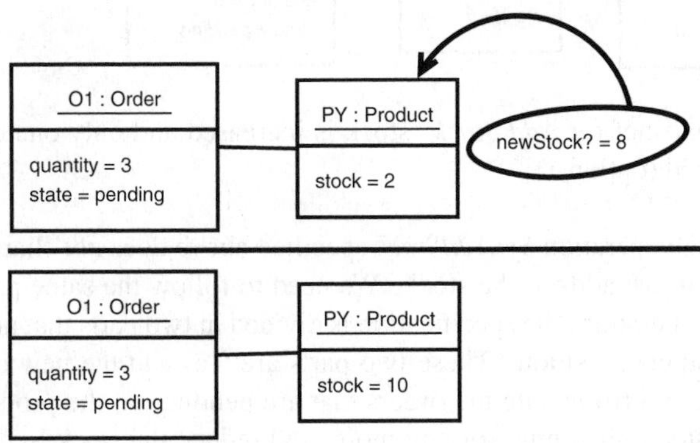

Figure 5.8: Snapshot for *Add Stock*: *Order* remains *pending*

Question 23: What happens when stock is added to products with pending orders? For example, in the snapshot, after the addition, there is enough stock to fulfill the order $O1$? Should $O1$ be changed to *invoiced* and stock subtracted the ordered amount?

Answer: The case study does not say what happens here. We assume that the pending order should be set to invoiced in this case. The snapshot should be corrected to reflect this: the after state of $O1$ would be *invoiced*, and *stock* value would be adjusted by $8 - 3$. This snapshot is valid in our model (proved in Z/Eves).

Question 24: But what if there were more than one order *pending* on *PY*?

Answer: Again, the case study is omissive. We assume that any order or orders are invoiced, until there is insufficient stock. We also decide not to impose any *ordering* to fulfill orders that are pending. This is is illustrated in Figures 5.9 and 5.10 – either of these diagrams can represent the effect of adding eight elements to the stock of *PY*. We model the fulfillment of orders after the addition of stock non-deterministically, which allows the developer to refine the model to enforce any ordering later in the development.

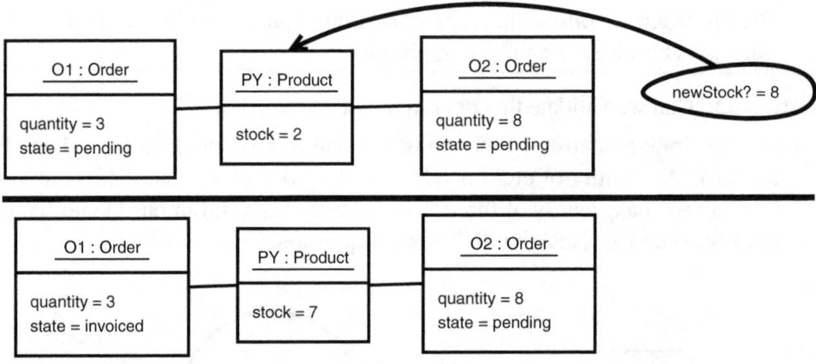

Figure 5.9: Snapshot for *Add Stock*: stock is increased and only one of the pending orders is invoiced (option 1)

Currently, the operation *SysAddStock* specified above does not change the state of *Order* objects, it just adds to the stock. We need to follow the same pattern used for the *New Order* operation: the specification is divided in two parts that are put together using sequential composition. These two parts are: (a) add the new quantity to the product's stock and (b) update the orders that are pending on the product until there is insufficient stock remaining for any more, and reduce the stock by the sum of the quantities of all orders that have been invoiced.

Above, we have specified part (a), so we just need to add part (b). First, we specify the component operation that updates a set of orders in the extension of *Order*. This needs to invoice a set of *Order* objects, which is defined using *multi-promotion* [STE 03][1]. $Order_{\Delta}Invoice$ is promoted to be executed on a set of *Order* objects (fully generated):

[1]Multi-promotion promotes operations on a set of objects, rather than a single object.

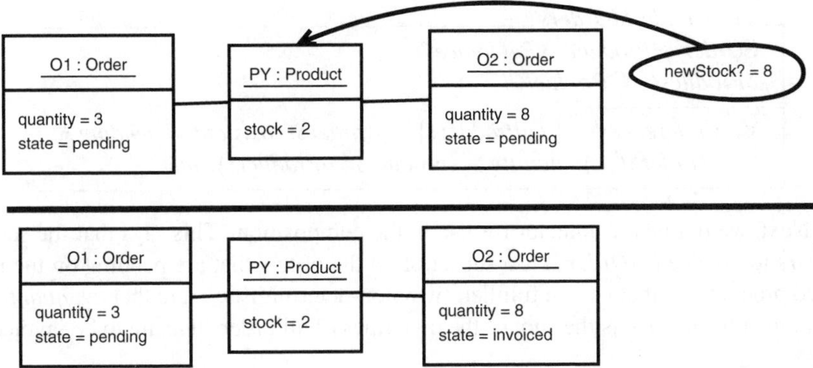

Figure 5.10: Snapshot for *Add Stock*: stock is increased and only one of the pending orders is invoiced (option 2)

$$
\begin{array}{l}
\_\_ \mathbb{S}_{\Delta} OrderInvoiceSet \_\_\_\_ \\
\Delta \mathbb{S}Order \\
osOrder? : \mathbb{P}(\mathbb{O}OrderCl) \\
\hline
osOrder? \subseteq orders \\
orders = orders' \\
osOrder? \lhd orderSt = osOrder? \lhd orderSt' \\
\forall o : osOrder? \bullet \exists \Delta Order \bullet \\
\qquad orderSt\ o = \theta Order \land orderSt'\ o = \theta Order' \land Order_{\Delta}Invoice
\end{array}
$$

The part (b) system operation is defined by composing component operations. First, we need a schema expressing the precondition for the operation; invoicing starts if there is at least one pending order on the product that can be fulfilled:

$$
\begin{array}{l}
\_\_ PreCondAddOrders \_\_\_\_ \\
\mathbb{S}Order; \mathbb{S}Product; \mathbb{A}References \\
oProduct? : \mathbb{O}ProductCl \\
\hline
\exists o : references^{\sim} (\!| \{oProduct?\} |\!) \bullet \\
\qquad (orderSt\ o).state = pending \\
\qquad \land (orderSt\ o).quantity \leq (productSt\ oProduct?).stock
\end{array}
$$

We have chosen to specify this operation non-deterministically, so we express the desired postcondition of the operation: after the operation is executed, there are no pending orders on the product that could be fulfilled:

$$
\begin{array}{|l}
\hline
\textit{PostCondAddOrders} \\
\mathbb{S}Order';\mathbb{S}Product';\mathbb{A}References' \\
oProduct? : \mathbb{O}ProductCl \\
\hline
\forall o : references'^{\sim}(\!|\ \{oProduct?\}\ |\!) \mid (orderSt'\ o).state = pending \bullet \\
\quad (orderSt'\ o).quantity > (productSt'\ oProduct?).stock \\
\hline
\end{array}
$$

Next, we define a connector for use in the composition. This says that the set of *Orders* to invoice (*osOrder*?) is a subset of all the orders that are pending on the updated product and that can be fulfilled (it is non-deterministic), and that the *quantity*? to subtract from stock is the sum of the quantities of all orders that are to be invoiced:

$$
\begin{array}{|l}
\hline
\textit{Connector} \\
\mathbb{S}Order;\ \mathbb{A}References;\ \mathbb{S}Product \\
oProduct? : \mathbb{O}ProductCl \\
quantity? : \mathbb{N} \\
osOrder? : \mathbb{P}(\mathbb{O}OrderCl) \\
\hline
osOrder? \subseteq \{\ o : references^{\sim}(\!|\ \{oProduct?\}\ |\!) \mid \\
\qquad (orderSt\ o).state = pending \\
\qquad \wedge\ (orderSt\ o).quantity \leq (productSt\ oProduct?).stock\ \} \\
quantity? = \Sigma\ \{\ o : osOrder? \bullet (o \mapsto (orderSt\ o).quantity)\ \} \\
\hline
\end{array}
$$

This uses the generic operator Σ from the Z toolkit of $UML + Z$:

$$
\begin{array}{|l}
\hline
[L] \\
\Sigma : (L \nrightarrow \mathbb{Z}) \rightarrow \mathbb{Z} \\
\hline
\Sigma\ \varnothing = 0 \\
\forall l : L; n : \mathbb{Z}; S : L \nrightarrow \mathbb{Z} \mid l \notin \mathrm{dom}\, S \bullet \Sigma\ (\{l \mapsto n\} \cup S) = n + \Sigma\ S \\
\hline
\end{array}
$$

The part (b) operation $SysAddStock_b$ is the composition of all these definitions: the operation says that if the precondition schema (*PreCondAddOrders*) is *true*, then orders are invoiced, otherwise nothing changes. The system operation, *SysAddStock*, composes the part (a) and part (b) specifications using sequential composition:

$$
\begin{array}{l}
\Psi AddStock_b == \Delta System \wedge \Xi \mathbb{A}References \\
SysAddStock_b == (\Psi AddStock_b \wedge \\
\qquad PreCondAddOrders \wedge \mathbb{S}_{\Delta}OrderInvoiceSet \\
\qquad\qquad \wedge\ Connector \wedge \mathbb{S}_{\Delta}ProductStockSubtract \wedge PostCondAddOrders \\
\qquad \vee\ \neg\ PreCondAddOrders \wedge \Xi System) \setminus (osOrder?, quantity?) \\
SysAddStock == SysAddStock_a \fatsemi SysAddStock_b
\end{array}
$$

Question 25: Is the new version of the operation consistent? What is its precondition? Are the snapshots valid in this new version?

Answer: The precondition remains the same, as expected. The validation proofs for the snapshots are provable in Z/Eves.

5.4 Natural language description of the specification

5.4.1 Case 1

An order references one product and a product may be referenced by zero or more orders. Orders may be in one of two states, *pending* or *invoiced*, depending on whether they are waiting to be fulfilled or if they have been fulfilled and invoiced; orders have a quantity, which is a positive whole number. An *Order* has the operation *invoice*, which changes the state of the *Order* from *pending* into *invoiced*. In the initial state of the system there are no orders and no products.

5.4.2 Case 2

Case 2 extends case 1 with three system operations to enter an order, to cancel an order, and to add stock.

The order entry operation stores the order as a new object, links it to the ordered product, and checks whether the order can be invoiced (in the same way as for case 1). If an order can be invoiced, then the order *quantity* is subtracted from the product *stock*, and the order *state* is set to *invoiced*. If not, then the product is unchanged, and the order *state* is set to *pending*.

Order cancellation applies only to orders in the *pending* state. The operation removes the order and the link between the cancelled order and the ordered product.

Entries of stock are explicitly additions to the product *stock*. When stock is received for a known product, it is added to the existing stock. The *pending* orders linked to that product are checked, and they are invoiced until no more orders can be met. There is no imposed ordering on this process, and no requirement to invoice as many orders as possible, but the non-deterministic ordering would allow such conditions to be added by refinement if required.

5.5 Conclusion

Our approach has produced a combined object-oriented and formal model of the system. Some aspects of the case studies were clarified simply by expressing the requirements in UML diagrams; the underlying Z representation of the UML diagrams forced us to be clear and precise in drawing UML diagrams. Many requirements were clarified through snapshot-based validation.

The Z model gives the precise meaning of the UML diagrams and enables formal verification and validation of UML-based models. We would like make the Z hidden to the user as much as possible, but this could not be fully achieved. At least one expert is required to write Z operation specifications and invariants that are not expressible diagrammatically. Nevertheless, the *UML* + *Z* framework offers the benefits of formal development, whilst allowing people who are not Z experts to engage in the modeling and analysis effort, by drawing class, state and object diagram.

An important feature of our approach is templates. The templates of the *UML* + *Z* catalogue are expressed in FTL [AMA 06]. All Z in this chapter is generated by instantiating templates from the catalogue. In most cases, the instantiation was fully generated from the diagrams; a few times, the developer needed to add extra information. The meta-theorems of the catalogue reduce the proof effort associated with checking the consistency of the *UML* + *Z* model; sometimes no proof at all was required (consistency conjectures were *true by construction*); at other times the meta-theorems simplified the proof to a point where it could be easily discharged in Z/Eves.

Our illustration of *UML* + *Z* validation has shown that errors in models can be found: (a) because the model does not capture what the developer intended; (b) because the model is inconsistent; (c) because the developer's intention is consistently expressed in the model but is not what the client wanted. The use of both diagrammatic and formalised snapshots is shown to be necessary to extract the various failings of the models.

Acknowledgements

Nuno Amálio is funded by the Portuguese Foundation for Science and Technology under grant 6904/2001.

Bibliography

[AMA 04] AMÁLIO N., STEPNEY S., POLACK F., "Formal Proof From UML Models", in DAVIES J. *et al.*, Eds., *ICFEM 2004*, vol. 3308 of *LNCS*, Springer, p. 418–433, 2004.

[AMA 05] AMÁLIO N., POLACK F., STEPNEY S., "An Object-Oriented Structuring for Z based on Views", in TREHARNE H. *et al.*, Eds., *ZB 2005: International Conference of B and Z Users*, vol. 3455 of *LNCS*, Springer, p. 262–278, 2005.

[AMA 06] AMÁLIO N., Frameworks based on templates for rigorous model-driven development, PhD thesis, Department of Computer Science, University of York, 2006.

[D'S 99] D'SOUZA D. F., WILLS A. C., *Objects, Components and Frameworks in UML: The Catalysis Approach*, Addison-Wesley, 1999.

[SAA 97] SAALTINK M., "The Z/EVES system", in *ZUM'97, Reading, UK*, vol. 1212 of *LNCS*, Springer, 1997.

[STE 03] STEPNEY S., POLACK F., TOYN I., "Patterns to Guide Practical Refactoring: Examples Targeting Promotion in Z", in BERT D. *et al.*, Eds., *ZB 2003, Turku, Finland*, vol. 2651 of *LNCS*, Springer, p. 20–39, 2003.

[WOO 96] WOODCOCK J., DAVIES J., *Using Z: Specification, Refinement, and Proof*, Prentice-Hall, 1996.

Chapter 6

ASM

Egon BÖRGER, Angelo GARGANTINI and Elvinia RICCOBENE

6.1 Overview of the ASM

The *Abstract State Machine* (ASM) method is a systems engineering method that guides the development of software and embedded hardware-software systems seamlessly from requirements capture to their implementation. Within a single precise yet simple conceptual framework, the ASM method supports and uniformly integrates the major software life cycle activities of the development of complex software systems. The process of *requirements capture* results into constructing rigorous *ground models* which are precise but concise high-level system blueprints ("system contracts"), formulated in domain-specific terms, using an application-oriented language which can be understood by all stakeholders. From the ground model, by piecemeal, systematically documented detailing of abstract models via stepwise refined models to code, the *architectural and component design* is obtained in a way which bridges the gap between specification and code. The resulting *documentation* maps the structure of the blueprint to compilable code, providing explicit descriptions of the software structure and of the major design decisions, besides a road map for system *(re-)use* and *maintenance*.

On the basis of a systematic separation of different concerns (e.g. design from analysis, orthogonal design decisions, multiple levels of definitional or proof detail, etc.), the ASM method allows a nowadays widely-requested *modeling technique* which integrates dynamic (*operational*) and static (*declarative*) descriptions, and an *analysis technique* that combines *validation* (by simulation and testing) and *verification* methods at any desired level of detail.

Even if the ASM method comes with a rigorous scientific foundation [BÖR 03], the practitioner needs no special training to use the ASM method since Abstract State Machines are a simple extension of Finite State Machines, obtained by replacing unstructured "internal" control states by states comprising arbitrarily complex data [BÖR 05], and can be understood correctly as pseudo-code or Virtual Machines working over abstract data structures. Control state ASMs, a basic class of Abstract State Machines, inherit from FSMs their standard graphical notation (see [BÖR 03, Figure 7.1]). Similarly, UML activity diagrams pass to their ASM models their graphical notation (see [BÖR 03, Figure 6.18, 6.19]), as do SDL programs or Petri nets to their ASM models.

A complete introduction on the ASM method can be found in [BÖR 03], together with a presentation of the great variety of its successful applications in different fields as: definition of industrial standards for programming and modeling languages, design and re-engineering of industrial control systems, modeling e-commerce and web services, design and analysis of protocols, architectural design, language design, verification of compilation schemes and compiler back-ends, etc.

6.2 Requirements capture and specification of case 1

We formulate seven categories of questions to be used as guidelines for the specification task leading from loosely formulated requirements to accurate, application-domain-oriented ground models. The questions are prompted by the application of the ASM method to the case 1 of the invoicing order system, although similar questions should be posed when using the ASM method for requirements capture and specification of other systems. Answers are preceded by explanations of some relevant ASM concepts.

6.2.1 Identifying the agents

An ASM can be intuitively viewed as pseudo-code or Virtual Machine program working on abstract data. The notion of ASMs moved from a definition which formalises simultaneous parallel actions of a single agent, either in an atomic way (*Basic ASMs*) or in a structured and recursive way (*Turbo ASMs*), to a generalisation where multiple agents interact in a synchronous/asynchronous manner[1] (*Synchronous/Asynchronous Multi-Agent ASMs*). The context in which an agent machine computes is represented by an external agent called *environment*.

Question 1: Who are the system *agents* and what are their relations? In particular, what is the relation between the system and its environment?

Answer: *R1* says that "the subject is to invoice orders". This leads us to define the *invoicing orders* specification in terms of a single-agent machine which may dispose of potentially unrestricted non-determinism and parallelism (appearing in the form of the "choose" and "forall" rules defined below) with flat programs (Basic ASM) or structured versions (Turbo ASM).

[1] For details and references on the treatment of *concurrency* in the ASM framework and on concurrent ASMs modeling threads in Java/C#, Petri nets, SDL, UML activity diagrams and state machines, etc., see [BÖR 03, Chapter 6].

6.2.2 Identifying the states

An ASM *state* models a machine state, i.e. the collection of elements and objects the machine "knows", and the functions and predicates it uses to manipulate them. Mathematically, a *state* is defined as an algebraic structure, where data come as abstract objects, i.e. as elements of sets (also called *domains* or *universes*, one for each category of data) which are equipped with basic operations (partial *functions*) and *predicates* (attributes or relations).

For the evaluation of terms and formulas in an ASM state, the standard interpretation of function symbols by the corresponding functions in that state is used. Without loss of generality we usually treat predicates as characteristic functions and constants as 0-ary functions. Partial functions are turned into total functions by interpreting $f(x)$ = *undef* with a fixed special value *undef* as $f(x)$ being undefined. The reader who is not familiar with this notion of structure may view a state as a "database of functions" (namely a set of function tables).

Question 2: What are the system states? What are the domains of objects and what are the functions, predicates and relations defined on them? This question is stressed by the object-oriented approach to system design[2].

Answer: By *R1* there is a set Orders and by *R2* there is a function orderState which yields the state of each order, which can be *invoiced* or *pending*. By *R3* there are two functions, referencedProduct[3] representing the product referenced in an order and orderQuantity, which returns the quantity in the order and which, by *R4,* is not injective, not constant. By *R3* we need a set Quantity (subset of Natural) to denote the quantity values, while by *R5* there is a function stockQuantity which represents the quantity of products in stock.

6.2.3 Identifying static and dynamic parts of the states

In support of the principles of separation of concerns, information hiding, data abstraction, modularisation and stepwise refinement, the ASM method makes a systematic distinction between *basic* functions which are taken for granted (typically those forming the basic signature of an ASM) and *derived* functions (auxiliary functions coming with a specification or computation mechanism given in terms of basic functions), together with a classification of basic functions into *static* and *dynamic* ones and of the dynamic ones into *monitored* (only read), *controlled* (read and write), *shared* and *output* (only write) functions. This functions classification reflects the different roles these functions can assume in a given machine. *Static* functions never change during

[2]For details on object-oriented ASMs, their theory (developed mainly in the work by Zamulin), their use for modeling object-oriented databases and languages, e.g. C++, Java, C#, SDL, and their incorporation into the language AsmL of .NET-executable ASMs, see [BÖR 03, Chapter 9].

[3]To allow an order to reference to several products, we should introduce a single function referencedProductQuantity: Orders $\times$ Products -> Quantity, which yields the quantity of products in an order (undef in case a product is not referenced in a given order).

any run of the machine so that their values for given arguments do not depend on the states of the machine; *dynamic* functions may change as a consequence of agent actions (or *updates*, see definition below) or by the *environment*, so that their values may depend on the states of the machine. By definition static functions can be thought of as given by the initial state, so that, where appropriate, handling them can be clearly separated from the description of the system dynamics. Whether the meaning of these functions is determined by a mere signature description, by axiomatic constraints, by an abstract specification or by an explicit or recursive definition depends on the degree of information-hiding the specifier wants to realize. Static 0-ary functions represent *constants*, whereas with dynamic 0-ary functions one can model *variables* of programming (not to be confused with logical variables). *Controlled* functions are dynamic functions which are directly updatable by and only by the machine instructions (known as *transition rules*: see below). Therefore, these functions are the ones which constitute the internally controlled part of the dynamic state of the machine; they are not updatable by the environment (or more generally by another agent in the case of a multi-agent machine). *Monitored* functions are dynamic functions which are read but not updated by a machine and directly updatable only by the environment (or more generally by other agents). These monitored functions constitute the externally controlled part of a machine state. As with static functions, the specification of monitored functions is open to any appropriate method. The only (but crucial) assumption made is that in a given state the values of all monitored functions are determined. Combinations of internal and external control are captured by interaction or *shared* functions that can be read and are directly updatable by more than one machine (so that typically a protocol is needed to guarantee consistency of updates). *Output* functions are updated but not read by a machine and are typically monitored by other machines or by the environment.

Question 3: What are the static and the dynamic parts of states? Who can update the dynamic functions?

Answer: By *R6a* the set Orders is static. By *R2* and *R5* the function orderState is dynamic and controlled by the system. By *R3* and *R6a* referencedProduct and orderQuantity are both static. By *R6a* the function stockQuantity is dynamic – a static interpretation is not reasonable – but it is unclear if the function is updated by the environment or by the system or by both of them (shared function). We make the *assumption* that *the stock is only updated by the system when it invoices an order*. The set of products and of quantities are assumed to be static. For writing down ASMs we use the AsmM language [ASMM] which has been derived from a metamodel of the ASMs and is endowed with a BNF grammar [SCA 05] and a syntax checker.

```
asm orderSystemCase1
 signature:
   static abstract domain Orders
   enum domain OrderStatus = { INVOICED | PENDING }
```

```
static abstract domain Products
static domain Quantity subsetof Natural
static referencedProduct: Orders -> Products
dynamic controlled orderState: Orders -> OrderStatus
static orderQuantity: Orders -> Quantity
dynamic controlled stockQuantity: Product -> Quantity
```

6.2.4 Identifying the transitions

Basic ASMs are finite sets of so-called *transition rules* of the form:

if *Condition* **then** *Updates*

which model the actions performed by the machine to manipulate elements of its domains and which result in a new state. The *Condition* (also called *guard*) under which a rule is applied is an arbitrary predicate logic formula without free variables, whose interpretation evaluates to true or false. *Updates* is a finite set of assignments of the form $f(t_1, t_2, \ldots, t_n) := t$, whose execution is to be understood as changing (or defining, if there was none) in parallel the value of the occurring functions f at the indicated arguments to the indicated value. More precisely, in the given state, first all parameters t_i, t are evaluated to their values, say v_i, v, then the value of $f(v_1, v_2, \ldots, v_n)$ is updated to v, which represents the value of $f(v_1, v_2, \ldots, v_n)$ in the next state. Such pairs of a function name f, which is fixed by the signature, and an optional argument $(v_1, v_2, \ldots, v_n)$, which is formed by a list of dynamic parameter values v_i of whatever type, are called *locations*. They represent the abstract ASM concept of basic object containers (memory units), which abstracts from particular memory addressing and object referencing mechanisms. Location-value pairs (*loc, v*) are called *updates* and represent the basic units of state change.

Non-determinism is a convenient way to abstract from details of scheduling of rule executions. It can be expressed by rules of the form:

choose *v* **in** *D* **with** G_v **do** $R(v)$

where *v* is a variable, *D* is a domain in which *v* takes its value, G_v is a term representing a boolean condition over v, and $R(v)$ is a transition rule which contains the free variable v. The meaning of such an ASM rule is to execute rule $R(v)$ with an arbitrary v chosen in D among those satisfying the selection property G_v. If there exists no such v, nothing is done.

Question 4: How and by which transitions (actions) do system states evolve? Under which conditions (guards) do the state transitions (actions) of single agents happen and what is their effect on the state? What is supposed to happen if those conditions are not satisfied?

Answer: By *R2* and *R5* there is only one transition to change the state of an order. It remains open whether the invoicing is done only for one order at a time, simultaneously for all orders, or only for a subset of orders (with a synchronisation for concurrent access of the same product by different orders). In case the update is meant to be made for one order at a time, it remains unspecified in which succession and with what successful termination or abruption mechanism this should be realized. The time model (duration of invoicing) is also not mentioned.

Modulo all those missing pieces of information, one can nevertheless reason upon possible rules for invoicing orders. A single-order rule can be formalised as follows[4]. Per step at most one order is invoiced, with an unspecified schedule (thus also not taking into account any arrival time of orders) and with an abstract deletion function:

```
rule r_InvoiceSingleOrder =
  choose $o in Orders with orderState($o) = PENDING and
    orderQuantity($o) <= stockQuantity(referencedProduct($o))
    do par
      orderState($o) := INVOICED
        r_DeleteStock[referencedProduct($o),orderQuantity($o)]
    endpar
```

Under the assumptions that stockQuantity is updated only by invoicing and only one order is processed at a time, the deletion function can be refined by the following macro rule:

```
rule macro r_DeleteStock($p in Products, $q in Quantity) =
    stockQuantity($p):= stockQuantity($p) - $q
```

The rule InvoiceSingleOrder has the disadvantage to invoice an order at a time, while some strategies could admit that the system can simultaneously invoice a certain number of orders at a time, if any. Simultaneous execution provides a convenient way to abstract from sequentiality where it is irrelevant for an intended design. In the ASM execution model, this *synchronous parallelism* is enhanced by the following notation to express the simultaneous execution of a rule R for each v satisfying a given condition G (where typically v will have some free occurrences in R which are bound by the quantifier):

forall v **in** D **with** G_v **do** $R(v)$

Question 5: Could the system actions be parallelised anyhow? Namely, in the case of invoicing orders, can the system invoice several orders in one step?

Answer: To speed up invoicing of orders, parallelism can be exploited in two directions. A first strategy consists of selecting a given product (possibly in a non-deterministic way) and then simultaneously invoicing all the corresponding orders, if possible. An alternative policy could be selecting, still non-deterministically, a set of orders to be invoiced in parallel.

[4]In AsmM a rule identifier begins with r_ and a logical variable identifier starts with $.

In case all orders for one product are simultaneously invoiced (or none if the stock cannot satisfy the request), an "all-or-none" strategy can be expressed by the following rule InvoiceAllOrNone which makes use of a function pendingOrders yielding the set of pending orders for a certain product, and of a (static) function totalQuantity returning the total quantity of a set of orders. The functions are defined below the rule:

```
rule r_InvoiceAllOrNone =
 choose $product in Products do
   let $pending = pendingOrders($product),
       $total = totalQuantity($pending) in
   if $total <= stockQuantity($product) then par
      forall $ord in $pending do orderState($ord) := INVOICED
     r_DeleteStock[$product, $total]
   endpar endif
```

where:

```
static function pendingOrders($p in Products): Powerset(Orders) =
    {$o | $o in Orders with orderState($o) = PENDING and
                            referencedProduct($o) = $p}

static function totalQuantity($so in Powerset(Orders)): Quantity =
   if (isEmpty($so)) then 0
   else let $first = first(asSequence($so)) in
     quantity($first) + totalQuantity(excluding($so,$first))
   endif
```

The previous definition of DeleteStock can be kept in this case as well. Indeed, the cumulative effect of updating the product quantity in stock is obtained by using the total quantity of the set of invoiced orders.
To avoid the system deadlock when the stock cannot satisfy any request, we formalise, by the following rule InvoiceOrdersForOneProduct, the second strategy introducing some non-determinism in the choice of a set of pending orders which can be invoiced according to the available quantity in stock:

```
rule r_InvoiceOrdersForOneProduct =
 choose $product in Products do
  let $pending = pendingOrders($product) in
  choose $ordSet in Powerset($pending)
     with totalQuantity($ordSet) <= stockQuantity($product)
  do par
     forall $ord in $ordSet do orderState($ord) := INVOICED
     r_DeleteStock[$product, totalQuantity($ordSet)]
  endpar
```

To parallelise invoicing orders over all products, a slight variant of the previous rule can be obtained replacing choose $product in Products with forall $product in Products. To further maximise a product quantity invoiced at the time, a new strategy is formalised by the rule InvoiceMaxOrdersForOneProduct. It consists of choosing a maximal invoicable subset of simultaneously invoiced pending orders for the same product. For this rule we need to define a static function maxQuantitySubsets defined on Powerset(Powerset(Orders)) to Powerset(Powerset(Orders)) which, given a set of set of orders, returns the set of all the sets having a maximum quantity:

```
rule r_InvoiceMaxOrdersForOneProduct =
 choose $product in Products do
   let $pending = pendingOrders($product),
         $invoicable = {$o | $o in Powerset($pending)
            with totalQuantity($o) <= stockQuantity($product) } in
  choose $ordSet in maxQuantitySubsets($invoicable) do par
     forall $ord in $ordSet do orderState($ord) := INVOICED
     r_DeleteStock[$product, totalQuantity($ordSet)]
  endpar
```

If the user requests a selection strategy which is not driven by a first choice of a product, another possible policy is to choose a set of pending orders, with enough referenced products in the stock, to be simultaneously invoiced. We reckon that this policy matches the intended behavior of the system better than the previous policies. The rule InvoiceOrders uses a predicate invoicable which is true on a set of pending orders with enough quantity of requested products in the stack, and a function refProducts which yields the set of all products referenced in a set of orders (the function is recursively defined below):

```
rule r_InvoiceOrders =
  choose $oSet in Powerset(Orders) with invoicable($oSet)
   do par
     forall $ord in $oSet do orderState($ord) := INVOICED
     forall $p in refProducts($oSet) do
               r_DeleteStock[$p, totalQuantity($oSet,$p)]
   endpar

static function invoicable($so in Powerset(Orders)) : Boolean =
  forall $o in $so with orderState($o) = PENDING and
   forall $p in Products with totalQuantity($so,$p) <= stockQuan-
     tity($p)

static function
      refProducts($so in Powerset(Orders)) : Powerset(Products) =
   if (isEmpty($so)) then {}
   else let $first = first(asSequence($so) in
            including(refProducts(excluding($so,$first)),
                                  referencedProduct($first))
   endif
```

Note that in all the previous examples, the non-deterministic selection of the orders to invoice could be performed by a monitored function which would formalise the user selection of a set of orders or the results of a particular scheduling algorithm.

6.2.5 Identifying the initial and final states

The *computation* of an ASM is defined in the standard way transition system *runs* are defined. Applying one step of the abstract machine M to a state S produces as next state another state S' of the same signature, which is obtained as follows: first evaluate in S, using the standard interpretation of classical logic, all the guards of all the rules of M, then compute in S, for each of the rules of M whose guard evaluates to true, all the arguments and all the values appearing in the updates of this rule; finally replace, simultaneously for each rule and for all the locations in question, the previous S-function value by the newly computed value if no two required updates contradict each other. The state S' thus obtained differs from S by the new values for those functions at those arguments where the values are updated by a rule of M which could fire in S. The effect of an ASM M, started in an arbitrary *initial* state S (generally provided by the user), is to repeatedly apply one step of M as long as an M-rule can fire. Such a machine terminates (in a *final* state) only if no rule is applicable anymore (and if the monitored functions do not change in the state where the guards of all the M-rules are false).

Question 6: What is the initialisation of the system and who provides it? Are there termination conditions and, if so, how are they determined? What is the relation between initialisation/termination and input/output?

Answer: No explicit initialisation is specified, although one can assume that all the orders are initially pending:

default init s_1: **function** orderState($o in Orders) = PENDING

No termination condition is given either. We assume that the system keeps to invoice orders as long as there are orders which can be invoiced (i.e. they are pending and there is enough product quantity in stock).

6.2.6 Exceptions handling and robustness

Usually, an ASM specification captures requirements concerning error handling by transition rules guarded by events[5] occurring in erroneous situations, and therefore separated by transition rules describing the normal machine execution.

[5]For details on event-driven ASMs, see [BÖR 03, section 6.5], which includes UML activity diagram ASMs. Event-driven ASMs also comprise Petri net ASMs [BÖR 03, sections 6.1,7.1.2], Abstract State Processes and Event-B ASMs [BÖR 03, section 4.2].

Furthermore, Turbo ASMs (see page 116) support exception-handling techniques to treat errors due to inconsistent updates. In Turbo ASMs, an abstract method for catching an inconsistent update set and of executing error handling rules is given by the **try-catch** rule. Let T be a set of terms. The semantics of **try** P **catch** T Q is to execute P, if the update set of P is consistent on the locations determined by elements of T, otherwise Q is executed.

Question 7: Which forms of erroneous use are to be foreseen and which exception handling mechanisms should be installed to catch them? What are the desired robustness features?

Answer: Since no exceptional computations are mentioned in the requirements and no inconsistent updates are allowed by the specification (see Question 8), we do not make use of the techniques supported by the ASM method to the error-handling purpose.

6.2.7 Identifying the desired properties (validation/verification)

The notion of ASM run makes the mechanical execution of ASM models possible, and various tools have been built for model *validation* by simulation and testing (see section 8.3 of [BÖR 03]). Furthermore, the rigorous mathematical definition of ASMs allows any standard mathematical *verification* technique to prove ASM model properties: from proof sketches over traditional or formalized mathematical proofs to tool supported interactive or automatic theorem proving or model checking (see sections 8.1 and 8.2 of [BÖR 03]).

Question 8: Is the system description complete and consistent?

Answer: *Completeness* with respect to the requirements can be verified for example by checking that every requirement has been analysed and captured by our specification. To validate a specification and its completeness with respect to user needs, it is important that the specification can be simulated by the user to uncover missing bits and pieces in the ground model. An ASM is *consistent* if it always performs consistent updates (i.e. it never tries to update in the same step the same location with different values). In our case there is a single rule which invoices one or more orders by updating simultaneously the status of the orders and the stock quantity. Since this single rule updates independently the status of different orders and updates the stock quantity of different products by means of a total quantity function which computes the cumulative effect of invoiced orders on the stock, the updates are always consistent.

Question 9: What are the system assumptions and what are the desired system properties? What do the requirements say about the state of the system?

Answer: No explicit assumptions or desired properties are given in the original specification. Through the requirements capture we have introduced several assumptions to fill missing information. For example, we have assumed that stockQuantity is updated only by the rule which invoices orders. Other assumptions can be introduced by means of auxiliary axioms. For example, the assumption that the quantity in every order must be greater than 0 is formalised as:

axiom over orderQuantity:
forall $o in Orders with orderQuantity($o) > 0

We have stated the following desired properties which express state invariants and correctness conditions. The first one states that the stock quantity is always greater than 0, i.e. the system cannot over invoice orders:

axiom over stockQuantity:
forall $p in Products with stockQuantity($p)>=0

Another property is that the state of every order is either pending or invoiced, but never undefined:

axiom over orderState:
forall $o in Orders with orderState($o) != undef

These properties have been proved by the method proposed in [GAR 00] and based on the theorem prover PVS. We report here only a sketch of the resulting encoding in PVS of the ASM for the order system. The controlled part of an ASM state is encoded in PVS as a record of functions representing the controlled ASM functions:

```
CTRLSTATE: TYPE =[#orderState:[Orders -> OrderStatus],
         stockQuantity :  [Products -> Quantity] #]
```

Each rule is a function that given a current state `c` and an intermediate controlled state `ctrl` returns a new controlled state in which the updates have been applied. The rule InvoiceSingleOrder is translated as follows, where the choose construct is substituted by the dynamic function `choose_order` (as explained in [GAR 00]):

```
InvoiceSingleOrder(c,ctrl) :  CTRLSTATE =
 let ord = choose_order(c) in
 let prod = referencedProduct(ord) in
 if orderState(c)(ord) = PENDING then ctrl with [
  orderState := orderState(c) with [(ord):= INVOICED],
  stockQuantity := stockQuantity(c) with [(prod) :=
       stockQuantity(c)(prod) + orderQuantity(ord)]]
 else ctrl endif
```

The properties are encoded as functions from `STATE` to `bool`. For example, the second property above is encoded as:

```
prop2(s:  STATE) :bool =
     forall (o:Orders):  orderState(s) (o) /= undef
```

and it is proved using induction and very simple PVS strategies.
Other more complex properties, which are not state invariants but which refer to execution paths, cannot be encoded in our verification method yet. For these properties, temporal logic and model checkers [DEL 00] could be used, although assumptions about the finiteness of the domains are necessary and uninterpreted domains are not allowed. For example, one may want to express that *an order o is eventually invoiced if it refers to a product available in the stock in enough quantity*. In CTL, this can be expressed as:

```
AF( AG( orderState(o) = INVOICED or
orderQuantity(o) > stockQuantity(referencedProduct(o)))
```

6.3 Requirements capture and specification of case 2

In this section we formulate for the answers to the very questions of case 1 only the changes needed for case 2.

Question 10: Who are the system *agents*?

Answer: The informal description does not specify the agents for dynamic manipulation of orders, stock and products, how they interact for shared data (namely the elements of Orders and the function stockQuantity), whether they act independently or following a schedule. For the sake of simplicity we assume that our system still has only one agent which performs all the requested actions. The main program executed by the agent (i.e. its main rule) will take care of the synchronisation of actions to avoid inconsistencies.

Question 11: What are the system *states*? What are the domains of objects and what are the functions, predicates and relations defined on them?

Answer: The domains Orders and Products and all the functions for case 1 remain. For the new operations of this case, we introduce the following three monitored functions that respectively yield the sequence of orders to add (as a sequence of pairs product and quantity), the sequence of orders to cancel, and the new quantities to add in the stock (as sequence of pairs product and quantity again):

monitored newOrders: Seq(Prod(Products,Quantity))
monitored ordersToCancel: Seq(Orders)
monitored newItems: Seq(Prod(Products,Quantity))

The value of these functions may be determined by the user or be the output produced by other system components in charge of computing orders to add or cancel and items to entry in the stock. They are considered system inputs.
The requirements do not specify whether a canceled order must be completely deleted from the system or whether it must be kept and marked as canceled. We assume that canceled orders are not deleted and their status changed to CANCELED. Therefore, the order status is modified as:

```
enum domain OrderStatus = {INVOICED | PENDING |CANCELED}
```

Question 12: What is the *classification* of domains and functions?

Answer: By *R6b* the set Orders is dynamic since new orders can be added and old orders can be deleted. Therefore, functions referencedProduct and orderQuantity are both dynamic and updated when a new order is inserted in Orders. The set Products is still assumed to be static since in *R6b* the entry of new products is not considered. The function stockQuantity is still dynamic and updated not only when an order or a set of orders is invoiced but also when new quantities of products are entered in the stock.

Question 13: How and by which *transitions* (actions) do system states evolve? How are the "internal" actions (of the system) related to "external" actions (of the environment)?

Answer: Besides the action of invoicing an order, *R6b* introduces other three operations: (1) cancelation of orders, (2) insertion of new orders, and (3) addition of quantities of products in the stock. We assume that these operations are driven by the monitored functions ordersToCancel, newOrders and newItems which return a sequence. The requested actions will be performed for every element in the sequence at each step. If the sequence is empty, the action has no effect. We introduce the following rule which is in charge of the cancelation of orders:

```
rule r_CancelOrders =
  forall $i in Natural with $i < length(ordersToCancel) do
      orderState(at(ordersToCancel,$i)) := CANCELED
```

Note that an order may be canceled even if it is already INVOICED. To allow only the cancelation of pending orders, the update of the order state must be guarded by orderState(at(ordersToCancel,$i))!= INVOICED.

Extending domains

So far we have updated locations, i.e. changed the value of functions on existing elements. If we want to introduce new orders in the Orders set, then we have to create or construct new orders. To construct new elements and to add them to domains, ASMs introduces the extend notation:

extend D **with** v **do** $R(v)$

where *D* is the name of the abstract type-domain to be extended, *v* is the logical variable which is bound to the new element imported in *D* from the *reserve* (see [BÖR 03]) and *R* is a transition rule executed after *v* is added to *D*. Generally *R* will perform some initialisation over *v*.

In order to deal with the problem of incoming new orders, we need to answer the following question:

Question 14: Could the domains be extended by adding new items? Namely, in the case of invoicing orders, can new orders be inserted?

Answer: We answer the question by the following rule AddOrders which extends the domain Orders with new elements and sets all functions on these new locations:

```
rule r_AddOrders =
 forall $i in Natural with $i < length(newOrders) do
  let  $p = first(at(newOrders,$i)),
       $q = second(at(newOrders,$i)) in
   extend Orders with $order do par
        orderQuantity($order) :=$q
        referencedProduct($order) :=$p
        orderState($order) := PENDING
   endpar
```

Sequentialisation and iteration

The characteristics of basic ASMs (simultaneous execution of multiple atomic actions in a global state) come at a price, namely the lack of direct support for practical composition and structuring principles. *Turbo ASMs* offer as building blocks sequential composition, iteration and parametrised (possibly recursive) sub-machines extending the macro notation used with basic ASMs. They capture the sub-machine notions in a black-box view hiding the internals of sub-computations by compressing them into one step. A Turbo ASM can be obtained from basic ASMs by applying finitely often and in any order the operators of *sequential composition*, *iteration* and *sub-machine call*. We report here only the definition of the *seq* and *iterate* constructors which we need for our purposes (namely to deal with the problem of incoming new items; see below). A complete overview of the Turbo ASMs can be found in [BÖR 03].

We denote the *sequential composition* of two ASM rules *P* and *Q* by P **seq** Q and define its semantics as the effect of first executing *P* in a given state *S* and then *Q* in the resulting (invisible micro-)state $S + U$ (if it is defined), where *U* is the set of updates produced by *P* in *S*. *Q* may overwrite a location which has been updated by *P*. The set of updates produced by *P* and then *Q* are merged only if *U* is consistent, so obtaining the new state S'; otherwise S' is the effect of applying *U* on *S*.

The construct **iterate** *R* iterates the sequential execution of a rule *R* encapsulating computations with a finite number of iterated steps into one step. It is defined by R_0 = **skip** (i.e. do nothing) and $R_{n+1} = R_n$ **seq** R. For iterated rule applications with *a priori* fixed bounds, we use the construct **while** (*cond*) *R* (= **iterate** (**if** *cond* **then** *R*)) when the stopping condition is specified, or **iterate** v **in** D **with** G_v **do** $R(v)$ to express the subsequent execution of a rule R for each v satisfying a given condition G. There are two natural stop situations for iterated rule applications without *a priori* fixed bounds, namely when the update set becomes empty (the case of *successful termination*) and when it becomes inconsistent (the case of *failure*).

We exploit the last form of the construct iterate to deal with the problem of entering new items. Requirements do not guarantee that two (or more) entries of a same product cannot arrive at the same time, so inconsistent updates may arise. The question is:

Question 15: How can location updates be sequentialized in order to avoid synchronous inconsistent updating? In the case study, how can the stock be updated when new quantities for the same product arrive at the same time?

Answer: The following rule AddItems performs the entry of quantities in the stock by increasing the value of the function stockQuantity for the entered products. Since the monitored sequence newItems could contain the same product several times, the function stockQuantity cannot be updated in parallel for each product in the sequence, otherwise inconsistent updates may appear (unless one assumes that a same product occurs no more than ones in the list newItems):

```
rule r_AddItems =
    iterate $i in Natural with $i < length(newItems) do
      let $p = first(at(newItems,$i)), $q = second(at(newItems,$i)) in
         stockQuantity($p) := stockQuantity($p) + $q
```

The three new rules CancelOrders, AddOrders and AddItems respectively update the function orderState for existing orders, the domain Orders, and the function stockQuantity. Therefore, they can be executed in parallel. The fourth action of the system to invoice orders (described in case 1) updates the functions orderState and stockQuantity, hence it cannot be executed in parallel with rules CancelOrders and AddItems. Some form of synchronization or scheduling must be introduced. Since this information is missing in the requirements, we decide to execute the first three actions in parallel and then perform the rule that invoices orders. The following main rule orderSystem which formalises the whole system behavior, reports the rule InvoiceOrders. However, any other rule presented in section 6.2.4 can be replaced according with the chosen selection strategy discussed for case 1.

```
main rule r_orderSystem =
    seq
      par
         r_AddOrders()
         r_CancelOrders()
         r_AddItems()
      endpar
      r_InvoiceOrders()
    endseq
```

6.4 The natural language description of the specification

6.4.1 Case 1

The system of invoicing orders is a single-agent machine. There is a set Orders which is static, namely new orders cannot be added, and every order has a state, which can be *invoiced* or *pending*. All the orders are initially pending. There is a set of products and new products cannot be added. Every order refers to a product for a certain quantity (greater than zero) and these data cannot be changed. The same product can be referenced by several different orders. Every product is in the stock in different quantity. The quantity of a product in the stock is only updated by the system when it invoices some orders. The system selects a set of orders which are invoicable, i.e. they are pending and refer to a product in the stock in enough quantity, it simultaneously changes the state of each order in this set from pending to invoiced, and updates the stock by subtracting the total product quantity in orders to invoice. The system keeps to invoice orders as long as there are orders which can be invoiced. The system guarantees that the state of an order is always defined and the stock quantity is always greater than or equal to zero.

6.4.2 Case 2

For the new operations foreseen in this case of *canceling orders, entering new orders*, and *adding new quantities of products in the stock*, the system takes three inputs: ordersToCancel, a sequence of orders to cancel, newOrders, a sequence of orders to add (as a sequence of pairs product and quantity), and newItems, which gives the new quantities to add in the stock (as a sequence of pairs product and quantity).

At every computation step, all the orders in ordersToCancel are not really deleted, but their status changed to CANCELED. Since new orders can be entered, the set Orders is dynamic in this case and all the orders in newOrders set are inserted in Orders in one step. The reference to a product and the quantity for a new order are set when this new order is entered. Furthermore, the system updates the stock quantities for all the products in newItems in one step taking into account the total quantity when the same product is present several times in newItems. The three new operations are performed in parallel. The fourth action of invoicing orders (described in case 1) is executed afterwards.

6.5 Conclusion

Elicitation of requirements is a notoriously difficult and most error-prone part of the system development activities. Requirements capture is largely a formalisation task, namely to realize the transition from natural language problem descriptions – which are often incomplete or interspersed with misleading details, partly ambiguous or even inconsistent – to a sufficiently precise, unambiguous, consistent, complete and minimal description which can serve as a basis for the *contract* between the customer or domain expert and the software designer. We have showed how the ASM method makes it possible to capture informal requirements by constructing a consistent and unambiguous, simple and concise, abstract and complete *ground model* which can be understood and checked (for correctness and completeness) by both domain experts and system designers.

During the formalisation process we have shown how requirements are often incomplete and assumptions must be stated in order to complete the specification. We have also shown how the ASM method is suitable to adapt the specification when different interpretations of the same requirements are possible (i.e. the discussion on different selection strategies of orders to be invoiced), and how the rigor of the ASM ground model allows formal (automatic) verification of properties. Furthermore, the documentation can be easily rephrased in natural language for an intuitive understanding of the formal description.

Bibliography

[ASMM] "The Abstract State Machines Metamodel (AsmM) website", http://www.dti.unimi.it/~riccobene/asmm/.

[BÖR 03] BÖRGER E., STÄRK R., *Abstract State Machines: A Method for High-Level System Design and Analysis*, Springer-Verlag, 2003.

[BÖR 05] BÖRGER E., "The ASM Method for System Design and Analysis. A Tutorial Introduction", in GRAMLICH B., Ed., *FroCoS 2005*, vol. 3717 of *Lecture Notes in Artificial Intelligence*, Vienna (Austria), Springer, p. 264-283, September 2005.

[DEL 00] DEL CASTILLO G., WINTER K., "Model Checking Support for the ASM High-Level Language", in GRAF S., SCHWARTZBACH M., Eds., *Proc. of TACAS*, vol. 1785 of *LNCS*, Springer-Verlag, p. 331–346, 2000.

[GAR 00] GARGANTINI A., RICCOBENE E., "Encoding Abstract State Machines in PVS", in GUREVICH Y., KUTTER P., ODERSKY M., THIELE L., Eds., *Abstract State Machines – Theory and Applications: International Workshop, ASM 2000*, vol. 1912 of *LNCS*, Monte Verità, Switzerland, Springer, p. 303–322, March 2000.

[SCA 05] SCANDURRA P., GARGANTINI A., GENOVESE C., GENOVESE T., RICCOBENE E., "A concrete syntax derived from the Abstract State Machine metamodel", in *Proc. of Abstract State Machines 2005*, 2005.

Chapter 7

TLA$^+$

Leslie LAMPORT

7.1 Overview of TLA$^+$

TLA$^+$ is a formal specification language based on set theory, first-order logic, and the Temporal Logic of Actions (TLA) [LAM 94, LAM 06]. In spirit, TLA$^+$ is close to Z. In fact, some aspects of TLA$^+$ were inspired by Z. I will therefore assume that the reader has read the chapter on Z, and I will explain the TLA$^+$ specification largely in terms of how it differs from the Z specification.

For reasons explained below, case 1 is problematic. I will therefore first present a complete specification for case 2 and only afterwards discuss case 1.

A complete description of TLA$^+$ and its tools can be found in [LAM 03]. Here I begin with a brief description of TLA and then describe the major differences between TLA$^+$ and Z.

7.1.1 TLA

A TLA specification is a temporal formula, often named *Spec*. The meaning of a temporal formula is a predicate on behaviors. A behavior represents a conceivable execution of a system. The behaviors satisfying *Spec* are the ones that represent correct behaviors of the system. More precisely, a behavior represents a conceivable history of a universe that may contain the system. A behavior satisfying specification *Spec* represents a history of the universe in which the system behaves correctly. To make this precise, we need some terminology.

A *state* is an assignment of values to variables. A *step* is a pair of states. A *behavior* is an infinite sequence of states; the *steps of* a behavior are its successive pairs of states. A *state predicate* is a formula whose meaning is a predicate (Boolean-valued function) on states. An *action* is a formula whose meaning is a predicate on steps. We often conflate a formula and its meaning. For example, if A is an action, then an *A-step* is defined to be a step that satisfies A. (Formally, the step satisfies the meaning of A, not the formula A.)

In TLA, actions are written as formulas containing primed and unprimed variables. Unprimed variables refer to the variables' values in the first state of the step; primed variables refer to their values in the second state. State predicates are actions with no primed variables.

Like most industrial specifications I have seen, the invoice system has the simplest possible non-trivial TLA specification – namely, it is a temporal formula *Spec* defined by:

$$Spec \triangleq Init \wedge \Box[Next]_{\langle v_1,\ldots,v_n \rangle}$$

where *Init* is a state predicate, $Next$ an action, and the v_i are the specification's variables. Formula *Spec* is true of a behavior σ iff *Init* is true of the first state of σ and every step (successive pair of states) of σ is either a $Next$ step (one that satisfies $Next$) or a "stuttering step" that leaves all the variables v_i unchanged. Nothing happens in a stuttering step, so it is impossible to observe that such a step has occurred. Hence, a specification should not be able to forbid stuttering steps. Allowing them permits implementation/refinement to be simple implication [LAM 83], and it permits composition to be conjunction [ABA 95]. However, since the specification exercise includes neither refinement nor composition, stuttering steps are irrelevant and can be ignored – except when a behavior ends in an infinite sequence of such steps. A behavior that ends this way represents an execution that terminates. Formula *Spec* allows terminating executions. Forbidding termination requires conjoining a liveness property [ALP 85] to the definition of *Spec*. Since there is no liveness requirement for the invoice system, I will ignore liveness.

A TLA specification consists of the definition of the formula *Spec* – that is, the one-line definition given above preceded by the definitions of *Init* and $Next$. These are ordinary mathematical formulas, involving no temporal logic. The $\Box$ in the line above is the only temporal-logic operator in the entire specification. (If we were specifying liveness properties, temporal operators would appear in the definitions of those properties as well.)

7.1.2 TLA$^+$ versus Z

The invoice system example reveals the following differences between the usual way of writing specifications in TLA$^+$ and Z. (There is another style of Z specification, not used in this book, in which sequences of states are described explicitly with ordinary mathematics.)

- A TLA$^+$ specification is a single temporal-logic formula. In Z, there is no single formula or object that mathematically constitutes *the* specification.
- One can assert in TLA$^+$ that a specification satisfies a property; Z has no mechanism for making such an assertion.

- Unlike Z, TLA+ is untyped. Type correctness of a TLA+ specification *Spec* is an invariance property asserting that, in every state reached during every possible execution satisfying *Spec*, each state variable is an element of an appropriate set (its type). One finds type errors by checking that invariance property. In principle, being untyped makes TLA+ significantly more expressive than Z. In practice, the inexpressiveness of Z's type system is at worst a minor nuisance for writing the specifications that typically arise in industry. There are advantages to a typed language, but I have found them not to be worth the extra complexity that types introduce. (Type checking is discussed in section 7.4.) However, eliminating types eliminates type declarations that can contain information helpful to the reader; such information needs to be included in comments.

- In Z, schemas are distinct from formulas and have their own logic. In TLA+, there are only formulas. What would be a schema in a Z specification usually becomes the definition of a formula in the corresponding TLA+ specification.

- While both TLA+ and Z use sets and functions, they have different built-in operators for describing them. For example, TLA+ has constructs for manipulating records that Z lacks; Z has a panoply of operators for describing sets of relations that TLA+ lacks. While TLA+ can easily define Z's mathematical operators, the Z syntax for them can be more convenient. Syntactic differences lead to stylistic differences in the specifications. A TLA+ specification might use records where a Z specification uses tuples or a schema, and it might use total functions where a Z specification uses partial functions.

- A TLA+ specification can distinguish between the system's interface, which must be implemented, and its internal state, which serves only to specify the behavior of the interface. This distinction can be made only informally in Z.

The following additional differences between ordinary TLA+ and Z specifications are not revealed by this simple example:

- TLA+ can be used to specify both safety and liveness properties [ALP 85]. Z lacks anything corresponding to the TLA+ operators for expressing liveness.

- TLA provides a simple mathematical definition of what it means for one specification to implement another. Implementation is implication. A specification $S1$ implements a specification $S2$ iff $S1 \Rightarrow S2$ is a valid formula. (There is no formal difference between a property and a specification; satisfying a property and implementing a specification are synonymous.)

For an engineer, the most significant difference between Z and TLA+ is probably the set of tools they provide for checking a specification. The tools currently available for checking TLA+ specifications are the SANY syntactic analyzer and the TLC model checker, which is described in section 7.4 below.

7.2 A specification of case 2

There is no such thing as *the* specification of a system. A specification is an abstraction that describes some aspects of the system and ignores others. It is like a map. One wants a different map of Texas for driving from Amarillo to Houston than for finding new deposits of helium. So the first question one should ask is:

Question 1: What is the purpose of the specification?

Answer: This question does not seem to have an answer. The invoice example is artificial because it does not indicate what the specification is to be used for. In my experience, engineers are most interested in specifications as a way of finding errors early in the design process. For that purpose, one writes a specification of a high-level design and checks that it satisfies certain properties. The description of the invoice system gives no nontrivial properties to be checked. Since I am just copying the Z specification, I do not have to answer this question. I will accept whatever answer is implicit in the Z specification.

The first question engineers who sit down to write a specification usually ask is:

Question 2: How do we begin?

Answer: Knowing how to begin is probably the hardest part of writing a specification. My best answer to this question is that one begins by informally writing a single correct behavior of the system. It can be written either as a sequence of states or a sequence of events. Doing this determines the grain of atomicity of the specification. For the invoicing system, it answers questions, such as is the placing of a new order represented as two events – the user places the order and the system replies – or as a single event?

Since I am mimicking the Z specification, knowing where to begin is not a problem. The Z specification tells us that placing an order is represented as a single event. Thus, the specification cannot describe a scenario in which one user places an order and, before the system responds, a second user places another order. If there are multiple users, which is not ruled out by the system description, such a scenario cannot be avoided. Whether abstracting away this real possibility ignores an irrelevant complication or hides potential problems depends on the purpose of the specification.

The next questions one asks are about the same for a TLA$^+$ specification as for a Z specification. I will therefore jump directly to an explanation of the complete specification, which appears in Figures 7.1 and 7.2. (Since the specification is explained in the text, I have omitted the explanatory comments that should appear in every specification.) If you have read the Z specification, then you already know pretty much what the TLA$^+$ specification says. I will therefore just explain the TLA$^+$ notation and the differences between the two specifications.

```
---------------------------- MODULE Invoice ----------------------------
EXTENDS Naturals
CONSTANTS OrderId, Product
VARIABLES stock, order, inp, out
-------------------------------------------------------------------------
ProdOrder ≜ {f ∈ [Product → Nat] : ∃ p ∈ Product : f[p] ≠ 0}

Order ≜ [state : {"pending", "invoiced"}, prods : ProdOrder]
          ∪ [state : {"none"}]
-------------------------------------------------------------------------
TypeOK ≜ ∧ stock ∈ [Product → Nat]
         ∧ order ∈ [OrderId → Order]

Init ≜ ∧ stock = [x ∈ Product ↦ 0]
       ∧ order = [x ∈ OrderId ↦ [state ↦ "none"]]
       ∧ inp = ⟨""⟩
       ∧ out = ⟨""⟩
-------------------------------------------------------------------------
InvoiceOrderOp(id) ≜
  ∧ inp' = ⟨"Invoice", id⟩
  ∧ IF order[id].state ≠ "pending"
       THEN ∧ out' = ⟨"order_not_pending"⟩
            ∧ UNCHANGED ⟨stock, order⟩
       ELSE IF ∀ p ∈ Product : order[id].prods[p] ≤ stock[p]
               THEN ∧ out' = ⟨"OK"⟩
                    ∧ order' = [order EXCEPT ![id].state = "invoiced"]
                    ∧ stock' =
                         [p ∈ Product ↦ stock[p] − order[id].prods[p]]
               ELSE ∧ out' = ⟨"not_enough_stock"⟩
                    ∧ UNCHANGED ⟨stock, order⟩

NewOrderOp(pOrder) ≜
  ∧ inp' = ⟨"NewOrder", pOrder⟩
  ∧ ∨ ∃ id ∈ OrderId :
          ∧ order[id].state = "none"
          ∧ out' = ⟨"OK", id⟩
          ∧ order' = [order EXCEPT ![id] = [state ↦ "pending",
                                             prods ↦ pOrder]]
          ∧ UNCHANGED stock
    ∨ ∧ ∀ id ∈ OrderId : order[id].state ≠ "none"
      ∧ out' = ⟨"IdError"⟩
      ∧ UNCHANGED ⟨stock, order⟩
```

Figure 7.1: The complete specification (beginning)

$$
\begin{array}{l}
\mathit{CancelOrderOp}(\mathit{id}) \triangleq \\
\quad \land\ \mathit{inp}' = \langle \text{“CancelOrder”},\ \mathit{id} \rangle \\
\quad \land\ \text{IF } \mathit{order}[\mathit{id}].\mathit{state} = \text{“pending”} \\
\qquad\quad \text{THEN } \land\ \mathit{out}' = \langle \text{“OK”} \rangle \\
\qquad\qquad\qquad \land\ \mathit{order}' = [\mathit{order} \text{ EXCEPT } ![\mathit{id}] = [\mathit{state} \mapsto \text{“none”}]] \\
\qquad\qquad\qquad \land\ \text{UNCHANGED } \mathit{stock} \\
\qquad\quad \text{ELSE } \land\ \mathit{out}' = \langle \text{“order\_not\_pending”} \rangle \\
\qquad\qquad\qquad \land\ \text{UNCHANGED } \langle \mathit{stock},\ \mathit{order} \rangle
\end{array}
$$

$$
\begin{array}{l}
\mathit{EnterStock}(\mathit{pOrder}) \triangleq \\
\quad \land\ \mathit{inp}' = \langle \text{“EnterStock”},\ \mathit{pOrder} \rangle \\
\quad \land\ \mathit{out}' = \langle \text{“OK”} \rangle \\
\quad \land\ \mathit{stock}' = [p \in \mathit{Product} \mapsto \mathit{stock}[p] + \mathit{pOrder}[p]] \\
\quad \land\ \text{UNCHANGED } \mathit{order}
\end{array}
$$

$$
\begin{array}{l}
\mathit{Next} \triangleq \\
\quad \lor\ \exists\, \mathit{id} \in \mathit{OrderId} : \mathit{InvoiceOrderOp}(\mathit{id}) \lor \mathit{CancelOrderOp}(\mathit{id}) \\
\quad \lor\ \exists\, \mathit{pOrder} \in \mathit{ProdOrder} : \mathit{NewOrderOp}(\mathit{pOrder}) \lor \mathit{EnterStock}(\mathit{pOrder})
\end{array}
$$

$$
\mathit{Spec} \triangleq \mathit{Init} \land \Box[\mathit{Next}]_{\langle \mathit{stock},\ \mathit{order},\ \mathit{inp},\ \mathit{out} \rangle}
$$

$$
\text{THEOREM } \mathit{Spec} \Rightarrow \Box\, \mathit{TypeOK}
$$

Figure 7.2: The complete specification (end)

TLA+ specifications are organized into modules. This simple specification consists of a single module named *Invoice*. The module begins with an EXTENDS statement that imports the standard module *Naturals*. This module defines the set *Nat* of natural numbers and the usual arithmetic operators.

The CONSTANT statement declares the constant parameters *OrderId* and *Product* that are the same as in the Z specification. The VARIABLES statement declares the specification's variables. (Unlike a constant, a variable can change its value in the course of a behavior.) The variable *stock* is as in the Z specification. I have replaced the two Z variables *orders* and *orderStatus* by a single record-valued variable *order*, where *order.prods* replaces *orders* and *order.state* replaces *orderStatus*. The variables *inp* and *out* represent the system's input and output. The Z specification assumes that each operation is performed as a single atomic action at the behest of some external agent. In the TLA+ specification, that action sets *inp* to the agent's input and *out* to the system's output. There is no variable *newids* because its value is a simple function of the other variables – namely, it equals *OrderId* minus the set of orders that are pending or invoiced. (Avoiding redundant variables is a stylistic choice; I find that it makes a specification clearer.)

Following the purely decorative horizontal line come definitions of two constant sets, *ProdOrder* and *Order*. The set *ProdOrder* represents the set of all non-empty bags of products. It would be easy to define a bag as a partial function, the way Z does. (The standard module *Bags* does just that.) However, here it's more convenient to represent a bag of products as a function b whose domain is the set *Product* of all products, where $b[p]$ is the number of copies of p in bag b, for any p in *Product*. The set *Order* is the set of all possible values of $order[id]$ for an id in *OrderId*. If id is an unused *OrderId*, then $order[id]$ is a record with just a *state* component whose value is the string "none". Otherwise it is a record whose *state* component is either "pending" or "invoiced" and whose *prods* field is an element of *ProdOrder*. (In TLA+, one typically uses a string like "pending" instead of introducing an unspecified constant *pending* as in the Z spec.) The definitions of *ProdOrder* and *Order* use the following TLA+ notation:

- $\{v \in S : P(v)\}$ is the subset of S containing all elements v satisfying $P(v)$.
- $[S \rightarrow T]$ is the set of all functions with domain S and range a subset of T.
- $[l_1 : S_1, \ldots, l_n : S_n]$ is the set of all records r with fields $l_1, \ldots, l_n$ such that $r.l_i \in S_i$ for each i. (A record is a function whose domain is the finite set of strings consisting of the names of its fields.)

The module next defines the type-correctness predicate *TypeOK* and the initial predicate *Init*. A type-correctness predicate asserts that each variable is an element of some set that is usually called its "type". This predicate is not part of the specification, meaning that it is not used in defining *Spec*. A theorem at the end of the module asserts that *TypeOK* is an invariant of *Spec*. It's helpful to state a type invariant early in the specification, because knowing the types of the variables makes the specification easier to read. I haven't bothered to specify the types of inp and out, since knowing their types isn't important for understanding the specification. The initial predicate *Init* specifies the initial values of the variables. The initial values of inp and out don't matter and could be left unspecified. However, the TLC model checker requires that all variables be initialized. Since the specification's actions always set inp and out to equal tuples, we initialize the variables to 1-tuples for uniformity. Predicate *Init* asserts that each variable equals a single value; an initial predicate often asserts that a variable is an element of some set. The definitions of *Init* and *TypeOK* introduce the following TLA$^+$ notation:

- A list bulleted by $\land$ or $\lor$ represents the conjunction or disjunction of the items. Indentation is used to eliminate parentheses in nested lists of conjunctions and/or disjunctions. This makes large formulas easier to read. We can also use $\land$ and $\lor$ as the customary infix operators.
- $[x \in S \mapsto e(x)]$ is the function f with domain S such that $f[x] = e(x)$ for all x in S.
- $\langle e_1, \ldots, e_n \rangle$ is an n-tuple, for any natural number n.
- $[l_1 \mapsto e_1, \ldots, l_n \mapsto e_n]$ is the record r with fields $l_1, \ldots, l_n$ such that $r.l_i = e_i$ for each i.

The next section of the module defines the next-state action $Next$, which specifies the allowed steps of the system. Jumping to the actual definition of $Next$, we see that it is a disjunction of a collection of actions. (I consider existential quantification to be a form of disjunction.) It defines a $Next$ step to be an $InvoiceOrderOp(id)$ or $CancelOrderOp(id)$ step for some id in *OrderId*, or else a $NewOrderOp(pOrder)$ or $EnterStock(pOrder)$ step for some $pOrder$ in *ProdOrder*. There is no formal significance to the names of these actions, or to this particular way of writing $Next$ as a disjunction. We could write the definition of $Next$ in any number of equivalent ways – for example, by eliminating the definitions of *InvoiceOrderop*, etc. and defining $Next$ as one large formula.

Of course, I defined $Next$ in this way to mimic the Z specification. There is the following correspondence between the TLA$^+$ actions and the Z operations:

- Action $InvoiceOrderOp(id)$ corresponds to an *InvoiceOrderOp* operation with its input $id?$ equal to id.
- Action $NewOrderOp(pOrder)$ corresponds to any Z operation *NewOrderOp* whose input $order?$ equals $pOrder$. (There may be many such operations – one for each possible output value $id!$.)
- Action $CancelOrderOp(id)$ corresponds to a *CancelOrderOp* operation with input $id?$ equal to id.
- Action $EnterStock(pOrder)$ corresponds to any *EnterStock* operation with input $newstock?$ equal to $pOrder$.

Knowing the meaning of the Z operations, you should be able to understand the definitions of these actions. The only new TLA$^+$ notation used in these definitions is the EXCEPT construct. The instances of this construct that are used here are explained by:

- $[f \text{ EXCEPT } ![i] = e]$ is the function g that is the same as f, except with $g[i] = e$.
- $[r \text{ EXCEPT } !.l = e]$ is the record s that is the same as r, except with $s.l = e$.
- $[f \text{ EXCEPT } ![i].l = e]$ equals $[f \text{ EXCEPT } ![i] = [f[i] \text{ EXCEPT } !.l = e]]$.

Observe that the actions all set the variables inp and out to tuples – either pairs or one-tuples. It is generally best to have the values of a variable all of a uniform "type". This is why, for example, the $EnterStock(pOrder)$ action sets out to the one-tuple $\langle$"OK"$\rangle$ rather than simply to the string "OK".

The expected definition of *Spec* follows the definition of $Next$. Formula *Spec* is the specification of the invoice system. However, it is not a satisfactory specification for several reasons. The first has to do with stuttering. Consider a behavior in which the action $NewOrderOp(\pi)$ is executed twice in a row, with the same product order π, when there is no unused *OrderId*. Both executions set inp to $\langle$"NewOrder", $\pi\rangle$, set out to $\langle$"IdError"$\rangle$, and leave $stock$ and $order$ unchanged. The second execution leaves all four variables unchanged, so it is a stuttering step. Since stuttering steps are unobservable, the second execution essentially never happens. Execution of the other actions could also produce a stuttering step in case of an error. The specification should distinguish between nothing happening and a second $NewOrderOp(\pi)$ operation being performed. For it to make this distinction, we must ensure that executing an action always changes the value of some variable. An easy way to do this is by adding another component to the tuple inp and/or out that is changed with every input or output. For example, we could let inp have a Boolean first component that is complemented on each action. In TLA$^+$, the ith element of a tuple t is $t[i]$, so the first conjunct of $NewOrderOp(pOrder)$ could then be written:

$$inp' = \langle \neg inp[1], \text{"NewOrder"}, pOrder \rangle$$

We would also have to modify the definition of *Init*, for example to assert that inp equals $\langle \text{TRUE} \rangle$.

Modifying the specification in this way highlights its second problem: the encoding of inputs and outputs is rather arbitrary. It would be more elegant simply to say that a $NewOrderOp(pOrder)$ step is performed by providing as input the operation name "NewOrder" and the product order $pOrder$, without specifying how those inputs are encoded in the value of inp. It is easy to do this in TLA$^+$; section 5.1 of [LAM 03] shows how. However, such elegance is of little concern to engineers.

The final problem with *Spec* as a specification of the invoice system is that it specifies the possible sequences of values assumed by all four variables $stock$, $order$, inp, out. A straightforward interpretation of the invoice system's description implies that only inp and out are directly visible. The values of variables $stock$ and $order$ can only be inferred from observing the inputs and outputs. An implementation must implement the input and output described by the variables inp and out, but it is under no obligation to implement $stock$ and $order$. A philosophically correct specification would hide those two variables. Such a specification is written informally as:

$$\exists\, stock, order \,:\, Spec$$

where $\exists$ is temporal existential quantification [LAM 94]. TLA$^+$ does not allow one to write this formula because its meaning is not at all clear. The problem with it has nothing to do with temporal logic; the meaning would be equally unclear with ordinary quantification and a non-temporal formula $Spec$. Logicians seem to be unaware of the problem because they never try to define formally what a definition means. The correct way to hide internal variables in TLA$^+$ is explained in section 4.3 of [LAM 03]. However, engineers are not concerned with philosophical correctness and don't bother hiding internal variables.

A comparison of the TLA$^+$ and Z specifications may lead one to ask:

Question 3: The Z specification decomposes the operations into conjunctions and disjunctions of simpler operations. Why doesn't the TLA$^+$ specification decompose the action definitions in a similar way?

Answer: It would have been easy to define the actions in terms of simpler ones. However, there is no point doing so for such simple actions. For most systems, the next-state action is naturally written as the disjunction of actions that each describe some single class of system events. Sometimes those actions may be grouped in a natural way, leading to a hierarchical definition of the next-state action as a disjunction of disjunctions. However, I have found that there is seldom anything to be gained by writing an action as the conjunction of separately-defined actions.

Question 4: But isn't modularity helpful – for example, in re-using specifications?

Answer: Almost everything you have learned about modularity and re-use is irrelevant for specification. Almost every TLA$^+$ specification ever written is no longer than about 2,000 lines (excluding comments). I have found that engineers usually want to specify their systems in as much detail as possible. However, they can't understand specifications that are longer than about 2,000 lines. If a specification starts becoming too long, an engineer starts over again and writes a less detailed, higher-level specification.

The TLA$^+$ module system permits the same kind of modularity that is provided by Z's schemas (and more). However, I have yet to see an engineer break up a specification into modules. Breaking definitions into simpler definitions within a single module provides all the modularity one needs for a 2,000-line specification. This is in large part because TLA$^+$ has a LET...IN construct that permits definitions that are local to a formula, so one can hierarchically structure a single definition.

Re-use of specifications is also a non-issue in practice. The hard part of specifying a system is understanding it and finding a suitable level of abstraction. The effort of writing 2,000 lines of formulas is minor. There is little point trying to make a specification reusable. If in the future we want to write a specification similar to that of the invoice system, we can just modify the invoice system's specification.

The specification ends with a theorem asserting type correctness. The temporal formula $\Box\, \mathit{TypeOK}$ is true of a behavior σ iff every state of σ satisfies the state predicate TypeOK. The formula $\mathit{Spec} \Rightarrow \Box\, \mathit{TypeOK}$ asserts of a behavior σ that, if σ satisfies Spec, then it satisfies $\Box\, \mathit{TypeOK}$. The theorem asserts that this formula is true for all behaviors. (Remember that a behavior is any sequence of states, not just one that satisfies some specification.)

7.3 The problematic case 1

A TLA+ specification describes a complete system and its environment. Thus far, I have been describing *closed-system* specifications that are satisfied by all behaviors in which both the system and its environment perform correctly. The distinction between the system and the environment is informal, and we must read the comments to discover which actions are to be implemented as part of the system and which are to be performed by the environment.

We can also write *open-system* specifications, also called *rely/guarantee* specifications, that are satisfied by all behaviors in which the system performs correctly as long as the environment does. The system and environment are then formally distinguished and the specification describes exactly what the system's implementer must implement. As explained in section 10.7 of [LAM 03], transforming a closed-system specification to an open-system one, or vice-versa, is usually trivial. It generally requires changing about three lines of the specification. Closed-system specifications are conceptually a bit simpler; they are the only ones that engineers write – largely because they're the only ones that TLC can check directly.

Our specification of the invoice system is unusual because a single step represents both an operation performed by the environment (providing input) and one performed by the system (changing the system state and producing output). By choosing such a representation, we committed ourselves to a closed-system specification that cannot be transformed into an open-system one.

The problem with case 1 is that it does not ask for a description of a complete invoice system. Instead, it asks for a description of one operation of such a system. We could transform this into a system-specification exercise by defining a system that performs only the invoicing operation and is used in an environment that performs the other operations of the invoicing system. To write such a specification, we would have to decide how abstractly to represent this "environment". If we represent those other operations at the same level of abstraction as we did in case 2, then a closed-system specification for case 1 becomes identical to our closed-system specification for case 2. All we change are the comments, indicating that all actions are performed by the "environment" except for *InvoiceOrderOp* actions, which are performed jointly by the "system" and the "environment". Had we written an open-system specification for case 2, we could have obtained the specification for case 1 by modifying it slightly to attribute all but the invoice system's invoicing actions to the environment.

While we could do all this, it is quite unnatural to consider the invoicing operation by itself to form a separate system. A more sensible interpretation of case 1 is that it asks for just the one part of a larger specification that describes the invoicing operation. The definition of *InvoiceOrderOp* in the *Invoice* module provides such a description.

7.4 Validation of the specification

We check a specification by checking that it satisfies certain desired properties. Most often checked in practice are invariance properties. With TLA$^+$, a property can be an ordinary specification – that is, a formula of the same form $Init \land \Box[Next]_{\langle \ldots \rangle}$ as *Spec*. If the specification includes liveness requirements, we can also check that it satisfies liveness properties.

The description of the invoicing system provides no properties that it should satisfy. Indeed, the system is so simple that it would be hard to find properties to check that would increase our confidence that the specification says what we want it to. The only thing we can check is the invariance property $\Box\, TypeOK$. Checking that *Spec* satisfies $\Box\, TypeOK$ essentially tells us that the specification is type correct. Invariance of a type-correctness predicate is a stronger property than is provided by automatic type checking in a typed language. For example, if s is a variable that has some sequence type, then the operation that assigns the tail of s to s will satisfy an automatic type checker. However, it will violate a type-correctness invariant if that operation can ever be executed when s equals the empty sequence.

I developed the logic TLA to provide a simple and elegant way of formalizing the correctness proofs of concurrent algorithms – the kind of proofs I had been writing for about 15 years. TLA$^+$ is well-suited to writing formal proofs; an example of a formal hand proof written in TLA$^+$ appears in [GAF 03]. However, very few engineers have the time or the training to write rigorous mathematical proofs. A couple of TLA$^+$ proofs have been checked mechanically by hand-translating them into the logic of a mechanical theorem prover, but there is not yet a mechanical proof checker for TLA$^+$.

Model checking is the most attractive form of verification for engineers, usually yielding by far the greatest confidence for the amount of effort expended. The TLC model checker, written by Yuan Yu, is described in Chapter 14 of [LAM 03]. It can check a finite model of a specification obtained by instantiating the constant parameters and, if necessary, specifying constraints to make the set of reachable states finite. One obtains a finite model of the invoice specification as follows, for particular values of α and β:

- Substituting specific finite sets for the parameters *OrderId* and *Product*.

- Replacing the set *ProdOrder* with the set of product orders containing at most α copies of any one item.
- Constraining TLC to examine only states in which $stock[p] \leq \beta$ for all products p.

With *OrderId* and *Product* each containing two elements, $\alpha = 2$, and $\beta = 3$, TLC finds about 70,000 reachable states and checks the type invariant in less than 30 seconds on my laptop. In the course of checking invariance, TLC also checks for the absence of deadlock, meaning that the system never reaches a state in which no action is enabled.

For most specifications, the kind of error that would be found by automatic type checking when using a typed language is found by TLC in a few seconds with a very small model.

7.5 Satisfying the specification

After writing a specification, the next step is to implement it. We would naturally like to check that the implementation satisfies the specification. In TLA, implementation, satisfaction and refinement all mean the same thing: logical implication. We can check that one TLA+ specification implies another, either by writing a proof or by using TLC.

In principle, it is straightforward to check that a TLA+ model of an implementation satisfies a TLA+ specification. This works quite well in practice for concurrent algorithms. One writes a simple TLA+ specification of what the algorithm is supposed to do, writes a TLA+ description of the algorithm, and shows that the algorithm implements its specification – see [GAF 03] for an example. The same idea can work for high-level system designs. One can write a TLA+ specification of what the system is supposed to do, write a TLA+ description of the design, and check that the design satisfies its specification. However, I have found that this is seldom done for real systems – with TLA+ or any other language. Engineers usually specify only the high-level design and check that it satisfies a few properties rather than a complete specification. I hope this changes as engineers gain more experience with specifications.

Ultimately, most systems must be implemented in a programming language or hardware-design language. One would also like to check that this implementation satisfies the TLA+ specification. In principle, this can be done by using a TLA+ representation of the implementation, obtained from a TLA+-based formal semantics of the implementation language. In practice, this kind of verification is economically feasible only for small, extremely critical applications. TLA+ now has no tools to support such low-level verification, so it is probably not an appropriate language for the task.

For most applications, the only feasible way of checking that an implementation satisfies a higher-level specification is by testing. This can be done by translating executions of the implementation into the corresponding higher-level behaviors and using

TLC to check that those behaviors satisfy the TLA$^+$ specification. The translation is performed by instrumenting the implementation in some way. There is no tool to help with the instrumentation, but engineers seem to find it easy to do on an *ad hoc* basis.

To my surprise, I have found that engineers are not very interested in this kind of checking. They seem confident in their ability to determine if an execution is correct without checking it against the specification. Instead, they want to use the specification to help generate tests. A promising approach that has been investigated is to use the specification to improve test coverage. Test executions are translated to behaviors that are used as input to TLC. However, instead of just checking that they satisfy the specification, TLC keeps track of which reachable high-level states the behaviors have not reached. This information is used to generate additional tests that drive the implementation into those unreached states [TAS 02].

7.6 The natural language description

No complicated formal specification can be understood without a natural language explanation. That explanation normally appears in comments within the module. The TLATEX program described in Chapter 13 of [LAM 03] can be used to typeset the commented ASCII specification in a more readable format. Figures 7.1 and 7.2 were generated automatically by TLATEX from the uncommented ASCII specification – the exact specification on which TLC was run. (However, that specification resided in an Emacs buffer while I wrote this chapter, so anything might have happened to it since TLC checked it.)

7.7 Conclusion

The simple invoice specification gives little insight into what TLA$^+$ is like in practice. For example, when first viewing TLA$^+$, a common complaint is the need for UNCHANGED conjuncts in the actions. The invoice specification might make that complaint seem justified, since 13% of its lines are UNCHANGED conjuncts. In a typical specification, the figure is more like 4%. One must use TLA$^+$ to realize that rather than being overhead, those UNCHANGED conjuncts provide useful redundancy. They allow TLC to discover if we have inadvertently neglected to specify the new value of a variable.

Significantly absent from the invoice example is concurrency. Concurrency is not mentioned in the example's description, and it is excluded from the Z specification. TLA$^+$ was designed for specifying and reasoning about concurrent systems. From a practical point of view, the differences between the TLA$^+$ and Z specifications of the invoice system are largely stylistic. The differences would be more significant for a concurrent system, especially if liveness were important. Liveness properties of sequential systems tend to be simple, asserting that an input action must be followed by the corresponding output action. An informal treatment of liveness is usually satisfactory. Liveness properties of concurrent systems can be subtle and can often be made clear only through formal specification.

In principle, a language's inability to express liveness could be a handicap. In practice, it seldom is. Experience has shown that most errors are violations of safety properties. Moreover, the computational complexity of model checking is larger for liveness properties than for safety properties. This means that model checking liveness properties is usually feasible only for small models – ones that may be too small to find subtle errors. The importance of liveness is more philosophical than practical.

Bibliography

[ABA 95] ABADI M., LAMPORT L., "Conjoining specifications". *ACM Transactions on Programming Languages and Systems*, 17(3):507–534, May 1995.

[ALP 85] ALPERN B., SCHNEIDER F.B., "Defining liveness". *Information Processing Letters*, 21(4):181–185, October 1985.

[GAF 03] GAFNI E., LAMPORT L., "Disk paxos". *Distributed Computing*, 16(1):1–20, 2003.

[LAM 83] LAMPORT L., "What good is temporal logic?" In R. E. A. Mason, ed., *Information Processing 83: Proceedings of the IFIP 9th World Congress*, pages 657–668, Paris, September 1983. IFIP, North-Holland.

[LAM 94] LAMPORT L., "The temporal logic of actions". *ACM Transactions on Programming Languages and Systems*, 16(3):872–923, May 1994.

[LAM 03] LAMPORT L., *Specifying Systems*. Addison-Wesley, Boston, 2003. Also available on the Web via a link at `http://lamport.org`.

[LAM 06] LAMPORT L., TLA – temporal logic of actions. A web page, a link to which can be found at URL `http://lamport.org`. The page can also be found by searching the Web for the 21-letter string formed by concatenating `uid` and `lamporttlahomepage`.

[TAS 02] TASIRAN S., YU Y, BATSON B., KREIDER S. "Using formal specifications to monitor and guide simulation: verifying the cache coherence engine of the Alpha 21364 microprocessor". in *In Proceedings of the 3rd IEEE Workshop on Microprocessor Test and Verification, Common Challenges and Solutions*. IEEE Computer Society, 2002.

Part II

Event-Based Approaches

Chapter 8

Action Systems

Jane SINCLAIR

8.1 Overview of action systems

Action systems [BAC 83] combine a definition of system state with an explicit description of how and when state-modifying events may occur. This example follows the work of Morgan [MOR 90] and Butler [BUT 92], in which these two aspects are given equal importance. Action systems describe both the succession of events in a system and the way in which system state changes. However, they are not tied to any one particular state-description notation and may be thought of as providing a framework which can, if required, be combined with other approaches. For example, the Z notation [SPI 92] offers significant advantages in the way state descriptions can be structured. This can be put to use within an action system as demonstrated below. The additional aspect of supporting event description and refinement means that features of event-based notations such as CSP [HOA 85] can be exploited for action systems too.

An action system consists of a *state*, an *initialisation* and a set *of labelled actions*. The state is a collection of variables, with an optional predicate (called an *invariant*) relating them. The values of state variables may be altered by the initialisation and by each action of the system. An action consists of a *guard* and a *command*. The guard is a predicate describing the states in which the action may be executed. The command describes how the state changes when the action is executed. One way to represent a command is using a statement from Dijkstra's Guarded Command Language [DIJ 76] (which uses simple assignment, sequencing, alternation and iteration) but other notations may also be used. The invariant provides an additional implicit constraint on the initialisation and all actions.

Execution of an action system proceeds by first performing the initialisation. The guards of all actions are then evaluated and actions whose guard is true are said to be *enabled*. The environment is offered the choice between all actions currently enabled. When one is chosen, the corresponding command is executed and the guards of all actions are then re-evaluated. This procedure is continued. If no action is enabled, the system is said to be *deadlocked*. If an action aborts (for example, with a non-terminating loop), the action system *diverges*, that is, it behaves unpredictably.

One way to view the execution of an action system is in terms of its state, considering the way the values of state variables change as execution proceeds. Another aspect concerns the possible sequences of actions which may occur. In referring to these, it is convenient to make use of *labels*. A label is an identifier, each action being associated with a label unique within the system. For example, if an action system has actions labelled *a* and *b* with the guard of each of these being *true*, then both actions are always enabled. Thus, after initialisation, any sequence of the actions *a* and *b* will be possible for the system. These sequences are referred to as *traces* of the system.

When an action system executes, several actions may be enabled at any point. The choice of which one should be selected is governed by the environment. For example, there may be a human user making decisions at each stage. Alternatively, there may be an interface with other components, which can themselves be specified using action systems. When action systems execute in parallel, commonly labelled actions occur together, providing communication channels between the separate action systems. Thus, action systems can provide a state-based approach to the development of distributed systems. Definitions and examples of parallel composition and refinement are given by Butler [BUT 92].

8.2 Analysis and specification of case 1

Case 1 of the requirements addresses the invoicing of orders. For an action system, both the state of the system and the required actions must be identified. Either may be addressed first. Once the actions have been decided upon, each one can be specified in detail by providing a guard and a command. Here, the state is considered first, with Z notation [SPI 92] used where appropriate. At the end of the section, the individual parts of the specification will be brought together and the action system for case 1 will be presented.

8.2.1 Modeling the state of the action system

The state variables must be identified. In addition, we have chosen a notation which provides information on the *type* of each variable (that is, the set of values over which it may range), so we must also consider how these should be defined.

Question 1: What are the state variables?

Answer: The orders are obviously important and will be updated when invoicing occurs. The stock should also be represented.

Question 2: What factors are important in defining types for these variables?

Answer: Relevant to an order are: the status, the product referred to, the quantity ordered. Also, since there can be many orders, we need a means of distinguishing between them. An order number can be used for this purpose. Each order should have a unique order number. For stock, there are products, each associated with a current stock level. These are all considered in detail below.

There is no need to provide any details about products, so we can simply regard them as being drawn from the set, *PRODUCT*, which represents the set of all possible products. In Z this is formally specified as:

$$[PRODUCT]$$

The status is a little different: it can take one of only two possible values. The following definition creates the type *STATUS* with precisely these two elements:

$$STATUS ::= pending \mid invoiced$$

The amount of an order, and the level of stock too, can both be represented as non-negative integers, that is, as elements of $\mathbb{N}$. For simplicity, we also assume that invoice numbers are drawn from $\mathbb{N}$. These basic building blocks can be used to construct suitable types for the state variables. A question arises:

Question 3: The requirements are ambiguous as to how many products may be referenced by a single order. How should they be interpreted?

Answer: It is assumed that each order references a single product.

As with many other aspects of specification, the way in which orders are defined is to some extent a matter of specification style. Of the four components of an order identified above, the order number is distinguished by being uniquely associated with an order. In view of this, we choose to specify *Order*, whose members each have a status, a product and an amount. Order numbers are then assigned via a function (see below). One way to define *Order* is as a Z schema, which specifies that any order has these three named components.

Order

$status : STATUS$
$product : PRODUCT$
$quantity : \mathbb{N}$

If o is an order, declared $o : Order$, then its individual components may be referred to as $o.status$, $o.product$ and $o.quantity$. Multiple orders can be represented by defining a function which associates an order number with an order. An existing order can be accessed by applying the function to the order number. Considering the domain of the function raises a further question:

Question 4: Can any number of orders be accommodated?

Answer: It is assumed that there will be some finite capacity.

This will allow us to explore the case where capacity is reached. We introduce *maxorders* for the maximum number of orders which can be held:

$$\mid \; maxorders : \mathbb{N}$$

The state variable which we have been working towards defining is the collection of orders. This can now be given as:

$$orders : 1 \mathrel{..} maxorders \rightarrowtail\!\!\!\!\!\!+\; Order$$

Each order in the system is associated with a unique order number drawn from the range $1 \mathrel{..} maxorders$. The function used is *partial*, that is, not every number in that range need currently be in use. The *domain* of the function (written $\operatorname{dom} orders$) gives the set of order numbers currently in use.

We now move on to consideration of the stock. It needs to be represented since invoicing can occur only when there is sufficient stock.

Question 5: Little guidance is given in the requirements about the nature of stock. Is the updating of stock to be included at this stage? Are all possible products known from the outset? Will it be possible for new products to be deleted and added?

Answer: Stock is decreased when an order is invoiced: this will be represented. No other stock-changing activity is included in case 1. The requirements make no reference at all to dealing with products. An arbitrary choice must be made. Here it is assumed that certain (but not necessarily all) products are known to the system. This would give scope for dealing with new and old products and unrecognised product identifiers, although this is beyond the current requirements.

Another partial function is used to represent the stock:

$$stock : PRODUCT \rightarrowtail\!\!\!\!\!\!+\; \mathbb{N}$$

Each product known to the system is associated with a number representing the stock level of that product. The set of products known to the system is referred to as $\operatorname{dom} stock$. Having decided upon the state variables *orders* and *stock*, it is appropriate to consider the relationship between them.

Question 6: Is an invariant needed?

Answer: Firstly, it is worth noting that the type information already given tells us quite a lot about these variables and must certainly be respected throughout the specification. Considering the relationship between *stock* and *orders*, there is a possible connection in terms of products; that is, we might wish to allow only those orders which have a known product number. However, we choose to allow orders with unknown product numbers. This will have implications for the definition of actions later on. Having made this decision, no invariant is needed.

8.2.2 Defining the actions

The initialisation and actions of the action system are now considered.

Question 7: What are the initial values of the state variables?

Answer: The requirements say that the stock and orders will be "given in an up-to-date state". We cannot say precisely what values they will each have, but they must be of the correct type.

The following initialisation reflects this answer by setting the values to be some (unspecified) member of the correct type:

$$orders :\in 1 \mathrel{..} maxorders \mathrel{+\!\!\!\!\to} Order$$
$$stock :\in PRODUCT \mathrel{+\!\!\!\!\to} \mathbb{N}$$

The symbol $:\in$ represents assignment of a value chosen from the set on the right hand side. This is *non-deterministic choice*, that is, it is made internally with no reference to the environment. When executed, this selects non-predetermined values for *orders* and *stock*. Given more precise requirements, the non-determinism could be resolved (that is, the choice narrowed down) accordingly.

Question 8: What actions are required?

Answer: The only action needed in this case is one to invoice orders.

Question 9: What are the inputs to the invoice action?

Answer: The answer to this depends on the way in which orders to be invoiced are to be chosen. Some possible ways to do this are:

- an order number is supplied as an input;
- a set of order numbers is supplied as an input;
- a pending order is automatically chosen and invoiced;
- all pending orders are automatically invoiced.

The last two cases again represent non-deterministic choices of the action system. The first approach is chosen here.

We write $o? : \mathbb{N}$ to represent the input order number. Note that *orders* $o?$ gives the order associated with $o?$. The status, for example, of that order can then be referenced by: $(orders\ o?).status$. For clarity, the following shorthand will be used:

Expression	**Shorthand**	**Refers to**
$(orders\ o?).status$	$status_{o?}$	status of order with number $o?$
$(orders\ o?).product$	$product_{o?}$	product of order with number $o?$
$(orders\ o?).quantity$	$quantity_{o?}$	quantity of order with number $o?$

Question 10: When will the invoiced action be enabled?

Answer: The answer to this question dictates the interface between the action system and its environment. There are several possibilities:

- the environment is allowed to choose the action at any point, but if invoicing is not possible for some reason, an *error case* may be appropriate;
- the environment is offered the invoiced action only when certain conditions are met (such as there being some orders whose status is currently *pending*).

Here, we choose the first possibility.

Question 11: Under what circumstances can an order (identified by $o?$) be successfully invoiced?

Answer: The following conditions must all be met:

$o? \in \mathrm{dom}\, orders$	• the order number is known
$status_{o?} = pending$	• the order has status pending
$product_{o?} \in \mathrm{dom}\, stock$	• the ordered product is known
$quantity_{o?} \leq (stock\ product_{o?})$	• there is sufficient stock

Question 12: What should the invoice action do in this case?

Answer: It should change the status of the order to *invoiced* and decrement the stock count.

To decrement the stock value for the product on the invoice we write:

$$stock\ product_{o?} := (stock\ product_{o?}) - quantity_{o?}$$

After this assignment, the product number we are interested in maps to a new stock value calculated by subtracting the ordered quantity from the old value. An assignment to change the status of the order may be specified:

$$status_{o?} := invoiced$$

Question 13: What should happen if the "successful case" conditions are not met? Should there be some response from the action system?

Answer: The requirements say nothing about this. A sensible option seems to be to leave the state unchanged. Responses indicating error (or indeed success) are also useful. An action system does not have to provide output, but in this case we choose to do so. For case 1, we distinguish simply between the case where all the conditions of Question 11 are met and the case in which they are not. That is, only one error message is used.

Since action systems provide the opportunity to consider the interface between the action system and its environment we ask:

Question 14: How and when should responses be delivered?

Answer: Even in a very simple case such as this, choices can be made concerning the way output is handled. Two possibilities are given:

- an output is given immediately by the invoicing action. In this case, the output is an indivisible part of the invoice action, that is, the output must occur before execution of the action system can proceed;
- the output activity is made into a separate action, allowing it to be split from the activity of updating state variables. This would allow, for example, for the buffering of outputs.

Here, the second option is chosen: the response will be given by a separate action (although buffering is not modeled here).

To do this, an additional state variable, *resp*, can be introduced to record the outcome of the invoice action. This can be used to trigger the output action, which we label *response*. When *resp* contains a reply waiting for output, *response* can be enabled. The situation of no reply waiting could be represented by some special value (*Nil*, say) for *resp*. A type for the reply is defined:

$$Reply ::= Ok \mid Error \mid Nil$$

The action *response* can then be defined as having output $r! : Reply$ and guard $resp \neq Nil$. The command part should set the output $r!$ to the current waiting value, and update *resp* to show that this output is no longer waiting. This is given by the following simultaneous assignment:

$$resp, r! := Nil, resp$$

The decision to include a response means that the answers to some previous questions have to be revised. The initialisation would now include:

$$resp := Nil$$

since no response is waiting initially. The *invoice* action will set *resp* to either *Ok* or *Error* as appropriate. Finally, if the *invoice* action were allowed to occur repeatedly without the output being dealt with, then *resp* would be overwritten. This can be prevented by allowing *invoice* to be offered only when *resp* has value *Nil*. The effect of this is discussed further below.

$$
Case1 == \left(\begin{array}{l}
\textbf{var} \;\; orders : 1 \mathrel{..} maxorders \rightarrowtail\!\!\!\!\!\!\!+\;\; Order; \\
\qquad stock : PRODUCT \rightarrowtail\!\!\!\!\!\!\!+\;\; \mathbb{N}; \\
\qquad resp : Reply \\
\textbf{init} \;\; orders :\in 1 \mathrel{..} maxorders \rightarrowtail\!\!\!\!\!\!\!+\;\; Order; \\
\qquad stock :\in PRODUCT \rightarrowtail\!\!\!\!\!\!\!+\;\; \mathbb{N}; \\
\qquad resp := Nil \\
\textbf{action}\ invoice\ \textbf{in}\ o? : \mathbb{N}\ :- \\
\qquad resp = Nil \longrightarrow \\
\qquad\qquad \textbf{if} \;\; o? \in \operatorname{dom} orders \wedge \\
\qquad\qquad\quad status_{o?} = pending \wedge \\
\qquad\qquad\quad quantity_{o?} \leq (stock\ product_{o?}) \\
\qquad\qquad \textbf{then} \;\; status_{o?} := invoiced; \\
\qquad\qquad\qquad (stock\ product_{o?}) := \\
\qquad\qquad\qquad\quad (stock\ product_{o?}) - quantity_{o?}; \\
\qquad\qquad\qquad resp := Ok \\
\qquad\qquad \textbf{else}\ resp := Error \\
\textbf{action}\ response\ \textbf{out}\ r! : Reply\ :- \\
\qquad resp \neq Nil \longrightarrow resp, r! := Nil, resp
\end{array}\right)
$$

Figure 8.1: Action system specification of the invoice case study: case 1

8.2.3 An action system for case 1

All the parts for constructing the specification have now been introduced and explained. This is brought together in Figure 8.1 as an action system which is given the name *case* 1. The additional syntactic features used in this definition are as follows. The keywords **var** and **init** are used to introduce the description of system state and initialisation as discussed above. The keyword **action** precedes each action, and is immediately followed by the label for that action. The keyword **in** indicates that input is required for this action as defined by the variables following the keyword. A similar convention is used for **out**. The action definition follows the symbol, : –, and is given in the format:

$$guard \longrightarrow command$$

Following the model of execution described above, immediately after initialisation, only *invoice* is enabled. Execution of *invoice* results in *response* being enabled. Thus, *invoice* alternates with *response* in traces of the system. Buffering using a sequence of waiting responses would provide a more flexible interface.

8.3 Analysis and specification of case 2

All our efforts in case 1 can be put to good use in case 2. The changes in requirements ask for additional features concerning stock control and management of orders. In this section the additional features are identified and specified.

8.3.1 Modeling the state for case 2

Question 15: Should the state be any different from that in Case 1?

Answer: No, the same variables are needed. Although we are required to perform some additional tasks, the state as already defined can support this.

To add a little extra interest, we consider how the specification should be modified if required to give separate error messages indicating which of the several unsuccessful cases has arisen. To do this, the type *Reply* is defined to include the necessary error cases:

$$\begin{aligned} \mathit{Reply} ::= \; & \mathit{OrderBookFull} \mid \mathit{StockAdded} \mid \mathit{InsufficientStock} \mid \mathit{AlreadyInvoiced} \\ & \mid \mathit{AddedOrder}\langle\!\langle 1 \mathinner{\ldotp\ldotp} \mathit{maxorders} \rangle\!\rangle \mid \mathit{InvalidOrder} \mid \mathit{Canceled} \mid \mathit{Invoiced} \end{aligned}$$

The only new syntax here concerns the case of adding a new order. It indicates that the reply, *AddedOrder*, will also include the order number of the new order.

8.3.2 Defining the actions

Question 16: What additional actions are required?

Answer: Case 2 should add orders, cancel orders and add stock.

Each action will be considered in turn before bringing the whole action system together. As in Case 1, the approach is to allow each action to be selected at any point as long as no output is waiting, so the guard in each case will be: $resp = Nil$. In defining the command part of an action, the more general **if** ... **fi** choice is used. This allows a number of branches to be specified. Branches are separated by the box symbol, $\Box$.

8.3.2.1 Adding an order

Question 17: When an order is added, how is its order number assigned?

Answer: It would be possible either to allow the order number to be given as an input or to allow the action system to choose a number from those currently unused. The latter option is chosen here.

The *addorder* action is defined in Figure 8.2. It requires alteration to the *orders* state component only. The product and quantity for the new order will be supplied as inputs. The command part of the action has two branches corresponding to the two

$$
\begin{array}{l}
\textbf{action}\ \mathit{addorder}\ \textbf{in}\ p? : \mathit{PRODUCT};\ n? : \mathbb{N}\ :-\\
\quad \mathit{resp} = \mathit{Nil} \longrightarrow\\
\quad\quad \textbf{if}\ \#(\mathrm{dom}\, \mathit{orders}) < \mathit{maxorders} \longrightarrow\\
\quad\quad\quad (\textbf{local}\ o :\in (1 \mathrel{..} \mathit{maxorders}) \setminus (\mathrm{dom}\, \mathit{orders})\ \textbf{in}\\
\quad\quad\quad\quad \mathit{orders} := \mathit{orders} \cup \{o \mapsto (\mu\, \mathit{ord} : \mathit{Order} \mid \mathit{ord.status} = \mathit{pending} \wedge\\
\quad\quad\quad\quad\quad \mathit{ord.product} = p? \wedge\\
\quad\quad\quad\quad\quad \mathit{ord.quantity} = n?)\};\\
\quad\quad\quad\quad \mathit{resp} := \mathit{AddedOrder}(o)\\
\quad\quad\quad)\\
\quad\quad \Box\ \neg\ (\#(\mathrm{dom}\, \mathit{orders}) < \mathit{maxorders}) \longrightarrow\\
\quad\quad\quad\quad \mathit{resp} := \mathit{OrderBookFull}\\
\quad\quad \textbf{fi}
\end{array}
$$

Figure 8.2: The action *addorder*

possible cases: either there is room to add a new order or there is not (with # giving the cardinality of the set). In the latter case, the response shows that no more orders can be taken. In the former, an unused order number, o, is selected using the non-deterministic choice described above. The expression $(1 \mathrel{..} \mathit{maxorders}) \setminus (\mathrm{dom}\, \mathit{orders})$ gives the set of all possible order numbers minus the set of those currently in use. The **local** construct allows o to be defined and referred to as a local variable within the command. With o selected, the new order can be added with status *pending*. The term $(\mu\, \mathit{ord} : \mathit{Order} \mid \ldots)$ constructs a value of type *Order* by giving a value for each of its components. The *maplet* notation, written $o \mapsto \ldots$ indicates that o indexes the new order.

8.3.2.2 Adding stock

To add stock, only the *stock* function is altered. This is defined in Figure 8.3. If required, a limit could be placed on the maximum levels of stock allowed.

$$
\begin{array}{l}
\textbf{action}\ \mathit{addstock}\ \textbf{in}\ p? : \mathit{PRODUCT};\ n? : \mathbb{N}\ :-\\
\quad \mathit{resp} = \mathit{Nil} \longrightarrow\\
\quad\quad (\mathit{stock}\ p?) := (\mathit{stock}\ p?) + n?;\\
\quad\quad \mathit{resp} := \mathit{StockAdded}
\end{array}
$$

Figure 8.3: The action *addstock*

$$
\begin{array}{l}
\textbf{action } \mathit{cancelorder} \textbf{ in } o? : \mathbb{N} \ :- \\
\quad \mathit{resp} = \mathit{Nil} \longrightarrow \\
\quad\quad \textbf{if } o? \notin \operatorname{dom} \mathit{orders} \longrightarrow \\
\quad\quad\quad \mathit{resp} := \mathit{InvalidOrder} \\
\quad\quad \Box\ (o? \in \operatorname{dom} \mathit{orders}) \wedge \mathit{status}_{o?} = \mathit{pending} \longrightarrow \\
\quad\quad\quad \mathit{orders} := \{o?\} \lhd \mathit{orders}; \\
\quad\quad\quad \mathit{resp} := \mathit{Canceled} \\
\quad\quad \Box\ (o? \in \operatorname{dom} \mathit{orders}) \wedge \mathit{status}_{o?} = \mathit{invoiced} \longrightarrow \\
\quad\quad\quad \mathit{orders} := \{o?\} \lhd \mathit{orders}; \\
\quad\quad\quad \mathit{resp} := \mathit{Canceled}; \\
\quad\quad\quad (\mathit{stock}\ \mathit{product}_{o?}) := (\mathit{stock}\ \mathit{product}_{o?}) + \mathit{quantity}_{o?} \\
\quad\quad \textbf{fi}
\end{array}
$$

Figure 8.4: The action *cancelorder*

8.3.2.3 Canceling an order

The action to be taken when an order is canceled is not clearly stated in the requirements, but it would seem to depend on the status of the order. If the order is still pending it can simply be removed. If it has already been invoiced, the situation is more complicated.

Question 18: What happens when canceling an order, particularly if it has already been invoiced?

Answer: In the absence of further guidelines, an arbitrary decision is made to allow invoiced orders to be canceled. The stock is replaced. This might be seen as modeling the return of unwanted goods. An alternative would be to allow cancelation of pending orders only.

The action *cancelorder* with input order number o is specified in Figure 8.4. Here, there are three alternatives in the command. If the order number is unknown, a response is assigned to indicate this. For a known order number, the cases depend on whether the order status is *pending* or *invoiced*, with the specification in each case according with the answer to the previous question. The notation $\{x\} \lhd f$ denotes the resulting function when x is removed from the domain of f.

8.3.2.4 Removing stock

Question 19: Should removal of stock be represented as a separate action?

Answer: Removal of stock is associated only with the invoicing of orders, so here it is incorporated with the *invoiceorder* action. It would also be possible to have a separate removal action which could form part of the interface.

$$
\begin{array}{l}
\textbf{action } \mathit{invoiceorder} \textbf{ in } o? : \mathbb{N} \ :- \\
\quad \mathit{resp} = \mathit{Nil} \longrightarrow \\
\qquad \textbf{if } o? \notin \operatorname{dom} \mathit{orders} \longrightarrow \\
\qquad\quad \mathit{resp} := \mathit{InvalidOrder} \\
\qquad \Box\ (o? \in \operatorname{dom} \mathit{orders}) \wedge (\mathit{status}_{o?} \neq \mathit{pending}) \longrightarrow \\
\qquad\quad \mathit{resp} := \mathit{AlreadyInvoiced} \\
\qquad \Box\ (o? \in \operatorname{dom} \mathit{orders}) \wedge (\mathit{status}_{o?} = \mathit{pending}) \wedge \\
\qquad\quad ((\mathit{stock}\ \mathit{product}_{o?}) < \mathit{quantity}_{o?}) \longrightarrow \\
\qquad\quad \mathit{resp} := \mathit{InsufficientStock} \\
\qquad \Box\ (o? \in \operatorname{dom} \mathit{orders}) \wedge (\mathit{status}_{o?} = \mathit{pending}) \wedge \\
\qquad\quad ((\mathit{stock}\ \mathit{product}_{o?}) \geq \mathit{quantity}_{o?}) \longrightarrow \\
\qquad\quad (\mathit{stock}\ \mathit{product}_{o?}) := (\mathit{stock}\ \mathit{product}_{o?}) - \mathit{quantity}_{o?}; \\
\qquad\quad \mathit{status}_{o?} := \mathit{invoiced}; \\
\qquad\quad \mathit{resp} := \mathit{Invoiced} \\
\qquad \textbf{fi}
\end{array}
$$

Figure 8.5: The action *invoiceorder*

8.3.2.5 Invoicing an order

The action to invoice an order requires the input of an order number. The order must have status *pending* and there must be sufficient stock available to cover the amount required. The action *invoiceorder* is described in Figure 8.5.

Question 20: Further questions concerning orders are raised. Should an order number represent a particular order once and for all time? Should each order identifier be completely fresh? Should there be some distinction between current orders and old orders?

Answer: Here, if an order is canceled then the index may be reused. There is no other way that an order “leaves” the system.

8.3.3 An action system for case 2

Before bringing the actions together in an action system, one question remains:

Question 21: How should case 2 be initialised?

Answer: It is assumed that *stock* and *orders* are initially empty, written, $\varnothing$.

The action system for case 2 is given in Figure 8.6. To prevent repetition, the definitions of the actions are not included here but are as defined in Figures 8.2 to 8.5.

$$Case2 == \left(\begin{array}{l} \textbf{var}\ \ orders : 1\,..\,maxorders \rightarrowtail Order; \\ \qquad stock : PRODUCT \rightarrowtail \mathbb{N}; \\ \qquad resp : Reply \\ \textbf{init}\ orders, stock, resp := \varnothing, \varnothing, Nil \\ \textbf{action}\ addorder\ \textbf{in}\ p? : PRODUCT;\ n? : \mathbb{N} \\ \textbf{action}\ cancelorder\ \textbf{in}\ o? : \mathbb{N} \\ \textbf{action}\ addstock\ \textbf{in}\ p? : PRODUCT;\ n? : \mathbb{N} \\ \textbf{action}\ invoiceorder\ \textbf{in}\ o? : \mathbb{N} \\ \textbf{action}\ response\ \textbf{out}\ r! : Reply\ \ : - \\ \qquad resp \neq Nil \longrightarrow resp, r! := Nil, resp \end{array}\right)$$

Figure 8.6: Action system specification of the invoice case study: case 2

8.4 Verification for action systems

The use of action systems allows verification of properties concerning the system state and of properties more usually associated with event-based approaches. A semantic basis for such proof can be provided by defining the *weakest precondition* (wp) for actions and sequences of actions. The wp for a statement s to establish a condition p is defined as the predicate describing the set of all states from which execution of statement s is guaranteed to terminate in a state satisfying p. For wp definitions, the reader is referred elsewhere [DIJ 76, MOR 90]. To show that, for example, a specification establishes and maintains invariant I we can verify:

$wp(init, I) = true$		"*init* establishes *I*"
$I \Rightarrow wp(a, I)$	for each action a	"if I is true before a then I is true after a"

This same approach can be used to prove that some general property holds for a specification. For example, to show that the limit of *maxorders* is not exceeded, the above conditions should be proved with I being: $\#orders \leq maxorders$. Other properties concerning change of state may also be verified. For instance, to show that the invoice action has no effect on the orders unless the status of the requested order is pending, we need to prove that for any input value o:

$$wp(invoiceorder.o, orders' \neq orders) \Rightarrow status\ o = pending$$

where *invoiceorder.o* represents the input action with input value o, and $orders'$ is the state of orders after the action has occurred.

Another area in which verification may be of use concerns the sequences of actions which may occur and the interface between the action system and its environment. It can be verified whether certain sequences of actions are possible traces of the system since a sequence s of actions is a trace if and only if execution of the initialisation followed by execution of each element of s in turn is guaranteed to terminate. This is again formalised using the wp definitions. We would find, for example, that an invoicing action cannot be immediately followed by another, that is:

$$\langle invoiceorder.o1, invoiceorder.o2\rangle$$

is not a possible trace. However, for certain values of $o1$ the following is a trace:

$$\langle invoiceorder.o1, response.InvalidOrder\rangle$$

As in CSP, not only traces but also *failures* and *divergences* may be defined. A failure is a trace, t, together with a set, S, of actions, where execution of t can lead to a state in which no action from S is enabled. A divergence is a trace which aborts. This allows a finer distinction between action systems than traces alone, since some action systems may have equivalent traces but different failures and divergences. Among the useful properties which can be verified for an action system is freedom from deadlock. This involves a proof that, no matter what trace has occurred, it is not possible for all actions to be denied to the environment. If G is defined to be the disjunction of all guards of the action system, then the action system is deadlock-free if G is invariant for the system.

Another aspect of verification for action systems is that of proving refinement. Refinement conditions for action systems are given by Woodcock and Morgan [WOO 90] and Butler [BUT 92]. An action system can be refined to a parallel composition of several subsystems. This corresponds to the development of the system to a distributed implementation. It is quite likely that a system for updating orders and stock levels could be accessed by a number of users acting concurrently. It is also possible that the system itself may be distributed. These situations can be represented by parallel composition of action systems, with refinement verified against a top level specification. With an action system representation, it is possible to refine a top level specification like those given here to a description of the system as the parallel composition of two or more separate subsystems which act in parallel. For example, here we might separate out the invoicing system and the stock control system. Certain operations could occur together, for example, orders could be placed in the system at the same time as stock was updated. Other actions, for example, two which update the stock, must still be consecutive rather than concurrent. Parallel composition for action systems allows communication to occur through shared actions. This additional communication can be hidden within the system to leave an external interface equivalent to the original.

Action systems provide a way of specifying and verifying many aspects of a system. However, the effort required for proof in anything but the smallest system is considerable. Research on machine-based support continues.

8.5 The natural language description of the specification

8.5.1 Case 1

Orders are identified by order number. There is a limit, *maxorders*, on the maximum number of orders that can be dealt with at any one time. Each order is for a specified amount of a single product and has a status of either *pending* or *invoiced*. The current stock level of each known product is recorded.

Initially, orders and stock are assumed to have some (unspecified) appropriate value. An action is required to *invoice* orders. This will be offered when no output is enabled and requires an order number as input. If the input order number is known, the status of the order is *pending*, and there is sufficient stock, then the order is invoiced. This involves setting its status to *invoiced* and decreasing the current stock level of the ordered product by the amount stated on the order. A reply indicates success. If one or more of the three conditions is not met, an error message is generated and both the order and the stock will remain unchanged.

The *response* action is enabled when a reply is waiting. The reply is output and a *Nil* value used to indicate that no further output is now waiting. When the action system is executed, the initialisation is first performed. After that, execution of the *invoice* action alternates with the *response* action.

8.5.2 Case 2

This extends case 1 by adding actions to add and cancel orders and to add stock. It also supplies a richer range of responses. The description of orders and stock levels is the same as in case 1. To add an order, details of the product and quantity ordered are supplied as inputs. A currently unused order number is assigned by the system. If the maximum number of orders has already been reached, an error message is generated and the order is not added. Canceling an order may be carried out irrespective of the status of the order. If the order has already been invoiced, the stock is returned. The order is deleted and the order number may later be reused. Stock may be added for any product. There is no limit to the amount of stock that can be held. Execution is similar to case 1, with the *response* action alternating with other actions in the system.

8.6 Conclusion

Action systems provide a notation for describing the interaction of events in a state-based system. During the development process, questions will naturally arise concerning both *what* the operations are required to do and *when* they can occur, highlighting any ambiguity in the requirements in both these aspects. It is a very useful combination for the invoice case study since, although description of the state seems fundamental, the interface and the interaction of events is important too. This becomes even more apparent if a distributed implementation is required. The action system notation, which gives equal importance to describing both state and actions, is well-suited to this task.

Although action systems have a precise formal semantics [MOR 90, BUT 92], there is no need to be prescriptive in the notation used. Here, it was shown that Z schemas can be slotted into the action system framework. This can allow users to work with their own favourite state-description notation and helps with structuring the description of system state and also of actions. Any notation which can be given a weakest precondition semantics is acceptable.

In common with other formal notations, action systems provide a basis for verification and refinement of the system. Both state-based properties (such as invariant properties) and event-based properties (such as freedom from deadlock) can be expressed and verified, as can steps of refinement. A single action system may be refined to a distributed implementation of subsystems working in parallel [BUT 92].

A disadvantage of the approach is that, currently, proofs are done by hand and can be difficult. Support for verification is under investigation and, although this could be a useful aid, it is unrealistic to suppose that the task will become a completely straightforward one. Another potential criticism is that, in allowing consideration of so many features, action systems are more complex than some other approaches. Rigidly fixing such aspects as the system interface from the very top level of specification might be too constraining in some circumstances.

Action systems are similar to a number of other notations combining state description and actions on state, for example, TLA [LAM 94] and Unity [CHA 88]. However, these notations and the state-based approach to action systems [BAC 83] allow communication between components based on shared state. Our event-based view models communication by synchronisation of commonly-labelled actions. Parallel components can be refined independently, unlike the state-based approach where constraints are placed on the environment. Unlike the state-based approach, the failures of a system may be observed and internal (non-deterministic) and external choice are distinguished. The event-based view associates action systems with CSP [HOA 85], and the two notations are thus very similar in many respects. However, action systems give equal consideration to both state and events, with both being treated uniformly in refinement [WOO 90, BUT 92, SIN 95]. Using action systems can also improve clarity of specification since, unlike CSP, the inputs or outputs connected with a single channel are gathered in one action. This makes them easily identifiable, a feature which is particularly useful for parallel composition.

Action systems also have a clear link with purely state-based description techniques such as Z, but go further in stating explicitly when events are enabled. This is different from the Z notion of precondition which may be weakened through refinement. Action systems provide additional structure to state-based approaches, admitting the definition of traces, failures and divergence. Issues of concurrency and distributed implementation can be addressed.

Bibliography

[BAC 83] Back R.J.R., Kurki-Suonio R. "Decentralisation of process nets with centralised control." In *2nd ACM SIGACT-SIGOPS Symp. on Principles of Distributed Computing*, pp 131–142, 1983

[BUT 92] Butler M.J. A CSP Approach to Action Systems. PhD thesis, Oxford University, UK, 1992

[CHA 88] Chandy K.M., Misra J. *Parallel Program Design.* Addison-Wesley, 1988

[DIJ 76] Dijkstra E.W. *A Discipline of Programming.* Prentice Hall, International Series in Computer Science, London, 1976

[HOA 85] Hoare C.A.R. *Communicating Sequential Processes.* Prentice Hall, International Series in Computer Science, London, 1985

[LAM 94] Lamport L. "The temporal logic of actions." *ACM Transactions on Programming Languages and Systems*, 16:872–923, 1994

[MOR 90] Morgan C.C. "Of wp and CSP." In W.H.J. Feijen *et al.* eds. *Beauty is our Business: A Birthday Salute to Edsger W. Dijkstra.* Springer-Verlag, pp 319–326, 1990

[SIN 95] Sinclair J., Woodcock J. "Event refinement in state-based concurrent systems." *Formal Aspects of Computing*, 7:266–288, 1995

[WOO 90] Woodcock J.C.P., Morgan C.C. "Refinement of State-based Concurrent Systems." *Proceedings of the VDM Symposium.* Springer-Verlag, LNCS 42, 1990

[SPI 92] Spivey J.M. *The Z Notation: A Reference Manual*, 2nd edn. Prentice Hall, International Series in Computer Science, London, 1992

Chapter 9

Event B

Dominique CANSELL and Dominique MÉRY

9.1 Introduction

What is the event B method? In the sequel, we refer to the original B method as classic B [ABR 96] and its event-based evolution as event B. The event B method [ABR 98, ABR 03a] reuses the set-theoretical and logical notations of the B method [ABR 96] and provides new notations for expressing abstract systems or simply models based on events. Moreover, the refinement over models is a key feature for incrementally developing models from a textually-defined system, while preserving correctness; it implements the proof-based development paradigm. Each development. includes proofs for invariance and refinement. Operations of the classic B method do not exist in the event B method and are substituted by events. Events modify the system state (or state variables), by executing an action when its guard holds. An event is not called but observed. When refining machines in classic B, one should maintain the number of operations both in the abstract machine and in the refinement; on the contrary, new events may be introduced in the refinement model and they may modify only new variables. New events bring new proof obligations for ensuring a correct refinement. Finally, an event B model is a closed system with a finite list of state variables and a finite list of events. If the system reacts to its environment, the event B model should integrate events of the environment. The B chapter introduces useful notations for the event B method like set theory, generalized substitution, predicate calculus.

Proof-based development. Proof-based development methods integrate formal proof techniques in the development of software systems. The main idea is to start with a very abstract model of the system under development. We then gradually add details to this first model by building a sequence of more concrete ones. The relationship between two successive models in this sequence is that of *refinement* [BAC 79, ABR 96, CHA 88]. It is controlled by means of a number of so-called *proof obliga-*

tions, which guarantee the correctness of the development. Such proof obligations are proved by automatic (and interactive) proof procedures supported by a proof engine. The essence of the refinement relationship is that it preserves already proved *system properties* including safety properties and termination properties. The invariant of an abstract model plays a central role for deriving safety properties and our methodology focuses on the incremental discovery of the invariant; the goal is to obtain a formal statement of properties through the final invariant of the last refined abstract model.

Refining formal models. Formal models contain *events* which preserve some invariant properties; they also include aspects related to the termination. Such models are thus very close to action systems introduced by Back [BAC 79] (see Chapter 8), to UNITY programs [CHA 88] and to TLA$^+$ specifications [LAM 94, LAM 02]. The refinement of formal models plays a central role in these frameworks and is a key concept for developing (sequential, distributed, communicating, ...) (computer-based) systems. When one refines a formal model, the corresponding more concrete model may have new variables and new events; it may also strengthen the *guards* of more abstract events. As already mentioned, some proof obligations are generated in order to prove that a refinement is correct. Notice that, if some proof obligations remain unproved, it means that either the formal model is not correctly refined or that an interactive proving session is required. The prover allows us to get a complete proof of the development and hence of the final system. No assumption is made about the *size* of the system, for instance, the number of nodes in a network, where the problem is to elect a leader [ABR 03e]. This contrasts with what should be done while using model-checking techniques.

Organization of the text. The text introduces in a very progressive way the different notations and concepts required for developing the case study. Section 9.2 analyzes the case study and extracts informations for constructing a first skeleton of B event-based model. The B event-based modeling technique is introduced in section 9.3 by writing an event B model. The first invoice case study model is given in section 9.4 and it completes the skeleton of the section 9.2. Section 9.5 defines the refinement of a event B model and it is used in the section 9.6 for deriving the second case study model; a refinement of this model is proposed and introduces an ordering over invoices. Sections 9.7 and 9.8 conclude our proof-based development of B event-based models for the case study. The complete B models are given in three figures.

9.2 Analyzing the text of the case study

The starting point of the incremental development of a event B model is the analysis of the requirements to extract pertinent details; the requirements are generally not very well structured and it may be helpful to structure them and then to derive logical and mathematical structures of the problem: sets, constants and properties over sets and constants. We produce the mathematical landscape through requirements elicitation.

B guidelines: *The concept of set is a central one in the B methodology; each basic object is a set; relations and functions should be considered primarily as sets.*

The lines of the case study are numbered; numbers will be used when we will analyze requirements. We will interleave questions asked by either the customer or the specifier, and we will answer to these questions.

1. The subject of the case study is **to invoice order**.

   Question 1: What is an order? How can we model an order? What does to invoice mean?

   Answer: In fact, an order is a member of a set, namely the set of orders. We define a set of orders by the name ALL_ORDERS; we do not know yet, if it is a quantity which may be modified. It is the set of all possible orders. The subject is explained later in the text.

2. To invoice is to change the state of an order (to change it from the state *pending* to *invoiced*).

   Question 2: Can you define what it means `to invoice order`?

   Answer: `To invoice order` is an action or an event which models a modification of the status of an order. The status of an order is either `invoiced` or `pending`; the action should modify the status from pending to invoiced. The action or the event is called *invoice_order* and is triggered for each pending order. The full condition is defined later in the item 5. However, let us detail the status of an order. An order is either pending or invoiced and the action invoice allows us to modify the state from pending to invoiced. It is then clear that we should be able to express the state of orders in our model and the state may change. We can use a set $STATUS$ with two elements `invoiced` and `pending`; the variable *orders_state* can be a function from the set of orders called ALL_ORDERS to the set $STATUS$ ($orders\_state \in$ ALL_ORDERS $\longrightarrow STATUS$); *orders_state* is a function because an order has at most only one possible status and it is a total function, because an order has at least one status. In fact, we can use a set called $invoiced\_orders$ containing the invoiced orders and which is a subset of the set of orders ALL_ORDERS.

   Question 3: Since the possible status of an order is either invoiced or pending, it means that it is a boolean structure and your state is in fact a predicate. Is it true?

   Answer: You point out a very interesting feature of a set-theoretical model; since the possible status of an order is either invoiced or pending, it means that we can use a state variable called *invoiced_orders* which contains the invoiced orders and the complement of *invoiced_orders* in the set of orders is the set of pending orders. At this point, we do not know if the set of orders can be modified and we leave unspecified the type of this variable.

3. On an order, we have one and only one reference to an ordered product of a certain quantity. The quantity can be different between orders.

Question 4: What is the structure between the features of an order?

Answer: The structure of an order is not clearly given; in fact, no new information on the orders is available. We have one and only one reference to a product of a certain quantity. This means that you can not have two different informations for the same product on the same order. If you want to order 4 products p and 5 products p, either you need to order 9 products p, or you order 4 products p and 5 products p, but you will have two different orders in the set of orders.

Question 5: But can we have several products on an order?

Answer: The answer is given in item 5: *ordered quantity* and *ordered product*. It seems that there is only one ordered product on an order. *The quantity can be different from other orders* means that the quantity is related to an order and not to a product.

Question 6: What are the consequences for the modeling decisions?

Answer: A set of orders can not be a subset of PRODUCTS $\times \mathbb{N}^*$ ($\mathbb{N}^*$ is the set of non-zero natural numbers) because two orders can have the same product and the same quantity. We can have a sequence of PRODUCTS $\times \mathbb{N}^*$, but it is not a good idea in a first abstraction. The simplest way to define the set of orders is the following one: we suppose that ALL_ORDERS is the abstract set which contains all orders (invoiced, pending and future) and orders is the set of existing orders.
We have the following safety property:

$$orders \subseteq \text{ALL\_ORDERS}.$$

Access operations are defined through the following functions:

$$reference \in orders \longrightarrow \text{PRODUCTS}$$

where $reference$ assigns a product to each order and is a function, because an order is related to one and only one ordered product.

$$quantity \in orders \longrightarrow \mathbb{N}^*$$

where $quantity$ assigns a quantity to each ordered product and we assume that if a product is ordered, the quantity is at least 1.
Another possible choice is to combine the two previous functions into a single one, as follows:

$$reference\_quantity \in orders \longrightarrow \text{PRODUCTS} \times \mathbb{N}^*$$

$reference\_quantity$ is a function for defining the set of pairs (product, quantity) of the current orders.

4. The same reference can be ordered on several different orders.

Question 7: So, there may be different orders with the same reference which is ordered?

Answer: Yes, you can order 4 bottles of wine and you (or another one) can order 4 bottles of wine so there are two different orders with the same reference (bottle) and the same quantity (4).

5. The state of the order will be changed into *invoiced*, if the ordered quantity is either less than or equal to the quantity which is in stock according to the reference of the ordered product.

   Question 8: What is the stock for? How do you use the stock feature in your model?

   Answer: When you invoice an order, you should check that there is enough quantity in stock. The text provides us the guard of the *invoice_order* event and the expression of the guard requires us to model the stock. The *stock* variable is a state variable, because the stock will evolve according to the occurrences of the *invoice_order* event and it assigns to each product the current quantity of available products in the stock:

   $$stock \in \text{PRODUCTS} \longrightarrow \mathbb{N}$$

   Another possible choice is to define *stock* as a partial function but the *invoice_order* event is more complex to write, since we should first check the definability of the function.

6. You have to consider the two following cases:
   (a) **Case 1**

   All the ordered references are references in stock. The stock or the set of the orders may vary:

   - due to the entry of new orders or canceled orders;
   - due to having a new entry of quantities of products in stock at the warehouse.

   We do not have to take these entries into account. This means that you will not receive two entry flows (orders, entries in stock). The stock and the set of orders are always given to you in an up-to-date state.

   Question 9: How do you take this point into account?

   Answer: We state that new events are maintaining the current invariant over variables and we do not care of the way the events are modifying the variables. We keep the invariant.

   (b) **Case 2**

   You do have to take into account the entries of:

   - new orders;
   - cancellations of orders;
   - entries of quantities in the stock.

Question 10: Is there any relation among the two cases?

Answer: All ordered references are references in stock. Item 5 already states this fact. In fact, we want to model the first case study model, Case 1 and then derive by refinement the second case study model Case 2. We will explain this process later. Perhaps the customer says that some order can arrive with an unreferenced product. It is not really difficult to handle, since such orders can be filtered in the next refinement.

Decision:
The mathematical structure is the set of all possible orders denoted ALL_ORDERS and the state variables of the system are $orders$, $stock$, $invoiced\_orders$, $reference$, $quantity$; the first case study model Case 1 explicitly states that *The stock or the set of the orders may vary* and we can now confirm the state variables, They satisfies the following properties:

- ALL_ORDERS $\neq \emptyset$: the set of all possible orders is not empty.
- $orders \subseteq$ ALL_ORDERS: the set of current existing orders is a subset of the set of all possible orders.
- $invoiced\_orders \subseteq orders$: The set of invoiced orders is a subset of the existing orders.
- $pending\_orders \subseteq orders$: The set of pending orders is a subset of the existing orders.
- $invoiced\_orders \cup pending\_orders = orders$ and $invoiced\_orders \cap pending\_orders = \emptyset$ are two safety properties linking the three variables.
- $reference \in orders \longrightarrow$ PRODUCTS.
- $quantity \in orders \longrightarrow \mathbb{N}^*$.
- $stock \in$ PRODUCTS $\longrightarrow \mathbb{N}$.

Question 11: What are the possible modifications over variables?

Answer: The text has already defined the *invoice_order* event; the item (a) defines two new events: a first event (new_orders) adds new orders and a second one ($cancel\_orders$) cancels orders. Moreover, the stock may vary and new quantities of products may be added to the stock: the $delivery\_to\_stock$ event.

Question 12: The pending orders disappear from your decisions?

Answer: No, in fact the set of current pending orders is defined by $orders - invoiced\_orders$ and we will understand later why we do not use the variable $pending\_orders$.

The first event B model, namely Case 1, is sketched in the next following lines; the model is not yet completed and the events should be defined.

MODEL
$Case$ 1
SETS
ALL_ORDERS; PRODUCTS
CONSTANTS
...
PROPERTIES
ALL_ORDERS $\neq \emptyset$
VARIABLES
$orders, stock, invoiced\_orders, reference, quantity$
INVARIANT
$orders \subseteq$ ALL_ORDERS $\wedge$
$stock \in$ PRODUCTS $\longrightarrow \mathbb{N} \wedge$
$invoiced \subseteq orders \wedge$
$quantity \in orders \longrightarrow \mathbb{N}^* \wedge$
$reference \in orders \longrightarrow$ PRODUCTS
ASSERTIONS
...
INITIALIZATION
$stock :=$ PRODUCTS $\times \{0\} \parallel$
$invoiced\_orders, orders, quantity, reference := \emptyset, \emptyset, \emptyset, \emptyset$
EVENTS
$invoice\_order = ...$
$cancel\_orders = ...$
$new\_orders = ...$
$delivery\_to\_stock = ...$
END

An event B model encapsulates variables defining the state of the system; the state should conform to the invariant and each event can be triggered when the current state satisfies the invariant. An abstract model has a name m; the clause SETS contains definitions of sets; the clause CONSTANTS allows one to introduce information related to the mathematical structure of the problem to solve and the clause PROPERTIES contains the effective definitions of constants: it is very important to list carefully properties of constants in a way that can be easily used by the tool Click'n'Prove [ABR 03c].

The second part of the model defines dynamic aspects of state variables and properties over variables using the *invariant* generally called *inductive invariant* and using *assertions* generally called *safety properties*. The invariant $I(x)$ types the variable x, which is assumed to be initialized with respect to the initial conditions, namely $Init(x)$, and which is supposed to be preserved by events (or transitions) enumerated in the EVENTS clause. Conditions of verification called *proof obligations* are generated from the text of the model using the SETS, CONSTANTS and PROPERTIES clauses for defining the mathematical theory and the INVARIANT, INITIALISATION and INVARIANT clauses to generate proof obligations for the preservation (when triggering events) of the invariant and proof obligations stating the correctness of safety properties with respect to the invariant.

B guidelines: *The requirements should be re-structured; basic sets should be identified.*

9.3 Event-based modeling

The B event-driven approach [ABR 03a] is based on the B notation [ABR 96]. It extends the methodological scope of basic concepts such as set-theoretical notations and generalized substitutions in order to take into account the idea of *formal models*. Roughly speaking, a B event-based formal model is characterized by a (finite) list x of *state variables* possibly modified by a (finite) list of *events*; an invariant $I(x)$ states some properties that must always be satisfied by the variables x and *maintained* by the activation of the events. The reader should be very careful and should not consider that the event B method and the classic B method are identical; they share foundational notions like generalized substitutions, refinement, invariance, proof obligations, but a B event-based model intends to provide a formal view of a reactive system, whereas an abstract machine provides operations which can be called and which also maintain the invariant.

In what follows, we briefly recall definitions and principles of formal models and explain how they can be managed with the help of the tool Click'n'Prove [CLE 04, ABR 05a].

Generalized substitutions provide a way to express the transformations of the values of the state variables of a formal model. In its simple form, $x := E(x)$, a generalized substitution looks like an assignment statement. In this construct, x denotes a vector build on the set of state variables of the model, and $E(x)$ a vector of expressions of the same size as the vector x. We interpret it as a *logical simultaneous substitution* of each variable of the vector x by the corresponding expression of the vector $E(x)$. There exists a more general form of generalized substitution. It is denoted by the construct $x \ :\mid P(x_0, x)$. This is to be read: "x is modified in such a way that the predicate $P(x_0, x)$ holds", where x denotes the *new value* of the vector, whereas x_0 denotes its *old value*. It is clearly non-deterministic in general. This general form could be considered as a *normal form*, since the simplest form $x := E(x)$ is equivalent to the more general form $x \ :\mid (x = E(x_0))$. In the next table, we give the correspondence of generalized substitutions with the normal form.

Generalized Substitution	Normalization
$x :\mid P(x_0, x)$	$x :\mid P(x_0, x)$
$x := E(x, y)$	$x :\mid (x = E(x_0, y))$
$x :\in A(x, y)$	$x :\mid (x \in A(x_0, y)$
$x_1 := E_1(x_1, x_2, y) \parallel$ $x_2 := E_2(x_1, x_2, y)$	$(x_1, x_2) :\mid \left(\begin{array}{l} x_1 = E_1((x_1)_0, (x_2)_0, y) \wedge \\ x_2 = E_2((x_1)_0, (x_2)_0, y) \end{array} \right)$

An event is essentially made of two parts: a *guard*, which is a predicate built on the state variables, and an *action*, which is a generalized substitution. An event can take one of the forms shown in the table below. In these constructs, *evt* is an identifier: this is the event name. The first event is not guarded: it is thus always enabled. The guard of the other events, which states the necessary condition for these events to occur, is represented by $G(x)$ in the second case, and by $\exists t \cdot G(t, x)$ in the third case. The latter defines a non-deterministic event where t represents a vector of distinct local variables. The so-called before-after predicate $BA(x, x')$ associated with each event shape describes the event as a logical predicate expressing the relationship linking the values of the state variables just before (x) and just after (x') the event "execution".

Event	Before-after Predicate $BA(x, x')$
BEGIN $x :\mid P(x_0, x)$ END	$P(x, x')$
WHEN $G(x)$ THEN $x :\mid Q(x_0, x)$ END	$G(x) \wedge Q(x, x')$
ANY t WHERE $G(t, x)$ THEN $x :\mid R(x_0, x, t)$ END	$\exists t \cdot (G(t, x) \wedge R(x, x', t))$

Proof obligations are produced from events in order to state that the invariant condition $I(x)$ is preserved. We next give general rules to be proved. The first one is the initialization rule which states that the invariant holds for each initial state:

$$\boxed{Init(x) \Rightarrow I(x)}$$

It follows immediately from the very definition of $BA(x, x')$, the before-after predicate, of each event:

$$\boxed{I(x) \land BA(x, x') \Rightarrow I(x')}$$

Notice that it follows from the two guarded forms of events that this obligation is trivially discharged when the guard of the event is false. When it is the case, the event is said to be "disabled". An event is essentially a reactive entity and reacts with respect to its guard $\mathsf{grd}(e)(x)$. An event should be *feasible* and the feasibility is related to the feasibility of the generalized substitution of the event: some next state must be reachable from a given state. Since events are reactive, related proof obligations should guarantee that the current state satisfying the invariant should be feasible. In the next table, we define, for each possible event, the feasibility condition.

Event : E	Feasibility : $fis(E)$
$x :\mid Init(x)$	$\exists x \cdot Init(x)$
BEGIN $x :\mid P(x_0, x)$ END	$I(x) \Rightarrow \exists x' \cdot P(x, x')$
WHEN $G(x)$ THEN $x :\mid P(x_0, x)$ END	$I(x) \land G(x) \Rightarrow \exists x' \cdot P(x, x')$
ANY l WHERE $G(l, x)$ THEN $x :\mid P(x_0, x, l)$ END	$I(x) \land G(l, x) \Rightarrow \exists x' \cdot P(x, x', l)$

For instance, the event BEGIN $x :\mid P(x_0, x)$ END is feasible, when the invariant ensures the existence of a next value x satisfying $P(x_0, x)$ (x_0 is the value of x, when the event is observed and x will be the value afterward). If we consider the following event BEGIN $a, b, c \ :| \ a = a_0 \wedge b = b_0 \wedge a_0, b_0, c_0 \in \mathbb{N} \wedge c = a \ div \ b$ END, the invariant should include a condition of the state of b ($b \neq 0$). Finally, predicates in the ASSERTIONS clause should be implied by the predicates of the INVARIANT clause; the condition is simply formalized as follows:

$$I(x) \Rightarrow A(x)$$

Now, we have defined the main concepts for deriving a B event-based model for the first case study.

9.4 Modeling the first event B model Case 1

The construction of an event B model is based on an analysis of data which are manipulated; each B model is organized according to clauses and requirements of the case study are incrementally added into the B model. In section 9.2, we have analyzed the requirements and we have derived a first sketch of a event B model. Events should now be completed and the model should be internally validated. The internal validation checks that proof obligations hold and is made with the help of the tool Click'n'Prove [CLE 04].

In the text of the description of the system, we use the following informations: *all the ordered references are references in stock* and we derive that the invoice_order event is triggered when there are enough items of a given reference in the current stock. Let o be a pending order ($o \in orders - invoiced\_orders$). If the quantity in stock of the product whose reference is $reference(o)$ is greater than the ordered one ($quantity(o) \leq stock(reference(o))$), then the order is invoiced, using:

$$invoiced\_orders := invoiced\_orders \cup \{o\}$$

and the stock is updated:

$$stock(reference(o)) := stock(reference(o)) - quantity(o) \ .$$

```
invoice_order =
  ANY
    o
  WHERE
      o ∈ orders − invoiced_orders   ∧
      quantity(o) ≤ stock(reference(o))
  THEN
      invoiced_orders := invoiced_orders ∪ {o}||
      stock(reference(o)) := stock(reference(o)) − quantity(o)
  END
```

The next three events are modeling the state changes for the variables attached to the stock and to the orders: *the stock or the set of the orders may vary.*

Question 13: How are variables modified? Can we cancel an invoiced order?

Answer: First of all, the text expresses that the stock and the set of orders may vary; either the variable $invoiced\_orders$ is not modified, since the invoiced orders are processed orders, or we can cancel invoiced orders. We can only modify the set $orders - invoiced\_orders$.

The modifications are to add a new order in the current set of orders and to set the order into the pending set, or to cancel a pending order from the set orders, or to modify the stock variable by incrementing the quantity of a product.

Question 14: Are your changes the most general ones?

Answer: I do not not understand *the most general notion.*

Question 15: Is it the most abstract model for the three events?

Answer: The specification text tells us that variables are modified and they are less precise than what we suggest. So we propose to require that the three events modify variables while the invariant is preserved, but the variable $invoiced\_orders$ is not modified by these events.

The event cancel_orders and the event new_orders modify the variables $orders, quantity, reference$ and the next values of these variables should satisfy:

$$\left(\begin{array}{l} orders \subseteq \text{ALL\_ORDERS} \wedge \\ invoiced\_orders \subseteq orders \wedge \\ quantity \in orders \longrightarrow \mathbb{N}^* \wedge \\ reference \in orders \longrightarrow \text{PRODUCTS} \end{array}\right).$$

We do not give details on the possible modifications and we do not care at this point.

Question 16: Why are you defining those events which have no effect on the variables?

Answer: These events are hidden in the first case but they are explicitly mentioned. They will be refined in the second case because the second case provides more details on those events. Finally, they illustrate the *keep* concept [ABR 05c], which expresses a possible change with respect to the invariant and which simplifies the refinement.

$$\begin{array}{l}\mathsf{cancel\_orders} = \\ \text{BEGIN} \\ \quad \begin{pmatrix} orders, \\ quantity, \\ reference \end{pmatrix} :| \begin{pmatrix} orders \subseteq \text{ALL\_ORDERS} \wedge \\ invoiced\_orders \subseteq orders \wedge \\ quantity \in orders \longrightarrow \mathbb{N}^* \wedge \\ reference \in orders \longrightarrow \text{PRODUCTS} \end{pmatrix} \\ \text{END}\end{array}$$

$$\begin{array}{l}\mathsf{new\_orders} = \\ \text{BEGIN} \\ \quad \begin{pmatrix} orders, \\ quantity, \\ reference \end{pmatrix} :| \begin{pmatrix} orders \subseteq \text{ALL\_ORDERS} \wedge \\ invoiced\_orders \subseteq orders \wedge \\ quantity \in orders \longrightarrow \mathbb{N}^* \wedge \\ reference \in orders \longrightarrow \text{PRODUCTS} \end{pmatrix} \\ \text{END}\end{array}$$

The event delivery_to_stock change the value of $stock$ and does not change other variable. We do not know how the stock is modified and we express that a modification is possible.

$$\begin{array}{l}\mathsf{delivery\_to\_stock} = \\ \quad \text{BEGIN} \\ \quad\quad stock :| (stock \in \text{PRODUCTS} \longrightarrow \mathbb{N}) \\ \quad \text{END}\end{array}$$

Question 17: The discourse of the event method reports on checking internal consistency. Did you check the internal consistency? Is the Case 1 model internally consistent?

Answer: The checking of internal consistency is established by proving nine proof obligations, stating that the invariant is initially true and that each event is maintaining the invariant. Each proof obligation is automatically discharged by the tool Click'n'Prove.

The client may be interested by an animation and one can use an animator for testing the possible behaviors of the global model.

Question 18: How do you express that only these events can modify variables of the model?

Answer: The set of variables of the model is the frame of the model; no other variable can be modified; if a variable is not explicitly modified, it is not changed. We assume that the model is closed.

9.5 Model refinement

The refinement of a formal model allows us to enrich a model using a *step by step* approach. Refinement provides a way to construct stronger invariants and also to add details to a model. It is also used to transform an abstract model into a more concrete version by modifying the state description. This is essentially done by extending the list of state variables (possibly suppressing some of them), by refining each abstract event into a corresponding concrete version, and by adding new events. The abstract state variables, x, and the concrete ones, y, are linked together by means of a so-called *gluing invariant* $J(x, y)$. A number of proof obligations ensure that (1) each abstract event is correctly refined by its corresponding concrete version, (2) each new event refines $skip$, (3) no new event takes control forever, and (4) relative deadlock-freeness is preserved (the relative deadlock-freeness states that the concrete model is not more blocked than the abstract one!).

We suppose that an Abstract Model AM with variables x and invariant $I(x)$ is refined by a Concrete Model CM with variables y and gluing invariant $J(x, y)$. The first proof obligation states the initial concrete states implies that there is at least one initial abstract state satisfying the abstract initial condition and related to the initial concrete state by the gluing invariant:

$$\boxed{INIT(y) \Rightarrow \exists x.(Init(x) \wedge J(x, y))}$$

If $BAA(x, x')$ (standing for Before-After Abstract event) and $BAC(y, y')$ (standing for Before-After Concrete event) are respectively the abstract and concrete before-after predicates of the same event, we have to prove the following statement:

$$\boxed{I(x) \wedge J(x, y) \wedge BAC(y, y') \Rightarrow \exists x' \cdot (BAA(x, x') \wedge J(x', y'))}$$

This says that under the abstract invariant $I(x)$ and the concrete one $J(x, y)$, a concrete step $BAC(y, y')$ can be simulated ($\exists x'$) by an abstract one $BAA(x, x')$ in such a way that the gluing invariant $J(x', y')$ is preserved. A new event with before-after predicate $BA(y, y')$ must refine $skip$ ($x' = x$). This leads to the following statement to prove:

$$\boxed{I(x) \wedge J(x, y) \wedge BA(y, y') \Rightarrow J(x, y')}$$

Moreover, we must prove that a variant $V(y)$ is decreased by each new event (this is to guarantee that an abstract step may occur). We have thus to prove the following for each new event with before-after predicate $BA(y, y')$:

$$\boxed{I(x) \wedge J(x, y) \wedge BA(y, y') \Rightarrow V(y') < V(y)}$$

Finally, we must prove that the concrete model does not introduce more deadlocks than the abstract one. This is formalized by means of the following proof obligation:

$$I(x) \wedge J(x, y) \wedge \mathsf{grds}(AM) \Rightarrow \mathsf{grds}(CM)$$

where $\mathsf{grds}(AM)$ stands for the disjunction of the guards of the events of the abstract model, and $\mathsf{grds}(CM)$ stands for the disjunction of the guards of the events of the concrete one.

9.6 Modeling the second event B model Case 2 by refinement of Case 1

According to the text of the specification, the second case study model *takes into account the entries of*:

- *new orders*;
- *cancellations of orders*;
- *entries of quantities in the stock.*

Question 19: Why do you choose that title for that section?

Answer: The behavior of Case 2 is more specialized than Case 1; in Case 1 we do not express how the variables are modified. We state that variables are modified by maintaining the invariant and it clear that Case 2 is more deterministic than case 1:

- $orders$ may change by adding new orders;
- $orders$ may change by removing pending orders from the current $orders$;
- $stock$ changes by adding new quantities of products in the stock.

No new event is added.

Decision:

The three last events of Case 1 should be refined to handle the modifications of the variables $orders$, $quantity$, $reference$ and $stock$ according to the three last items:

- *new orders*: the new_orders event modifies $orders$, $quantity$, $reference$; it adds a new order called o which is not yet existing in the current set of orders called $orders$; $quantity$ and $reference$ are updated according to the ordered quantity q and reference p;
- *cancellations of orders*: the cancel_orders event modifies $orders$, $quantity$, $reference$; it removes a order called o which is pending in the current set of orders called $orders$; $quantity$ and $reference$ are updated;

- *entries of quantities in the stock*: the delivery_to_stock event adds a given quantity q of a given product p in the stock.

The text for Case 2 is very clear and it mentions specific ways to modify variables $orders$, $quantity$, $reference$ and $stock$. Events will simply translate these expressions.

```
new_orders =
  ANY
    o, q, p
  WHERE
    o ∈ ALL_ORDERS − orders
    q ∈ ℕ*
    p ∈ PRODUCTS
  THEN
    orders := orders ∪ {o}||
    quantity(o) := q||
    reference(o) := p
  END
```

Let o be an order which is not yet either pending or invoiced. It is a future order which is added to the current set of orders ($orders$) and the quantity of product is set to q; the identification of the product of the o order is set to p.

```
cancel_orders =
  ANY
    o
  WHERE
    o ∈ orders − invoiced_orders
  THEN
    orders := orders − {o}||
    quantity := {o} ⩤ quantity||
    reference := {o} ⩤ reference
  END
```

Let o be an order which is pending. The event deletes the order from the set $orders$ and the two functions $quantity$ and $reference$ are updated by removing o from the set of orders which is the domain of those functions.

Question 20: What happens if we forget the condition over invoiced orders in the guard of the event cancel_orders?

Answer: The refinement conditions generate a proof obligation like $o \in orders \Rightarrow invoiced\_orders \subseteq orders - \{o\}$ and it is clearly not provable without the guard $o \notin invoiced\_orders$.

```
delivery_to_stock =
  ANY
    p, q
  WHERE
    q ∈ ℕ*
    p ∈ PRODUCTS
  THEN
    stock(p) := stock(p) + q
  END
```

The stock can only be increased and the event increases by q units the quantity of the product p. The stock for p is increased by q.

Question 21: Is the concrete event delivery_to_stock more deterministic than the abstract one?

Answer: Yes, the concrete event only modifies the quantity of one product. The abstract event can also decrease quantities of products.

In the case study, customers mention the following statement:

But, we do not have to take these entries into account. This means that you will not receive two entry flows (orders, entries in stock). The stock and the set of orders are always given to you in a up-to-date state.

The last question leads to a new case study, called Case 3; it takes into account the flow of orders. The new model captures the notion of flow by a set; it means that the ordering of arrival is not expressed, for instance. We can require some fairness assumption over some events to obtain a deadlock and live-lock-free model. It is clear that we can not state any kind of fairness in B and the reason is that the B language does not provide this facility; Méry [MER 99] analyzes the extension of B scope with respect to liveness and fairness properties. However, the key question is to refine models while fairness constraints are stated and Cansell et al [CAN 00b] propose predicate diagrams to deal with these questions. In fact, it is possible that an order remains always pending and is never invoiced, because there are always other orders which are processed. Another problem is that the quantity may be not sufficient for a while and it is infinitely often sufficient for a given quantity of a given product.

If the referenced quantity changes in the stock (event delivery_to_stock), one can also invoice another order with the same referenced product. Modeling this fact in an abstract way requires strong fairness on event delivery_to_stock. A first idea is to use a sequence of orders and to invoice the first suitable order in the sequence. In this case we have no starvation if the event delivery_to_stock is fair enough. For the customer, it is not a good solution because the delay for delivery to the stock is too long and so one can invoice other orders. We decide to add a time to each order to sort orders ($time \in orders \rightarrowtail \mathbb{N}$) and to invoice the most recent possible order. The event new_orders gives to each new order its time using a variable t ($t \in \mathbb{N}$) which always contains the next ordered time ($\forall i \cdot (i \in \mathbf{ran}(time) \Rightarrow i \leq t)$).

The variable $time$ records the time when the order was added and the new condition strengthens the guard of the previous event invoice_order:

$$\forall d \cdot \left(\begin{array}{l} d \in orders - invoiced\_orders \ \wedge \\ quantity(d) \leq stock(reference(d)) \\ \Rightarrow \\ time(o) \leq time(d) \end{array} \right)$$

The variable $time$ is an total injection from $orders$ into $\mathbb{N}$, which is defining a total ordering over $orders$.

invoice_order =
  ANY
    o
  WHERE
    $o \in orders - invoiced\_orders \ \wedge$
    $quantity(o) \leq stock(reference(o)) \wedge$
    $\forall d \cdot \left(\begin{array}{l} d \in orders - invoiced\_orders \ \wedge \\ quantity(d) \leq stock(reference(d)) \\ \Rightarrow \\ time(o) \leq time(d) \end{array} \right)$
  THEN
    $invoiced\_orders := invoiced\_orders \cup \{o\} ||$
    $stock(reference(o)) := stock(reference(o)) - quantity(o)$
  END

new_orders =
  ANY
    o, q, p
  WHERE
    $o \in$ ALL_ORDERS $- orders$
    $q \in \mathbb{N}^*$
    $p \in$ PRODUCTS
  THEN
    $orders := orders \cup \{o\} ||$
    $quantity(o) := q ||$
    $reference(o) := p ||$
    $time(o) := t ||$
    $t := t + 1$
  END

The variable t is a new shared variable which models the evolution of the timestamps; we use the same variable to be sure that we obtain a total ordering over orders. $time$ is updated according to the current value of the variable t.

```
cancel_orders =
  ANY
    o
  WHERE
    o ∈ orders − invoiced_orders
  THEN
    orders := orders − {o}||
    quantity := {o} ⩤ quantity||
    reference := {o} ⩤ reference||
    time := {o} ⩤ time
  END
```

When one cancels an order, *time* should be updated by removing the canceled order from the domain of *time*.

9.7 The natural language description of the event B models

The new description appears in our development including B models; the initial text is quite clear. The refinement-based development (starting from a very abstract model) helps us to gradually improve the understanding of the case studies. The first reading attempts to detect informations from the informal text itself and leads to the first abstract model. The new natural language description is the old one enriched by new informations derived from the question/answer game. We add the following text to the initial one:

We have one and only one reference to a product of a certain quantity per order. This means that you can not have two different informations for the same product on the same order. If you want to order 4 products p and 5 products p, either you need to order 9 products p, or you order 4 products p and 5 products p, but you will have two different orders in the set of orders. Each invoiced order can not be canceled according to the customer of the specification. The second case is simply a refinement of the first one and it gives a more precise view of the environment actions, namely stock variations or orders creation/cancelation.

The implementation of a fairness assumption was obtained by a time-stamp over orders.

9.8 Conclusion

The case study provides us a framework for introducing the main concepts of the event B method; the statement of the development should include a table with the required proof obligations:

Model	Unproved PO	PO	Interactive PO
Case 1	0	9	0
Case 2	0	14	3
Case 3	0	18	5

Each proof obligation requires less than one interaction step using the Click'n'Prove tool. We emphasize the central role of the model refinement in the construction of formal models; it simplifies proofs by providing a progressive and detailed view of a system through different models.

Bibliography

[ABR 96] Jean-Raymond Abrial. *The B book.* Cambridge University Press, 1996.

[ABR 98] Jean-Raymond Abrial. *On B* In Bert [BER 98], pages 1–8.

[ABR 02] Jean-Raymond Abrial, Dominique Cansell, and Guy Laffitte. *"higher-order" mathematics in B* In Bert *et al.* [BER 02], pages 370–393.

[ABR 03a] Jean-Raymond Abrial. *$B^{\#}$: Toward a synthesis between Z and B* In Bert *et al.* [BER 03], pages 168–177.

[ABR 03b] Jean-Raymond Abrial. *Event based sequential program development: Application to constructing a pointer program* In Araki *et al.* [ARA 03], pages 51–74.

[ABR 03c] Jean-Raymond Abrial and Dominique Cansell. *Click'n'Prove: Interactive proofs within set theory* In Basin and Wolff [BAS 03], pages 1–24.

[ABR 03d] Jean-Raymond Abrial, Dominique Cansell, and Dominique Méry. *Formal derivation of spanning trees algorithms* In Bert *et al.* [BER 03], pages 457–476.

[ABR 03e] Jean-Raymond Abrial, Dominique Cansell, and Dominique Méry. *A mechanically proved and incremental development of IEEE 1394 tree* identify protocol. *Formal Asp. Comput.*, 14(3):215–227, 2003.

[ABR 05a] Jean-Raymond Abrial and Dominique Cansell. *Click'n'Prove* 2004,2005. http://www.loria.fr/cansell.

[ABR 05b] Jean-Raymond Abrial and Dominique Cansell. *Formal Construction of a Non-blocking Concurrent Queue Algorithm (a Case Study in Atomicity) Journal of Universal Computer Science*, 11(5):744–770, May 2005.

[ABR 05c] Jean-Raymond Abrial, Dominique Cansell, and Dominique Méry. *Refinement and reachability in Event B* In Treharne *et al.* [TRE 05], pages 222–241.

[ABR 98] Jean-Raymond Abrial and Louis Mussat. *Introducing dynamic constraints in B* In Bert [BER 98], pages 83–128.

[ARA 03] Keijiro Araki, Stefania Gnesi, and Dino Mandrioli, eds. *FME 2003: Formal Methods, International Symposium of Formal Methods Europe, Pisa, Italy, September 8-14, 2003, Proceedings*, volume 2805 of *Lecture Notes in Computer Science*. Springer, 2003.

[BAC 79] Ralph Back. *On correct refinement of programs Journal of Computer and System Sciences*, 23(1):49–68, 1979.

[BAS 03] David A. Basin and Burkhart Wolff, eds. *Theorem Proving in Higher Order Logics, 16th International Conference, TPHOLs 2003, Rom, Italy, September 8-12, 2003, Proceedings*, volume 2758 of *Lecture Notes in Computer Science*. Springer, 2003.

[BER 98] Didier Bert, editor. *B'98: Recent Advances in the Development and Use of the B Method, Second International B Conference, Montpellier, France, April 22-24, 1998, Proceedings*, volume 1393 of *Lecture Notes in Computer Science*. Springer, 1998.

[BER 02] Didier Bert, Jonathan P. Bowen, Martin C. Henson, and Ken Robinson, eds. *ZB 2002: Formal Specification and Development in Z and B, 2nd International Conference of B and Z Users, Grenoble, France, January 23-25, 2002, Proceedings*, volume 2272 of *Lecture Notes in Computer Science*. Springer, 2002.

[BER 03] Didier Bert, Jonathan P. Bowen, Steve King, and Marina A. Waldén, eds. *ZB 2003: Formal Specification and Development in Z and B, Third International Conference of B and Z Users, Turku, Finland, June 4-6, 2003, Proceedings*, volume 2651 of *Lecture Notes in Computer Science*. Springer, 2003.

[CAN 00a] Dominique Cansell and Dominique Méry. *Abstraction and refinement of features* In Ryan Stephen, Gilmore and Mark, eds, *Language Constructs for Designing Features*. Springer Verlag, 2000.

[CAN 00b] Dominique Cansell, Dominique Méry, and Stephan Merz. *Diagram Refinements for the Design of Reactive Systems Journal of Universal Computer Science*, 7(2):159–174, 2001.

[CAN 02] Dominique Cansell, Ganesh Gopalakrishnan, Michael D. Jones, Dominique Méry, and Airy Weinzoepflen. *Incremental proof of the producer/consumer property for the PCI* protocol. In Bert *et al.* [BER 02], pages 22–41.

[CHA 88] K. Mani Chandy and Jay Misra. *Parallel Program Design A Foundation* Addison-Wesley, 1988. ISBN 0-201-05866-9.

[CLE 04] ClearSy, Aix-en-Provence (F). *B4FREE* 2004. http://www.b4free.com.

[DIJ 76] Edgster W. Dijkstra. *A Discipline of Programming* Prentice-Hall, 1976.

[EHR 85] Hart Ehrig and Bernt Mahr. *Fundamentals of Algebraic Specification 1, Equations and Initial Semantics* EATCS Monographs on Theoretical Computer Science. Springer Verlag, W. Brauer and R. Rozenberg and A. Salomaa eds, 1985.

[LAM 94] Leslie Lamport. *A temporal logic of actions ACM Transactions on Programming Languages and Systems*, 16(3):872–923, May 1994.

[LAM 02] Leslie Lamport. *Specifying Systems: The TLA+ Language and Tools for Hardware and Software Engineers*. Addison-Wesley, 2002.

[MER 99] Dominique Méry. *Requirements for a temporal B: assigning temporal meaning to abstract machines ... and to abstract systems.* In A. Galloway and K. Taguchi, eds, *IFM'99 Integrated Formal Methods 1999*, York, June 1999.

[MOR 05] C. Morgan, T.S. Hoang, and Jean-Raymond Abrial. *The challenge of probabilistic event B - extended abstract* In Treharne *et al.* [TRE 05], pages 162–171.

[TRE 05] Helen Treharne, Steve King, Martin C. Henson, and Steve Schneider, eds. *ZB 2005: Formal Specification and Development in Z and B, 4th International Conference of B and Z Users, Guildford, UK, April 13-15, 2005, Proceedings*, volume 3455 of *Lecture Notes in Computer Science*. Springer, 2005.

Chapter 10

VHDL

Laurence PIERRE

10.1 Overview of VHDL

VHDL [MAZ 95, BER 93] is not a formal language, it is a Hardware Description Language, i.e. a language devoted to the description of hardware components at various levels of abstraction. It has been standardised by the IEEE under the names *VHDL'87* and *VHDL'93* [IEE 88, ANS 93]; the features added to VHDL'93 are useless here, hence we employ the VHDL'87 version. Three different description styles are commonly used: the *behavioral* style (clocked or asynchronous concurrent "processes" execute algorithmic specifications and communicate through common "signals"), the *dataflow* style (the architecture of the device is described by means of a set of equations; this style roughly corresponds to the *Register Transfer* level of abstraction), and the *structural* style (the device is described as a set of interconnected components). In this chapter, we show that the *behavioral* style is appropriate for describing systems like the case study of this book. A VHDL simulator can be used to run and debug the specification.

VHDL as well as the other standardised language Verilog [IEE 95, THO 98] are widely used by the community of hardware designers. A variety of commercial CAD tools support these languages, providing complete design environments with capabilities for schematic capture, simulation, gate-level or high-level synthesis. VHDL has a "simulation semantics", i.e. a semantics based on an event-driven simulation engine. Since the publication of the first official VHDL Language Reference Manual, many efforts have been devoted to defining the language formally (see for instance [KLU 95, DEL 95, HYM 03]). The semantics of the VHDL constructs introduced hereafter give their meaning in terms of the successive simulation cycles; a physical time and a logical time are attached to each simulation cycle.

A VHDL description is composed of an "entity" and one or several "architectures". The *entity* is a black box that only specifies the interface of the device (i.e. the input/output ports also called primary inputs and outputs). It can have "generic" parameters that parameterise the description; for instance, the size of some structures (vectors, arrays) can be specified using generic parameters. Each *architecture* gives a particular view of the structure or behavior of the system, depending on its style of description. An *architecture* contains a set of concurrent statements. The only concurrent statement that we use in the rest of this chapter is the "process" . A *process* includes a set of sequential statements that are executed at each simulation cycle in which the *process* is *active*. There are two ways of specifying when a *process* should be active: the keyword "process" is followed by a *sensitivity list*, or the *process* includes at least one "wait" statement. Only the construct of *sensitivity list* will be used hereinafter.

Prior to explaining the role of a *sensitivity list*, we have to define what a "signal" is. Signals are used to model hardware communication channels (wires, buses) or storage elements (latches, flipflops); *processes* can communicate through signals. Usual algorithmic "variables" can also be used, but have to be local to the *processes*. When a *variable* is modified (assignment operator :=), its new value is immediately available in the current simulation cycle. Conversely, the value assigned to a *signal* (assignment operator <=) during a simulation cycle is only available in a future cycle. More precisely, if the assignment statement includes no "after" clause to specify an explicit delay, then the signal value is available in the next simulation cycle, otherwise it is available in the simulation cycle that corresponds to the physical time computed by adding the delay of the *after* clause to the current simulation time. A *sensitivity list* is a list of *signals*, the *process* sensitive to these *signals* resumes each time there has been an *event* on at least one of these *signals* (the value of the *signal* has changed). Upon resumption, it executes its sequential statements and then it suspends its execution until the next reactivation event. This is the usual way *processes* asynchronously communicate in VHDL: each time a *process* updates a *signal*, the *processes* that are sensitive to that *signal* resume (in the future) because of that event, and take into account this new value. They do not have to synchronize with sending/receiving actions. The *sensitivity list* can include primary inputs, hence external events can also be taken into account.

While *variables* are declared locally to *processes*, *signals* are shared by *processes*. Their values can be read by every *process* but only one of them is allowed to modify the value of each *signal*, unless a *resolution function* is defined. A *resolution function* manages conflicts in case of multi-source signals; it is a user-defined function that is used by the simulator to determine unambiguously the value to be assigned to the *signal* (for instance, in circuit descriptions, resolution functions often represent wired ORs or ANDs). In VHDL'93, the concept of *shared variables* has been introduced, but it must be used very carefully to avoid inducing nondeterminism.

VHDL is a strongly typed language with some predefined data types (Boolean, natural, etc.). By default, the initial value of an object is the "lowest" value of range for its type. The user can define other types and sub-types, in particular enumerated types, records and arrays. Array types can be unconstrained (i.e. their size is not fixed), but instances of these types must be constrained. The user can also define functions/procedures. Type definitions and function/procedure signatures are given in a "package", while function/procedure definitions are given in the corresponding "package body".

10.2 Analysis and specification of case 1

The goal of the invoicing system is to consider a stock of products and a set of orders, and to invoice orders when it is possible (i.e. if the ordered quantity is less or equal to the quantity in stock). In case 1, we simply have to consider that the stock and the set of orders are given in a up-to-date state.

10.2.1 Identifying data structures

VHDL is a strongly typed language, and various kinds of user data types can be defined. The first questions we ask are related to the choice of the data types.

Question 1: Which data type can be used to represent the orders?

Answer: An order is characterized by a number, the reference of the ordered product, and the quantity ordered. These elements can be the fields of a record type `Orders`; these fields are represented by natural numbers. When an order is invoiced, its state has to be changed from "pending" to "invoiced". Thus, we have another field `stat` whose value is either `pending` or `invoiced`. We define an enumerated type `State_of_order` for these values.

```
type State_of_order is (pending, invoiced);
type Orders is record      -- record type for the orders
      number, ref, quant : natural;
      stat : State_of_order;
end record;
```

Question 2: Which data type can be used to represent the products?

Answer: Products can also be modeled as records. The type `Products` has two fields that represent the reference of the product and the quantity in stock.

```
type Products is record   -- record type for the products
     s_ref, s_quant : natural;
end record;
```

Question 3: Which data types can be used to represent the set of orders and the set of products?

Answer: They can be modelled using one-dimensional arrays. The types `List_of_orders` and `State_of_stock` are unconstrained (i.e. their size is not specified) one-dimensional arrays of `Orders` and `Products` respectively.

```
type List_of_orders is array(natural range <>) of Orders;
type State_of_stock is array(natural range <>) of Products;
    -- "natural range <>" means that the arrays
    -- are unconstrained
```

All these types, together with the associated functions, are declared in a *package* called `Invoice`. The function definitions are given in the corresponding *package body*, see the next section.

10.2.2 Identifying operations

As explained in the introductory section, the VHDL description of a component starts with the definition of its *entity* (i.e. external view).

Question 4: What should the external view of the invoicing system be?

Answer: The user should be able to observe on the *output* of the system a response (which orders have been invoiced) to the up-to-date state of stock and of orders. The system should also return information about the modifications it has made to the stock and to the orders. Therefore, we decide that the system *inputs* the up-to-date state, and *outputs* every order that can be invoiced, as well as the modified state. This corresponds to the external view depicted on Figure 10.1. The device inputs the current state of orders (port `ord` of the VHDL description) and the current state of the stock (port `st` of the VHDL description). It outputs the invoiced orders (port `outord` of the description), and updates the state of orders and the state of stock. The ports `ord` and `st` are consequently declared as *inout* ports in the VHDL description.
This corresponds to the following entity `invoicing1` which has two generic parameters `nbord` and `nbpr` that parameterise the description on the number of orders and on the number of products that can be considered:

```
entity invoicing1 is
      generic (nbord,nbpr:positive);
      port (ord: inout List_of_orders(0 to nbord);
            st: inout State_of_stock(0 to nbpr);
            outord: out Orders);
end invoicing1;
```

Question 5: How are the orders processed?

Answer: The orders contained in the list `ord` are iteratively scanned (using a for..loop VHDL statement) in order to try to invoice the pending orders. For each order, if the quantity ordered is less or equal to the quantity that is in stock for the

Figure 10.1: External view of case 1

ordered product, then the order is output on the port `outord`, its state (field `stat`) becomes `invoiced`, and the corresponding quantity is removed from the stock `st`.

Question 6: Which operators/functions are needed?

Answer: Simple assignment statements are necessary to express that the order is output on the port `outord` and that its state becomes `invoiced`. To implement the withdrawal of the corresponding quantity from the stock, we define a function called `remove`:

```
function remove(s:State_of_stock; r,q:natural)
return State_of_stock is    -- returns the stock s where the
            -- quantity q of the product r has been removed
variable sres:State_of_stock(s'range);
                      -- result, which has the same range as s
begin
    for i in 0 to s_actualsize(s) loop
       sres(i).s_ref:=s(i).s_ref;
       if s(i).s_ref=r then
         sres(i).s_quant:=s(i).s_quant - q;
       else
         sres(i).s_quant:=s(i).s_quant;
       end if;
    end loop;
    return sres;
end remove;
```

Other functions are needed: `o_actualsize` computes the actual size of a vector of orders (used in the for..loop which scans the orders), `s_actualsize` computes the actual size of a vector of products (used in `remove`), and `get_quantity` returns the available quantity of a product, given its reference.

Thus, here is the complete definition of the package `Invoice` and of its package body with the function definitions:

```
package Invoice is
 type State_of_order is (pending, invoiced);
 type Orders is record      -- record type for the orders
    number, ref, quant : natural;
    stat : State_of_order;
 end record;
 type Products is record   -- record type for the products
    s_ref, s_quant : natural;
 end record;
 type List_of_orders is array(natural range <>) of Orders;
 type State_of_stock is array(natural range <>) of Products;
 function o_actualsize(o:List_of_orders) return integer;
 function s_actualsize(s:State_of_stock) return integer;
 function get_quantity(s:State_of_stock; r:natural)
    return natural;
 function remove(s:State_of_stock; r,q:natural)
    return State_of_stock;
end Invoice;

package body Invoice is
  function o_actualsize (o: List_of_orders) return integer is
     -- computes the actual size of the vector of orders o
  variable i:natural;
  begin
    i:=0;
    while (i<=o'right) and (o(i).ref/=0) loop
    -- while the right bound has not been reached and there
    -- is an actual reference
        i:=i+1;
    end loop;
    return i-1;
  end o_actualsize;

  function s_actualsize (s: State_of_stock) return integer is
     -- computes the actual size of the vector of products
  variable i:natural;
  begin
    i:=0;
    while (i<=s'right) and (s(i).s_ref/=0) loop
        i:=i+1;
    end loop;
    return i-1;
  end s_actualsize;
```

```
function get_quantity(s:State_of_stock; r:natural)
   return natural is
   -- returns the available quantity of the
   -- product r in the stock s
begin
  for i in 0 to s_actualsize(s) loop
     if s(i).s_ref=r then
       return s(i).s_quant;
     end if;
  end loop;
  return 0;
end get_quantity;

function remove(s:State_of_stock; r,q:natural)
   return State_of_stock is
variable sres:State_of_stock(s'range);
begin
  for i in 0 to s_actualsize(s) loop
     sres(i).s_ref:=s(i).s_ref;
     if s(i).s_ref=r then
       sres(i).s_quant:=s(i).s_quant - q;
     else
       sres(i).s_quant:=s(i).s_quant;
     end if;
  end loop;
  return sres;
end remove;
end Invoice;
```

Question 7: How many VHDL processes are required?

Answer: Our specification corresponds to the behavior of a single process, called operative_part, which is sensitive to the signals ord and st. It resumes each time an event occurs on one of these signals. This process is the body of the architecture arch1 of the entity invoicing1:

```
architecture arch1 of invoicing1 is
begin
  operative_part:process(ord,st)  -- sensitive to ord and st
  variable s:State_of_stock(st'range);
  begin
    s:=st;
    -- tries to invoice every pending order in the set
    -- of orders:
```

```
    for i in 0 to o_actualsize(ord) loop
      -- for every pending order
      if (ord(i).stat=pending) then
        -- if the available quantity of product is
        -- sufficient
        if (ord(i).quant <= get_quantity(s,ord(i).ref))
          then
            -- the invoiced order is output,
            outord <= ord(i);
            -- its state changes (ord is updated),
            ord(i).stat <= invoiced;
            -- and ord(i).quant articles are removed
            -- from the stock:
            s:=remove(s,ord(i).ref,ord(i).quant);
        end if;
      end if;
    end loop;
    st <= s;  -- st is updated
  end process;
end arch1;
```

Note: our aim is to emphasize the *dynamic* aspects of VHDL (behaviors, communications). It could have been possible to consider the fact that the same reference can be requested on several different orders, but we have not explicitly taken this into account, as it is simply related to *static* aspects (data). By default, our implementation arbitrarily selects the *oldest* order, since our type `List_of_orders` behaves as a FIFO.

10.3 Analysis and specification of case 2

Now we have to take into account the entries of new orders/cancellations of orders and the entries of quantities in the stock.

Question 8: What should the external view of the system be?

Answer: Now, we should observe on the output `outord` a response to these entries: new orders (port `neword`), order cancellations (port `cancel`), and new quantities in the stock (port `newst`).
This corresponds to the entity `invoicing` given below; the sizes of the vector of orders and of the vector of products are generic parameters. The port `cancel` receives the numbers of the orders to be canceled:

```
entity invoicing is
     generic (nbord,nbpr:positive);
     port (neword: in Orders; newst: in Products;
```

```
            cancel: in natural;
            outord: out Orders);
end invoicing;
```

Question 9: How are the new entries processed?

Answer: We can identify three cases:

- if a new order is received, then it must be added to the current set of orders;
- if an existing order is cancelled, then we simply change its state from `pending` to `invoiced`;
- if a new quantity of a given product is to be added to the stock, then the state of the stock is updated accordingly.

Question 10: Do we need additional operators/functions?

Answer: The first two cases of the answer to Question 9 only require the assignment statement. For the third case, we define an ad hoc function called `update`:

```
function update(s:State_of_stock; r,q:natural)
return State_of_stock is  -- returns s with the additional
                          -- quantity q of the product r
variable sres:State_of_stock(s'range);
variable found:boolean:=false;
  begin
    for i in 0 to s_actualsize(s) loop
       sres(i).s_ref:=s(i).s_ref;
       if s(i).s_ref=r then  -- quantity added
         sres(i).s_quant:=s(i).s_quant + q;
         found:=true;
       else
         sres(i).s_quant:=s(i).s_quant;
       end if;
    end loop;
    if (not found) then  -- product added
      sres(s_actualsize(s)+1):=Products'(r,q);
    end if;
    return sres;
end update;
```

Now we can give the updated definition of the package `Invoice` and of its package body:

```
package Invoice is
 type State_of_order is (pending, invoiced);
 type Orders is record      -- record type for the orders
```

```
      number, ref, quant : natural;
      stat : State_of_order;
   end record;
   type Products is record   -- record type for the products
      s_ref, s_quant : natural;
   end record;
   type List_of_orders is array(natural range <>) of Orders;
   type State_of_stock is array(natural range <>) of Products;
   function o_actualsize(o:List_of_orders) return integer;
   function s_actualsize(s:State_of_stock) return integer;
   function get_quantity(s:State_of_stock; r:natural)
      return natural;
   function remove(s:State_of_stock; r,q:natural)
      return State_of_stock;
   function update(s:State_of_stock; r,q:natural)
      return State_of_stock;
  end Invoice;

  package body Invoice is
    function o_actualsize (o: List_of_orders) return integer is
       -- computes the actual size of the vector of orders o
    variable i:natural;
    begin
      i:=0;
      while (i<=o'right) and (o(i).ref/=0) loop
         i:=i+1;
      end loop;
      return i-1;
    end o_actualsize;

    function s_actualsize (s: State_of_stock) return integer is
       -- computes the actual size of the vector of products
    variable i:natural;
    begin
      i:=0;
      while (i<=s'right) and (s(i).s_ref/=0) loop
         i:=i+1;
      end loop;
      return i-1;
    end s_actualsize;

    function get_quantity(s:State_of_stock; r:natural)
       return natural is
       -- returns the available quantity of the
```

```
      -- product r in the stock s
   begin
     for i in 0 to s_actualsize(s) loop
        if s(i).s_ref=r then
          return s(i).s_quant;
        end if;
     end loop;
     return 0;
   end get_quantity;

   function remove(s:State_of_stock; r,q:natural)
      return State_of_stock is
   variable sres:State_of_stock(s'range);
   begin
     for i in 0 to s_actualsize(s) loop
        sres(i).s_ref:=s(i).s_ref;
        if s(i).s_ref=r then
          sres(i).s_quant:=s(i).s_quant - q;
        else
          sres(i).s_quant:=s(i).s_quant;
        end if;
     end loop;
     return sres;
   end remove;

 function update(s:State_of_stock; r,q:natural)
 return State_of_stock is  -- returns s with the additional
                           -- quantity q of the product r
 variable sres:State_of_stock(s'range);
 variable found:boolean:=false;
   begin
     for i in 0 to s_actualsize(s) loop
        sres(i).s_ref:=s(i).s_ref;
        if s(i).s_ref=r then  -- quantity added
          sres(i).s_quant:=s(i).s_quant + q;
          found:=true;
        else
          sres(i).s_quant:=s(i).s_quant;
        end if;
     end loop;
     if (not found) then  -- product added
       sres(s_actualsize(s)+1):=Products'(r,q);
     end if;
```

```
        return sres;
    end update;
    end Invoice;
```

Question 11: How many processes will be involved?

Answer: The behavior of the whole system can be decomposed as illustrated by Figure 10.2:

- a process, referred to as the "operative part", takes into account the stock and the set of orders, and is in charge of invoicing the orders if possible (this corresponds to the process described in section 10.2);
- another process, subsequently referred to as the "control part", receives the entries of new orders or cancellations of orders, and the entries of quantities in the stock, and its role consists in updating the set of orders or the state of stock as specified in the answer to Question 9.

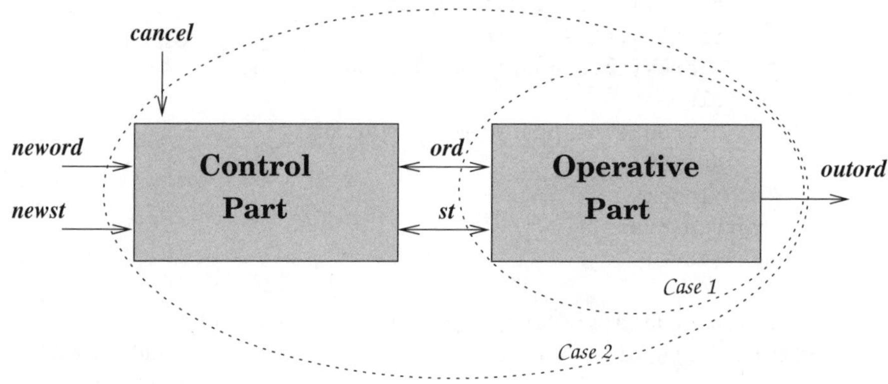

Figure 10.2: Representation of case 2

The concurrent composition of these two processes fulfils the requirements of case 2. Note that each process should access and modify the state of orders `ord` and the state of the stock `st`; this is shown as double arrows in the figure.

Question 12: How do the different processes access to the common data `ord` and `st`?

Answer: A typical solution would consist of declaring `ord` and `st` as signals shared by the VHDL processes that implement the operative and control parts.

However, we just mentioned that both processes have to modify these data. Hence the corresponding signals would be multi-source signals and such a solution would require the definition of resolution functions, as explained in our introductory section. We have decided to reject this solution because it entails the definition of resolution functions on composite (record) types; such a function can have a complicated definition, and moreover is not supported by every

VHDL compiler. To guarantee determinism, we also avoid a solution based on shared variables, implementable in VHDL'93.
A simple and safe solution consists in using four signals, the actual signals `ord` and `st`, and two copies `ord_tmp` and `st_tmp`. The control part is definitely responsible for modifying `ord` and `st`, the operative part modifies `ord_tmp` and `st_tmp`. The operative part is sensitive to the events on `ord` and `st`, whereas the control part is sensitive to the events on `ord_tmp` and `st_tmp`.

As expressed by the answers to the previous questions, our architecture `myarch1` of the entity `invoicing` should include two processes, one for the operative part (called `operative_part` below) and one for the control part. For the sake of clarity, we split the control part into two processes that play distinct roles: `control_part_ord` manages new orders/cancellations, and `control_part_st` manages new items into the stock:

```
architecture myarch1 of invoicing is
signal ord, ord_tmp: List_of_orders(0 to nbord);
signal st, st_tmp: State_of_stock(0 to nbpr);
begin
```

The process `operative_part` is only sensitive to the two internal signals `ord` and `st`. Each time an event occurs on one of these signals, the process resumes and behaves as the process `operative_part` of the description of section 10.2. However, in order to let the processes `control_part_st` and `control_part_ord` have the entire responsibility of managing the stock and the list of orders, the process `operative_part` only updates the auxiliary signals:

```
operative_part:process(ord,st)  -- sensitive to ord and st
variable s:State_of_stock(st'range);
variable o:List_of_orders(ord'range);
begin
  s := st;
  o := ord;
  -- tries to invoice every pending order in the
  -- set of orders
  for i in 0 to o_actualsize(ord) loop
    if (ord(i).stat=pending) then
       if (ord(i).quant <= get_quantity(s,ord(i).ref))
         then
           -- the invoiced order is output
           outord <= ord(i);
           -- its state changes
           o(i).stat := invoiced;
           -- and ord(i).quant articles are removed
```

```
                    -- from the stock:
                    s := remove(s, ord(i).ref, ord(i).quant);
                end if;
             end if;
        end loop;
        st_tmp <= s;
        ord_tmp <= o;
    end process;
```

The process control_part_st is sensitive to the port newst and to the local signal st_tmp (an event on st_tmp indicates that the computations of the operative part give rise to modifications in the stock). The modifications (if any) induced by the operative part are stored in a local variable s. Then, if there has been an event on the port newst, a new stock is computed thanks to the function update:

```
control_part_st:process(newst, st_tmp)
                                --sensitive to newst and st_tmp
variable s:State_of_stock(st'range);
begin
  if (st_tmp'event) then  -- if st_tmp has been modified
    s := st_tmp;
  else
    s := st;
  end if;
  -- if a new quantity in stock is entered
  if (newst'event) then
    -- a new stock is computed, with the
    -- additional quantity
    s := update(s, newst.s_ref, newst.s_quant);
  end if;
  st <= s;  -- the actual stock is updated
end process;
```

Finally, the process control_part_ord is sensitive to the input ports neword and cancel, and to the local signal ord_tmp (an event on ord_tmp indicates that the computations of the operative part give rise to modifications in the list of orders). If a new order is input on neword, then it is added at the end of the vector ord, and if an order is canceled, then its state becomes invoiced (but this order is not output on outord):

```
control_part_ord:process(neword, cancel, ord_tmp)
variable o:List_of_orders(ord'range);
begin
  if ord_tmp'event then o := ord_tmp;
```

```
        else o := ord;
        end if;
        if (neword'event) then    -- a new order is received
          o(o_actualsize(o)+1) := neword;
        end if;
        if (cancel'event) then  -- order cancellation received
          for i in 0 to o_actualsize(ord) loop
            if (o(i).number=cancel) then
              -- instead of removing the order, we give it
              -- the status "invoiced"
              o(i).stat := invoiced;
            end if;
          end loop;
        end if;
        ord <= o;
      end process;
    end myarch1;
```

Note: the process `operative_part` iterates on the whole set of pending orders and this iteration is *atomic* from the point of view of the simulation engine. Inside a process, the statements are sequentially executed within the same simulation cycle (the simulation time is unchanged).

10.4 The natural language description of the specification

10.4.1 Case 1

An order is characterized by a number, the reference of the ordered product, and the ordered quantity. All of these data are natural numbers. When an order is invoiced, its state changes from `pending` to `invoiced`. A product is represented by its reference and its quantity in stock. The set of orders and the stock (set of products) are encoded as one-dimensional arrays.

The system has two inputs: the current state of orders (port `ord`) and the current state of the stock (port `st`). It outputs the invoiced orders (port `outord`), and updates the state of orders and the state of stock (inputs are in fact inouts). Each time there has been an external event (the state of orders or the state of stock has changed), the orders are iteratively scanned to invoice the pending ones: for each order, if the quantity ordered is less than or equal to the quantity that is in stock for the ordered product, then the order is output by the device, its state becomes `invoiced`, and the corresponding quantity is removed from the stock.

10.4.2 Case 2

The behavior described for Case 1 becomes the behavior of the *operative part* of the system. Modifications to the state of orders or stock no longer correspond to external events but to events coming from the *control part*.

This *control part* reacts to external events (new orders, cancellations, or new products are input respectively on the ports `neword`, `cancel` or `newst`) and to the events coming from the *operative part* (orders have changed from `pending` to `invoiced`, or quantities have been removed from the stock). Each time there is a new order, it is added to the set of orders (i.e. it is put into the corresponding vector). When an order is cancelled, its state is changed to `invoiced`. When a new product or a new quantity is entered, the stock is modified accordingly.

10.5 Conclusion

This example involves elaborate data types and associated operators, features communications between the system and its environment and communications between sub-systems. We have shown that we can deal with all these aspects in VHDL; in particular, this case study highlights the VHDL constructs that make it possible to model processes that communicate asynchronously. While the structural style of this language is well-suited to the description of hardware devices using libraries of components, the behavioral style can be used to develop much more abstract specifications.

One of the advantages of this approach is that there are VHDL simulators that can provide accurate information about the temporal behavior of the description and that can be useful for debugging the specification: the designer can observe the behavior of the system for some well-chosen input stimuli, generated at different time points.

For example, Figure 10.3 gives an excerpt from a simulation waveform for case 2 (made with the free version of VHDL Simili [VHD]). A waveform is associated with each signal; it contains the successive values of this signal. For instance, at this point of the simulation (22 min), the signal `st`, which is an array of five elements, contains three products: 2 items of product number 378, 15 items of product 252 and 5 items of product 836; this value will change at time 25 min. An order for 30 items of product number 252 arrives at time 23 min (see the value of the signal `neword`). This order cannot be invoiced because there is not enough quantity in stock, it is put after the other orders in the array `ord` (which is not visible here). At time 25 mn, 25 new items are delivered (see the value of the signal `newst`), the order can then be invoiced and it is output on the port `outord` (see the value of this signal). Only 10 items remain in stock (see the new value of the signal `st`). Let us note that it is very easy to specify delays in a VHDL description; it would have been possible to take into account in the VHDL specification a duration for processing an order (for instance, a delay of 3 mins for invoicing an order).

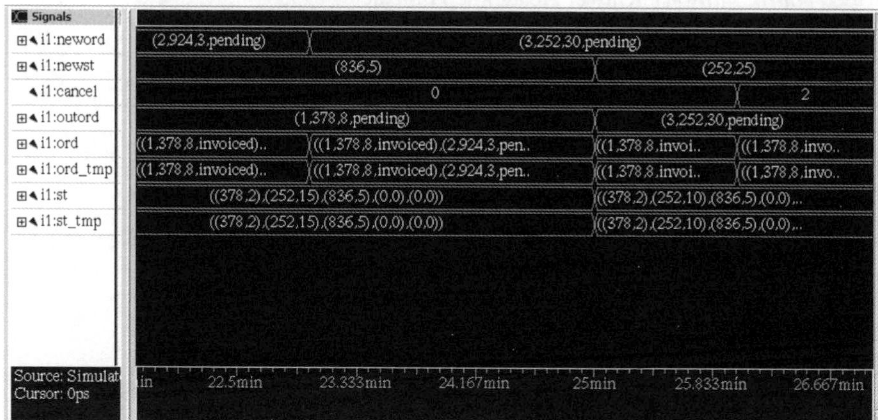

Figure 10.3: Excerpt from a simulation waveform

Series of well-chosen stimuli can be used to corroborate every typical situation of the expected behavior. A high-level synthesis tool can also be used to synthesize a behavioral VHDL specification into a more concrete realisation, provided that a *synthesizable subset* of VHDL is used (the high-level description proposed here is not restricted to this VHDL subset).

Bibliography

[KLU 95] Kluwer Academic Publishers *Formal Methods in System Design*. 7(1/2), 1995

[BER 93] Bergé J.M., Fonkoua A., Maginot S., Rouillard J. *VHDL'92: The New Features of the VHDL Hardware Description Language*. Kluwer Academic Publishers, 1993

[DEL 95] Delgado Kloos C., Breuer P. (Eds.) *Formal Semantics for VHDL*. Kluwer Academic Publishers, 1995

[HYM 03] Hymans C. "Design and Implementation of an Abstract Interpreter for VHDL". In Geist D., Tronci E. (Eds.) *International Conference on Correct Hardware and Verification Methods*. LNCS 2860, Springer-Verlag, 2003

[IEE 88] IEEE *Standard VHDL Language Reference Manual*. IEEE, 1988

[ANS 93] ANSI/IEEE *Standard VHDL Language Reference Manual, IEEE Standard 1076-1993*. IEEE Computer Society, 1993

[IEE 95] IEEE *1364-1995 IEEE Standard Description Language Based on the Verilog(TM) Hardware Description Language*. IEEE, 1995

[MAZ 95] Mazor S., Langstraat P. *A Guide to VHDL*. Kluwer Academic Publishers, 1995

[THO 98] Thomas D.E., Moorby P.R. *The Verilog Hardware Description Language (Fourth Edition)*. Kluwer Academic Publishers, 1998

[VHD] VHDL Simili. `http://www.symphonyeda.com`

Chapter 11

Estelle

Eric LALLET and Jean-Luc RAFFY

11.1 Overview of the FDT Estelle

Estelle [BUD 85, BUD 87] is a Formal Description Technique standardised by ISO [ISO 97]. Its main application field is the formal specification of distributed systems such as communication protocols [BRE 97]. Estelle permits a clear split between the definition of the global architecture of the system and the internal behavior of its components.

An Estelle specification describes a collection of hierarchical communicating components that can be nested in a parent/child relationship. A component is an instance of a generic module definition composed of a single header definition and one or more associated body definitions. These instances may be statically or dynamically created by means of a header/body pair.

The header definition describes the external communication part of the module and specifies a synchronous parallel or a non-deterministic serial execution. The communication interface of a module is defined by ports called interaction points (IPs). Each IP refers to a channel which defines two sets of interactions (messages sent and received). Nested modules can also communicate by sharing exported variables. The attribute declared in the header part may be either *systemprocess* (or process) and it leads to a synchronous parallel execution or *systemactivity* (or activity) and it leads to a non-deterministic serial execution.

The body definition describes the behavior of the component. It uses the extended finite state machine (EFSM) paradigm. It is composed of three parts: a declaration part, an initialisation part and a transition part where the EFSM is described. Within the EFSM, each transition part is made of two different parts, a clause group and a transition block. The clauses within a clause group define the transition firing conditions where the transition block defines the action part of the transition.

The syntax uses standard Pascal [ISO 83].

11.2 Analysis and specification of case 1

As stated above, we have to specify the architecture and then describe the behavior of the different components.

We must first clarify some points because of the incompleteness of the user requirements.

Question 1: Could an order contain several products?

Answer: We assume that, as it is only stated that "on an order, we have one and only one reference to an ordered product", an order could contain several products.

Moreover, as the user requirements states that a same reference can be ordered on several different orders and that an order will be changed to "invoiced" if the ordered quantity is either less than or equal to the quantity which is in stock, two more points arise:

- firstly, the orders have to be invoiced one by one;
- secondly, as no specific sequence among the orders is given, we must use a non-deterministic structure.

11.2.1 Defining the architecture of the specification

11.2.1.1 Identifying the independent systems

The first question one should ask is:

Question 2: How many independent systems must be specified?

Answer: The only system required is *invoiceCase1*. This system will contain sub-systems called modules.

11.2.1.2 Identifying the global behavior and the sub-systems

As stated above, we will use a non-deterministic behavior. In Estelle, it is expressed by the attribute "systemactivity".

Question 3: What are the sub-systems within the system?

Answer: As, in the first case study, the stock and the set of orders are given in a up-to-date state, we can use a static structure. Different choices could be made. In order to show some features of Estelle, we chose to have as many Order modules as actual orders. As in Estelle, we only declare generic modules and we need only one Order module. Thus, the sub-systems are the Stock module and the Order module. All the orders will be instances of the generic Order module.

11.2.1.3 Identifying the information sent and the communication links

Estelle allows some decisions to be left to the implementation phase. As we do not know how many orders are given, or how many products (and in which quantity) are in stock, we will use the keyword *any* to state that it may be any value taken in a range of values:

```
TYPE
    (we declare a new type with a range of values).
    Max = 0..100000;
```

Comments can be added in Estelle code under 2 forms:

```
    {this is a comment}
    (*this is a comment, as well*)
```

```
CONST
    { All the constants may take one of the values in range of Max. }
    MaxOrder = any Max;
    MaxRef = any Max;
    MaxInList = any Max;
    MaxInStock = any Max;
    MaxOrdered = any Max;

TYPE
    { We do not know at the specification phase, either the actual number of
    orders or the number of products referenced. }
    NbOrder = 0..MaxOrder;
    Reference = 1..MaxRef;
    { We assume that a product is known by its reference number and its quan-
    tity. }
    Product = RECORD
        ref : Reference;
        nb : 1.. MaxOrdered
    END;
    { We assume that an order is made of an array of Product. }
    ProductList = ARRAY [0..MaxInList] OF Product;
```

We have now to decide which messages are exchanged by the modules.

Question 4: What kind of information does an order send to the stock?

Answer: Let assume that the Order module sends only the list of products (with their quantities).

Question 5: What is the answer of the stock?

Answer: We assume that the Stock module answers a Boolean to indicate if the order can be executed (and thus invoiced) or not.

A channel of communication is first declared with two opposite roles. Second, the messages to be sent are given for each role:

```
CHANNEL OrderStockChan (order,stock);
    { Parameters can be sent within messages. }
    BY order: destock (list:ProductList);
    BY stock: result (ack:boolean);
```

We can now declare the headers of the modules. They represent the external interface of the modules. We specify the interactions points (IPs) and the role they have, related to the channel declaration.

The Stock module has an array of IPs because of the number of orders it has to deal with. As the dimension of the array is not known, it is set to NbOrder. The parameter *stockList* is initialised with the initial stock. An exported variable, *Done*, is provided to communicate with the specification level. When all the orders have been taken into account the variable *Done* will be set to true. It will stop the execution:

```
MODULE Stock ACTIVITY (stockList:ProductList);
    IP
        ToOrder:ARRAY[NbOrder] OF OrderStockChan (stock);
    EXPORT
        Done: BOOLEAN;
END; { MODULE HEADER Stock }
```

As said previously, we have to declare only one Order module. It has a single interaction point because it exchanges messages only with the Stock module. It uses an exported variable to indicate if the order is invoiced or not. The parameter *order* is initialised with the list of product to be ordered.

```
MODULE Order ACTIVITY (order:ProductList);
    IP
        ToStock: OrderStockChan (order);
    EXPORT
        Invoiced: BOOLEAN;
END; { MODULE HEADER Order }
```

11.2.2 Defining the behavior

11.2.2.1 Defining the initialisation of the architecture

We first have to declare the module variables with the keyword *modvar*. The initialisation part is a normal transition beginning by the keyword *initialize*. It is the first transition to be fired. In this transition, we have to initialise the modules, i.e. associate a body to the module variable (which has a type "module header"). Then connections have to be made. Recall that in Estelle, dynamic creation and deletion of modules is permitted. We will see the use of this feature in the second case:

```
MODVAR
    { We declare the module variables before instantiation. }
    ProductsInStock : Stock;
    OrderForm: ARRAY [NbOrder] OF Order;
VAR
    itemsList : ProductList;

STATE
    wait, stop; {The EFSM is composed of 2 states}

INITIALIZE TO wait
NAME initPart:
BEGIN       {Initialisation of a Stock module}
    itemsList := fillStock;
    INIT ProductsInStock WITH StockBody(itemsList);
    { StockBody is the part of the specification where the behavior of the mod-
    ule Stock is specified. }
    ProductInStock.Done := FALSE;
    ALL nbOfOrderForms : NbOrder DO
        {Initialisation of Order modules }
        BEGIN
        itemsList := fillOrder(nbOfOrderForms);
        INIT OrderForm[nbOfOrderForms]
            WITH OrderBody (itemsList);
        OrderForm[nbOfOrderForms].Invoiced := FALSE;
        { We create the links between Order modules and the Stock module. }
        CONNECT OrderForm[nbOfOrderForms].ToStock
        TO ProductsInStock.ToOrdel[nbOfOrderFormS];
        END;
END;
```

We use a function *fillOrder()* to fill in the order form. As nothing is said about it, we leave it for the implementation. In Estelle, such function is declared as follows:

```
FUNCTION fillOrder(nbOrd: NbOrder):ProductList; PRIMITIVE;
```

We use the same for the function *fillStock()*:

```
FUNCTION fillStock:ProductList;        PRIMITIVE;
```

When all the orders are taken into account, the result of the invoicing operation will be printed out.

```
TRANS
    FROM wait
    TO stop
    PROVIDED ProductsInStock.Done
    BEGIN
    END;

    FROM stop
    TO stop
    BEGIN
        ALL oo:NbOrder DO
            printResults (oo, OrderForm [oo].Invoiced);
    END;
```

11.2.2.2 Defining the behavior of the modules

The Stock module receives a message from an order module with a list of products as parameter. It answers a Boolean depending of the state of the stock.

As stated above, no ordering is given to the orders. Thus we use a non-deterministic feature of Estelle given by the keyword *any*.

Question 6: What to do if an order can only be partly served?

Answer: As no information is given in the informal specification to explain what to do, we will use a function removeFromStock() whose description is postponed to the implementation.

The Stock module must take into account all the orders and then tell the specification module that it has ended. The behavior can be described by means of an EFSM with 2 states, exec and close. The transition part is made of 2 transitions. The first one makes it possible to take all the orders into account, the second one makes it possible to tell the specification module that the job is done. As these 2 transitions start from the same state, *exec*, we have to specify which one will be first fired. In Estelle, we will use the clause *Priority*; that clause is used with a positive integer. The smaller the integer, the higher the priority:

```
BODY StockBody FOR Stock;
{behavior of the Stock Module }
STATE
    exec, close; {The EFSM is composed of 2 states}

TRANS
    FROM exec
    TO exec
    PRIORITY 0 {The highest priority}
```

```
{The any clause permits to specify a non-deterministic behavior.}
ANY oo:NbOrder DO
WHEN ToOrder[oo].destock(list)
VAR
    ack:BOOLEAN;
NAME checkAndUpdate:

BEGIN
    { removeFromStock() description is postponed to the implementation.
    }
    ack := removeFromStock(list,stockList);
    OUTPUT ToOrder[oo].result(ack)
END;

FROM exec
TO close
NAME closing;
BEGIN
    Done := TRUE;
END;
END;{ MODULE BODY StockBody }
```

Each Order sends a message to the Stock module to destock. Then depending on the answer given by the Stock module, the order will be set to invoiced or not by means of the exported variable *Invoiced*:

```
BODY OrderBody FOR Order;
STATE pendingState, invoicedState; {The EFSM is composed of 2 states}
{The Order module asks the Stock module if it can provide the required
  products}
INITIALIZE TO pendingState
    NAME destock:
    BEGIN
        OUTPUT ToStock.destock(order);
    END;

TRANS

    FROM pendingState
    TO invoicedState
    WHEN ToStock.result(ack)
    NAME ackInvoice:
    BEGIN
        IF ack THEN
```

```
            Invoiced := TRUE;
      END;

   END; { MODULE BODY OrderBody}
```

11.3 Analysis and specification of case 2

Question 7: What are the new required operations?

Answer: In case 2, Orders can be added or deleted and products can be added to the Stock.

Thus, we have to add some new functions and procedures. As nothing is said about how and when all these operations could occur, we leave the description of these functions and procedures to the implementation:

```
FUNCTION initial_nb_of_order: NbOrder; PRIMITIVE;
{permits to begin the job with a set of orders}

FUNCTION NewItemsForStock: BOOLEAN; PRIMITIVE;
FUNCTION NewItemList: ProductList ; PRIMITIVE;
PROCEDURE AddToStock(list:Productlist,VAR stock:ProductList);
    PRIMITIVE;
{permit the addition of products to the stock}

FUNCTION OrderToDelete: BOOLEAN; PRIMITIVE;
FUNCTION OrderToDeleteId:NbOrder; PRIMITIVE;
FUNCTION NewOrderId:NbOrder; PRIMITIVE;
FUNCTION NewOrderToCreate: BOOLEAN; PRIMITIVE;
{permit to add or delete orders}
```

11.3.1 Defining the new architecture

As we don't know how many orders would be added or canceled, we will have to use a dynamic architecture. It means that order modules will be connected one after the other to the Stock module.

Question 8: What happens to the order module which cannot be invoiced?

Answer: We assume that the order could be presented later because of the possible refilling of the stock by the system.

Question 9: How many times could it be presented?

Answer: We assume that the process could last a certain period of time. The exact amount of time is left to the implementation. Thus, the exported variable *Done*, declared in the header of the Stock module (in the first case), becomes useless.

We use a clause called **DELAY** in a transition of the system. That clause postpones the firing of the transition until the delay given by a positive integer. This integer represents a number of time units defined by the **TIMESCALE** statement.

```
TIMESCALE Second;

TRANS
    TO stop
    DELAY (MaxTimeToFinish)
    PRIORITY 0
    NAME stop_with_some_orders_not_invoiced:
    BEGIN
    END;
```

11.3.1.1 Identifying the information sent and the communication links

The Stock module has to deal with the system to update its stock. Thus, we have to add another interaction point to the Stock module and an internal interaction point to the system. We have to declare a channel of communication between the System and the Stock modules. We assume that the Stock module accepts any refilling of its stock. Thus, a single message has to be declared:

```
CHANNEL SystemStockChan (system,stock);
    BY system:
        addstock (list:ProductList);

MODULE Stock ACTIVITY (stockList:ProductList);
    IP
        ToOrder : OrderStockChan (stock);
        ToSystem: SystemStockChan (stock);
END; { MODULE HEADER Stock }

IP {Internal interaction point of the system }
    ToStock: SystemStockChan(system)
```

11.3.2 Defining the behavior

11.3.2.1 Defining the initialisation of the architecture

We assume that the process begins with some orders. First, we initialise the Stock module and connect it to the System module. Then we initialise the order modules. The System automaton is composed of three states: no_order_connected, stop and one_order_connected:

```
INITIALIZE TO no_order_connected
```

```
VAR
    OrderId: NbOrder;
    itemsList: ProductList;

NAME initPart:
BEGIN
    itemsList := fillStock;
    INIT ProductsInStock WITH StockBody(itemsList);
    CONNECT ProductsInStock.ToSystem TO ToStock;
    FOR OrderId := 1 TO initial_nb_of_order DO
        BEGIN
        itemsList := fillOrder(OrderId);
        INIT OrderForm WITH OrderBody (itemsList);
        OrderForm.OrderId := OrderId;
        END;
END;
```

The system must connect one Order module to the Stock module. It has to look for Order modules whose exported variable to_do is set to to_wait. It is done in Estelle by the statement *Exist* ... *Suchthat*. If at least one such an Order module exists, the system has to select one and only one to connect it to the Stock module. It is done in Estelle by the statement *Forone* ... *Suchthat*:

```
TRANS

FROM no_order_connected
TO one_order_connected
PROVIDED EXIST oo: Order SUCHTHAT (oo.to_do = do_wait)
PRIORITY 1
NAME system_connects_order:
BEGIN
    FORONE oo: Order SUCHTHAT
        (oo.to_do = do_wait)
    DO
        BEGIN
        CONNECT oo.ToStock TO ProductsInStock.ToOrder;
        oo.to_do := do_order;
        OrderConnected := oo.OrderId;
        END;
END;
```

As soon as the Order module has got its answer, the system disconnects it:

```
FROM one_order_connected
```

```
TO no_order_connected
PROVIDED EXIST oo: Order SUCHTHAT
((oo.OrderId = OrderConnected) AND (oo.to_do <> do_order))
NAME system_deconnects_order:
BEGIN
    DISCONNECT ProductsInStock.ToOrder;
END;
```

The system stops either when all the orders are invoiced or when the timeout is expired.

As the following transition has no Priority clause, it will be fired only if the transition with the priority set to 1 is not fireable:

```
FROM no_order_connected
TO     stop
NAME all_orders_are_Invoiced:
BEGIN
END;

TRANS
TO stop
DELAY (MaxTimeToFinish)
PRIORITY 0
NAME stop_whith_some_order_not_invoiced:
BEGIN
END;
```

In Estelle, dynamic creation and deletion of modules are permitted. The deletion is done by the statement *Terminate*. The creation is done exactly as in the static case:

```
TRANS
FROM no_order_connected
TO no_order_connected
PROVIDED OrderToDelete
PRIORITY 0
VAR
    OrderId: NbOrder;
NAME System_deletes_order:

BEGIN
    OrderId := OrderToDeleteId;
    FORONE oo: Order SUCHTHAT
        ((oo.OrderId = OrderId) AND (oo.to_do = do_wait))
    DO
        TERMINATE oo;
```

```
END;
```

The two following transitions have neither **from** clause nor **to** clause. The meaning of this structure is that these transitions may be fired from any state to the same one:

```
TRANS
PROVIDED NewOrderToCreate
VAR
    OrderId: NbOrder;
    itemsList : ProductList;
NAME System_Creates_new_order:
BEGIN
    OrderId := NewOrderId;
    ItemsList := fillOrder(OrderId);
    INIT OrderForm WITH OrderBody (itemsList);
    OrderForm.OrderId := OrderId;
END;
```

The following transition permits the addition of some products to the stock:

```
PROVIDED NewItemsForStock
VAR
    itemsList : ProductList;
NAME System_adds_items_to_stock:
BEGIN
    itemsList := NewItemList;
    OUTPUT ToStock.AddStock(itemsList,stockList);
END;
```

11.3.2.2 Defining the behavior of the Stock module

Question 10: What new operation must be done by the Stock module?

Answer: The only new operation is the update of the stock done by the system. Thus, we have to add a new transition:

```
WHEN ToSystem.addstock(list)
NAME add_to_stock:
BEGIN
    AddToStock(list,stockList);
END;
```

11.3.2.3 Defining the behavior of the Order module

Order modules can have different status:

- waiting for connection;

- waiting for the answer from the stock module after being connected;
- waiting for the end of the transaction.

We use an exported variable, *to_do*, to state the status. To describe the behavior we need 3 states:

- *initState*, when the module is not connected and not invoiced;
- *pendingState*, when the module is connected and waiting for the answer from the stock;
- *invoicedState*, when the order is invoiced.

```
{Body of Module Order}
BODY OrderBody FOR Order;
STATE InitState, PendingState, InvoicedState;
INITIALIZE TO InitState
NAME init_of_order:
BEGIN
    to_do := do_wait;
END;

TRANS

FROM InitState
TO PendingState
PROVIDED (to_do = do_order)
NAME send_order:
BEGIN
    OUTPUT ToStock.destock(order_list);
END;

FROM PendingState
TO InitState
WHEN ToStock.result(ack)
PROVIDED NOT ack
NAME order_fail:
BEGIN
    to_do := do_wait;
END;

FROM PendingState
TO InvoicedState
WHEN ToStock.result(ack)
PROVIDED ack
NAME order_success:
```

```
BEGIN
    to_do := do_end;
END;
END; { MODULE BODY OrderBody }
```

11.4 Validating the specification

Once the decisions left to the implementation are made, a simulation can be performed to validate the specification. Some tools, such as EDT (Estelle Development Toolset) [BUD 92], permit a random and/or a user-driven simulation. Moreover, with EDT, what you simulate is what you implement; it is not necessary to rewrite the validated specification. It means that it is the same code you use to test and to implement the specification. It is also possible to implement your specification as a distributed system with no change [CAT 97]. Unfortunately you cannot use formal proof tools or model checking for validation (see drawbacks below).

11.5 The natural language description of the specifications

11.5.1 Case 1

The system is composed of two modules. An Order module which is instantiated as many times as the number of orders to serve and a Stock module which has only one instance. A product list is given to each Order module instance as a parameter. An initial stock is given to the Stock module. Each Order module sends its order list to the Stock module. Depending of the state of the stock, the Stock module sends back an acknowledgement. When an order is invoiced its variable called *invoiced* is set to true. The system stops when the Stock module has sent all the acknowledgements.

11.5.2 Case 2

As new orders as well as refilling of stock can happen during execution, the specification level has to control it. As such, its behavior changes. One and only one Order module is now connected at a time to the Stock module. Either it can be invoiced or not: if not, it could be reconnected later. The number of successive connections is not set. The system stops when a timer is out. At any time the system can add some products to the stock.

The behavior of the Stock module remains the same except for the adding of new products. An intermediate state has been added to the behavior of order modules. It makes it possible to come back to the initial state in case of non-invoicing.

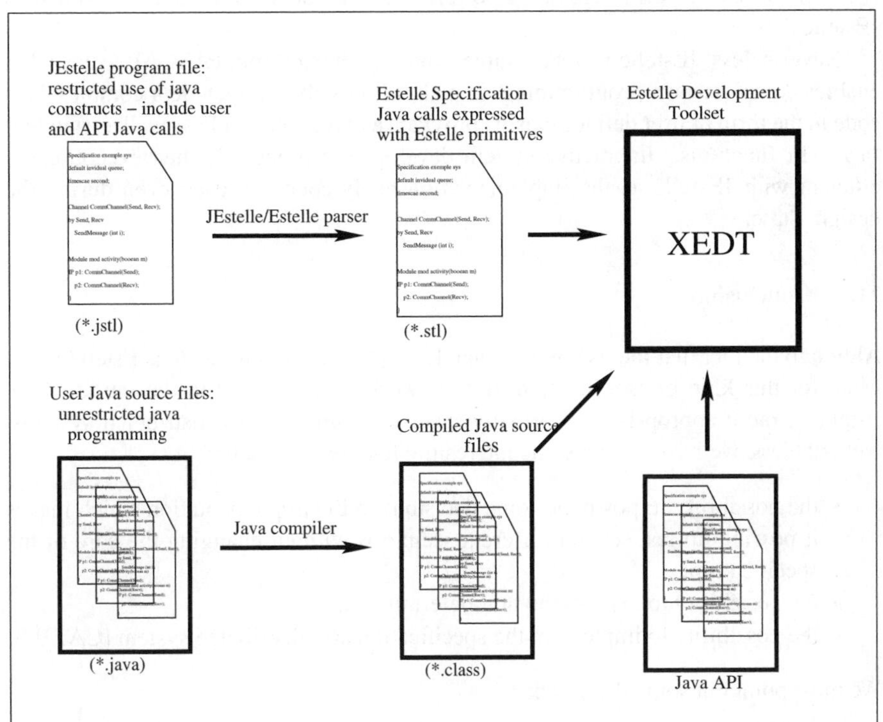

Figure 11.1: JEstelle development process

11.6 JEstelle (Estelle with Java)

JEstelle [CZE 03] has been created to make a fusion of the Estelle formalism and the ease-of-use of Java intead of PASCAL. As the formal feature of Estelle should be kept, there must be one Estelle equivalent for every JEstelle specification. In order to achieve this, the Java syntax used has been restricted. Thus, we do not lose any consistency. The side effect of Java syntax restrictions is that it is still possible to use the existing Estelle dedicated tools to check the JEstelle specification correctness. All static checking performed using powerful Estelle tools can be done as well with JEstelle.

Nevertheless, JEstelle is not a simple syntax exchange from PASCAL to Java, but enables complete Java programming. It makes it possible to include a complex Java code in the form of user defined classes provided as Java *.class file as well as standard Java API functions. Interactive system development process is then exceptionally efficient with JEstelle as the implementation-ready code can used even during the design phase.

11.7 Conclusion

Although the fact that the use of a formal description technique such as Estelle is not usual for this kind of specification, it does work. But, as said in the introduction, Estelle is more appropriate to formally specify communicating distributed systems. Nevertheless, we have shown some interesting features of Estelle:

- the possibility to postpone some decisions to the implementation which makes it possible to test several different scenarios without changing the core of the specification;
- the possibility to express the non-determinism;
- the possibility to implement the specification as a distributed system [CAT 97].

We must point out some drawbacks:

- the use of Estelle does not prevent incorrect descriptions of the user requirements, even if it permits to clarify some points;
- it does not provide any formal method to validate operations on data.

Finally, we think that it could be worthwhile to combine formal methods, such as the B method, and Estelle, to be able to cover all the aspects of the formal specification problem.

Bibliography

[BRE 97] Bredereke J. Communication Systems Design with Estelle. Thesis D 386, Kaiserslautern University, Shaker Verlag, Aachen, 1997

[BUD 85] Budkowski S. "Generation of a global system description from the description of cooperating subsystems". In: Yemini Y., Strom R., Yemini S. (Eds.) IFIP WG 6.1 Fourth International Workshop on Protocol Specification, Testing, and Verification, June 11-14, 1984, North-Holland, 1985

[BUD 87] Budkowski S., Dembinski P. "An Introduction to Estelle: A Specification Language for Distributed Systems". Computer Networks and ISDN Systems 14:3–23, 1987

[BUD 92] Budkowski S. "Estelle Development Toolset". Computer Networks and ISDN Systems 25:63-82, 1992

[CAT 97] Catrina O., Lallet E., Budkowski S. "Automatic implementation using Estelle Development Toolset (EDT)". In: research report, Institut National des Télécomunications, RR 97 10 01, October 1997

[ISO 97] ISO/IEC Information technology – Open Systems Interconnection – Estelle: A formal description technique based on an extended state transition model. ISO/IEC 9074:1997, International Organization for Standardisation, Geneva, Switzerland, 1997

[ISO 83] ISO/IEC Programming language – Pascal. ISO/IEC 7185, International Organization for Standardisation, Geneva, Switzerland, 1983

[CZE 03] Czenko M., Raffy J-L JEstelle, novel approach to the distributed Java systems specification and development, Proceedings of the 2nd international conference on Principles and practice of programming in Java, Kilkenny City, Ireland, 2003, p 213-218, ISBN:0-9544145-1-9

Chapter 12

SDL

Pascal POIZAT

12.1 Overview of SDL

SDL (Specification and Description Language) is a specification language with a formal semantics that has been developed and standardised [CCI 92] by ITU-T[1]. It is based on an extended finite state machine (EFSM) model for the description of system behavior together with abstract data types (ADT) features. Developments such as non-determinism and object-oriented features have led to the definition of SDL-92 [ELL 97]. SDL comes with two equivalent notations: GR (Graphical Representation) and PR (Phrase Representation). Here we use the GR representation since it is more readily understood. Please refer to SDL related literature [CCI 92, ELL 97] for GR and PR equivalence.

SDL is mainly used for the specification of telecommunication protocols and services, but may be used more widely on any reactive system. SDL is supported by several tools, like the Telelogic Tau SDL Suite. A more comprehensive list of tools can be found in the SDL Forum Society website (`http://sdl-forum.org/`).

SDL is a "mixed specification language" in the sense that it has both a dynamic part – for communication aspects – and a static part – coping with data types.

An SDL specification describes a *system* as several communicating extended finite state machines. These machines exchange messages called *signals* that may carry typed data values (and hence provide a simple way for data exchange between them). The machines support the *process* concept. A process is a common description of the behavior that is shared by its *instances*. Each process instance has a single different process identifier (PId). These PIds are particularly useful for addressing messages

[1]International Telecommunication Union, has replaced in 1993 the former International Telephone and Telegraph Consultative Committee (CCITT).

between processes instances. The processes own data values (hence the term "extended" for the machines). Exchange of data between processes is possible by way of signals or variable sharing.

The system may also communicate with the external environment which is assumed to behave like any SDL process instance (for example, it is assumed to own a PId which is different from all the system components PIds).

SDL offers basic types (types are called *sorts* in SDL) for use in process behaviors. These include the usual ones like integers or Booleans but also time (to model timers), duration and PId (to work on process instances). User-defined sorts can be defined by means of *abstract data types*: constants (called *literals*), typed signatures for the operations (called *operators*) available on the sort and equations (called *properties*) for their semantics. SDL-92 defines object-oriented concepts. We will not present them here since we do not use them.

12.2 Analysis and specification of case 1

There are various ways to make a specification from scratch (informal requirements) in SDL as in other formal description techniques that have both a dynamic and a static (data type) part [POI 99, TUR 93]. We will first work on the system structure, then we will make the process graphs and finally define the sorts used in the previous steps.

12.2.1 System structure

The first task is to find out all the system functionalities (signals triggered by the system environment). The system is about invoicing orders and the unique available functionality is `invoice`. A user (in the environment) is assumed to send the corresponding signal to the system.

This operation raises several questions. We will give them together with the solution we adopted.

Question 1: What are the `invoice` operation parameters? Does the user just ask the system to invoice all the orders it can or does the user ask the system to invoice a particular order?

Answer: (1) The user asks to invoice a particular order. The `invoice` signal carries some information on the order that is to be invoiced (its identifier to stay at an abstract level). (2) The user asks to invoice all invoiceable orders (but in which order?). (3) The system runs independently to invoice one (or several) orders; in this case, the `invoice` operation is not triggered by the environment. We choose the first solution.

We then have to give the `invoice` operation dynamic semantics in more detail.

Question 2: What shall the system do if the order does not exist?

Answer: Return a specific signal (named `error`) to the user.

Question 3: What shall the system do if the order cannot be invoiced?

Answer: Return an error signal. Another solution would have been to save the `invoice` signal for later use.

Question 4: May the user invoice the same order several times?

Answer: Surely not. This should output the `error` signal.

We also have to give more details on the operation conditions.

Question 5: Under which conditions is invoicing an order possible?

Answer: At this (abstract) level, we assume an `invoiceable` Boolean operation in some SDL sort to check if an order may be invoiced. Questions on this operation's semantics will be deferred to the work on sorts in section 12.2.3.

Question 6: Do there exist wrong orders (i.e. orders with products not referenced in stock)?

Answer: This could have been the case, and an error message could have been sent, somewhere! Since we do not have an operation to create orders in this case, this would make no sense. This question and related ones will be delayed to case 2.

Now that we have the system functionalities, we split the system into subparts to have a good architecture to work on. This split may be done several times until we have a good level of detail with sequential processes running in parallel.

SDL offers the means to structure a specification. The system is made up of several connected *blocks*. There are *block substructures* and *block diagrams*. They differ only in the fact that block diagrams are at the end of the decomposition process. Whereas block substructures may contain other block substructures or block diagrams, a block diagram may only contain processes.

The connections are modeled by *channels*. Channels may not connect more than two blocks. They may carry the signals defined in their *signal list*. Channels are uni- or bi-directional. A signal list is associated to each direction. Channels between processes are called *signal routes*.

Connection points link block channels with their enclosing superstructure. Like the blocks, the channels may be decomposed into subcomponents (blocks and channels). This may be used for example when modeling unreliable media.

As with processes, blocks (including the system) and channels give a common definition shared by their instances. SDL has a simple name scope rule: any definition is available in the current and sub-blocks. Note that in blocks one may use definitions or references to remote specifications. References are useful as placeholders. They also provide a more readable structuring of systems and blocks by separating abstraction levels.

We model the case study with two subcomponents: a process that manages the stock and a process that manages the set of orders. We will have a single block for the system. This block will contain references to a STOCK process and a SET_ORDERS process. Note that this is a matter of choice. We might also have used a single component.

In order to model the other types (orders and products), we have to make a choice between active (process) and passive (sort) objects. We here make the choice to use passive objects. Orders could have been modeled using active objects with different PIds as identifiers.

This decomposition leads us to ask questions about the subcomponent signal exchanges (between each other and the environment):

- What are the channels and signal routes between the system and the environment?
  The `invoice` signal comes from the external environment (user) and is received by the SET_ORDERS process. If the order is not correct, an `error` signal is sent back.
- What are the channels and signal routes between inner blocks?
  The SET_ORDERS process when receiving a correct `invoice` signal asks the STOCK using an `ask` signal if the order may be invoiced. The STOCK may then reply using either an `ok` or a `not_ok` signal.
- What are the new signal parameters?
  The whole order information is to be used by the STOCK. Full orders will then be used as parameters for the `ask` signal. `ok` and `not_ok` (return signals) have no parameters.

All these questions and the corresponding answers lead to the system architecture given in Figures 12.1 and 12.2. SDL notations are given in Figure 12.2.

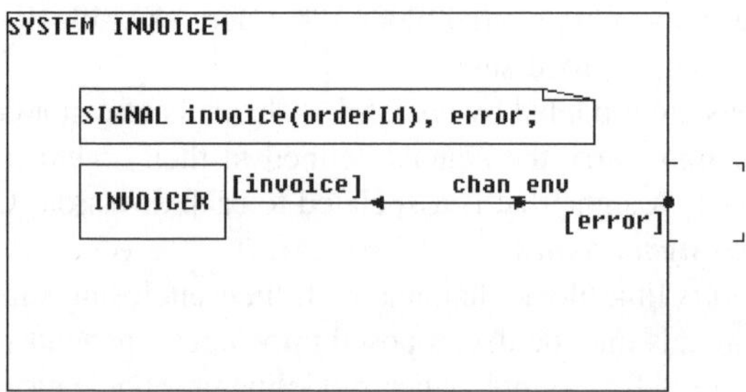

Figure 12.1: The system architecture for case 1

SDL allows one to give an initial and a maximum number of instances in process references. In the case study, there is a unique STOCK instance and a unique SET_ORDERS instance.

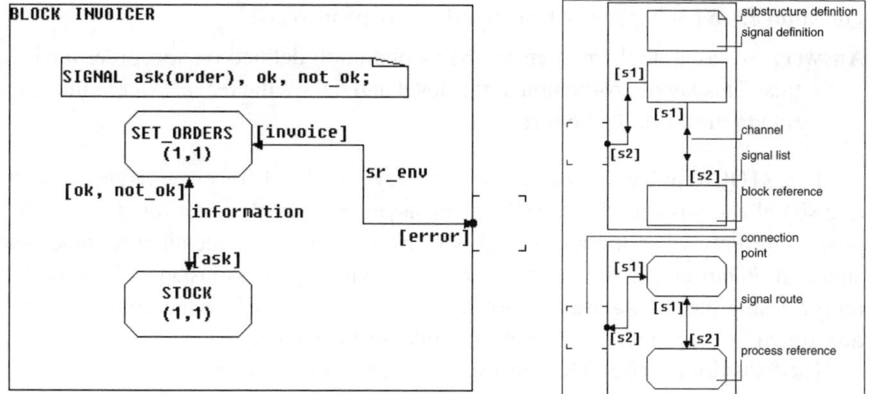

Figure 12.2: The INVOICER block for case 1/system structuring notation

12.2.2 Process graphs

In this part, we specify the behavior of the processes.

Process behaviors are given by means of process graphs. A process instance may be in several *states* where it may receive or send different sets of signals. Process instances are created (at system initialisation or dynamically by another process instance in the same block) in a special state called the *initial state* (the states without names on the process graphs). The semantics for the behavior of the system is given in terms of its instance process behaviors.

Process instance communication is *asynchronous*. Senders do not block on signal sending. Receivers own an (unlimited) buffer where valid signals (i.e. signals that the process may treat in some state) are held until consumption or discard. If a signal can be treated in the current state of a process instance, the process instance initiates a *transition*, consumes the signal, does some optional *activity* and then goes into the target state. If the message cannot be treated in the current state, the instance discards it (there is also a way to save the message for later). The buffers, also called *input ports*, behave in a first-in/first-out way (except for saved signals).

Signals are a way to exchange values. A process instance p may send signals (i) implicitly to the unique process instance connected to it via the system structure, (ii) to all processes instances linked to a certain signal route (via signal routes and channels), or (iii) to a specific process instance using process identifiers (remember there is a unique identifier for each process). Destination keywords include: *self* (the process instance itself), *sender* (the process instance that sent the last message), *offspring* (the last process instance created by p) or *parent* (the process instance that created p).

STOCK. The STOCK process receives requests from the SET_ORDERS process to ask if some order is `invoiceable`. As we have already said, we assume that the sort associated with the stock has an operation to reply to this question.

Question 7: What happens when an order may be invoiced?

Answer: We assume there is an `invoice` operation defined on sort orderStock for this. This keeps abstraction at this level and delays the real answer to this question to the work on the sorts.

The STOCK process behavior is then very simple. It receives requests via the `ask` signal and answers them. SDL, being asynchronous, does not force the STOCK process to reply when the `ask` signal is received. There may be already some other signal in its buffer. So the question arises: to which process instance does STOCK reply? Using the `to sender` keywords of SDL, the STOCK, when treating a given `ask` signal, is able to reply to the exact sender of the signal.

The behavior of the STOCK process is given in Figure 12.3.

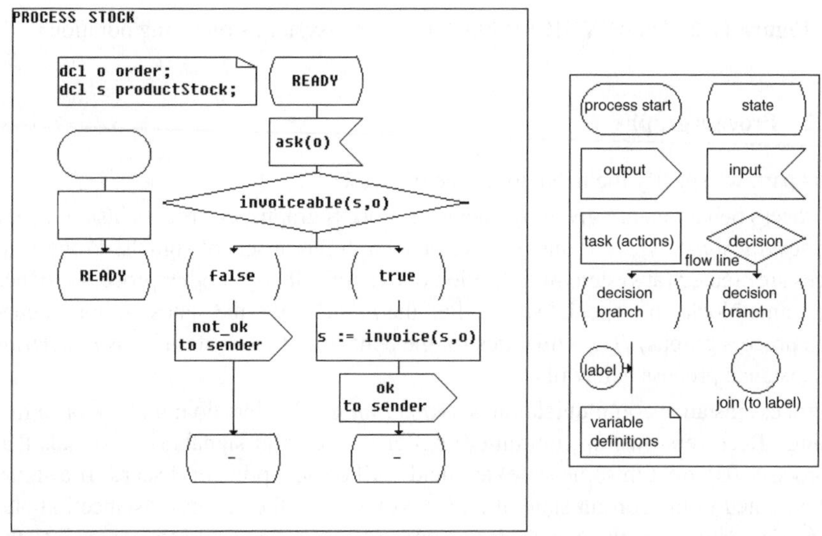

Figure 12.3: The STOCK process behavior for case 1/process notation

SET_ORDERS. The SET_ORDERS process receives invoice requests from the environment. If the order does not exist or has already been invoiced, an `error` signal is output. Otherwise, the STOCK is asked for the order invoiceability. If the order is not invoiceable an error signal is `output`, otherwise the order is invoiced. Errors are returned (as signals) to the sender of the `invoice` signal. The PId of this sender has to be kept in a variable (`lastsender`).

Question 8: Apart from passing the order from state pending to invoiced, what becomes of the order?

Answer: (1) The order may be suppressed or (2) it may be kept in the set of orders. We choose the second solution.

We saw that the SET_ORDERS process sends ask signals to the STOCK in order to check the invoiceability of orders. Thereafter, the SET_ORDERS process may either work on other invoicing requests after sending this signal or wait until reception of an ok or not_ok signal. Since the first approach could lead to orders affecting the stock several times before being invoiced, we will choose the first one.

The behavior of SET_ORDERS is given in Figure 12.4.

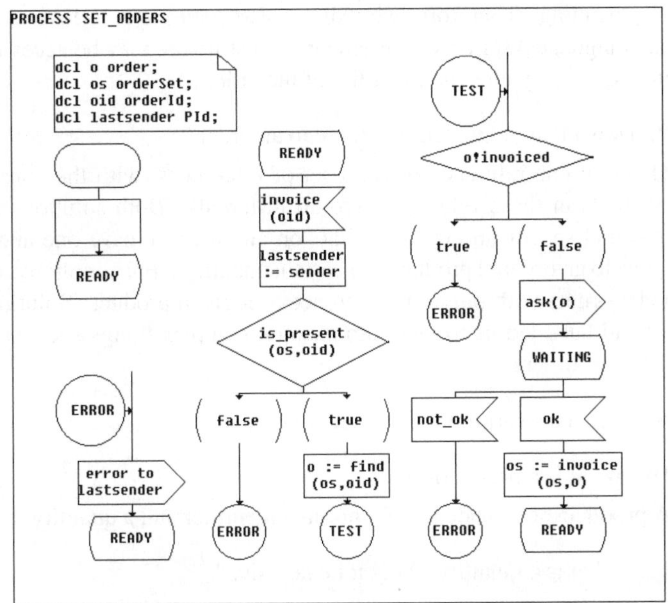

Figure 12.4: The SET_ORDERS process behavior for case 1

12.2.3 Sort definitions

In earlier phases we focused on system decomposition or signal exchange conditions. Here we give the corresponding operator properties. For each sort we use a constructive approach. Basic operators are defined and then semantics for all other operators used in process graphs are given in terms of these basic operators.

The sorts used in earlier phases (process graphs) are: `orderId`, `order`, `orderSet`, and `productStock`. Other sorts are SDL predefined sorts (PId). Each non-SDL predefined sort has to be defined.

Sorts orderId (and productId[2]). These two sorts are used as identifiers. This may be achieved using the `Natural` sort.

[2]The `productId` sort will be used later on.

We use the SDL *syntype* concept that enables one to define (rename) a sort with a restricted (or here equal) set of values with respect to the type it is based on:

```
syntype orderId = Natural
endsyntype;
```

```
syntype productId = Natural
endsyntype;
```

Sort order. Orders have an identifier. We assume identifiers are unique. Orders also contain references to certain quantities of products. Orders may be invoiced or (alternatively) pending. Therefore, we will use a *structure* type (close to records in programming languages) for orders. Elements in a structure may be accessed using a "!" notation (e.g. `o!id` yields the identifier of the order `o`).

Question 9: How many references are there to an order?

Answer: (1) Only one reference or (2) a set of references (with the constraint that the products in these references are all different). Both solutions cope with the informal specification stating that "on an order we have one and only one reference to an ordered product of a certain quantity". For simplicity, we choose to model orders with only one reference to a given product. Solution number two would have led us to take into account complex things such as "partially invoiceable" orders.

Sort productRef. This sort models product references.

Question 10: What is a productRef?

Answer: A productRef is made up of a product identifier and a quantity.

Question 11: What is a quantity? May it be negative?

Answer: A quantity may not be negative.

In SDL, we may model such numbers using naturals:

```
newtype order struct
  id orderId;
  ref productRef;
  invoiced Boolean;
endnewtype;
```

```
newtype productRef struct
  id productId;
  qty Natural;
endnewtype;
```

Sorts orderSet and productStock. These two sorts are sets. SDL enables one to define sets by means of the *powerset* generator. The usual operations on sets (`incl` to add an element, `del` to remove an element, `in` to test if an element is in a set, and `empty` for the empty set) are available (amongst others):

```
newtype basicOrderSet
  powerset(order)
endnewtype;
```

```
newtype basicProductStock
  powerset(productRef)
endnewtype;
```

These basic sorts must be extended to define operators used in the process graphs that are not defined in basic sets. This can be done using the SDL *inheritance* concept.

All that is defined in the parent sort is inherited, and more can be defined using the `adding` keyword. Partial inheritance (or renaming) can be specified on literals and/or operators.

The operators needed for sort orderSet are the following. An operator `invoice: orderSet, order → orderSet` (it takes an `orderSet`, an `order`, and it returns an `orderSet`) marks the order in the order set as invoiced. An operator `is_present: orderSet, orderId → Boolean` will be used to check if an order of a certain orderId is in the set. An operator `find: orderSet, orderId → order` is also needed to find the order corresponding to a certain identifier:

```
 newtype orderSet
inherits basicOrderSet
   literals all;
   operators all;
adding
   operators
      invoice : orderSet, order -> orderSet;
      find : orderSet, orderId -> order;
      is_present : orderSet, orderId -> Boolean;
axioms
 for all os in orderSet (
 for all o1,o2 in order (
 for all oid in orderId (
  invoice(empty, o2) == empty;
  (o1!id = o2!id)==> invoice(incl(o1,os),o2) ==
      incl(invoice(o1),os);
  (o1!id /= o2!id)==> invoice(incl(o1,os),o2) ==
      incl(o1,invoice(os,o2));

  is_present(empty, oid) == false;
  (o1!id = oid)==> is_present(incl(o1,os),oid) == true;
  (o1!id /= oid)==> is_present(incl(o1,os),oid) ==
      is_present(os,oid);

  (o1!id = oid)==> find(incl(o1,os),oid) == o1;
  (o1!id /= oid)==> find(incl(o1,os),oid) == find(os,oid);
 ););
endnewtype;
```

The operators needed for sort productStock are the following. Operators `invoice: productStock, order → productStock` and `invoiceable: productStock, order → Boolean` are needed.

Question 12: When is an order invoiceable?

Answer: When the product it references is present in the stock and in a sufficient quantity.

Question 13: What is the effect of invoicing an order on the stock?

Answer: There are several solutions: (1) no effect, (2) the stock may be reduced by a corresponding amount, or (3) the corresponding amount of the required product may be marked as being reserved (for example until some customer pays for it). We choose the second solution:

```
newtype productStock
inherits basicProductStock
   literals all;
   operators all;
adding
   operators
      invoice : productStock, order -> productStock;
      invoiceable : productStock, order -> Boolean;
axioms
 for all s in productStock (
 for all o in order (
 for all p in productRef (
  invoice(empty,o) == empty;
  (o!ref!id = p!id)==> invoice(incl(p,s),o) ==
     incl(subtractQty(p,o!ref!qty),s);
  (o!ref!id /= p!id)==> invoice(incl(p,s),o) ==
     incl(p,invoice(s,o));

  invoiceable(empty,o) == false;
  (o!ref!id = p!id)==> invoiceable(incl(p,s),o) ==
     (o!ref!qty <= p!qty);
  (o!ref!id /= p!id)==> invoiceable(incl(p,s),o) ==
     invoiceable(s,o);
 ););););
endnewtype;
```

Modifications in productRef. An operator `subtractQty: productRef, Natural` $\rightarrow$ `productRef` is needed due to prior sort definitions. Its definition makes use of `*!` operators. These operators are to be used in structure type definitions. The operator *Make!(...)* builds a structure from its fields, an operator like *IDExtract!(record)* is used to extract the value of some field *ID* in the record, and an operator like *IDModify!(record,value)* is used to replace the value of some field *ID* in the record:

```
newtype productRef
struct
 ...
adding operators
   subtractQty : productRef, Natural -> productRef
axioms
 for all pr in productRef (
 for all qtySub in Natural (
  (qtyExtract!(pr) >= qtySub)==> subtractQty(pr,qtySub) ==
```

```
      qtyModify!(pr,qtyExtract!(pr) - qtySub);
   ););
   endnewtype;
```

Modifications in order. An operator `invoice: order` → `order` is needed due to prior sort definitions:

```
    newtype order struct
    ...
   adding operators
      invoice : order -> order
   axioms
    for all o in order (
     invoice(o) == invoicedModify!(o,true);
    );
   endnewtype;
```

12.2.4 Comments on the first case study

The first case-study specifies that the stock and set of orders are always up to date. On the other hand, it is said that no other operation than invoicing should be defined. This causes a problem since SDL is dynamic and does not specify static properties (invariants) of the system. In order to have a fully working system, we should have modeled operations for initialisation and adding of orders/products in stock.

12.3 Analysis and specification of case 2

Case 2 is an extension of case 1. This is reflected in the SDL specification.

12.3.1 System structure

There is still the `invoice` functionality. New ones are `addProduct` to add a certain quantity of a given product in stock, `createOrder` to create new orders and `cancelOrder` to cancel an order.

Question 14: What are their parameters?

Answer: `addProduct` takes a product identifier and a certain quantity as parameter. This pair is of sort productRef as seen earlier. `createOrder` takes an order as parameter. `cancelOrder` takes an order identifier (of sort orderId) as parameter.

Question 15: Are there any conditions on `addProduct`?

Answer: We choose to impose non-negative quantities. Another choice would have been to treat negative quantities and to either return an error when there is not a sufficient product quantity in stock, or to keep the request for later (saving the signal).

Question 16: What shall be done when `addProduct` is used to add a quantity of a product that does not exist in stock (yet)?

Answer: The product is created in stock with an initial amount equal to the quantity given in `addProduct`.

Question 17: Are there any conditions on `createOrder`?

Answer: This is not said in the informal specification. We assume the product reference should exist in stock, and if this is not the case return an error. Another choice would have been to save the `createOrder` signal.

Question 18: What shall be done if the order identifier already exists?

Answer: Return an error signal.

Question 19: What is/should be the initial status of orders?

Answer: Orders may be created in (1) any status or (2) in a pending state. We choose the second solution. If the order given as parameter for `createOrder` is invoiced, return an error signal.

Question 20: Are there any conditions on `cancelOrder`?

Answer: The order with the given identifier has to exist. If this is not the case, an error signal is returned.

Question 21: Can invoiced orders be canceled?

Answer: No. Return an error signal if a `cancelOrder` is received for an invoiced order.

As far as the system structure is concerned, the architecture of case 1 is still relevant for case 2. Again (see case 1) the structuring leads us to reply to the questions:

- What are the channel and signal routes?
  The channel and signal routes for case 1 are kept. New signals corresponding to the new operations are added where needed. A new channel and a new signal route are created between the environment and the STOCK concerning the `addProduct` operation. A new signal is created for SET_ORDERS to ask the STOCK if the product referenced in a newly created order is valid or not. This signal will be called `askValid`. The STOCK will use `valid` and `not_valid` signals to answer.
- What are the new signal parameters?
  Information needed for testing the validity of a product consists of a product identifier. Return signals have no parameters.

The architecture of case 2 is given in Figures 12.5 and 12.6.

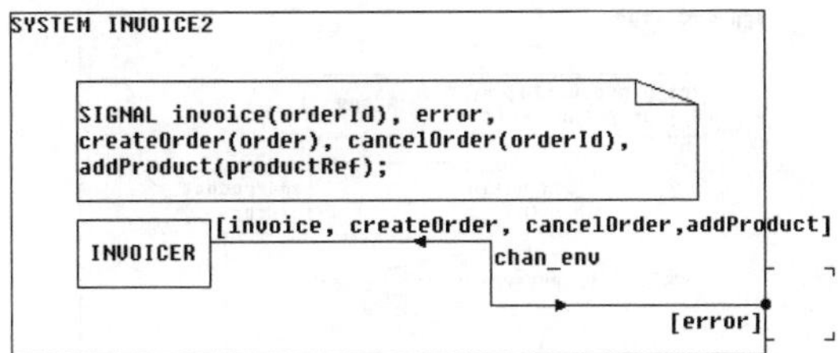

Figure 12.5: The system architecture for case 2

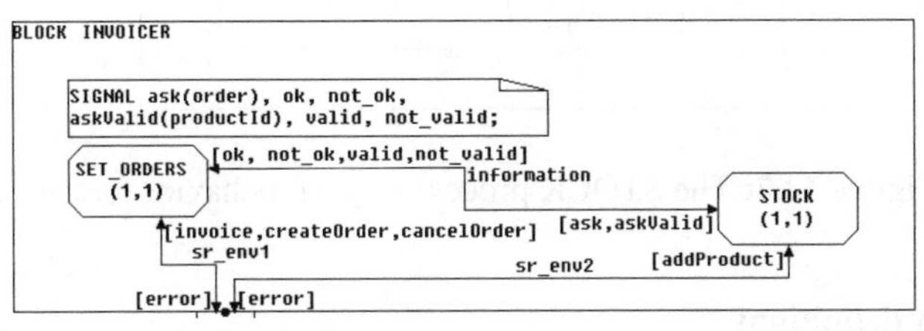

Figure 12.6: The INVOICER block for case 2

12.3.2 Process graphs

STOCK. We have to take into account the new communication scheme corresponding to the SET_ORDERS process asking the STOCK process if a given product identifier is valid or not. This will be modeled using a transition, a decision to test the validity, and corresponding output signals. As far as the `addProduct` signal is concerned, we just call an `addProduct` operation that has to be defined on the sort `productRefStock`: as usual, the exact semantics of operations are to be defined later, in the sorts part of the specification, the dynamic conditions being in the process graph.

Figure 12.7 gives only what should be added to the definition given in Figure 12.3.

SET_ORDERS.

Question 22: What happens when canceling an order?

Answer: There are two solutions: (1) mark it as being canceled, or (2) remove it from the set of orders. The first solution would require modifications to the existing process graph (when invoicing, we should verify that the order is not canceled). So we choose the second solution.

As with STOCK, Figure 12.8 gives only what should be added to the definition given in Figure 12.4.

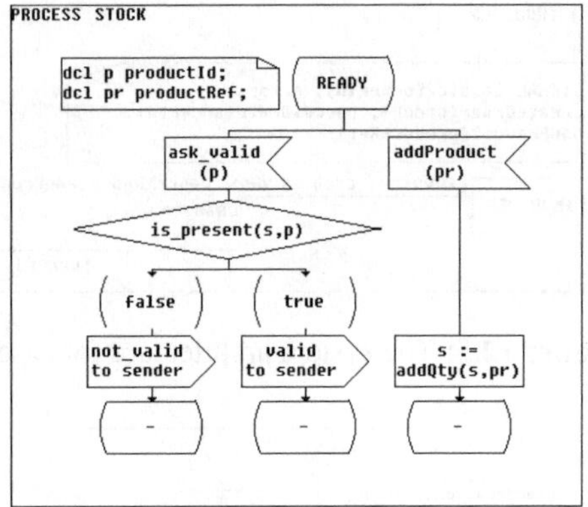

Figure 12.7: The STOCK process (added) behavior for case 2

12.3.3 Sort definitions

The new process graphs introduce new operators. We herein give the parts that are to be added to the sorts defined in section 12.2.3. Another solution would have been to use the SDL inheritance concept to define the new sorts, and to modify the process graphs to take this into account.

Sorts orderSet and productStock. As far as sort `productStock` is concerned, new operators `is_present : productStock, productId` $\rightarrow$ `Boolean` and `addQty : productStock, productRef` $\rightarrow$ `productStock` are needed. Operator `is_present` is like the operator with the same name defined in orderSet (we may have defined a new set type constructor by specializing `Powerset`):

```
 newtype productStock
inherits basicProductStock
   literals all;
   operators all;
adding
   operators
      ...
      is_present : productStock, productId -> Boolean;
      addQty : productStock, productRef -> productStock;
axioms
 for all s in productStock (
 for all p1,p2 in productRef (
 for all id in productId (
  ...
  is_present(empty, id) == false;
  (p1!id = id)==> is_present(incl(p1,s),id) == true;
  (p1!id /= id)==> is_present(incl(p1,s),id) == is_present(s,id);
```

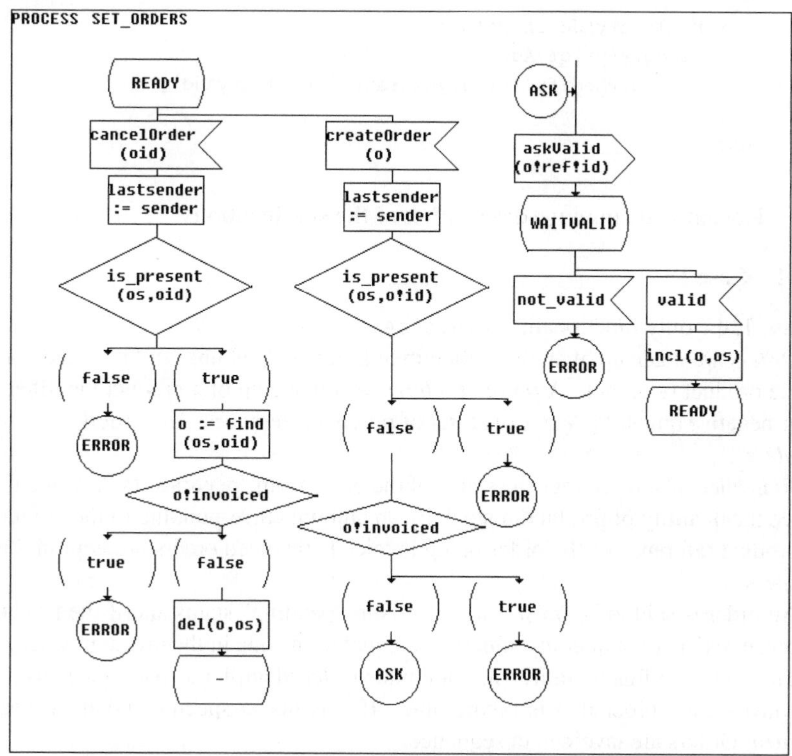

Figure 12.8: The SET_ORDERS process (added) behavior for case 2

```
    addQty(empty,p2) == incl(p2,empty);
    (p!id = p2!id)==> addQty(incl(p,s),p2) ==
       incl(addQty(p,p2!qty),s);
    (p!id /= p2!id)==> addQty(incl(p,s),p2) ==
       incl(p,addQty(s,p2));
     ...
   );););
endnewtype;
```

Sort productRef. Due to prior sort definitions, an operator `addQty: productRef, Nat` $\rightarrow$ `productRef` is needed:

```
   newtype productRef
 operators
     ...
     addQty : productRef, Natural -> productRef;
 axioms
     for all pr in productRef (
```

```
    for all qtyAdd in Natural (
      addQty(pr,qtyAdd) ==
          qtyModify!(pr,qtyExtract!(pr) + qtyAdd);
  ););
endnewtype;
```

12.4 The natural language description of the specifications

12.4.1 Case 1

In Case 1, the only functionality is `invoice`.

Orders are made up of an order identifier, a status ("pending" or "invoiced") and a unique product reference. A *product reference* is made up of a product identifier and a non-negative quantity. A *stock* is a set of product references. The orders are in a *set of orders*.

To invoice means: change the status of the order from "pending" to "invoiced" and reduce the quantity of product in stock by an amount corresponding to the amount in the product reference of the order being invoiced. Invoiced orders are kept in the set of orders.

An order is said to be *invoiceable* if it is in "pending" status and if the product it references exists (in a quantity superior or equal to the one in the order) in stock.

The `invoice` functionality takes a unique order identifier as parameter. Its effect is to invoice the order if it is invoiceable. If it is not, a specific signal (`error`) is returned. Orders are invoiced in sequence.

12.4.2 Case 2

Case 2 is an extension of Case 1. New functionalities are `addProduct`, `createOrder` and `cancelOrder`.

`addProduct` takes a product identifier and a certain non-negative quantity as parameters. If the product does not exist in stock, it is created (with the given quantity as initial amount), elsewhere, the quantity of the product in stock is increased by the given quantity.

`createOrder` takes an order as parameter. The product in the order must exist in stock or a specific signal (`error`) is returned. This signal is also returned if the order identifier exists in the set of orders or if the order is created in invoiced status.

`cancelOrder` takes an order identifier as parameter. If the order does not exist in the set of orders or if it has already been invoiced, then a specific signal (`error`) is returned; elsewhere the order is removed from the set of orders.

12.5 Conclusion

As shown by the invoicing system, informal specifications, even of small case studies, are inherently incomplete and not precise. Being formal, SDL enables us to express the system requirements in a more precise way (raising questions) and to validate the specification using a wide range of tools (theorem provers for the data part, simulation, model-checking).

Like other "mixed" formal specification languages or methods [ISO 89a, ISO 89b], SDL makes it possible to describe both the dynamic and the static parts of systems. This is really a great advantage as the semantics of operations and the order and conditions under which they may be applied are equally important. Clearly separating the specification into structuring, process graphs and data types makes mixed specification easy.

SDL comes with both a textual and a graphical representation. This provides the specifier with a wider specification toolbox. The SDL graphical concepts are intuitive. They enable the specifier to work at different abstraction levels using the structuring mechanisms. They also make the extension of existing specifications easier (see the passage from case 1 to case 2, for example). The system structuring may be extended adding blocks and channels. The process graphs may be extended adding new transitions. Finally, data types may be extended using the SDL inheritance concept.

SDL asynchronous buffered communication semantics are closer to real-world communication mechanisms – closer to an implementation in terms of (asynchronously) communicating objects – than some other specification languages such as LOTOS. Moreover, requirements involving time may be expressed in SDL using timers.

If these SDL strengths were used in case 2, case 1 showed its main weakness. Unlike model-based specification methods such as Z [LIG 91] or B [ABR 96], SDL is inherently dynamic and requirements like "the set of orders and the stock are always given in an up-to-date state" (a state invariant) cannot be expressed.

Acknowledgements

I would like to thank Professor K. J. Turner for his careful reading and comments about an earlier version of this chapter.

Bibliography

[ABR 96] ABRIAL J.-R., *The B Book – Assigning Programs to Meanings*, Cambridge University Press, August 1996.

[CCI 92] CCITT, Recommendation Z.100: Specification and Description Language SDL, blue book, volume x.1 edition, 1992.

[ELL 97] ELLSBERGER J., HOGREFE D., SARMA A., *SDL : Formal Object-oriented Language for Communicating Systems*, Prentice-Hall, 1997.

[ISO 89a] ISO/IEC, ESTELLE: A Formal Description Technique based on an Extended State Transition Model, ISO/IEC no. 9074, International Organization for Standardization, 1989.

[ISO 89b] ISO/IEC, LOTOS: A Formal Description Technique based on the Temporal Ordering of Observational Behaviour, ISO/IEC no. 8807, International Organization for Standardization, 1989.

[LIG 91] LIGHTFOOT D., *Formal Specification using Z*, Macmillan, 1991.

[POI 99] POIZAT P., CHOPPY C., ROYER J.-C., "Concurrency and Data Types: A Specification Method. An Example with LOTOS", in FIADEIRO J., Ed., *Recent Trends in Algebraic Development Techniques, Selected Papers of the 13th International Workshop on Algebraic Development Techniques (WADT'98)*, vol. 1589 of *Lecture Notes in Computer Science*, Lisbon, Portugal, April, 2-4, 1998, Springer-Verlag, p. 276–291, 1999.

[TUR 93] TURNER K. J., Ed., *Using Formal Description Techniques, An Introduction to Estelle, LOTOS and SDL*, Wiley, 1993.

Chapter 13

E-LOTOS

Kenneth J. TURNER and Mihaela SIGHIREANU

13.1 Overview of the LOTOS notation and method

This section introduces the LOTOS and E-LOTOS languages, and how they may be used in requirements capture.

13.1.1 The *LOTOS* and *E-LOTOS* languages

LOTOS (Language of Temporal Ordering Specification [ISO 89]) is a standardised FDT (Formal Description Technique) originally intended for the specification of communications and distributed systems. There exist several tutorials for LOTOS [BOL 88, TUR 93]. The design of LOTOS was motivated by the need for a language with a high abstraction level and a strong mathematical basis, suitable for the specification and analysis of complex systems. LOTOS consists of two integrated sub-languages for specifying data types (ADTs –Abstract Data Types) and behavior (process algebra). LOTOS has been used to specify and analyse a variety of systems. Many of these have been communications standards, but LOTOS has been successfully used in a number of other fields. LOTOS is supported by tools for specification, simulation, compilation, test generation and formal verification. LOTOS toolsets include CADP (CÆSAR/ALDÉBARAN Development Package [FER 96]), LITE (LOTOS Integrated Tool Environment) and LOLA (LOTOS Laboratory). More information about LOTOS, tools, applications and publications can be found online [TUR 00].

Although LOTOS has proved to be widely applicable, ISO has been developing a revised version called E-LOTOS (Enhancements to LOTOS [ISO 01]). New language features of particular relevance to the invoicing case study include modularity, functional (constructive) data types, classical programming constructs, a controlled imperative style and strongly typed gates. Since E-LOTOS standardisation was not quite complete at the time of writing, the authors have used a snapshot of the language.

In LOTOS and E-LOTOS, a system (the entity being specified) is modeled as one or more processes that communicate with each other and with their environment (whatever is outside a process, e.g. its user). The communication ports of a process are called (event) gates. LOTOS processes are parameterised by their gates and the values they maintain. Inputs and outputs correspond to LOTOS events, i.e. interactions at a gate between two processes such as the system and its environment. It will be seen later that the inputs of Figure 13.1 correspond to event offers made in the specifications. In LOTOS, an event occurs when two parties synchronise on matching event offers. An event offer indicates a willingness to communicate at a gate. Since several events may be offered, a choice may have to be made of which event offers are synchronised and therefore which event actually occurs. This choice may affect the future behaviour of the system.

13.1.2 Requirements capture in *LOTOS*

LOTOS is often used to specify a system as a black box, and therefore to concentrate on its boundary, inputs and outputs. A LOTOS specifier will try to write a high-level specification of requirements, avoiding implementation-oriented concerns. The emphasis will be on specifying the partial ordering of (observable) events. Other factors that influence the approach include the balance chosen between processes and data in the specification, and the choice of specification style (if one is explicitly adopted). Various methods have been investigated for LOTOS, e.g. [BOL 95, TUR 90], but because the case study was so small, the authors followed only general LOTOS principles:

- delimit the boundary of the system to be specified;
- define the interfaces of the system (inputs, outputs, parameters);
- define the functionality of the system (the relationship among inputs and outputs);
- for incomplete requirements, choose an abstract or simple interpretation that will give some freedom later for adopting a more specific interpretation.

LOTOS is a constructive specification language: any specification will exhibit some structure (usually hierarchic, though a monolithic style is also possible). The subject of specification style has been investigated in considerable depth for LOTOS. Indeed it might be fairly said that LOTOS specifiers are pre-occupied with specification style! The choice of style for specifying requirements has a big impact on how the specification is structured. Another way of putting this is to say that LOTOS specifiers care about the high-level architecture of a system. (In the sense of [TUR 97], the architecture of a specification means its structure and style.) Several LOTOS workers have considered general 'quality' principles for specification architecture [SCO 93, TUR 97].

Because LOTOS combines a data type language with a process algebra, the specifier must choose an appropriate balance when using these two aspects of the language

[LED 87]. This partly depends on the preferred specification style, partly on the intended use of the specification (e.g. for analysis or refinement), and partly on the application. Some applications focus on the representation and manipulation of data (e.g. a database), and so are more naturally specified using the data part of LOTOS. Other applications focus on dynamic (reactive) behaviour, and so are more naturally specified using the process algebra part of LOTOS.

The case study treated in this book is data-oriented in nature since it effectively describes a database. For this reason, its LOTOS specification makes significant use of data types. However, there is a modeling choice to be made of whether to represent stocks and orders as processes or as data values. For this reason, *two* specification approaches were used by the authors. These give some idea of the range of styles open to the LOTOS specifier.

A LOTOS-based approach to requirement capture raises the following kinds of questions:

Environment: Who are the users of the system? What is the context of the system? What is the boundary of the system? What functions can the system rely on in the environment?

Interfaces: What are the interfaces to the environment? What are the data flows into and out of the system? What is the structure and content of these data flows?

Functionality: What functions must the system perform? What is the relationship among inputs and outputs?

Limitations: What limits apply to system inputs, outputs and functions?

Non-functional aspects: What timing and performance aspects must be specified? What other organisational issues should be considered?

Methodology: How should the formal model be developed? Which specification style is appropriate? How should the specification be validated (by testing and/or verification)?

The case study deals with requirements capture, analysis, specification and verification of the invoicing system. Of necessity this chapter presents only an overview of the specifications and their verification. Full details can be found in [SIG 98]. The act of formalisation typically raises many questions that would normally be discussed with the client. In a realistic situation, the systems analyst would raise such questions with the client. This would allow ambiguities, errors and omissions in the requirements to be resolved. As in this case study, it is sometimes not possible to approach a client with questions. For example, it may be necessary to carry out a *post hoc* formalisation of something that already exists (e.g. a legacy system or an international standard).

It was necessary for the authors to raise questions about the invoicing requirements and to provide answers in a sensible fashion. Analysis was performed according to the method outlined above. Some answers (**Answer** in the following) came from a common-sense reading of the requirements. Others (**Answer+**) required interpretation or extension of the requirements. As will be seen, the volume of questions is much greater than the informal problem statement! Of course, this demonstrates the value of a formal method.

Each portion of a formal specification is preceded by an informal explanation. In the specifications that follow, the authors have used their own convention for the case of identifiers (keywords in bold, variables in lower case, other identifiers with an initial capital).

13.2 Analysis and specification of case 1

The first case is discussed in this section though, as will be seen, it is treated as a simple abstraction of the second case.

13.2.1 Analysis

13.2.1.1 Methodology

Question 1: Is case 1 a simplification/abstraction of case 2? Is case 2 an extension/refinement of case 1?

Answer+: It is not clear what the relationship between the cases is meant to be. In the authors' opinion, case 1 does not make sense in isolation from case 2. Note that this is a methodological issue, not a ***LOTOS*** issue. From the ***LOTOS*** point of view, case 1 could have been specified without reference to case 2. Orders cannot realistically be satisfied from stock under all circumstances, even if the informal problem statement permits this assumption. Sometimes it is better if the analyst does not literally accept everything the client says! The system could be placed in an impossible situation if the assumption were violated. The informal description of case 1 also supposes some unidentified agency that maintains orders and stocks. For both these reasons, the authors do not regard case 1 as meaningful in its own right – only as a simplification of case 2. It was therefore decided to treat case 2 as primary, with case 1 being an abstraction of this. The analysis in this section is therefore confined to those questions that arise from case 1 alone.

13.2.1.2 Interfaces

Question 2: What does being 'given stock and the set of orders' imply?

Answer: This means that the first case study deals with a closed system that does not directly accept stock or order changes. It also means that the system has direct access to the current stock and orders. It follows that these must be maintained by some other sub-system.

13.2.1.3 Functionality

Question 3: Why is it said that all ordered references are in stock?

Answer+: This is presumably a hint that stock levels should not be checked before an order is invoiced. However it is not a realistic assumption. It is therefore prudent to check stock levels in this case, even if the check proves to be redundant.

Question 4: It is said that there will be no entry flows to the system, yet the system is 'given stock and orders in an up-to-date state'. Being 'given' such information is equivalent to an entry flow. How should such apparently contradictory requirements be resolved?

Answer+: The only interpretation that begins to make sense is that the information is somehow separate from the invoicing function and is updated by some other agency. The system can then consult this information at any time. Presumably the information is up-to-date only in respect of current stocks and order requests: that is, the order status is presumably not up-to-date or the system would be pointless! This interpretation does not directly affect the specification, but is a necessary stage in understanding the requirements.

13.2.2 Specification

Case 1 is viewed as an abstraction of case 2. There is therefore no externally observable behavior since the system is closed. For case 2, the process-oriented style introduces some internal structure to the specification. The structure of the specifications to be presented is pictured in Figure 13.1. The outer ovals in this figure represent the boundaries of alternative models. These correspond to the specifications for case 1, case 2 in data-oriented form, and case 2 in process-oriented form. In each specification, the inner details are hidden from external view. There are thus three alternative levels of abstraction. Case 1 has no inputs, and thus has no externally observable behaviour. The inputs in case 2 are *Request* (place an order), *Cancel* (remove an order) and *Deposit* (supply new stock). The process-oriented version of case 2 introduces an internal communication *Withdraw* (satisfy an order from stock).

Since case 1 is treated as a simple modification of case 2, the primary specifications are given in Section 13.3. Note that this was a modeling choice and is not intrinsic to how LOTOS might have been used. In fact the modifications for case 1 are trivial, requiring only the internal communication channels to be hidden. For example, the process-oriented E-LOTOS specification has the following added:

```
hide Request:(Reference, Product, Amount)            (* hide internal gates *)
  Cancel:Reference, Deposit:(Product, Amount),
    Withdraw:(Product, Amount) in ...       (* in remainder of specification*)
```

13.3 Analysis and specification of case 2

The meat of this chapter lies in analysing and specifying the second case. Four specifications will be presented, using E-LOTOS and LOTOS in process-oriented and data-oriented styles.

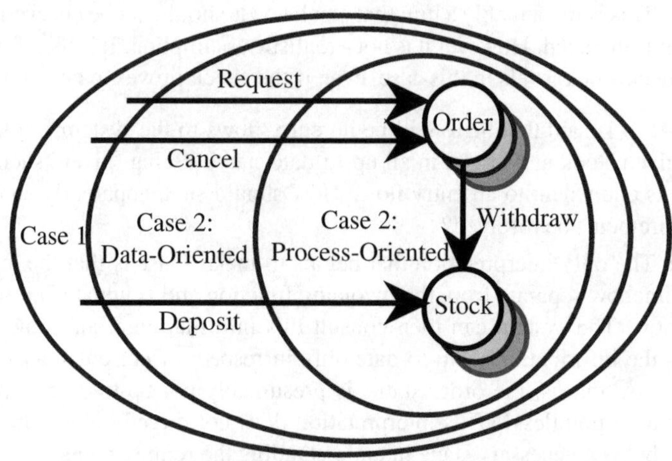

Figure 13.1: Structure of the alternative models/specifications

13.3.1 Analysis

13.3.1.1 Environment

Question 5: Is it necessary to know how many users there are?

Answer: This is not stated in the informal requirements. If there were only one user, it would not be necessary to identify orders (assuming that they were processed in sequence). If there were several users and it were necessary to issue invoices (or other messages to users), it would be necessary to identify users or orders. Invoices and the like would then have to carry an identification. Since the informal requirements do not ask the system to do anything (e.g. produce an invoice or deliver a product), this question is purely for understanding the requirements. It does not affect the ***LOTOS*** specifications directly.

13.3.1.2 Interfaces

Question 6: At what point is the status of an order updated? If the status is updated when the stock or set of orders changes, how does the system know that there has been a change? If the status is updated following a periodic check, how frequently should the system check?

Answer+: Updating on change of stocks or orders is a simpler interpretation and is therefore preferred. It follows that the system must be told of new stocks or orders. This information thus becomes input to the system. The system must update the stock and orders, which by implication are stored within the system since no outputs are mentioned. The system to be specified is thus an embedded sub-system of some larger system.

Question 7: Are new stocks or orders notified individually or in batches to the system?

Answer+: For simplicity it is assumed that inputs occur individually.

Question 8: How is invoicing triggered, how is the information obtained, and how is the decision made to update orders?

Answer+: Since the requirements imply that some internal agency manages stocks and orders, it is presumed that this agency supplies information to the system as required and triggers an update.

Question 9: How is it possible to identify an order to be canceled?

Answer+: The only sensible solution is if an order carries a reference that can subsequently be quoted in a cancellation. Other information such as the original product code or requested quantity would be redundant on cancellation and so is omitted.

Question 10: Who, then, is responsible for creating an order reference?

Answer+: It could be supplied by the user or generated automatically by the system. In normal ordering practice, the user generates the order number, so this might seem to be more natural. However, it creates a new problem: how to handle a duplicate order number. Solving this would require mechanisms to force users to use unique numbers, or to reject a duplicate. In fact it is simpler to adopt a more abstract approach that simply requires unique numbers, whether generated by the user or the system (or both, in cooperation).

13.3.1.3 Functionality

Question 11: What is the meaning of being able to "change the state of an order"?

Answer: It is presumed that the system merely inspects the state of current orders and adjusts their status according to the current stock.

Question 12: Should the system issue an invoice when 'changing the state of an order'?

Answer: Normally such a system would actually issue an invoice. However, there is no mention of this in the informal problem statement. The conclusion is that the system operates on a set of orders whose status is updated by the system. If an invoice had to be generated, there would be other questions about what it should contain: order reference, product code, quantity, price, etc. However, these matters can be ignored in the case study.

Question 13: What is implied by the system changing the state of an order from "pending" to "invoiced"?

Answer+: It is not clear whether this means that orders should be explicitly associated with a status. Presumably so, though the status of an order might be implicit (e.g. if unfulfilled orders are held separately).

Question 14: It is said that several orders may cite the same product code. This seems an almost unnecessary remark, but it hints that several orders may be outstanding for the same product. In this case, how should stock be allocated to orders?

Answer+: The stock is limited by implication, so the choice of allocation strategy may lead to different results. For example the smallest – or the largest – outstanding order for a product might be satisfied first. In the interests of abstractness, it is presumed that orders are satisfied in some "random" manner. Specifically, the allocation algorithm is not visible to or influenced by the system environment, i.e. it is non-deterministic.

Question 15: If an order can be fulfilled from stock, its state must be changed to "invoiced". What should happen if an order cannot be fulfilled because the stock is insufficient?

Answer+: In this situation the order might be ignored, it might be explicitly rejected, or it might be held until stock becomes available. The first possibility is rather unfriendly and is therefore not considered. As already concluded, the system produces no outputs so the second possibility is rejected. The third possibility is therefore adopted, and is more consistent with the informal requirements.

Question 16: What should be done if an order is held until stock becomes available?

Answer+: When the system is given new stock it must re-examine any unfulfilled orders to see if they can be satisfied. As discussed in Question 14, there is then an issue of how stock should be allocated. Again, a "random" algorithm is assumed.

Question 17: What does canceling an order mean?

Answer+: This suggests an explicit request rather than just omitting an order from the updated list. At what point can an order be canceled: before it is received by the invoicing system, after reception but before invoicing, after invoicing but before delivery, after delivery? In a real system these questions would have to be answered concretely. However, as discussed above the purpose of the system seems to be just maintaining a set of current orders. Cancelation must therefore mean removing an order from the pending set. Canceling a non-existent or invoiced order is assumed to be forbidden.

Question 18: Is any concurrent or distributed processing required?

Answer+: There is nothing explicit in the requirements, but some implicit possibilities exist. For example, the processing of stock and order updates might be handled concurrently. The invoicing system might also be sub-divided into distributed components. Since these issues are open a decision should not be forced, though they may be permitted by the specification.

13.3.1.4 Limitations

Question 19: Is it required that an order carry a product code?

Answer: This is implicit.

Question 20: Is there any restriction on the product quantity carried by an order?

Answer+: Presumably the quantity must be a positive integer. Negative quantities might correspond to returned products. A zero-quantity order is conceivable, but does not seem very useful and should be forbidden. Fractional quantities might be meaningful for products that can be broken down into smaller units, but for simplicity this was not allowed. Similarly, stock deposits are assumed to be strictly positive integers.

Question 21: Are there any orders or stocks initially?

Answer+: This is not explicitly stated in the informal requirements. Conceivably there could be an initial setup of orders or stocks, but for simplicity it is presumed that these are empty at start-up.

13.3.1.5 Non-functional properties

Question 22: As would normally be expected, are there any non-functional requirements such as cost, delivery schedule, performance, reliability, integration and testing?

Answer: Performance specification and testing have been studied in *LOTOS*-based development. However, non-functional aspects can be ignored since the only requirements available are strictly functional.

Question 23: Must an uncancelled order be satisfied eventually?

Answer: It is assumed that the system behaves fairly and does not indefinitely delay the processing of an order.

Question 24: Must the system be free from deadlocks?

Answer: This requirement is implicit and leads to a formal property of the specification that should be checked.

Question 25: Must the system be free from livelocks (i.e. unbounded loops of internal actions)?

Answer: This requirement is implicit, and leads to a formal property of the specification that should be checked.

13.3.2 Specification

Since E-LOTOS is the future form of the language, the authors felt it would be interesting to show how its specification style differs from LOTOS. Both E-LOTOS and LOTOS specifications of the case study have therefore been prepared. Since the languages differ, each has been written in its native style; the specifications are not just syntactic translations of each other. There are thus eight specifications in total, corresponding to {Case 1, Case 2}×{process-oriented, data-oriented}×{E-LOTOS, LOTOS}. For space reasons, these have not been presented in full.

13.3.2.1 Process-oriented specifications

Process-oriented E-LOTOS specification. Gates in E-LOTOS are typed, allowing static checks on the kinds of values that are communicated. E-LOTOS event offers such as *Request(!ref, ?prd, ?amt)* may be synchronized (matched) with others. A fixed value in an event offer is preceded by '!', whereas a value to be determined in an event offer is preceded by '?'. These notations are also used in pattern-matching of expressions. Although '!' and '?' in event offers can usually be interpreted as output and input respectively, there is technically no distinction between these in LOTOS. This is because '?' is just a shorthand way of offering all the values from a set (e.g. '*?prd*' means 'offer any product reference').

The process-oriented specification of the invoicing system might be regarded as object-based. Orders and stock items are individual objects that encapsulate an identity (order reference or product code), state (order or stock status) and services (request order, deposit stock, etc.). The identity of an order or stock item allows that object, out of the whole collection, to synchronize on the messages intended for it. The specification allows several pending orders to compete simultaneously for the same product (whose stock levels may not be sufficient to satisfy all the orders). Since these orders are handled concurrently, the sequence in which they are satisfied is non-deterministic.

The data types and processes are specified here in a separate module *OrderStock* for convenience. As in normal software engineering practice, an E-LOTOS module is a re-usable and self-contained collection of definitions. Modules are maintained separately from the specification proper that describes the whole system.

For clarity, separate types are introduced for an order *Reference*, a *Product* code, and a product *Amount*. For simplicity, these types simply rename the natural number type (non-negative integers); library types like this can be used without explicit importing. If desired, structured types could be introduced for order references and product codes:

```
module OrderStock is                              (* order-stock definitions *)
  type Reference renames Nat endtype                    (* order references *)
  type Product renames Nat endtype                         (* product codes *)
  type Amount renames Nat endtype                        (* product amounts *)
```

The status of an order is defined using an enumerated type. Orders start out blank, i.e. their product and amount have not yet been defined. Such an order is said to have status *None*. The complete type for an order is given as a record containing product, amount and status fields:

```
type Status is enum None, Pending, Invoiced endtype      (* order status *)
type Order is                                                   (* order *)
   record Prod:Product, Amt:Amount, Stat:Status
endtype
```

A blank order is filled in when an *Order* object accepts an order *Request*. A pending order may accept a *Cancel* and be annulled. A pending order may also *Withdraw* from stock. A choice is made from these possibilities using the '[]' (choice) operator that offers alternative behaviours. One of these is selected by matching event offers with the environment of the *Order* object. Other common LOTOS operators include ':=' (for assignment) and ';' (for sequential behaviour).

An event offer may be qualified by a condition (written in brackets after the offer). For example, a new order is permitted only if the order is blank (status *None*) and the amount being ordered is positive (*amt* > *0*); the order status then becomes *Pending*. Cancellation is allowed only if the order is pending, at which point the order ceases to exist (i.e. its status becomes *None*). A pending order may ask for withdrawal of stock. The stock object with the corresponding product will synchronise on this offer if there is sufficient stock. If the order cannot be currently satisfied, the withdrawal request remains open until sufficient stock exists. At this point the order becomes invoiced:

```
process Order [Request, Cancel, Withdraw]     (* order object gates, ... *)
 (ref:Reference, prd:Product, amt:Amount, sta:Status) is  (* parameters *)
  loop                                            (* loop indefinitely *)
    Request(!ref, ?prd, ?amt)     (* new order if blank, amount positive *)
     [(sta == None) and (amt > 0)];
      ?sta := Pending                             (* set status pending *)
  []                                                            (* or *)
    Cancel(!ref) [sta == Pending];           (* cancel order if pending *)
    ?sta := None                               (* set status not in use *)
  []                                                            (* or *)
    Withdraw(!prd, !amt)         (* withdraw product for pending order *)
     [sta == Pending];
      ?sta := Invoiced                           (* set status invoiced *)
  endloop                                             (* end main loop *)
endproc                                              (* end order object *)
```

A *Stock* object repeatedly accepts deposits from the environment and withdrawals from order objects. New stock (of positive amount) is added to the current stockholding. Withdrawal is permitted if the requested amount can be taken from current stock:

```
process Stock [Deposit, Withdraw]                    (* stock object gates, ... *)
  (prd:Product, amt:Amount) is                                  (* parameters *)
   var newamt:Amount in                               (* variable declaration *)
     loop                                                (* loop indefinitely *)
       Deposit(!prd, ?newamt)               (* deposit stock if amount positive *)
        [newamt > 0];
       ?amt := amt + newamt                           (* increase stock amount *)
     []                                                                (* or *)
       Withdraw(!prd, ?newamt) (* withdraw stock if sufficient amount *)
        [newamt <= amt];
       ?amt := amt − newamt                           (* decrease stock amount *)
     endloop                                                (* end main loop *)
   endvar                                         (* end variable declaration *)
endproc                                                  (* end stock object *)
```

The module concludes by defining unbounded sets of processes for *Orders* and *Stocks*, each running independently in parallel (denoted '|||'). These are obtained by explicit recursion over the order reference and stock product code. An order is initialized with its reference and 'not in use' status. A stock item is initialized with its product code and a zero amount:

```
process Orders [Request, Cancel, Withdraw]              (* orders gates, ... *)
  (ref:Reference) is                                          (* parameter *)
   Order [Request, Cancel, Withdraw] (ref, 0, 0, None)        (* one order *)
|||                                          (* independently in parallel with *)
   Orders [Request, Cancel, Withdraw] (ref + 1)             (* more orders *)
endproc                                                      (* end orders *)
process Stocks [Deposit, Withdraw]                      (* stocks gates, ... *)
  (prd:Product) is                                            (* parameter *)
   Stock [Deposit, Withdraw] (prd, 0)                     (* one stock item *)
|||                                          (* independently in parallel with *)
   Stocks [Deposit, Withdraw] (Succ(prd))             (* more stock items *)
endproc                                                      (* end stocks *)
endmod                                           (* end order-stock definitions *)
```

The overall specification imports the module for orders and stocks. The communication gates (all inputs in this case) are introduced, and the types of values they carry are specified:

```
specification Invoicing imports OrderStock is   (* use order-stock module *)
  gates Request:(Reference, Product, Amount),    (* gates and their types *)
   Cancel:Reference, Deposit:(Product, Amount)
  behaviour                                     (* specification behavior *)
```

Communication between orders and stocks is via an internal gate *Withdraw* (see Figure 13.1). The order and stock processes synchronise on withdrawal. An operator such as '|[*Withdraw*]|' names the gates on which parallel behaviors must synchronise. The first order reference and product code are given as 0. As new orders and stocks arrive, the processes will update their state and will communicate to satisfy orders:

```
      hide Withdraw:(Product, Amount) in          (* hide withdrawal gate *)
        Orders [Request, Cancel, Withdraw] (0)                (* orders *)
      |[Withdraw]|                     (* synchronising on withdrawals with *)
        Stocks [Deposit, Withdraw] (0)                        (* stocks *)
  endspec                                           (* end specification *)
```

Process-oriented LOTOS specification. The equivalent process-oriented specification in LOTOS is similar, except that modules are not available. The specification is self-contained behaviour that continues indefinitely ('**noexit**').The natural number type is selected from the standard library. Since this type does not define subtraction, a definition of this is given (though not here, for brevity):

```
  specification Invoicing [Request, Cancel, Deposit] : noexit     (* gates *)
    library NaturalNumber endlib                (* use naturals in library *)
```

As for the E-LOTOS process-oriented specification, order references, product codes and product amounts are specified by renaming naturals. These types, along with the similar status type, are omitted here. The overall behavior is also left out as it is similar to the E-LOTOS version. Except for syntactic differences, the *Order* and *Stock* objects are similar to their E-LOTOS counterparts. Loops must be achieved by explicit process recursion in LOTOS:

```
    process Order [Request, Cancel, Withdraw]   (* order object gates, pars *)
     (ref:Reference, prd:Product, amt:Amount, sta:Status) : noexit :=
      [sta = None] ->                              (* status is blank order? *)
        Request !ref ?prd:Product        (* order request for positive amount *)
         ?amt:Amount [amt gt 0];
        Order [Request, Cancel, Withdraw]              (* set pending status *)
         (ref, prd, amt, Pending)
    []                                                                (* or *)
      [sta = Pending] ->                         (* status is pending order? *)
        (
          Cancel !ref;                                      (* cancel order *)
          Order [Request, Cancel, Withdraw]              (* set blank status *)
           (ref, 0 of Product, 0 of Amount, None)
        []                                                            (* or *)
          Withdraw !prd !amt;                             (* withdraw stock *)
          Order [Request, Cancel, Withdraw]           (* set invoiced status *)
           (ref, prd, amt, Invoiced)
        )
    endproc                                             (* end order object *)
```

```
    process Stock [Deposit, Withdraw]                 (* stock object gates, ... *)
     (prd:Product, amt:Amount) : noexit :=                      (* parameters *)
      Deposit !prd ?newamt:Amount               (* deposit if positive amount *)
       [newamt gt 0];
      Stock [Deposit, Withdraw]                (* repeat with increased stock *)
       (prd, amt + newamt)
    []                                                                (* or *)
      Withdraw !prd ?newamt:Amount         (* withdrawal if sufficient amount *)
       [newamt le amt];
      Stock [Deposit, Withdraw]                (* repeat with decreased stock *)
       (prd, amt – newamt)
    endproc                                               (* end stock object *)
  endspec                                                (* end specification *)
```

13.3.2.2 Data-oriented specifications

Data-oriented E-LOTOS specification. In this approach, orders and stocks are defined by data values rather than processes. Invoicing is then an operation on these values. The simple data types are not given here since they closely resemble the process-oriented E-LOTOS ones. A collection of orders is treated as an associative array indexed by order reference. A collection of stocks is similar, but the array is indexed by product code and the values are amounts. An array element is accessed by operation *Get* and stored by *Put*. Similar operations are used with record fields, e.g. *Get_Stat* and *Set_Stat* for the order status field.

Invoicing orders is performed by function *Invoice* that takes current orders and stocks. Each order is checked in a loop, from first reference number to last. The *Next* function finds the next array index since there may be gaps in order numbers. Orders are thus fulfilled in reference number sequence, whereas the process-oriented specifications deal with them non-deterministically. Non-determinism could have been achieved, but only by complicating the specification. The current reference is used to extract the product, amount and status of a record. The product code is used to extract the stock level. If the order is pending and there is sufficient stock, the order is marked as invoiced and the stock level is updated. After all orders have been processed, the function exits with the updated orders and stocks. If an order cannot be fulfilled, it may be satisfied later when invoicing is repeated on receipt of new stock:

```
function Invoice(ords:Orders, stks:Stocks) :  (* invoicing parameters, ... *)
 (Orders, Stocks) is                                          (* results *)
  var ref:Reference, prd:Product, amt,          (* variable declarations *)
   stk:Amount, sta:Status in
    for (?ref := First(ords); ref <= Last(ords);   (* first to last order *)
      ?ref := Next(ords, ref)) do
       (?prd, ?amt, ?sta) := Get(ords, ref);          (* get order details *)
```

```
        ?stk := Get(stks, prd);                      (* get stock for product *)
        if (sta == Pending) and                               (* pending ... *
         (amt <= stk) then                                     (* in stock? *)
          ?ords :=                                     (* set order invoiced *)
           Put(ords, ref, Set_Stat(Get(ords, ref), Invoiced));
          ?stks := Put(stks, prd, stk – amt)      (* decrease stock level *)
        endif                                 (* end pending order check *)
      endfor                                          (* end order loop *)
      (ords, stks)                      (* return resulting orders, stocks *)
    endvar                                (* end variable declarations *)
  endfunc                                    (* end invoicing function *)
endmod                                    (* end order-stock definitions *)
```

The system specification is like that for the process-oriented E-LOTOS version except that local variables are introduced for orders, stocks, order reference and product code. Orders and stocks are initialized to be empty. The main behaviour repeatedly accepts order requests, order cancellations and stock deposits. The logic is as already seen, except that the existence of an order is checked against the *Orders* array. Each branch of the loop updates orders or stocks as appropriate. The *Invoice* function is then called to deal with pending orders and to alter stocks accordingly:

```
      loop                                          (* loop indefinitely *)
        (                             (* choice of request, cancel, deposit *)
          Request(?ref, ?prd, ?amt)        (* new order, positive amount? *)
           [NotIn(ords, ref) and (amt > 0)];
          ?ords :=                       (* update orders with pending order *)
           Put(ords, ref, Order(prd, amt, Pending))
        []                                                        (* or *)
          Cancel(?ref)                 (* cancel order if exists and pending *)
           [IsIn(ords, ref) andthen
            (Get_Stat(Get(ords, ref)) == Pending)];
          ?ords := Delete(ords, ref)                        (* delete order *)
        []                                                        (* or *)
          Deposit(?prd, ?amt) [amt > 0];        (* deposit positive amount *)
          ?stks := Put(stks, prd,           (* update with extra/new amount *)
            if IsIn(stks, prd) then Get(stks, prd) + amt else amt endif)
        );                                                (* end choice *)
        (?ords, ?stks) := Invoice(ords,stks)      (* get new orders, stocks *)
      endloop                                           (* end main loop *)
    endvar                                (* end variable declarations *)
endspec                                           (* end specification *)
```

Data-oriented LOTOS specification. This specification begins in much the same way as the process-oriented LOTOS version, except that Boolean equality for status values has to be defined. Boolean equality is defined for two status values so that compound Boolean expressions involving status can be written. Following normal LOTOS practice, equality is defined using an auxiliary function that maps values to the natural numbers. The reference, product, amount and status types are imported as components of an order. Stock is built from product and amount types. Since LOTOS does not have a record construct, *MkOrder* and *MkStock* operations are needed.

Orders and stocks might have been defined using the generic *Set* type in the library. However, orders and stocks have been specified from scratch since sets are not entirely appropriate. (Stocks of the same product need to be amalgamated, so stock is not strictly a set. Identical orders should be allowed, so a bag rather than a set is needed.) *NoOrders* is an empty collection of orders. An order may be added to or removed from this using the *AddOrder* and *RemOrder* operations. *StatOrder* is introduced to retrieve the status of an order in the collection. Each operation is defined by equations that show its evaluation for each pattern of parameters. In this case, the distinct forms of operation parameter to be considered are a collection with no orders and with at least one order. Conditional equations (*condition* ⇒ *equation*) apply only if the condition holds:

```
type Orders is Order, Status                              (* order list *)
  sorts Orders                                     (* name for order list *)
  opns                                                     (* operations *)
    NoOrders : -> Orders                         (* empty list of orders *)
    AddOrder : Order, Orders -> Orders               (* add order to list *)
    RemOrder : Order, Orders -> Orders        (* remove order from list *)
    StatOrder : Reference, Orders -> Status (* get status for reference *)
  eqns                                                      (* equations *)
    forall ref1,ref2:Reference, prd1,prd2:Product,   (* global variables *)
     amt1,amt2:Amount, sta1,sta2:Status, ords:Orders
      ofsort Status                        (* operations yielding status *)
        StatOrder(ref1, NoOrders) = None;         (* no orders, no status *)
        ref1 eq ref2 =>                     (* order references match? *)
          StatOrder(ref1,                                  (* get status *)
           AddOrder(MkOrder(ref2, prd2, amt2, sta2), ords)) = sta2;
        ref1 ne ref2 =>                     (* order references differ? *)
          StatOrder(ref1,                          (* check other orders *)
           AddOrder(MkOrder(ref2, prd2, amt2, sta2), ords)) =
            StatOrder(ref1, ords);
      ofsort Orders                        (* operations yielding orders *)
        ref1 eq ref2 =>                     (* order references match? *)
          RemOrder(                           (* remove order from list *)
           MkOrder(ref1, prd1, amt1, sta1),
            AddOrder(MkOrder(ref2, prd2, amt2, sta2), ords)) = ords;
        ref1 ne ref2 =>                     (* order references differ? *)
          RemOrder(             (* keep current order, check later ones *)
```

```
            MkOrder(ref1, prd1, amt1, sta1),
             AddOrder(MkOrder(ref2, prd2, amt2, sta2), ords)) =
              AddOrder(MkOrder(ref2, prd2, amt2, sta2),
               RemOrder(MkOrder(ref1, prd1, amt1, sta1), ords));
endtype                                          (* end order list *)
```

A stock collection is defined in a similar way. The operations particular to stocks are *InStock* (to check if a product is stocked) and *StockOf* (to check the stock level). As has just been seen, LOTOS data types are reasonably straightforward but lengthy. The *Stocks* type is therefore omitted here.

A LOTOS operation can return only one result, unless results are grouped in a composite type. Invoicing is therefore computed by two separate operations: *UpdateOrders* and *UpdateStocks*. In both cases, the collection of orders is processed one by one. As in the data-oriented E-LOTOS specification, this means that order fulfilment is deterministic, although not in the fixed order of reference numbers. If an order is pending and the stocks are sufficient for the requested amount, the order status is set to invoiced and the stock level is updated:

```
type Updates is Orders, Stocks                      (* order-stock updates *)
  opns                                                      (* operations *)
    UpdateOrders : Orders, Stocks -> Orders              (* update orders *)
    UpdateStocks : Orders, Stocks -> Stocks              (* update stocks *)
  eqns                                                       (* equations *)
    forall ref:Reference, prd:Product, amt:Amount,    (* global variables *)
     sta:Status, ords:Orders, stks:Stocks
      ofsort Orders                             (* operations yielding orders *)
        UpdateOrders(NoOrders, stks) =              (* no orders, no update *)
         NoOrders;
        (sta eq Pending) and             (* pending order, sufficient stock? *)
         (StockOf(prd, stks) ge amt) =>
          UpdateOrders(    (* update orders by setting order invoiced *)
           AddOrder(MkOrder(ref, prd, amt, sta), ords), stks) =
            AddOrder(MkOrder(ref, prd, amt, Invoiced),
             UpdateOrders(ords, RemStock(MkStock(prd, amt), stks)));
        (sta eq Invoiced) or             (* invoiced or insufficient stock? *)
         (StockOf(prd, stks) lt amt) =>
          UpdateOrders(      (* update orders by leaving order alone *)
           AddOrder(MkOrder(ref, prd, amt, sta), ords), stks) =
            AddOrder(MkOrder(ref, prd, amt, sta),
             UpdateOrders(ords, stks));
      ofsort Stocks                             (* operations yielding stocks *)
        UpdateStocks(NoOrders, stks) =              (* no orders, no update *)
         stks;
        (sta eq Pending) and             (* pending order, sufficient stock? *)
```

```
            (StockOf(prd, stks) ge amt) =>
              UpdateStocks(          (* update stocks by decreasing stock *)
                AddOrder(MkOrder(ref, prd, amt, sta), ords), stks) =
                  UpdateStocks(ords, RemStock(MkStock(prd, amt), stks));
            (sta eq Invoiced) or            (* invoiced or insufficient stock? *)
            (StockOf(prd, stks) lt amt) =>
              UpdateStocks(       (* update stocks by leaving stock alone *)
                AddOrder(MkOrder(ref, prd, amt, sta), ords), stks) =
                  UpdateStocks(ords, stks);
    endtype                                  (* end order-stock updates *)
```

The overall behaviour is similar to that for the E-LOTOS data-oriented specification, though the syntax is different. Explicit process recursion is used to express a loop. Each branch of the choice produces an updated pair of order-stock values. A recursive call to the *Invoice* process updates the orders and stocks following invoicing.

13.4 Validation and verification of the LOTOS specifications

The terms 'validation' and 'verification' are used with various meanings in the literature. The authors use these terms to mean testing and proof respectively. Since E-LOTOS had not quite reached its final form at time of writing, tools for the language were still under development. The E-LOTOS specifications should hence be regarded as preliminary, although they were statically checked using the TRAIAN compiler developed by INRIA Rhône-Alpes. However they are similar to the LOTOS specifications and have been independently reviewed, so there is a high degree of confidence in them. The following discussion therefore refers to automated analysis of only the LOTOS specifications.

13.4.1 Validation

The LOTOS specifications were initially validated using the LITE toolset in a form of white-box testing. The data type definitions were checked by evaluating operations on test values conforming to each distinct form of parameter. For example, *RemOrder* was checked with an empty list of orders (*NoOrders*) and a list containing at least one order (*RemOrder(SomeOrder, MoreOrders)*). The latter has two sub-cases: the order reference exists in the list of orders, and the order reference does not exist.

Behavioral aspects were checked using scenarios that exercised each significant case. For order requests the scenarios included duplicated references, zero amounts, products not currently in stock, amounts less than current stock, amounts exactly equal to current stock, and multiple orders for the same product. For order cancellations the scenarios dealt with non-existent references, pending and invoiced orders. For stock deposits the scenarios included new product codes, existing product codes, zero amounts, and stocks for pending orders. Validation was documented by executing the scenarios and recording the reactions of the specified system. Normally the client would be asked to confirm the completeness and correctness of testing, but that was not possible in this case study. Instead the authors reviewed the behaviour exhibited by the specifications. This uncovered some small specification errors, notably in the LOTOS data types (which are rather complex).

13.4.2 Verification

13.4.2.1 Model generation

Validation cannot ensure the correctness of the specification. Neither is it possible to prove equivalence between various specifications. To achieve this requires formal verification, for which the authors used model-checking [CLA 83] and equivalence-checking [FER 91]. These procedures are automated, but apply only to a system with a finite state space.

CADP (CÆSAR/ALDÉBARAN Development Package [VAS 05]) provides several tools for the design and verification of communications protocols and distributed systems. The CADP tools used in the case study will be mentioned only briefly. CÆSAR and CÆSAR.ADT are compilers that translate a LOTOS specification into a (possibly infinite) LTS (Labelled Transition System) that encodes all possible execution sequences. ALDÉBARAN is a verification tool for comparing or minimising LTSs with respect to various equivalence relations [MIL 89]. XTL (Executable Temporal Language) is a functional-like programming language for compact implementation of various temporal logics.

An LTS is formally defined as a quadruple $M = \langle Q, A, T, q_{init} \rangle$. Q is the set of states, A is the set of actions, and $T \subseteq Q \times A \times Q$ is the transition relation between the states. A transition $\langle q_1, a, q_2 \rangle \in T$ (also written $q_1 \xrightarrow{a} q_2$) means that it is possible to move from state q_1 to state q_2 by performing action a. State $q_{init} \in Q$ is the initial one. The translation of a LOTOS specification into an LTS respects the operational semantics of LOTOS. A state of an LTS represents a point in the behaviour of a specification, and each transition from a state is labeled with a possible action of the behaviour.

To compile data operations efficiently, CÆSAR.ADT needs to know which operations are the constructors (i.e. the primary operations that build values). Also, data type equations are considered as rewriting rules (that change the left-hand expression to the right-hand one), and equations between constructors are not allowed. For tool use, the data types are therefore annotated and some transformations are applied [GAR 89].

To ensure finiteness, the domains of various parameters were restricted for verification purposes. Specifically, an upper bound was set on the highest value for order references, product codes and order amounts (denoted *MaxRef*, *MaxProd*, and *MaxAmt*). An infinite number of parallel processes is implied by the specifications since the number of orders and stock items is unlimited. A specific number of process instances was used according to the upper bound chosen for the parameters. As a practical limitation, only certain combinations of parameter bounds were investigated:

MaxRef values of 1 or 2, *MaxProd* values of 0 and 1, *MaxAmt* values of 1 and 2. In principle this generates 8 LTSs for each specification under consideration.

Verification requires knowledge of all the actions performed by the system. Specifications of case 2 can be used directly. However, those for case 1 cannot because visible actions are deliberately made internal. Models are therefore generated only for case 2. Execution times in Tables 13.1 and 13.2 were obtained when using the CADP tools on a SUN computer (Ultra Sparc-1, 143 MHz processor, 256 MBytes memory).

Model generation for the process-oriented specification of case 2 is summarised in Table 13.1. This is limited by state explosion. The three last rows of the table indicate the incomplete LTSs generated before memory is exhausted. The reason for the state explosion is the high degree of parallel interleaving in this specification. Note that the LTS size increases by one order of magnitude when *MaxRef* or *MaxAmt* is incremented. Moreover, it increases more sharply with *MaxAmt* than with *MaxRef*.

MaxProd	*MaxRef*	*MaxAmt*	States	Transitions	Time (mins.)
0	1	1	5,890	16,130	0.1
0	1	2	39,371	170,754	0.5
0	2	1	25,846	96,430	0.4
0	2	2	323,459	1,826,512	5.9
1	1	1	7,698,453	35,655,750	132.8
1	1	2	$>$ 6,531,532	$>$ 49,232,000	164.5
1	2	1	$>$ 8,213,739	$>$ 49,896,000	383.0
1	2	2	$>$ 4,524,531	$>$ 43,904,000	237.1

Table 13.1: Model generation for the process-oriented specification of case 2

Model generation for the data-oriented specification of case 2 is summarised in Table 13.2. The limit here is execution time not memory occupancy: the last row of the table stays within memory limits but takes an inordinate amount of time. The reason is that parallel interleaving in the process-oriented specification is replaced by data computations. The functions used by the data-oriented specification perform several traversals over the lists containing the orders and the stocks, and these are relatively complex structures. It is interesting to note that the LTS size increases by one order of magnitude when either *MaxRef* or *MaxAmt* is incremented. In the data-oriented case the model size increases more sharply with *MaxRef* than with *MaxAmt*.

13.4.2.2 Verification using model checking

The generated LTSs are verified against formal properties stated in XTL. Since the informal requirements do not state formal properties, these have to be inferred. As the dynamic semantics of LOTOS is event-based, it is natural to express the properties as temporal logic formulae concerning actions. The XTL language supports data types for states, transitions and labels. It also supports functions for manipulating them.

MaxProd	*MaxRef*	*MaxAmt*	States	Transitions	Time (mins.)
0	1	1	14,975	20,195	0.5
0	1	2	88,023	165,792	4.0
0	2	1	82,403	117,386	5.6
0	2	2	848,067	1,603,478	165.3
1	1	1	> 5,236,886	> 9,761,401	31935.4

Table 13.2: Model generation for the data-oriented specification of case 2

The informal requirements were interpreted as described in sections 13.2.1 and 13.3.1. The new requirements can be split into three (overlapping) classes: those that cannot be formalised, those are self-evidently reflected in the specifications, and those that lead to formal properties. The last class of requirements was formalised as safety or liveness properties. Safety properties state that something bad never happens, while liveness properties state that something good eventually happens.

For conciseness, only the first property below is presented in full detail. The text gives an informal statement, a more precise formulation (in italics), a formalisation in XTL, and an explanation of this. For the other properties, only the informal statement and the more precise formulation are given. The full formulation of these properties may be found in [SIG 98].

Property 1: A safety property is that the quantity carried by an order must be a positive integer. *All Requests have strictly positive amounts*:

> **not exists** L : **label in**
> L -> [Request _ _ ?amt : **integer where** amt ≤ 0]
> **end_exists**

The **exists** operator checks here for existence of a label in the LTS corresponding to a *Request* with an amount that is not positive. Of course, such a label should not exist. Formulae are written in brackets as above. XTL is able to access the parameters of an event; the '_' notation stands for any value of event parameter.

Property 2: A safety property is that an order reference must be unique. Duplicate references to an order (i.e. more than one *Request* with the same reference) are allowed only if the order has not been invoiced (i.e. a *Cancel* for the order reference has been accepted). *Between two subsequent Requests with the same reference* ($0 \leq ref \leq MaxRef - 1$)*, a Cancel action with the same reference must occur.*

Property 3: A safety property is that only existing orders may be cancelled. *A Cancel action with some reference* ($0 \leq ref \leq MaxRef - 1$) *can appear only if there has been a Request with the same reference.*

Property 4: A liveness property is that an uncancelled order will eventually be invoiced. Note that this property makes a statement about the state variables of the specifications (i.e. the status of an order). Since the underlying model of LOTOS is an LTS, a state variable cannot be checked directly. Instead, only properties over transitions can be verified. It is therefore necessary to introduce an explicit *Invoice* event that notes when invoicing occurs. *After a Request with some reference* ($0 \leq ref \leq MaxRef - 1$), *if a Cancel with the same reference does not occur, then eventually an Invoice action for the reference will occur.*

Property 5: System behaviour should always progress. *The system is free from deadlock.*

Property 6: System behaviour should not get stuck in an internal loop. The need for this property arises because of internal actions in the specifications. These are due to hiding gates (*Withdraw*) or indirectly due to the enabling operator ($\gg$). *The system does not livelock, i.e. there are no cycles of internal actions.*

The six properties were evaluated on the complete LTS models using the XTL model-checker. The models were first minimised using strong equivalence in order to reduce their size. In every case the properties were verified in less than one minute. Properties 1, 2, 3, 5 and 6 are true of all the models. With the introduction of an *Invoice* event to verify property 4, all the properties were shown to hold.

13.4.2.3 Verification using bisimulation

As an alternative to model-checking, verification using bisimulation was also performed using ALDÉBARAN. The goal was to prove that the process-oriented and data-oriented LOTOS specifications of case 2 are equivalent by checking their LTSs. ALDÉBARAN supports several notions of equivalence, ranging from strong bisimulation equivalence (each specification can mimic the other) to safety equivalence (neither specification violates safety properties of the other). The ALDÉBARAN tool was used to check all the possible forms of equivalence. Branching equivalence and observational equivalence cannot be checked since the specifications contain internal events.

It was found that the data-oriented specification is included in the process-oriented one, but not equivalent to it when using safety equivalence. This equivalence does not hold because the process-oriented specifications allow *Cancel* events after *Deposit* events if the order is not yet treated. In the data-oriented specification this cannot occur since the list of orders is immediately updated after each *Deposit* event.

This difference can be removed by not immediately updating the stocks and orders in the data-oriented specification. Instead, an internal event is required before updating can occur. This has the positive effect of making the data-oriented and process-oriented specifications safety equivalent. Unfortunately it also introduces livelock due to continual updating of stocks and orders. Although this violates Property 6, a more complex modification of the specification would avoid livelock.

13.5 Natural language description of the specifications

The following summarises how the two cases have been interpreted in the E-LOTOS and LOTOS specifications.

13.5.1 Case 1

As discussed under Question 1, case 1 is considered to be an abstraction of case 2. Its specifications merely hide (make internal) the actions that *Request* orders, *Cancel* orders, and *Withdraw* products from stock. This applies equally to the LOTOS/E-LOTOS and process-oriented/data-oriented variants.

13.5.2 Case 2

The E-LOTOS variants have separate modules for handling orders and stocks. This cleanly separates the subsidiary operations from the main specification. Modules do not exist in LOTOS, so specifications have to be written in isolation. For E-LOTOS and LOTOS, basic types are defined for an order *Reference*, a *Product* code, a product *Amount*, and an order *Status*. These are used to define the main type for an *Order*

In the process-oriented E-LOTOS specification, *Order* and *Stock* items are represented as processes. A blank *Order* may be filled in by a *Request*. A pending *Order* may be annulled by a *Cancel* or it may *Withdraw* stock. A *Stock* item may accept the *Deposit* of new stock, or may allow an *Order* to *Withdraw* stock. Sets of *Orders* and *Stocks* synchronise on *Withdraw* actions that are hidden from external view. The process-oriented LOTOS specification is broadly similar to its E-LOTOS counterpart, except that the main loop must be specified using explicit process recursion.

In the data-oriented E-LOTOS specification, lists of *Orders* and *Stocks* are maintained as data values rather than as processes. An *Invoice* function is called to allocate pending orders to available stocks. The main behavior simply loops, accepting *Request*, *Cancel* and *Deposit* actions. The data-oriented LOTOS specification is forced to use complex data types that achieve the effect of invoicing. Lists of *Orders* and *Stocks* are specified in data types with auxiliary operations on orders and stock items. The *Updates* type defines operations equivalent to the *Invoice* function. *UpdateOrders* yields the new order list following invoicing, while *UpdateStocks* does the same for the stock list.

13.6 Conclusion

This chapter has shown how E-LOTOS and LOTOS may be used for requirements analysis, formal specification, validation and verification. Through the procedure of formal specification and verification, 25 questions were raised about the informal requirements. This in itself is an indication of the value of applying a formal technique.

The LOTOS approach of black-box specification is useful in obtaining a high-level formalisation of a system. Although LOTOS shares its behavioral approach with other process algebras, LOTOS is relatively unusual in having an integration of behaviour with data specification. This is convenient for specification since different aspects of a problem can be treated as behaviour or data. The process-oriented and data-oriented specifications show that these aspects can be balanced according to the system being specified.

Of the four case 2 descriptions, the authors are most satisfied with the E-LOTOS process-oriented specification. It is clear that E-LOTOS offers a much cleaner and more compact style of specification compared to current LOTOS. In particular, modularity, typed gates and functional data types are felt to be much preferable. The data types used in LOTOS have been rather disliked for the verbosity that is evident from the specifications of the case study. The LOTOS data type library is also somewhat distant from conventional programming practice. Some syntactic LOTOS data typing shorthands have been developed for these reasons [PEC 93].

The process-oriented and data-oriented specifications make an interesting comparison. In E-LOTOS there is little to choose between them regarding clarity or compactness. However, in LOTOS, the data-oriented specification is tedious because of the verbose data part. In general, there are good reasons to prefer the process-oriented approach. It takes an object-based view, and is thus closer to conventional analysis. The approach also hints at possible concurrent or distributed implementation, and so allows a range of realisations.

Verification with CADP supports LOTOS with state-of-the-art techniques. As far as the authors know, CÆSAR and CÆSAR.ADT are the only model checkers that support dynamic data structures. It is useful to have the choice of verification through model-checking or equivalence-checking. Model-checking requires system properties to be explicitly formalised. It is not always obvious what these properties should be, nor whether 'enough' properties have been defined. Nonetheless, formulating system properties is a valuable exercise in its own right. For the case study, the properties highlighted some important issues that might otherwise have been overlooked.

The main difficulty with model checking is state-space explosion. This is, of course, not unique to LOTOS. To generate finite and tractable LTSs it is necessary to modify the original LOTOS specifications. Although these changes are relatively straightforward, they are nonetheless changes. The need to modify data types will disappear with E-LOTOS since this has constructive type definitions. However, it will continue to be necessary to limit the number of parallel processes considered during verification. Despite the restrictions imposed during verification, state-space explosion continued to be a problem. The source of this is the high degree of non-determinism in the process-oriented specifications and the complex data types in the data-oriented specifications. It is hoped that ongoing development of CADP will help to minimise state-space explosion by producing reduced LTSs.

Equivalence checking was relatively straightforward, although a minor change still had to be made in the specifications to prove equivalence. However, this reflects the different ways that the process-oriented and data-oriented specifications were written. The need for a change was thus for modeling rather than theoretical reasons.

Acknowledgements

Thanks are due to the following for carefully reviewing the papers that formed the basis of this chapter: Hubert Garavel (INRIA Rhône-Alpes), Radu Mateescu (INRIA Rhône-Alpes) and Carron Shankland (University of Stirling). Mihaela Sighireanu was employed by INRIA Rhône-Alpes during most of the work reported here.

Bibliography

[BOL 88] BOLOGNESI T., BRINKSMA E., "Introduction to the ISO Specification Language LOTOS", *Computer Networks*, vol. 14, no. 1, p. 25–59, Elsevier Science Publishers, January 1988.

[BOL 95] BOLOGNESI T., VAN DE LAGEMAAT J., VISSERS C. A., Eds., *The LOTOSPHERE Project*, Kluwer Academic Publishers, London, UK, 1995.

[CLA 83] CLARKE E., EMERSON E. A., SISTLA A. P., "Automatic Verification of Finite-State Concurrent Systems using Temporal Logic", in *Proc. 10th Annual Symposium on Principles of Programming Languages*, 1983.

[FER 91] FERNÁNDEZ J.-C., MOUNIER L., "A Tool Set for Deciding Behavioral Equivalences", in *Proc. CONCUR'91*, Amsterdam, Netherlands, August 1991.

[FER 96] FERNÁNDEZ J.-C., GARAVEL H., KERBRAT A., MATEESCU R., MOUNIER L., SIGHIREANU M., "CADP (CÆSAR ALDÉBARAN Development Package): A Protocol Validation and Verification Toolbox", in ALUR R., HENZINGER T. A., Eds., *Proc. 8th. Conference on Computer-Aided Verification*, no. 1102, Lecture Notes in Computer Science, p. 437–440, Springer, Berlin, Germany, August 1996.

[GAR 89] GARAVEL H., "Compilation of LOTOS Abstract Data Types", in VUONG S. T., Ed., *Proc. Formal Description Techniques II*, North-Holland, Amsterdam, Netherlands, December 1989.

[ISO 89] ISO/IEC, *Information Processing Systems – Open Systems Interconnection – LOTOS – A Formal Description Technique based on the Temporal Ordering of Observational Behaviour*, ISO/IEC 8807, International Organization for Standardization, Geneva, Switzerland, 1989.

[ISO 01] ISO/IEC, *Information Processing Systems – Open Systems Interconnection – Enhanced LOTOS – A Formal Description Technique based on the Temporal Ordering of Observational Behaviour*, ISO/IEC 15437, International Organization for Standardization, Geneva, Switzerland, 2001.

[LED 87] LEDUC G. J., "The Intertwining of Data Types and Processes in LOTOS", in RUDIN H., WEST C. H., Eds., *Proc. Protocol Specification, Testing and Verification VII*, p. 123–136, North-Holland, Amsterdam, Netherlands, May 1987.

[MIL 89] MILNER A. J. R. G., *Communication and Concurrency*, Addison-Wesley, Reading, Massachusetts, USA, 1989.

[PEC 93] PECHEUR C., "Vlib: Infinite Virtual Libraries for LOTOS", in DANTHINE A. A. S., LEDUC G., WOLPER P., Eds., *Proc. Protocol Specification, Testing and Verification XIII*, p. 29–44, North-Holland, Amsterdam, Netherlands, May 1993.

[SCO 93] SCOLLO G., On the Engineering of Logics, PhD thesis, Department of Informatics, University of Twente, Enschede, Netherlands, March 1993.

[SIG 98] SIGHIREANU M., TURNER K. J., Requirement Capture, Formal Description and Verification of an Invoicing System, Report no. RR-3575, Institut National de Recherche en Informatique et Automatique, Le Chesnay, France, December 1998.

[TUR 90] TURNER K. J., "A LOTOS-Based Development Strategy", in VUONG S. T., Ed., *Proc. Formal Description Techniques II*, p. 157–174, North-Holland, Amsterdam, Netherlands, 1990, Invited paper.

[TUR 93] TURNER K. J., Ed., *Using Formal Description Techniques – An Introduction to ESTELLE, LOTOS and SDL*, Wiley, New York, January 1993.

[TUR 97] TURNER K. J., "Specification Architecture illustrated in a Communications Context", *Computer Networks*, vol. 29, no. 4, p. 397–411, Elsevier Science Publishers, March 1997.

[TUR 00] TURNER K. J., "World-wide Environment for Learning LOTOS", June 2000, http://www.cs.stir.ac.uk/well/.

[VAS 05] VASY TEAM, "CADP (CAESAR/ALDÉBARAN Development Package): A Software Engineering Toolbox for Protocols and Distributed Systems", June 2005 http://www.inrialpes.fr/vasy/cadp/.

Chapter 14

EB^3

Frédéric GERVAIS, Marc FRAPPIER and Richard ST-DENIS

14.1 Introduction

EB^3 (entity-based black box) [FRA 03] is a formal language specially created for specifying information systems (IS). EB^3 is inspired from the JSD (Jackson system development) [CAM 89, JAC 83] method and from the black box concept of Cleanroom [MIL 86, PRO 99]. A *black box* is a function from sequences of inputs to outputs.

The JSD process is decomposed into the following phases: i) entity action; ii) entity structure; iii) initial model; iv) function; v) system timing; and vi) implementation. The first two steps, in which entities are identified and the valid sequences of actions for each entity are defined, are of interest for Cleanroom black boxes. JSD entities are indeed specified using an *entity structure diagram*, which is essentially the abstract syntax tree of a regular expression.

In EB^3, an extension of JSD's entity structure diagram, constructed using a process algebra inspired from CSP [HOA 85], CCS [MIL 89] and LOTOS [BOL 87], is used to specify IS entities as Cleanroom's black boxes. An IS entity can be considered as an object of the IS. Hence, the terms *entity type* and *entity* are used in EB^3 instead of class and object. Thus, the core of EB^3 includes a process and a formal notation to describe a complete and precise specification of the input-output behavior of IS. An EB^3 specification consists of the following elements:

1. a user requirements class diagram which includes entity types, associations, and their respective actions and attributes. These diagrams are based on entity-relationship model concepts [ELM 04];
2. a process expression, denoted by $main$, which defines the valid input traces;
3. input-output rules, which assign an output to each valid input trace;

4. recursive functions, defined on the valid input traces of $main$, that assign values to entity and association attributes.

The denotational semantics of an EB^3 specification is given by a relation R defined on $\mathcal{T}(main) \times O$, where $\mathcal{T}(main)$ denotes the finite traces accepted by process $main$ and O is the set of output events. Let t denote the system trace, which is a list of the *valid* input events accepted so far in the execution of the system. Let $t :: \sigma$ denote the right append of an input event σ to trace t, and let [] denote the empty trace. The operational behavior is defined as follows:

$t :=$ [];
forever do
  receive input event σ;
  if $main$ can accept $t :: \sigma$ **then**
    $t := t :: \sigma$;
    send output event o such that $(t, o) \in R$;
  else
    send error message;

A complete description of EB^3 can be found in [FRA 03].

14.2 Analysis and specification of case 1

In case 1, the problem has been reduced to its bare essentials in the sense that action Invoice_Order is described without any reference to a business domain. Case 1 is essentially a state-based description. It refers to the status of an order, which must be changed from "pending" to "invoiced". Consequently, it would be better described by a state box in Cleanroom than by a black box in EB^3. A *state box* is a transition function from inputs and states to outputs and states. Contrary to black boxes, the output depends on the last input only in a state box. A black box can be refined into a state box, since it abstracts from states by using the history of inputs to determine the output. However, EB^3 is based on black box specification; hence, a solution is given in this section in terms of a black box.

14.2.1 Entity types and actions

The first two questions are closely related because answers to one can hold the answer to the other and vice versa. Indeed, a problem can be tackled by using different strategies: one in which emphasis is placed on entities, one in which emphasis is placed on actions, or one that is a mix of the two. An *action* in EB^3 is an atomic operation of the system.

Question 1: What are the actions performed by the system?

Answer: The only action identified from case 1 is Invoice_Order.

Question 2: What is the entity type that performs this action?

Answer: The entity type that performs action Invoice_Order is order.

The answers to the two previous questions establish the boundary of the software system. The next question concerns action Invoice_Order.

Question 3: What is the signature of this action?

Answer: The *signature* of an action consists of the declaration of its input and of its output parameters, along with their respective types. The signature of action Invoice_Order is the following:

$$\text{Invoice\_Order}(oId : ORDERID, items : ITEMS,$$
$$status : STATUS, stock : STOCK) : (msg : STRING)$$

This action has four input parameters and one output. Obviously, input parameter oId, whose type is $ORDERID$, is the order to invoice. $ORDERID$ is the given set (i.e. the set of all the existing and possible entities) of orders. Since the stock and the set of orders are always known in case 1, we have chosen to give the list of referenced products, the status of the order and the list of stocked products as input parameters of action Invoice_Order. Input parameters $items$ and $stock$ represent the set of referenced products and the current state of the stock, respectively. Their types are defined as follows:

$$ITEMS \triangleq PRODUCTID \nrightarrow NAT$$
$$STOCK \triangleq PRODUCTID \rightarrow NAT$$

where $PRODUCTID$ is the set of all the existing products. In $items$, each referenced product of the order is associated with the ordered quantity; hence an element of type $ITEMS$ is a partial function ($\nrightarrow$) from $PRODUCTID$ to the set of naturals (NAT). In parameter $stock$, each product is associated with its quantity in stock. Thus, each element of type $STOCK$ is a total function ($\rightarrow$) from $PRODUCTID$ to NAT. The type of input parameter $status$ is defined by the following enumerated set: $STATUS = \{$"pending", "invoiced"$\}$. We note that parameters $items$ and $status$ depend on order oId.

The only output of the action is a confirmation message msg. The reason behind this decision is essentially to introduce some aspects of EB^3 to the reader earlier because action Invoice_Order is an update action that normally has no output (denoted by special type $void$ in EB^3).

14.2.2 Process expressions

Question 4: What is the behavior of entity type order?

Answer: The behavior of an entity type is specified in EB^3 by a process expression using a process algebra adapted to IS. The process expression for entity type order is defined as follows:

$$
\begin{array}{l}
\mathsf{order}(oId : ORDERID) \triangleq \\
\quad |\ items, status, stock\ :\ ITEMS, STATUS, STOCK\ : \\
\quad\quad status = \text{“pending”} \wedge \\
\quad\quad \exists pId \in dom(items) : items(pId) > 0 \wedge \\
\quad\quad \forall pId \in dom(items) : items(pId) \leq stock(pId) \\
\quad\quad \Rightarrow \\
\quad\quad \mathsf{Invoice\_Order}(oId, items, status, stock)
\end{array}
$$

The quantified ($|\ items, status, stock : ...$) choice denotes that a value for each of the variables $items$, $status$ and $stock$ is chosen among $ITEMS$, $STATUS$ and $STOCK$, respectively. In EB^3, there are no free variables in a process expression; hence, the model of this specification must be closed and the quantified choice represents a user choice for the input parameters $items$, $status$ and $stock$ of action Invoice_Order.

A valid input trace for entity type order is a trace in which every invoice action refers to an order that includes at least one ordered product. In other words, there exists at least one product such that its associated quantity is greater than zero. Moreover, the status of the order must be “pending” and the ordered quantity of each product is either less than or equal to the quantity in stock. These constraints are specified by the predicate before the symbol “$\Rightarrow$”, which represents the guard of action Invoice_Order. The action can be executed only if the guard is satisfied.

Question 5: What is the behavior of the system?

Answer: In case 1, we do not need to specify the behavior of the whole system. We just know that several orders can exist together. The main process expression is therefore defined as follows:

$$main \triangleq (\ |||\ oId : ORDERID : \mathsf{order}(oId)^*\ )$$

Quantified interleaving ($|||$) denotes that several entities of type order exist at the same time. The Kleene closure (*) denotes that the process expression for order will be executed an arbitrary number of times for each order oId.

14.2.3 Input-output rules

Question 6: What is the output of action Invoice_Order?

Answer: A message “Order xxx invoiced” is displayed.

This is formally translated in the following input-output rule:

RULE R1
INPUT Invoice_Order$(oId, items, status, stock)$
OUTPUT "Order" $\cdot$ oId $\cdot$ "invoiced"
END

where "$\cdot$" denotes the concatenation of strings. By this input-output rule, whenever action Invoice_Order is accepted as a valid input event by process $main$, then the expression in clause OUTPUT is evaluated and output by the system.

A legitimate question that could be raised is "What is the output for an input trace that does not satisfy the global behavior described by process $main$?". Then, following the operational semantics of EB^3 (see section 14.1), the system generates an error message to notify the user.

14.3 Analysis and specification of case 2

Contrary to case 1, the problem now takes the entries of orders and of new quantities of products in stock into account. Hence, action Invoice_Order can be described in relation to a business model of the software system.

14.3.1 Entity types, associations and actions

The first task is to determine the user requirements class diagram of the software system. Essentially, case 2 raises the same questions as case 1, but they are repeated for each entity, action, and attribute.

Question 7: What are the actions performed by the system?

Answer: In addition to Invoice_Order, several other actions are required. According to the requirements of case 2, at least four new actions must be defined. Two new actions are introduced to create and cancel orders: Create_Order and Cancel_Order. Moreover, an action is required to display the list of orders: DisplayListOrders. A new action is also defined to add new quantities of products in stock: Add_Stock.

Question 8: What are the entity types of the system?

Answer: By analyzing the actions performed by the system, we deduce at least two entity types: order and product.

The actions performed by entity type order are the following ones: Create_Order, Cancel_Order, Invoice_Order and DisplayListOrders. Entity type product represents the products in stock and performs action Add_Stock. We note that Invoice_Order can be considered as the consumer of an order and/or the producer of an invoice; hence, a third entity type invoice could be defined. In this chapter, we consider only entity types order and product.

Question 9: What are the associations of the system?

Answer: Only one association is determined. Since products in stock can be referenced by orders, a binary association reference is defined between entity types order and product.

Question 10: What is the cardinality of the association?

Answer: This question exhibits an ambiguity in the case study. Indeed, item 3 of the case study states that: "On one order, we have one and one only reference to a certain quantity of an ordered product". However, two meanings are possible: either an order contains only one reference; or it can contain several references, but a product can appear at most once in the set of references. By analyzing case 1, this ambiguity has not been detected, because action Invoice_Order is described without any reference to a business model of the software system. Hence, the second option has been implicitly taken in the specification of case 1 (see section 14.2.1). For case 2, if the first option is chosen, then reference is a $1..N$ association, with product at the 1 side; otherwise, it is an $M..N$ association. In the first case, each order can reference only one product, while many products can be referenced in the second case. In both cases, a product appears at most once in an order, since the entities of reference are distinct. As in case 1, we consider the second option for case 2.

Question 11: What are the actions of the association?

Answer: Three new actions are introduced to add, modify and remove references: Add_Reference, Modify_Reference and Remove_Reference.

Question 12: What are the signatures of the actions?

Answer: The signatures are:

Create_Order($oId : ORDERID$) : $void$
Cancel_Order($oId : ORDERID$) : $void$
Invoice_Order($oId : ORDERID$) : $void$
DisplayListOrders($void$) : $(msg : (ORDERID \times STATUS)^*)$
Add_Stock($pId : PRODUCTID, qty : NAT$) : $void$
Add_Reference($oId : ORDERID, pId : PRODUCTID, qty : NAT$)
  : $void$
Modify_Reference($oId : ORDERID, pId : PRODUCTID, qty : NAT$)
  : $void$
Remove_Reference($oId : ORDERID, pId : PRODUCTID$) : $void$

The first four actions are performed on entity type order. We note that the signature of action Invoice_Order is not the same as in case 1. It no longer includes the list of referenced products, the order status and the state of the stock. It depends only on order oId. Action Add_Stock adds a quantity qty of product pId in stock. The last

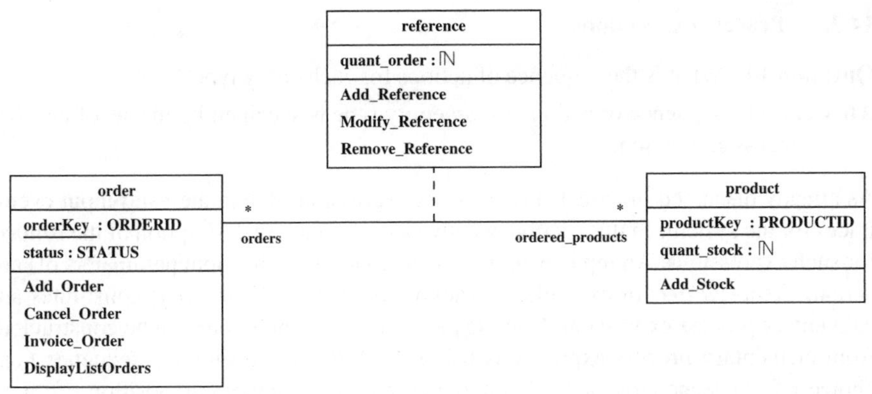

Figure 14.1: User requirements class diagram for case 2

three actions are performed on association reference; they require both order oId and the referenced product pId as input parameters. The only action that has an output is DisplayListOrders which returns the list of order identifiers and their associated status. In the type of output parameter msg, the symbol "*" denotes a list of elements; in that case, the elements are from type $ORDERID \times STATUS$.

Question 13: What are the attributes of the entity types and associations?

Answer: The attributes that are relevant for case 2 are the following ones. A *key* must be identified for each entity type and association. As usual, a key uniquely identifies an entity. The following keys are defined for the entity types: attribute $orderKey$ for entity type order and attribute $productKey$ for entity type product. The key of association reference is composed of two attributes: $(orderKey, productKey)$. In entity type order, we define non-key attribute $status$ that represents the status of the order. In entity type product, the quantity of products in stock is represented by attribute $quant\_stock$. In association reference, the quantity ordered for the referenced product is defined by non-key attribute $quant\_order$.

Hence, the user requirements class diagram of the software system has been determined for case 2. It is shown in Figure 14.1. As discussed in Question 10, reference is an $M..N$ association, denoted by symbol "$*$" at each side of the association. We note that reference involves two roles: $orders$ for entity order and $ordered\_products$ for product.

14.3.2 Process expressions

Question 14: What is the sequence of actions for each entity type?

Answer: The sequence of actions for an entity type is specified by means of an EB^3 process expression.

As already discussed in case 1, EB^3 process expressions define the valid input event traces for the system. In this section, we give a more detailed description of the syntax for such expressions. An input event is an instantiation of (the input parameters of) an action, Create_Order for example. An action like Create_Order(oId) constitutes an elementary process expression. Complex EB^3 process expressions can be constructed from elementary process expressions using the following operators: sequence (.), choice (|), Kleene closure (*), interleaving (|||), parallel composition (||, i.e. CSP's synchronization on shared actions), guard ($\Rightarrow$), process call, and quantification of choice ($|x : T : ...$) and of interleaving ($|||x : T : ...$). The complete syntax of EB^3 process expressions can be found in [FRA 03].

The EB^3 process expression for entity type order is:

$$
\begin{array}{l}
\mathsf{order}(oId : ORDERID) \triangleq \\
\quad \mathsf{Create\_Order}(oId)\ . \\
\quad (\ |||\ pId : PRODUCTID : \mathsf{reference}(oId, pId)^{\star}\ )\ . \\
\quad (\\
\qquad (\\
\qquad\quad (\exists pId \in productKey(t) : ((oId, pId) \in referenceKey(t) \\
\qquad\qquad \wedge\ quant\_order(t, oId, pId) > 0) \wedge \\
\qquad\quad \forall pId \in productKey(t) : (oId, pId) \in referenceKey(t) \\
\qquad\qquad \Rightarrow quant\_order(t, oId, pId) \leq quant\_stock(t, pId)\ ) \\
\qquad\quad \Rightarrow \\
\qquad\quad \mathsf{Invoice\_Order}(oId) \\
\qquad) \\
\quad | \\
\qquad \mathsf{Cancel\_Order}(oId) \\
\quad)
\end{array}
$$

where t denotes the current trace of the software system. A valid input sequence for an order oId first consists of the creation of the order (Create_Order). Then, zero or several products can be referenced in the order. Indeed, process expression "$|||\ pId : PRODUCTID : ...$" means that the process expression for association reference, which will be defined later in the chapter, is a valid sequence of actions for each of the product in $PRODUCTID$. The Kleene closure on process reference implies that each product can be referenced, but it is not required. Moreover, the process expression reference will prevent a product being referenced more than once (see the next question). In our solution, the input event trace for an order ends either when action Invoice_Order can be executed, or if the order is cancelled. An order can be invoiced if there exists at least one referenced product whose ordered quantity is greater than zero and if all the referenced products are available in stock. Action Invoice_Order is then guarded by a predicate that formalizes these conditions. The expression $referenceKey$ denotes the key of association reference. We recall that $status$, $quant\_order$ and $quant\_stock$ are attributes of the system. Their definition will be given in section 14.3.4.

The process expression for entity type product is:

$$\begin{array}{l} \mathsf{product}(pId : PRODUCTID) \triangleq \\ \qquad (\ ||| \ oId : ORDERID : \mathsf{reference}(oId, pId)^\star) \\ \quad ||| \\ \qquad \mathsf{Add\_Stock}(pId, \_)^\star \end{array}$$

We suppose that all the products already exist in entity type product, but their quantity is set to zero if they are not available. We recall that action Add_Stock adds a new quantity of a product in stock. In the process expression, the special symbol "_" is used as an actual parameter of an action to denote an arbitrary value of the corresponding type. For a particular product pId, either it is referenced in an order, or a new quantity is added. The quantified interleaving on oId allows one product to be referenced by several orders.

Question 15: What is the sequence of actions for the association?

Answer: The EB^3 process expression for reference is:

$$\begin{array}{l} \mathsf{reference}(oId : ORDERID, pId : PRODUCTID) \triangleq \\ \quad pId \notin ordered\_products(t, oId) \Rightarrow \mathsf{Add\_Reference}(oId, pId, \_) \ . \\ \quad \mathsf{Modify\_Reference}(oId, pId, \_)^\star \ . \\ \quad (\ \lambda \mid \mathsf{Remove\_Reference}(oId, pId)) \end{array}$$

Once a reference is added, it can be modified until it is removed. The symbol "λ" denotes the action that does nothing. Here it corresponds to the end of the process when the order is invoiced. By the guard on action Add_Reference, a product is referenced at most once in an order.

Question 16: What is the global behavior of the system?

Answer: The main process expression is:

$$\begin{array}{l} main \triangleq \\ \qquad (\ |||oId : ORDERID : \mathsf{order}(oId)^\star\ ) \\ \quad || \\ \qquad (\ |||pId : PRODUCTID : \mathsf{product}(pId)^\star\ ) \\ \quad ||| \\ \qquad \mathsf{DisplayListOrders}^\star \end{array}$$

14.3.3 Input-output rules

Question 17: What is the output of action DisplayListOrders?
Answer: A list of the order identifiers associated with their status is displayed.

We recall that an input-output rule has two clauses, INPUT and OUTPUT, and that the expression in clause OUTPUT is evaluated whenever the action in clause INPUT is accepted as a valid input event by process $main$. The output of an input-output rule is specified either by a recursive function or by an SQL statement of the form SELECT FROM WHERE. Thus, there are two ways to specify the input-output rule for action DisplayListOrders. By using a recursive function, the rule is of the following form:

```
RULE R2
INPUT DisplayListOrders()
OUTPUT listOrders(t)
END
```

where $listOrders$ is a recursive function on the trace that evaluates the list and t is the current trace of the software system (i.e. the list of the valid input events accepted so far by the system). This function will be defined in section 14.3.4.

When the action output consists of a list of attribute values, then a SELECT statement can be used to specify the output. Indeed, an action like DisplayListOrders corresponds to the query of attribute values in the system; hence, the definition of a recursive function such as $listOrders$ can be redundant with respect to the attribute definitions. By using an SQL statement, the definition of the input-output rule is simplified and the SELECT statement can be directly used to query the database represented by the EB^3 attribute definitions:

```
RULE R2'
INPUT DisplayListOrders()
OUTPUT
    SELECT orderKey, status
    FROM order;
END
```

In the remainder of the chapter, we consider rule R2 in order to illustrate the specification of a recursive function distinct from the attribute definitions. We note that function $listOrders$ must be defined such that R2 and R2' are equivalent. R2 is the unique input-output rule defined for case 2, since only action DisplayListOrders provides an output.

14.3.4 Attribute definitions

Question 18: How are the attribute values evaluated?
Answer: In EB^3, recursive functions on the valid traces of the system are defined for each key and for each non-key attribute to evaluate their values.

The functions are total and are given in a functional style, as in CAML [COU 98]. They output the attribute values that are valid for the state in which the system is, after having executed the input events in the trace. A key definition outputs a set of key values, while a non-key attribute definition outputs the attribute value for a key value given as an input parameter. The complete syntax of attribute definitions can be found in [GER 05b].

The key definition of entity type order is of the following form:

$$
\begin{array}{l}
orderKey(t : \mathcal{T}(main)) : \mathbb{F}(ORDERID) \triangleq \\
\quad \textbf{match } last(t) \textbf{ with} \\
\qquad \perp : \emptyset, \\
\qquad \mathsf{Create\_Order}(oId) : orderKey(front(t)) \cup \{oId\}, \\
\qquad \mathsf{Cancel\_Order}(oId) : orderKey(front(t)) \; - \; \{oId\}, \\
\qquad \_ : orderKey(front(t));
\end{array}
$$

where expression $\mathbb{F}(ORDERID)$ denotes the set of finite subsets of $ORDERID$. Standard list operators are used, such as *last* and *front* which respectively return the last element and all but the last element of a list; they return the special value "$\perp$" when the list is empty. Expressions of the form $input \, : \, expr$, where $input$ can be "$\perp$", "_" or an instantiation of action, are called the *input clauses* of the function. EB^3 attribute definitions always include "$\perp$", that matches with the empty trace, to represent undefinedness. Moreover, any reference to an attribute $attr$ in the definition is always of the form $attr(front(t), ...)$. In the remainder of the chapter, expression $front(t)$ is omitted for the sake of concision. For instance, expressions $orderKey()$ and $status(oId)$ stand for $orderKey(front(t))$ and $status(front(t), oId)$, respectively.

When an attribute definition is executed, then all the input clauses of the attribute definition are analyzed, and the first pattern that holds is the one executed. Hence, the ordering of the input clauses is important. The pattern matching analysis always involves the last input event of trace t. If one of the expressions $input$ matches with $last(t)$, then the corresponding expression $expr$ is computed; otherwise, the function is recursively called with $front(t)$, that is, t truncated by removing its last element. This case corresponds to the last input clause with symbol "_".

The other key definitions for case 2 are:

$$
\begin{array}{l}
productKey(t : \mathcal{T}(main)) : \mathbb{F}(PRODUCTID) \triangleq \\
\quad \textbf{match } last(t) \textbf{ with} \\
\qquad \perp : PRODUCTID, \\
\qquad \_ : productKey();
\end{array}
$$

$$
\begin{array}{l}
referenceKey(t : \mathcal{T}(main)) : \mathbb{F}(ORDERID \times PRODUCTID) \triangleq \\
\quad \textbf{match } last(t) \textbf{ with} \\
\qquad \perp : \emptyset, \\
\qquad \mathsf{Add\_Reference}(oId, pId, \_) : referenceKey() \cup \{(oId, pId)\},
\end{array}
$$

$$\begin{aligned}&\mathsf{Remove\_Reference}(oId, pId) : referenceKey() - \{(oId, pId)\},\\&\mathsf{Cancel\_Order}(oId) : referenceKey() -\\&\quad\{(oId, pId) \mid pId \in ordered\_products(oId)\},\\&\_ : referenceKey();\end{aligned}$$

We note that for the input clause Cancel_Order in key definition $referenceKey$, the evaluation of the key values depends on the role $ordered\_products$. Hence, each referenced product in order oId is removed from association reference. The roles of this association are defined in EB^3 as abbreviations of the following form:

$$\begin{aligned}&orders(t : \mathcal{T}(main), pId : PRODUCTID) \triangleq\\&\quad\{oId \in orderKey(t) \mid (oId, pId) \in referenceKey(t)\}\\&ordered\_products(t : \mathcal{T}(main), oId : ORDERID) \triangleq\\&\quad\{pId \in productKey(t) \mid (oId, pId) \in referenceKey(t)\}\end{aligned}$$

Non-key attribute definitions output the attribute values for the key values given as input parameters. For instance, non-key attribute $status$ is defined in EB^3 in the following way:

$$\begin{aligned}&status(t : \mathcal{T}(main), oId : ORDERID) : STATUS \triangleq\\&\quad\mathbf{match}\ last(t)\ \mathbf{with}\\&\qquad\bot : \bot,\\&\qquad\mathsf{Create\_Order}(oId) : \text{“pending”},\\&\qquad\mathsf{Invoice\_Order}(oId) : \text{“invoiced”},\\&\qquad\mathsf{Cancel\_Order}(oId) : \bot,\\&\qquad\_ : status(oId);\end{aligned}$$

This recursive function returns the status of order entity oId. In particular, the status is undefined (denoted by symbol "$\bot$") if the order has been cancelled. We note that since the status of a new order is set to "pending" and that it is not changed to "invoiced" until action Invoice_Order is executed, then it is not required to specify as in case 1 predicate $status =$ "pending" as a guard of action Invoice_Order in the process expression of order.

The other non-key attribute definitions for case 2 are:

$$\begin{aligned}&quant\_order(t : \mathcal{T}(main), oId : ORDERID, pId : PRODUCTID) : \mathbb{N}^{\star}\\&\triangleq\\&\quad\mathbf{match}\ last(t)\ \mathbf{with}\\&\qquad\bot : \bot,\\&\qquad\mathsf{Add\_Reference}(oId, pId, qty) : qty,\\&\qquad\mathsf{Modify\_Reference}(oId, pId, qty) : qty,\\&\qquad\mathsf{Remove\_Reference}(oId, pId) : \bot,\\&\qquad\mathsf{Cancel\_Order}(oId) : \mathbf{if}\ pId \in ordered\_products(oId)\\&\qquad\qquad\qquad\qquad\quad\mathbf{then}\ \bot\\&\qquad\qquad\qquad\qquad\quad\mathbf{end},\end{aligned}$$

$\_ : quant\_order(oId, pId);$

$$
\begin{array}{l}
quant\_stock(t : \mathcal{T}(main), pId : PRODUCTID) : \mathbb{N} \triangleq \\
\quad \textbf{match } last(t) \textbf{ with} \\
\quad\quad \bot : 0, \\
\quad\quad \mathsf{Add\_Stock}(pId, qty) : quant\_stock(pId) + qty, \\
\quad\quad \mathsf{Invoice\_Order}(oId) : \textbf{if } pId \in ordered\_products(oId) \\
\quad\quad\quad\quad \textbf{then } quant\_stock(pId) - quant\_order(oId, pId) \\
\quad\quad\quad\quad \textbf{end}, \\
\quad\quad \_ : quant\_stock(pId);
\end{array}
$$

We note that conditional terms of the form **if then end** are used when several key values to delete, update or insert are concerned. For instance, when order oId is invoiced by action Invoice_Order, then for each referenced product in the order, the ordered quantity is removed from its quantity in stock (see attribute $quant\_stock$).

Question 19: How is the output of action DisplayListOrders evaluated?

Answer: An additional recursive function with the same general form as those of the attribute definitions is required to evaluate the list of orders and their associated status:

$$
\begin{array}{l}
listOrders(t : \mathcal{T}(main)) : (ORDERID \times STATUS)^{\star} \triangleq \\
\quad \textbf{match } last(t) \textbf{ with} \\
\quad\quad \bot : [], \\
\quad\quad \mathsf{Create\_Order}(oId) : listOrders() :: (oId, \text{“pending”}), \\
\quad\quad \mathsf{Invoice\_Order}(oId) : listOrders() \\
\quad\quad\quad\quad - (oId, status(oId)) :: (oId, \text{“invoiced”}), \\
\quad\quad \mathsf{Cancel\_Order}(oId) : listOrders() \; - \; (oId, status(oId)), \\
\quad\quad \_ : listOrders();
\end{array}
$$

where symbol “–” denotes the removal of an element from a list, while symbol “::” represents the concatenation of an element to a list. This function is used in rule R2 (see section 14.3.3).

14.4 The natural language description of the specification

14.4.1 Case 1

The system provides only one action, Invoice_Order. This action accepts as input an order, the list of referenced products in the order, the status of the order and the current state of the stock. In the list, each product identifier is associated with an ordered quantity. The status of an order is either “pending” or “invoiced”. The stock associates a quantity in stock with each product identifier. This action produces an output message of the form “Order xxx invoiced”, when the next three conditions are satisfied: i) the order status is "pending"; ii) the quantity in stock is greater than the ordered quantity, for each reference in the order; and iii) at least one referenced product has an ordered quantity greater than zero. The action can be successfully invoked only once for each order.

14.4.2 Case 2

The system provides eight actions. An action allows a new quantity of product to be added in the stock. Two other actions allow orders to be created or cancelled. References to an order may be added, modified or removed. A product appears at most once in an order. An order may be invoiced if the next two conditions are satisfied: i) it contains at least one referenced product; and ii) there is enough stock for each referenced product. When an order is invoiced, references can no longer be added, modified or removed. The quantity in stock for a product is increased by action Add_Stock. Action Invoice_Order decreases the stock for each reference to the order. The quantity in stock must never be negative. Finally, a query action provides status information about orders.

14.5 Conclusion

EB^3 is a trace-based formal language created for the specification of information systems. The behavior of the entities of the system is specified by means of process expressions. EB^3 differs from the other process algebraic languages by the following characteristics. First of all, EB^3 is inspired from Cleanroom; hence, the specification of the inputs and of the outputs of the system is divided in two parts. The semantics of EB^3 is a trace-based semantics. Process expressions represent the valid input traces of the IS, while outputs are computed from valid traces. The syntax of process expressions has been simplified and adapted to IS with respect to other process algebraic languages like CSP [HOA 85]. In particular, EB^3 process expressions are close to regular expressions, with the use of the sequence operator and the Kleene closure. Attributes, linked to entities and associations of an IS, are computed in EB^3 by recursive functions on the valid traces of the system.

The APIS project [FRA 02b] aims at synthesizing IS from EB^3 specifications. There exists an interpreter, called EB3PAI [FRA 02a], for interpreting EB^3 process expressions. Moreover, an algorithm has been developed in order to generate relational database transactions that correspond to EB^3 actions from the input-output rules and the EB^3 attribute definitions [GER 05a]. The objective of the project is to efficiently interpret EB^3 specifications for the purpose of software prototyping and requirements validation.

Concerning the case study, the black box approach adopted in EB^3 is less suitable for case 1, because the problem is stated at a lower level of abstraction. It refers to the internal system state (i.e. the order status); hence, it is essentially a state box problem. To model case 1 with a black box, the system state has to be included both as an input and output parameter of the action Invoice_Order. Moreover, the output of the invoice action depends only on the last input; the history of inputs is not used at all. EB^3 is more suitable for case 2, because the behavior of each action can be described in terms of the input history. The list of referenced products in an order is then represented by a binary association between the orders and the products in stock. Moreover, the status of the order and the current state of the stock, which are specified as attributes of the software system, are evaluated by means of recursive functions defined on EB^3 traces. In particular, attribute definitions are used in the guards of the EB^3 process expressions to constrain the sequences of valid input events of the system.

Bibliography

[BOL 87] BOLOGNESI T., BRINKSMA E., "Introduction to the ISO Specification Language LOTOS", *Computer Networks and ISDN Systems*, vol. 14, no. 1, p. 25–59, 1987.

[CAM 89] CAMERON J., *JSP and JSD: The Jackson Approach to Software Development*, IEEE Computer Society Press, 2nd edition, 1989.

[COU 98] COUSINEAU G., MAUNY M., *The Functional Approach to Programming*, Cambridge University Press, Cambridge, 1998.

[ELM 04] ELMASRI R., NAVATHE S., *Fundamentals of Database Systems*, Addison-Wesley, 4th edition, 2004.

[FRA 02a] FRAIKIN B., FRAPPIER M., "EB3PAI: an Interpreter for the EB^3 Specification Language", in *15th Intern. Conf. on Software and Systems Engineering and their Applications (ICSSEA 2002)*, Paris, France, CMSL, 3-5 December 2002.

[FRA 02b] FRAPPIER M., FRAIKIN B., LALEAU R., RICHARD M., "APIS – Automatic Production of Information Systems", in *AAAI Spring Symposium*, Stanford, USA, AAAI Press, p. 17–24, 25-27 March 2002.

[FRA 03] FRAPPIER M., ST-DENIS R., "EB^3: an Entity-Based Black-Box Specification Method for Information Systems", *Software and Systems Modeling*, vol. 2, no. 2, p. 134–149, 2003.

[GER 05a] GERVAIS F., FRAPPIER M., LALEAU R., "Generating Relational Database Transactions From Recursive Functions Defined on EB^3 Traces", in *3rd IEEE International Conference on Software Engineering and Formal Methods (SEFM 2005)*, Koblenz, Germany, IEEE Computer Society Press, p. 117–126, 7-9 September 2005.

[GER 05b] GERVAIS F., FRAPPIER M., LALEAU R., BATANADO P., EB^3 Attribute Definitions: Formal Language and Application, Report no. 700, CEDRIC, Paris, France, 2005.

[HOA 85] HOARE C., *Communicating Sequential Processes*, Prentice-Hall International, 1985.

[JAC 83] JACKSON M., *System Development*, Prentice-Hall International, 1983.

[MIL 86] MILLS H., LINGER R., HEVNER A., *Principles of Information Systems Analysis and Design*, Academic Press, Orlando, FL, 1986.

[MIL 89] MILNER R., *Communication and Concurrency*, Prentice-Hall International, 1989.

[PRO 99] PROWELL S., TRAMMELL C., LINGER R., POORE J., *Cleanroom Software Engineering: Technology and Process*, Addison-Wesley, 1999.

Part III

Other Formal Approaches

Chapter 15

CASL

Hubert BAUMEISTER and Didier BERT

15.1 Overview of the CASL notation

The acronym CASL stands for *Common Algebraic Specification Language* [CAS 04a, CAS 04b]. It is a language designed by the IFIP WG1.3[1] working group to provide a unified notation for writing algebraic specifications. For an easy introduction to the language see [MOS 99]. Case studies written in CASL are available on the web[2].

Two main principles underlie the algebraic specification technology. The first one is *representation independence*. This means that data representation is not known and does not need to be known early in the specification process. Fixing actual implementation of data is deferred as much as possible. This was made popular by the *abstract data type* paradigm. All the data defined in the algebraic formalism are "abstract" in that sense. The second principle is a consequence of the previous one. Because representation is not given the only way to use data values is to provide *sets of operations* on these data. By way of illustration, the data type integer, available in usual programming languages, is an example of an abstract data type. Its values are accessible only via constants $(0, 1, \ldots)$ and operations $(+, \times, \ldots)$. Data abstractly defined with functional operations are called *algebras* in mathematics, which explains the word "algebraic" in the formalism name. For the underlying theory of algebraic specification, one can see [EHR 85, BER 89, WIR 90]. For examples of applications, see [VAN 89] among others.

A simple algebraic specification contains a part called the *signature* where new names are declared. The names can be data names, called *sorts*, operation and predicate names. Operation and predicate names are declared together with a *profile* which

[1] Foundations of System Specification, URL: www.fiadeiro.org/jose/IFIP-WG1.3/.

[2] CASL Case Studies, URL: www.pst.informatik.uni-muenchen.de/~baumeist/CoFI/case.html.

indicates the expected sorts of arguments and, for the operations, the sort of the result. So a signature provides a way to form expressions, also called *terms*, by combining operations, constants and variables. Terms are *well-formed* if the sorts of the arguments are compatible with the profiles of the operations. All the well-formed terms denote "values" of a given sort. The CASL language also admits declaration of subsorts to characterize subsets of values.

Once a "discourse domain" is defined through a signature, one can declare *properties* on it. Properties are expressed in a standard logic formalism very close to the Z or B specification notation. They are introduced in a specification by declarations of *axioms*.

In CASL specifications may be *structured*, that is, built by using structuring primitives. This provides a very powerful mechanism to reuse specification modules and to adapt old specifications in order to match with new requirements. The main structuring primitives are renaming, hiding, union and extension. Specifications can also be generic, that is, parameterised by other specifications. Thus, new specifications can be built by instantiating generic specifications. Semantic relations between specifications are achieved by declarations of *views*. However, it has been noticed that structuring choices at the specification level does not always yield a good structure at the program level. So the CASL language provides primitives to build *architectural specifications* which are intended to reflect the program structure.

To conclude this overview, note that CASL is a *property-oriented* specification language. That means that a specification does not build directly a model of the problem. Rather, it is intended to express the properties which must hold in the final realisation. So the semantic meaning of a specification is a *class of models*, not one model only.

15.2 Analysis and specification of case 1

The given requirements of the case study clearly settle the aim of the final software product: "the subject is to invoice orders". Not all the used words are defined in the requirements, but the domain is assumed to be known by the specifier. When some details are missing in the requirements, the expression "*we assume*" indicates what are the hints given by the user. When several solutions are possible to specify a part of the problem, the expression "*we choose*" indicates a choice made by the specifier.

In the algebraic specification method, the first task is to identify "sort" names that denote data (i.e. sets of values) of the problem and operations and predicates on these sorts. If some data do not refer to any standard data types, then new sorts are introduced. All names should be derived from the informal requirements for the sake of traceability.

Question 1: What are the data of the invoicing problem?

Answer: The requirements introduce the data of orders, stock and products. Moreover, there is a notion of *quantity* because the ordered quantity must be compared to the quantity in stock.

For the three first data we choose to use new sorts, respectively called *Order*, *Stock* and *Product*. For the "quantity" data we have two possibilities in CASL: we can introduce a new sort, say "Qty", and a total order predicate "$\leq$" to denote the quantity values and the ordering, or we can use a data specification of the predefined library [ROG 00]. In that case an obvious solution is to take the data type of natural numbers defined in the specification *NAT*, with the sort "*Nat*" and all the usual operators and predicates. We assume that a quantity cannot be negative, otherwise we should take the sort "*Int*" from the specification of integers.

Question 2: What is the state of an order?

Answer: The state of an order is either "*pending*" or "*invoiced*".

So the order set denoted by the sort *Order* is divided into pending orders and invoiced orders. This can be specified by two predicates characterizing disjoint sets of order values. In the CASL texts below, keywords are boldfaced; comments are introduced by "%%" and terminate at the end of line:

preds %% declaration of two predicates
  is_pending, is_invoiced : *Order* %% on the orders.
axiom %% declaration of an axiom:
  $\forall o : Order \bullet \neg\, is\_pending(o) \Leftrightarrow is\_invoiced(o)$

Another view of this notion would be to define the state as an *attribute* of the orders. In that case *state* becomes an operation from *Order* to *State*, where *State* is the sort of the state values: *pending* and *invoiced*. In CASL, an enumerated set of values can be directly introduced with the sort declaration:

free type *State* ::= *pending* | *invoiced*;

The operation $state$ and the axioms relating it to the predicates are then:

op $state : Order \rightarrow State$ %% declaration of an operation
var $o : Order$ %% declaration of variables for the axioms
  • $is\_pending(o) \Leftrightarrow state(o) = pending$
  • $is\_invoiced(o) \Leftrightarrow state(o) = invoiced$

From now on we only consider the predicative description of the state, not the description by an attribute.

Question 3: What are the operations on the orders?

Answer: The requirements indicate the operations that observe the content of the orders. They are the "reference" to a product and the "quantity" of the ordered product.

We assume that the quantity of the ordered product is not zero (otherwise it is useless to order the product). The requirements are rather ambiguous on the point of the references. An interpretation of the sentence: "On an order, we have one and one only reference to an ordered product of a certain quantity" is that there is one reference on an order. Another interpretation is that there may be several references, but it is forbidden that the same reference should occur several times on an order. We choose here the first interpretation which seems confirmed by the sentence "according to the reference of the ordered product".

We have stressed that an algebraic specification contains sorts, operators and predicates. A good specification-writing method is to gather all the strongly connected declarations into a specification module. So the specification *ORDER* below declares the sorts *Order* together with the "observer" operations. Nothing is said about the effective construction of the *Order* values. The specification also introduces the sort *Product*, which is needed to define the reference attribute. In CASL, the set of positive natural numbers is denoted by the sort *Pos*, which is a subsort of *Nat*. A specification module can be built as an *extension* of other specifications. Here the *ORDER* specification needs the specification *NAT*, which must be "imported":

spec *ORDER* = *NAT* %% *NAT* is imported.
then %% extension by new declarations.
  sorts *Order*, *Product*;
  ops *reference* : *Order* $\rightarrow$ *Product*;
    ordered_qty : *Order* $\rightarrow$ *Pos*;
  preds *is_pending*, *is_invoiced* : *Order*;
  vars *o* : *Order* %% axiomatisation of the predicates.
  • $\neg$ *is_pending*(*o*) $\Leftrightarrow$ *is_invoiced*(*o*)
end

Question 4: What about the stock?

Answer: In the requirements one can find the expressions "the references in stock" and "the quantity (of a product) which is in stock".

We infer that there is an operation *qty* which, given a reference to a product and a (current value of the) stock, returns the quantity of the product. We assume that there are operations to *add* and to *remove* product items in the stock. We specify also a predicate $p\ is\_in\ s$ which holds if the product p is referenced in the stock s. The operations *qty*, *add* and *remove* are partial, that is, are only defined on the domain of the products which are effectively in the stock. Moreover, the remove operation can be applied only if there are enough items of the product. The function symbol of partial operations is denoted by "$\rightarrow?$". The definition domain of partial operations is specified through a "definedness predicate" introduced by the keyword **def**. The notation "ϕ_1 **if** ϕ_2" is just another way to write "$\phi_2 \Rightarrow \phi_1$". The axiomatisation of *add* and *remove* is achieved by their effect on the result of the operation *qty*. This is called an *observational* specification of the operations. So, the specification of the stock is given by:

spec *STOCK* $=$ *NAT* **then**
sorts *Stock*, *Product*;
ops *qty* : *Product* $\times$ *Stock* $\rightarrow?$ *Nat*;
add, *remove*:*Product* $\times$ *Pos* $\times$ *Stock* $\rightarrow?$ *Stock*
pred *__is_in__* : *Product* $\times$ *Stock*
vars p, p' : *Product*; n : *Pos*; s : *Stock*
• **def** $qty(p, s) \Leftrightarrow p\ is\_in\ s$
• **def** $add(p, n, s) \Leftrightarrow p\ is\_in\ s$
• **def** $remove(p, n, s) \Leftrightarrow p\ is\_in\ s \wedge qty(p, s) \geq n$
• $qty(p, add(p, n, s)) = qty(p, s) + n$ **if** $p\ is\_in\ s$
• $qty(p', add(p, n, s)) = qty(p', s)$ **if** $p'\ is\_in\ s \wedge p\ is\_in\ s \wedge p' \neq p$
• $qty(p, remove(p, n, s)) = qty(p, s) - n$ **if** $p\ is\_in\ s \wedge qty(p, s) \geq n$
• $qty(p', remove(p, n, s)) = qty(p', s)$
if $p'\ is\_in\ s \wedge p\ is\_in\ s \wedge p' \neq p \wedge qty(p, s) \geq n$
end

Question 5: What are the inputs and outputs of the main operation that we shall call "*invoice_order*"?

Answer: Clearly the operation "*invoice_order*" gets an order and the stock as inputs, because the quantity of the ordered product must be compared to the quantity in stock. The operation may modify the order and the stock, because the state of the order can change and the stock is modified; more precisely, the quantity in stock of the product must be updated if this quantity is large enough.

Because the algebraic formalism is *functional*, the read (or input) values are the parameters of the operation and the modified (or output) values are the results. However, in CASL, the profile of an operation gets only one result. So, the regular solution is to gather both values into a new one, the sort of which is a product type of the two respective sorts. It is easy to define a specification of a sort which is a product type of several other sorts. Similar as for enumeration types like *State* above, CASL provides an abbreviation for product types which generates all the declarations of a product at once. In the *OrdStk* declaration below "*mk_os*" is a new operation that takes two values of sort *Order* and *Stock* respectively and returns a value of sort *OrdStk*. It is called a *constructor* operation. The operations *order_of* and *stock_of* select the corresponding information from an *OrdStk* value. They are called *selectors*:

free type *OrdStk* ::= *mk_os*(*order_of* : *Order*; *stock_of* : *Stock*);

This free type declaration generates the following signature and axioms:

ops
mk_os : *Order* $\times$ *Stock* $\rightarrow$ *OrdStk*;
order_of : *OrdStk* $\rightarrow$ *Order*;
stock_of : *OrdStk* $\rightarrow$ *Stock*;

vars o : *Order*; s : *Stock*; os : *OrdStk*
• $mk\_os(order\_of(os), stock\_of(os)) = os$
• $order\_of(mk\_os(o, s)) = o$
• $stock\_of(mk\_os(o, s)) = s$

Question 6: What are the required conditions to invoice an order?

Answer: At a first glance, the requirements indicate that an order can be invoiced if at least three conditions are satisfied: (1) the state of the order is "pending", (2) "the ordered references are references in stock" and (3) "the ordered quantity is either less or equal to the quantity which is in stock".

All these conditions can be expressed by CASL formulas on the two parameters of the operation $invoice\_order$, o : *Order*; s : *Stock*. The first one is obviously: "*is_pending*(o)". For the other conditions new predicates are introduced through "definitions", that is, profile and meaning at the same time. For instance, the second condition can be expressed by the definition:

$$\textbf{pred}\ \textit{referenced}(o : Order;\ s : Stock) \Leftrightarrow \textit{reference}(o)\ is\_in\ s$$

which is a short form of: **pred** *referenced* : $Order \times Stock$
vars $o : Order;\ s : Stock$
• $\textit{referenced}(o, s) \Leftrightarrow \textit{reference}(o)\ is\_in\ s$

Then we define the predicates $enough\_qty$ (condition *(3)*) and $invoice\_ok$ which formalize the precondition of the $invoice\_order$ operation:

$$enough\_qty(o : Order;\ s : Stock) \Leftrightarrow ordered\_qty(o) \leq qty(\textit{reference}(o), s);$$
$$invoice\_ok(o : Order;\ s : Stock) \Leftrightarrow$$
$$\textit{is\_pending}(o) \wedge \textit{referenced}(o, s) \wedge enough\_qty(o, s);$$

In the sequel of the specification we choose a "defensive" style, which means that the operation *invoice_order* is defined to be total on its parameters. The profile is then:

$$\textit{invoice\_order} : Order \times Stock \longrightarrow OrdStk$$

However, we could choose a "generous" style with partial operation and preconditions. Of course, this style requires that the preconditions are checked by the calling programs. For this operation the conditions *(1)* and *(2)* would be left as preconditions.

Question 7: What is the effect of the operation "*invoice_order*"?

Answer: Within the conditions defined above, the state of the order becomes invoiced and the quantity of the ordered product in the stock is reduced by the ordered quantity. The requirements do not prescribe the behaviour of the operation when the conditions are not fulfilled. We assume that the parameters are not changed in that case.

Following again the observational specification style, the effect of the operation *invoice_order(o,s)* is determined by the modification of the attributes of the order o (*reference*, *ordered_qty*) and of the stock s (*qty*). However, for the stock we can use the modification operations already defined. The first set of axioms state what happens when the conditions for invoicing an order hold:

- $is\_invoiced(order\_of(invoice\_order(o, s)))$ **if** $invoice\_ok(o, s)$
- $stock\_of(invoice\_order(o, s)) = remove(reference(o), ordered\_qty(o), s)$ **if** $invoice\_ok(o, s)$

If the conditions are not fulfilled, the order and the stock are not modified:

- $invoice\_order(o, s) = mk\_os(o, s)$ **if** $\neg\ invoice\_ok(o, s)$ $\quad (*)$

Moreover, the other attributes of the order are not changed by the $invoice\_order$ operation. We need to make these properties explicit through extra axioms:

- $reference(order\_of(invoice\_order(o, s))) = reference(o)$
- $ordered\_qty(order\_of(invoice\_order(o, s))) = ordered\_qty(o)$

Assume now that we want messages to be issued for the various cases of the results of the *invoice_order* operation. This is not expressed by the requirements, but can be useful for the users. The messages are defined by the following free type:

free type *Msg* ::= *success* | *not_pending* | *not_referenced* | *not_enough_qty*

The profile of the operation *invoice_order* becomes:

free type *OSM* ::= $mk(order\_of : Order;\ stock\_of : Stock;\ msg\_of : Msg)$;
op $invoice\_order : Order \times Stock \rightarrow OSM$

The axiom (*) from above needs to be changed and the following axioms have to be added to the specification:

- $msg\_of(invoice\_order(o, s)) = success$ **if** $invoice\_ok(o, s)$
- $msg\_of(invoice\_order(o, s)) = not\_pending$ **if** $\neg\ is\_pending(o)$
- $msg\_of(invoice\_order(o, s)) = not\_referenced$ **if** $is\_pending(o) \wedge \neg\ referenced(o, s)$
- $msg\_of(invoice\_order(o, s)) = not\_enough\_qty$ **if** $is\_pending(o) \wedge referenced(o, s) \wedge \neg\ enough\_qty(o, s)$

All the definitions from Question 5 should be gathered in a specification module named *INVOICE* to achieve the specification which concludes the first part of the case study.

15.3 Analysis and specification of case 2

In case 2 we have to take into account the "dynamics" of the invoicing system and to specify the "two entry flows (orders, entries in stock)".

Question 8: What are the operations involved in this part?

Answer: On the orders, it is said that we have to specify:
– "*new_order*" to introduce a new pending order.
– "*cancel_order*" to cancel an order.
On the stock, the operation requested by the requirements is:
– "*add_qty*" to add a certain quantity of a product in the stock.

The requirements do not mention another fundamental operation that we shall name "*deal_with_order*". This operation tries to invoice a pending order. If invoicing succeeds, the order becomes an "invoiced" order. It is the heart of the invoicing process. This operation should use the already specified operation "*invoice_order*". In addition, a constant "*init*" is needed to represent the initial state of the invoicing system.

Question 9: Could you explain the scenario of the invoicing process?

Answer: The invoicing process evolves from the initial state by invocation of the four operations: *new_order*, *cancel_order*, *deal_with_order* and *add_qty*. Firstly, orders are put in a set of pending orders, then they can be transferred to the set of invoiced orders if the invoicing operation can be applied. A question arises when an order cannot be invoiced by lack of product quantity in the stock. In that case the order remains pending, but the system must be aware that there are orders which have not been invoiced for the reason of lack of product quantity. Independently, the stock can be supplied. Finally, orders can be canceled at any time.

Question 10: Is there an ordering to choose the orders which must be invoiced by the system?

Answer: This point is left open in the requirements. The usual treatment is to invoice orders on the basis of the first-in first-out policy. However, the orders not invoiced by lack of product quantity should be invoiced as soon as the ordered product is supplied in the stock.

This ordering assumption is an important design decision. The scenario is now much more defined. The pending orders should be organized in a queue, at least at the abstract level. The oldest orders are the first ones in the queue. So the invoicing system must try to invoice the oldest orders which satisfy the conditions to be invoiced.

The next step now is to specify the queue data type. As explained in the introduction, this is not an implementation decision, because the specification is independent from the concrete data structures which will be used later. These queues are matter of thinking of the problem, not of giving an implementation. In CASL, queues are not provided as basic data types [ROG 00]. However, there is a specification of the generic data type "*LIST*" which can be adapted to our purpose. This provides an example of using structuring primitives to build new specifications. The heading of the "*LIST*" specification presents the minimal signature required for the instantiations (here the sort of the elements):

spec *LIST* [**sort** *Elem*] = ...

The body of the *LIST* specification contains declarations and axioms about lists. The operations are as usual: *nil*, $a :: l$ (for *cons*), *first*, *last*, *rest*, $l_1 ++ l_2$ (for concatenation), etc. Inside the generic module, the sort of element list is denoted by "*List*[*Elem*]". We instantiate *LIST* by the *ORDER* specification. The sort generated by the instantiation mechanism is *List*[*Order*]. Then we build a new specification by renaming (keyword **with**) the sort *List*[*Order*] into *OQueue*. The operations and predicates on lists are inherited and their profiles are changed accordingly. Finally, we declare a new infix predicate "∈" and give the specification the name *ORDER_QUEUE*. Note that we must be able to decide if two orders are equal or not ("=" predicate):

spec *ORDER_QUEUE* =
  { *LIST* [*ORDER* **fit** *Elem* ↦ *Order*] **with** *List*[*Order*] ↦ *OQueue* }
then
  pred $\_\_ \in \_\_ : Order \times OQueue$;
  vars $o, o' : Order;\ oq : OQueue$;   %% This predicate is specified
    • $\neg\, o \in nil$ %% by the case for nil, then by
    • $o' \in (o :: oq) \Leftrightarrow o' = o \vee o' \in oq$ %% the case for $cons$.
end

In the next specification named *QUEUES*, we define three subsorts of *OQueue*: the subsort *UQueue* of queues with uniquely identified, distinct orders; the subsort *PQueue* of queues with pending orders and the subsort *IQueue* of queues containing only invoiced orders. This will be done using the subsorting facilities of CASL, which allows us to declare subsorts defined by predicates:

spec *QUEUES* = *ORDER_QUEUE* **then**
  preds $unicity, pqueue, iqueue : OQueue$;
  vars $o : Order;\ oq : OQueue$;
    • $unicity(nil)$
    • $unicity(o :: oq) \Leftrightarrow \neg (o \in oq) \wedge unicity(oq)$
    • $pqueue(oq) \Leftrightarrow \forall x : Order \cdot (x \in oq \Rightarrow is\_pending(x))$
    • $iqueue(oq) \Leftrightarrow \forall x : Order \cdot (x \in oq \Rightarrow is\_invoiced(x))$
  sorts
    $UQueue = \{oq : OQueue \bullet unicity(oq)\}$;
    $PQueue = \{uq : UQueue \bullet pqueue(uq)\}$;
    $IQueue = \{uq : UQueue \bullet iqueue(uq)\}$;
end

Question 11: What is the global state of the invoicing process and what are the conditions which should be fulfilled by the global state values?

Answer: The global state is composed of the orders and of the stock. The requirements state that "all the ordered references are references in stock". Moreover, we have seen that if orders can be cancelled then they must be uniquely identified.

From now on, specification texts are expressed within a specification module named *WHS* (for warehouse). In our analysis of the problem, we divide the orders in two distinct queues: the pending orders and the invoiced orders. The global state can be defined through a free type product declaration:

$$\textbf{free type } GState = mk\_gs(porders : PQueue;\ iorders : IQueue;\ the\_stock : Stock);$$

The requirements state that all orders in the queues are distinct and that the references are references in the stock. Therefore, we define the predicate $consistent$ on queues yielding true if and only if the requirements are satisfied and declare the subsort *VGS* (valid global state) of *GState* containing only consistent queues. Notice the overloading of the predicate *referenced*. The distinction between both predicates is made from the sort analysis of the arguments. The same mechanism is applied to disambiguate overloaded operation symbols. The first line below is an *operation definition* in CASL:

$$\begin{aligned}
&\textbf{op} \quad the_orders(gs : GState) : OQueue = porders(gs) +\!\!+\, iorders(gs)\\
&\textbf{preds}\ referenced(oq : OQueue;\ s : Stock) \Leftrightarrow\\
&\qquad\qquad \forall x : Order \cdot (x \in oq \Rightarrow referenced(x, s));\\
&\quad consistent(gs : GState) \Leftrightarrow unicity(the_orders(gs))\\
&\qquad\qquad \wedge\ referenced(the_orders(gs), the_stock(gs))\\
&\textbf{sort}\ VGS = \{gs : GState \bullet consistent(gs)\}
\end{aligned}$$

Question 12: What is the effect of the operations identified at the very beginning of this section (Question 8)?

Answer: Their effect is mainly to change the global state according to the given scenario.

We are now able to write the specification of the operations identified at Question 8. As in the first part of the case study, parameters specify the sorts of the values that are read and the result specifies the sort of the values that are modified. As such, each operation takes as one parameter a global state value and returns a global state value:

$$\begin{aligned}
new_order &: Product \times Pos \times VGS \rightarrow VGS;\\
cancel_order &: Order \times VGS \rightarrow VGS;\\
add_qty &: Product \times Pos \times VGS \rightarrow VGS;\\
deal_with_order &: VGS \rightarrow VGS;
\end{aligned}$$

Following the recommendations of the defensive specification style, we have declared all operations as total. However, if some conditions on parameters are not fulfilled, the operations may do nothing (this will be made clear by the axioms). In the first part of the case study, the operation $invoice\_order$ was axiomatised through its effect on the attributes of the order to be invoiced and on those of the stock (observational specification method). Here because all the operations return a value of sort *VGS*, we could axiomatise them by giving the values of the global-state attributes, that is to say, the values of $porders$, $iorders$ and the_stock after the execution of the operations. Instead, we shall use the *constructive* method, which means that the value of the global state after each operation will be effectively built through the constructor operation *mk_gs*. The constructive method is very close to a "model-oriented" specification style for the operations. The observational method is more abstract in the sense that the axioms defined by this method can be deduced as logical consequences of the constructive axiomatisation while the inverse is usually not possible. For the axiomatisation below, we use the following variables:

$$\textbf{vars} \quad o : Order;\ p : Product;\ n : Pos;\ vgs : VGS;$$

The $new\_order(p, n, vgs)$ operation takes as parameters an ordered product p, a quantity n and the global state. The global state is not modified if the product is not referenced in the stock. Otherwise a pending order ordering n units of the p product is added at the end of the queue of the pending orders. We need a new operation:

$$mk\_order : Product \times Pos \times VGS \longrightarrow Order$$

such that $mk\_order(p, n, vgs)$ builds a pending order with product p and ordered quantity n which is different from those already in *vgs*. More formally:

- $is\_pending(mk\_order(p, n, vgs))$
- $\neg\, mk\_order(p, n, vgs) \in the\_orders(vgs)$
- $reference(mk\_order(p, n, vgs)) = p$
- $ordered\_qty(mk\_order(p, n, vgs)) = n$

Moreover, we use the operation: "$q <\!\!-\ a$" that appends an element a at the end of the queue q. Let t be of sort s', then the notation "t **as** s" forces t to be of subsort s of s' provided that t satisfies the subsorting constraints. In the second axiom below, the constructive axiomatisation makes clear which parts of the global state are modified or not:

- $new\_order(p, n, vgs) \;=\; vgs \ \textbf{ if } \neg\, p \ is\_in \ the\_stock(vgs)$
- $new\_order(p, n, vgs) \;=$
$$mk\_gs((porders(vgs) <\!\!-\ mk\_order(p, n, vgs)) \textbf{ as } PQueue,\ iorders(vgs),\ the\_stock(vgs)) \ \textbf{ if } p \ is\_in \ the\_stock(vgs)$$

Question 13: The meaning of *cancel_order* is clear when the order in pending. But what does it mean to cancel an order which has already been invoiced?

Answer: This corresponds to the case when a product is not accepted by the customer and when it is returned at the warehouse. So, the order is canceled and the stock is updated.

The operation *cancel_order*(o, vgs) removes the order o from the queue it is on in the global state *vgs*. Moreover, if the order is invoiced, the stock is supplied by the ordered quantity of the referenced product. The operation which removes an order o from an order queue q is denoted by *remove*(o, q). If the order o does not belong to the orders of the global state, then the state is unchanged. We can notice that the *unicity* property on the orders is needed to make the specification of *cancel_order* sound. Actually, the following property holds:

$$o \in porders(vgs) \wedge unicity(the\_orders(vgs)) \Rightarrow \neg\, o \in iorders(vgs)$$

and symmetrically with the *iorders* queue. The axiomatisation of *cancel_order* is given through three cases, the last one being the case: $\neg\,(o \in the\_orders(vgs))$. It uses the *add* operation of the stock data type. The notation: "t_1 **when** c_1 **else** t_2 **when** c_2 **else** ..." is a "conditional term". It means that when the condition c_1 holds then the value of the whole term is t_1, otherwise when c_2 holds, then the value is t_2 and so on:

- $cancel\_order(o, vgs) =$
  $mk\_gs(remove(o, porders(vgs))$ **as** $PQueue, iorders(vgs),$
  $the\_stock(vgs))$ **when** $o \in porders(vgs)$
  else $mk\_gs(porders(vgs), remove(o, iorders(vgs))$ **as** $IQueue,$
  $add(reference(o), ordered\_qty(o), the\_stock(vgs)))$
  when $o \in iorders(vgs)$
  else vgs

The operation *add_qty*(p, n, vgs) adds the quantity n to the product p, if the reference is in the stock. This operation uses again the *add* operation on stocks. So the axioms of the operation *add_qty* are simply:

- $add\_qty(p, n, vgs) = vgs$ **if** $\neg\, p\ is\_in\ the\_stock(vgs)$
- $add\_qty(p, n, vgs) =$
  $mk\_gs(porders(vgs), iorders(vgs),$
  $add(p, n, the\_stock(vgs)))$ **if** $p\ is\_in\ the\_stock(vgs)$

The operation *deal_with_order*(vgs) tries to invoice a pending order. The order which is invoiced is the oldest order in the pending order queue for which the quantity in stock is greater than the ordered quantity. By the consistency property of the global state, the references of the pending orders are references in the stock. So *invoice_ok* is satisfied and the invoice operation succeeds. The order is put in the queue of the invoiced orders. It is clear that if there are orders older than the invoiced one, then these orders are waiting for the stock to be supplied with a large enough quantity of the ordered product. We need to define the condition on which an order in the pending queue can be invoiced, "*invoiceable*", and what is the first order which should be dealt with:

preds $invoiceable(pq : PQueue;\ s : Stock) \Leftrightarrow$
$\exists o : Orders \cdot (o \in pq \wedge enough\_qty(o, s));$

op $\mathit{first\_invoceable} : \mathit{PQueue} \times \mathit{Stock} \rightarrow ?\ \mathit{Order}$
vars $o : \mathit{Order}$; $pq : \mathit{PQueue}$; $s : \mathit{Stock}$;
• **def** $\mathit{first\_invoceable}(pq, s) \Leftrightarrow \mathit{invoiceable}(pq, s)$
• $\mathit{first\_invoceable}((o :: pq)\ \textbf{as}\ \mathit{PQueue}, s) = o$ **when** $\mathit{enough\_qty}(o, s)$
else $\mathit{first\_invoceable}(pq, s)$

If no order in the pending queue is invoiceable, then the operation *deal_with_order* leaves the global state unchanged (first axiom), otherwise the first invoiceable order of the pending queue is effectively invoiced (second axiom). The *invoice_ok* conditions are well fulfilled, because the order is pending, the product is referenced in stock (property of the global state) and the product quantity has just been checked. The notation "u = **let** $x : s = t$ **in** v" is a readable shortcut for the formula $\forall x : s \cdot (x = t \Rightarrow u = v)$:

• $\mathit{deal\_with\_order}(\mathit{vgs}) = \mathit{vgs}$
if $\neg\, \mathit{invoiceable}(\mathit{porders}(\mathit{vgs}), \mathit{the\_stock}(\mathit{vgs}))$
• $\mathit{deal\_with\_order}(\mathit{vgs}) =$
let $o_1 : \mathit{Order} = \mathit{first\_invoceable}(\mathit{porders}(\mathit{vgs}), \mathit{the\_stock}(\mathit{vgs}))$
in let $os : \mathit{OrdStk} = \mathit{invoice\_order}(o_1, \mathit{the\_stock}(\mathit{vsg}))$
in let $o_2 : \mathit{Order} = \mathit{order\_of}(os)$ %% the order after invoicing
$s_2 : \mathit{Stock} = \mathit{stock\_of}(os)$ %% the stock after invoicing
in $\mathit{mk\_gs}(\mathit{remove}(o_1, \mathit{porders}(\mathit{vgs}))\ \textbf{as}\ \mathit{PQueue},$
$(\mathit{iorders}(\mathit{vgs}) \leftarrow o_2)\ \textbf{as}\ \mathit{IQueue}, s_2)$
if $\mathit{invoiceable}(\mathit{porders}(\mathit{vgs}), \mathit{the\_stock}(\mathit{vgs}))$

One can notice that within the condition $\neg\, \mathit{isEmpty}(\mathit{porders}(\mathit{vgs}))$, if we have:

$$\mathit{first\_invoiceable}(\mathit{porders}(\mathit{vgs}), \mathit{the\_stock}(\mathit{vgs})) \neq \mathit{first}(\mathit{porders}(\mathit{vgs}))$$

then there are orders for which the number of items of the ordered product is not sufficient in stock. If required by the user (see answer to Question 9) this information can be exploited to specify a notification mechanism for such sold out products.

15.4 Architectural specification

A feature that distinguishes CASL from other specification languages is its possibility to specify the design of a software system by defining the program modules that have to be implemented and how these modules are combined to an implementation of the specification.

The specifications given in the previous sections denote a signature and a class of algebras; the use of structuring methods on this level does not imply any structure for the program satisfying the specification. However, it is also desirable to be able to specify, in an abstract way, the construction of the resulting program from program modules. In CASL, this is done using architectural specifications. The following architectural specification specifies a possible design of a program implementing the case study:

arch spec *Warehouse* =
  units
    NatAlg : *NAT* ;
    StockFun : *NAT* → *STOCK* ;
    StockAlg = *StockFun*[*NatAlg*] ;
    WhsFun : *STOCK* → *WHS* ;
  result
    WhsFun [*StockAlg*]
end

The notation *NatAlg* : *NAT* means that *NatAlg* is some algebra satisfying the *NAT* specification and implies the task of providing such an implementation. The definition of *StockFun* implies the task of implementing a module taking an implementation of *NAT* and yielding an implementation of *STOCK*. Thus, *StockFun* applied to *NatAlg*, *StockFun*[*NatAlg*], is an algebra satisfying the *STOCK* specification.

Identically, the definition of *WhsFun* represents the task of implementing a module taking an implementation of *STOCK* and yielding an implementation of *WHS*.

The result of the architectural specification *Warehouse* is a construction of an implementation of *WHS* using the modules defined before.

15.5 The natural language description of the specification

15.5.1 Case 1

The specification of the orders declares the *Order* data type and two disjoint predicates characterizing the pending orders and the invoiced orders. It provides two operations on the orders which respectively return the reference to the ordered product and the ordered quantity. The specification of the stock provides the *Stock* data type, a predicate which asserts itself if a product is referenced in the stock and three operations: the first two change the number of items of a product in stock and the third returns the number of items of a product in stock. Then the *invoice_order* operation takes an order and the stock as parameters. If the order is pending, the referenced product is in stock and the quantity in stock of the product is sufficient enough, then the invoicing operation changes the state of the order and removes the ordered quantity from the stock; otherwise the operation is without effect. Moreover, messages are issued to inform the user about the success or failure of the invoicing operation together with the reasons for any failure.

15.5.2 Case 2

The invoicing software system is specified using a global state and four operations changing the global state. The global state consists of a queue of pending orders, a queue for the already invoiced orders and the stock. The operation *new_order* creates a new order and puts it at the end of the queue of pending orders. The operation *cancel_order* removes an order from the queue it is on and does nothing if the order is not on some queue. Moreover, if the order is removed from the queue of invoiced orders, then the ordered quantity of that order is added to the stock. The third operation, *add_qty*, supplies the stock with new items of a product if the product was referenced in the stock; it has no effect otherwise. Finally, the operation *deal_with_order* invoices the first invoiceable order on the queue of pending orders, which is also the oldest invoiceable order, and puts it at the end of the queue of invoiced orders. If such an order does not exist, *deal_with_order* does nothing.

15.6 Conclusion

In the case study, no particular problem has been encountered for the specification of data types given in the requirements: *Order*, *Stock*, *OQueue*, etc. The CASL language allows data types and operations to be specified either in an *observational* or a *constructive* style. Examples of the former style are given in the *STOCK* specification and in the axioms of *invoice_order*. Examples of the latter style are the axioms of the operations on the global state in the second part. We stress that the observational style is very useful at the very beginning of the specification phase. It allows the specifier to formulate some assertions about the model without building it at all. This set of formal assertions can be discussed with the user or the customer, in order to validate the first assumptions made about the model.

Some particular features of the CASL language have been revealed as being very useful in the specification process. One of them is the notion of partial or total operations. It forces the specifier to be aware of the definition domains of operations. Definedness conditions provide guarantees about operation call correctness through the proof of lemmas (proof obligations). Another powerful feature, the subsort mechanism, is well designed to impose constraints on some data in the same way as invariant properties for model-oriented languages. Subsort checking proofs increase the confidence on a sound usage of the subsorted values. CASL environments do not yet provide proof-obligation generators, so our specifications were not checked for this aspect.

However, the functional style of the algebraic specifications makes the description of states (in the usual sense) painful. A state is often described by a tuple of variables. In CASL this tuple must be a part of the parameters and of the result of the operations. So the profiles might look rather strange compared with the final implementation of the operations in an imperative programming language. Theoretical and practical research is in progress to facilitate description and axiomatisation of states in the algebraic formalism. The CASL language is open to such extensions.

The invoicing case study is not a large problem, at least not at the very high specification level. So, few CASL structuring primitives have been exemplified. Only simple mechanisms, such as extension (importation) and instantiation, were needed. Finally, we showed how to build an architectural specification of the case study in the last part of the chapter.

Bibliography

[CAS 04a] Bidoit, M., Mosses, Peter D. CASL *User Manual.* LNCS 2900, Springer-Verlag, 2004

[CAS 04b] Mosses, Peter D. (Ed.) CASL *Reference Manual.* LNCS 2960, Springer-Verlag, 2004

[BER 89] Bergstra, J. A., Heering, J., Klint, R. *Algebraic Specification.* Addison-Wesley, Reading, MA, 1989

[EHR 85] Ehrig, H., Mahr, B. *Fundamentals of Algebraic Specification 1.* EATCS Monograph 6, Springer-Verlag, Berlin, 1985

[VAN 89] van Horebeek, I., Lewi, J. *Algebraic Specifications in Software Engineering.* Springer-Verlag, 1989

[MOS 99] Mosses, Peter D. "CASL: A Guided Tour of its Design". In José Luiz Fiadeiro (ed.), *Recent Trends in Algebraic Development Techniques*, Proceedings, LNCS 1589, Springer-Verlag, pp. 216-240, 1999

[ROG 00] Roggenbach, M., Mossakowski, T., Schröder, L. Basic Datatypes in CASL, Version 0.4, 2000 URL: http://www.brics.dk/Projects/CoFI/Notes/L-12

[WIR 90] Wirsing, M. "Algebraic Specifications". In J. van Leeuwen (ed.), *Handbook of Theoretical Computer Science*, North-Holland, Elsevier, pp. 675-788, 1990

Chapter 16

Coq

Philippe CHAVIN and Jean-François MONIN

This chapter is an attempt to provide a formal specification which is as faithful as possible to the informal one and consistent. The powerful type system of Coq is used to make our specification both very abstract and eventually executable. This ensures that an implementation can be found. Indeed, we *construct* mathematical structures or functions whenever possible, instead of specifying them with axioms. If the axiomatic way turns out better, we look for structures satisfying the axioms we need. We also insist on the quest for proof opportunities in order to get further confidence that specified objects are the right ones.

16.1 Introduction to Coq

Coq [COQ 04, BER 04] is a tool for developing mathematical specifications and proofs. Specifying an application using Coq is then just writing a (hopefully relevant) piece of mathematics. The main difference with other techniques such as algebraic specifications [BID 91] or Z is that Coq is not based on set theory, but on constructive type theory, which naturally deals with computational objects such as data structures and algorithms. Using Coq we can put emphasis on verification: Coq includes a proof checker and a means to build formal proofs.

As a specification language, Coq is both a higher order logic – quantifiers may be applied on natural numbers, on functions of arbitrary types, on propositions, predicates, types, etc. – and a typed lambda-calculus enriched with an extension of primitive recursion. For instance, 0 has the type `nat` which has itself the type Set. This is formally written `0 : nat` and `nat :` Set. Besides objects such as natural numbers, we have logical objects, such as propositions. Explanations come below with the use of new notions. The reader may find further details in [COQ 04, BER 04] and [HUE 04].

Let us stress some practical consequences of the use of type theory instead of set theory. First, recall that set theory is essentially untyped. Using type theory, we gain accurate and decidable type checking (note that Z and B [ABR 96] use restricted versions of set theory endowed with a limited notion of type). Conversely, subsets are sometimes less easy to represent with types. Here is an interesting illustration of the accuracy of type theory, due to the fact that functions are a primitive notion. If f is a function from A to B, we know not only that f is a binary relation between A and B, as in the type system of Z or B, but also that for any x in A there is a unique y in B related to x by f. Moreover, existence and uniqueness are given for free (no proof obligation is raised), as type checking is decidable. Lemmas about f are then simpler to prove. This is used here, for formalizing sentences such as "on an order, we have one and only one reference to, etc.". The type of functions from A to B is denoted by $A \rightarrow B$.

The main pitfall in a specification is to introduce personal assumptions (sometimes unknowingly) over data structures, system properties, implementation requirements, etc. Here, we are asked not to provide an implementation, but to formalize the text of a problem written in natural language. Using Coq greatly eases this purpose: higher order logic, unusual in other formal methods, allows one to reason in a very abstract way, without yielding the consideration of implementation; for instance, we pack together some sets with the few hypotheses we make on them and then hide this behind an *ad hoc* notion of separable sets; we are even able, as shown in section 16.4.2, to quantify over abstract algebraic structures when needed, without additional complications in the specification. Still, we are able, given succinct refinement, to provide specification animation through scenarios: see section 16.6. This freedom is due to the fact that we are not *a priori* coerced into any model, as opposed to B for instance, where we have to work within a particular model of set theory.

16.2 Analysis of the text

16.2.1 Stock and orders

Informally, we have two sets (order and stock), an operation (invoice), and two attributes referring both to orders and to the stock (reference and quantity). Nothing is said about products to be ordered. We consider them as an abstract notion: a product will be represented by a reference. In fact references can serve as identifiers of products, while they cannot serve as identifiers of orders, because "the same reference can be ordered on several different orders". The original statement says that an order has a state, which we call *status* below. This status can take at least two values, pending and invoiced. Now we express mathematical properties on the aforementioned types.

Question 1: Does an order consists of exactly one reference, or of several references?

Answer: In our understanding of the sentence "the state of the order will be changed into 'invoiced' if the ordered quantity is either less than or equal to the quantity which is in stock according to the reference of the ordered product", an order has exactly one reference.

The sentence "the same reference can be ordered on several different orders" seems to be there only to state that the relation between orders and references is not one-to-one. We consider that this sentence has been added only in order to prevent references to be used as identifiers for orders (see Question 9), hence we simply discard it in our informal version of the specification (and similarly for "the quantity can be different to other orders").

Besides orders, we have a notion of a stock.

Question 2: What is a stock?

Answer: stock defines for each reference the quantity (of the corresponding product) in stock.

Formalizing this notion is easy: we simply use a function.

16.2.2 Operations

The world is not static: the status of an order can change, new orders can arise and so on. Then we consider operations, which are transformations from a world to a new world. We will define a type state of worlds, and operations will be functions from state (and possibly further arguments) to state.

Question 3: Can operations be applied to any state?

Answer: Operations can be applied only if their preconditions are satisfied; in a high level specification, we are concerned with intended normal behavior. Further considerations such as exception raising should be postponed until implementation-level refinement.

The first operation to be considered is invoice, which changes the status of an order from pending to invoiced. The other operations are considered in "Case 2"; they are: adding an order, canceling an order, and entering quantities in the stock. Pre- and post-conditions are studied later.

Question 4: What is the ordering for operations?

Answer: The text does not say anything about this issue; we can consider sequential or parallel composition. For the sake of simplicity, we choose a sequential ordering.

Question 5: Do we have a fairness requirement? Should every pending order be invoiced at some time?

Answer: The sentence "the state of the order *will be* changed into invoiced *if*..." can be interpreted as a requirement for fairness, or as the formulation of the existence of a precondition to invoice. Again, nothing is said about ordering, triggering or whatever concerning timings, so we consider it a precondition.

If we wanted to interpret it as a requirement for fairness of behaviors of the system, we would introduce a temporal logic, using Coq-Unity for instance [HEY 96].

16.2.3 Requirements on quantities

Question 6: What are quantities? Mathematically speaking, what operations are available on quantities?

Answer: Since nothing is said about the nature of the products, we only assume the customer uses a "traditional" notion of quantity.

We should respect a preservation principle: no operation considered in this case study may "create" or "destroy" quantities – the sum of quantities of a given product after an operation should be equal to the sum of quantities of this product before this operation. Hence, we need an addition on quantities. We also know, from the description of invoicing, that quantities can be compared. Altogether, we suppose that the type for quantities (called quant) is endowed with a binary relation leq which is reflexive, antisymmetric and transitive (it is a total order relation). We also consider that the mathematical structure of quantities includes a zero (a neutral element for addition) which is also less than or equal to any quantity. We call such a structure a *measure system.*

Question 7: Do all products share the same measure system?

Answer: We stick to the text, which makes no assumption on this point. We just attach a measure system to each reference in stock.

Actually, there is no reason to compare a quantity of kiwis to a quantity of oil, even if both are represented by natural numbers. Moreover, oil may perfectly be measured with real numbers. There is even no point in adding kilograms of potatoes to pieces of kiwis. Therefore, we consider in section 16.4.2 a *family* of types of quantities, one for each reference, where each instance of quant is endowed with its own version of leq, zero, +, etc. Natural numbers are an obvious model for quantities and we stick to this model in our first specification.

16.3 A specification for case 1

16.3.1 Basic types

Coq uses a type theory: every value inhabits a (unique) type. For instance, we need a type for the status of an order, a type for references, a type for quantities and a type for orders. They are respectively called status, ref, quant and order. From them we can construct more complex types, e.g. for stocks (ref $\rightarrow$ quant) or for worlds (state; see below).

The type status has exactly two inhabitants, pending and invoiced. Here we declare an enumerated type, as in Pascal but with a different syntax:

Inductive status : Set := pending : status |invoiced : status.

The standard library of Coq constructs in the same way the type bool, inhabited by true and false, as well as the type nat of natural numbers, whose constructors are O (zero) and S (successor):

Inductive nat : Set := O : nat | S: nat → nat.

Here we understand better the name *inductive*, because natural numbers are constructed in a recursive way. Inductive types are actually the fundamental way of constructing data types in Coq. An important property of inductive types is that the *only* values in them are constructed by their constructors, e.g. true and false for bool. Coq automatically infers induction principles for these types.

Question 8: Should the sets of references and their associated quantity measure system be considered as constant during the whole system lifetime?

Answer: We consider them as parameters of the system.

Indeed, there is no requirement for an operation which could add, or delete, a reference. The set of references seems to be constant: they are available for this system as well as for a user of this system.

Parameter ref : Set.

In this section, quantities are just natural numbers (the general case for quantities is postponed to section 16.4.2). Indeed, the standard library of Coq defines the traditional operations on them, as well as a number of useful lemmas. This makes nat a good candidate for the type of quantities:

Definition quant := nat.

Now we can express a stock as an inhabitant of ref → quant. The operation invoice takes such a function s, and it returns a function that, given a reference r, yields $s(r)$ except for one reference – the ordered reference. To this effect we clearly need a computable function for testing whether two elements of ref are equal or not. We call a type endowed with such a function a *separable* type. For instance, finite types such as status and bool are separable; nat is also separable, though it is infinite; but functional types over infinite sets (even separable) such as nat → bool are not separable. Formally, we say that a type A is separable if:

$$\forall xy : A, \{x = y\} + \{\neg x = y\},$$

which reads as follows: for all x and y of type A, we can compute an inhabitant of $\{x = y\} + \{\neg x = y\}$, that is a Boolean whose value is true if $x = y$ and false if $\neg x = y$. Sep is then defined as the type of separable sets.

Given a separable type A, a type B, a function f from A to B, a value a in A and a value b in B, we can define the function f' of type $A \rightarrow B$ such that $f'(a_0) = f(a_0)$ if $a_0 \neq a$ and $f(a_0) = b$ if $a_0 = a$. As functions are first class objects, it is easy to define a (higher order) function assign which, applied to f, a and b (A and B are then implicit), yields f'.

To sum up, we need to assume a type ref and to ensure that it is separable.

Question 9: Should we specify identifiers for orders?

Answer: Using Coq we do not need to build up an order identification system; we can let orders be an abstract type and work directly with it.

We must avoid a pitfall: formalizing an order by a triple $\langle r, q, s\rangle$, where r is a reference, q a quantity and s a status is not satisfactory, because we do not necessarily want to confuse two different orders with the same components! We could try to identify orders in some way, but how?

Question 10: What is the space of all possible orders?

Answer: We are not given size limit or other properties for the set of orders. We make as few assumptions as possible in order to fit the text: orders is just a separable set.

16.3.2 State and operation

Now we can define a type for the states (of the world) we consider. It is just a mathematical structure composed of a stock, a set of orders and information saying that each order has one and only one reference, quantity and status. We know that functions are just the ticket for the latter requirements. The type of orders must be separable, because the operation invoice will change status_of_ord in the same way as stock:

```
Record state : Type := mkstate {
  stock : ref → quant ;
  orders : Sep ;
  ref_of_ord : orders → ref ;
  quant_of_ord : orders → quant ;
  status_of_ord : orders → status }.
```

It is actually just syntactic sugar for an inductive type with one constructor (mkstate here) and related projections (stock, order, ref_of_ord, etc.). For instance, if st is a state, stock st yields the stock in state st (Coq uses the notation f x y for applying a function to arguments).

16.3.3 Operation "invoice"

Each operation is modeled by a function that takes an initial state, additional arguments (e.g. an order) and required properties on them, and returns a new state. Then, for each operation, we have to ask "what is the initial state?", "what are the possible values for arguments", etc. In the sequel we make such questions explicit only when the answer is not clearly stated in the text. The first of them concerns the new state returned by invoice.

Question 11: Does invoicing an order affect the stock?

Answer: This operation could change the state only by changing the status of the order, or it could also have side effects on the stock by withdrawing the ordered quantity. We consider the latter: the ordered product is not available from the stock after invoicing.

This prevents the system invoicing twice the same instance of a product. Moreover, invoice seems to be the only operation considered in "case 1", so we decide it is up to this operation to maintain the stock consistently with relation to invoiced orders. This point is also raised when we specify operations using a preservation principle.

Question 12: What is the precondition of the invoicing operation?

Answer: It is easy to show that in order to respect the preservation principle, the ordered quantity of product should be in stock when we attempt to deliver it: on non-negative numbers, $x - a + a$ is equal to x only if $a \leq x$; this is exactly the precondition formalized below on invoice.

Given a state st and an order o in st, we have to specify the quantity q of ordered product remaining in stock after invoicing. By the preservation principle mentioned above, q is a quantity such that q, added to the ordered quantity quant_of_ord st o, yields the quantity in stock just before invoicing stock st (ref_of_ord st o). We can use the type of elements x of A such that $P\ x$, which is denoted by $\{x : A \mid P\ x\}$, with suitable x, A and P:

$$\{\ \mathsf{q{:}quant} \mid \mathsf{q} + (\mathsf{quant\_of\_ord\ st\ o}) = \mathsf{stock\ st\ (ref\_of\_ord\ st\ o)}\}.$$

Let us denote this type simply by spec_remains st o. Therefore we define a function with two arguments st and o, using the following notation:

Definition spec_remains (st:state) (o: orders st) :=
{ q:quant | q + (quant_of_ord st o) = stock st (ref_of_ord st o)}.

Assume a function remains taking as arguments a state st, an order o (in st) satisfying a suitable precondition (see below) and yielding a result of type spec_remains st o. The type of remains is more precisely[1,2]:

∀ (st:state) (o:orders st),
quant_of_ord st o ≤ stock st (ref_of_ord st o) → spec_remains st o.

The operation invoice is then simply specified by:

[1] Let A and B be two types, then $A \to B$ is the type of functions from A to B. We may want to give a name to the argument (not only to its type): then we use the notation $\forall a : A, B$ instead of $A \to B$. This is especially useful if B is itself an expression depending on a. In the example considered here, the type of the second argument depends on the first, the type of the third and the type of the result depend on the two first arguments.

[2] The type of the third argument is a proposition. This means that the function should be applied to a state, an order, and a *proof* of the precondition: in Coq proofs are also considered as objects; this is why the syntax is uniform. But we can simply interpret $\forall a : A, P\ a \to B$ as the type of functions taking an argument a of A such that $P\ a$ and returning an element of B.

```
Definition invoice (st:state) (o:orders st) :
   (status_of_ord st o)=pending →
   (quant_of_ord st o) ≤ (stock st (ref_of_ord st o))
 → state :=
 fun pre1 pre2 ⇒
 (mkstate
    (assign (stock st) (ref_of_ord st o) (pr1 (remains st o pre2)))
    (order st)
    (ref_of_ord st)
    (quant_of_ord st)
    (assign (status_of_ord st) o invoiced) ).
```

The part of this expression before := is the type of invoice; the second, the content of the definition, exhibits an inhabitant of this type.

We have to explain the role of the function pr1. The type $\{x : A \mid P\ x\}$ is not a subtype of A, it is an inductive type with one constructor taking two arguments, an x of A and a proof of $P\ x$. When we apply the projection pr1 to an element of this type, we get the underlying element of type A (in our case, A is quant), satisfying the predicate P. Thanks to the definition of spec_remains above, the value of q returned by the function remains is:

stock st (ref_of_ord st o) - quant_of_ord st o.

We forbid negative values for quantities, therefore, we need the precondition:

quant_of_ord st o ≤ stock st (ref_of_ord st o)

in order to prove that q does satisfy the equality specified in spec_remains. This explains why the function remains has an argument for this precondition.

16.4 A specification for case 2

16.4.1 Using general operations over sets

In case 1, the set of orders and the stock were considered as constants, but including operations such as adding orders, adding quantities in stock, etc., leads us to consider more advanced features of Coq.

We could introduce a set orders representing the set of all possible orders – including non-existent ones – at a given state. Instead, we make explicit the assumption that we can always find a fresh order. More precisely, given a (separable) Set A, we assume that we can get a new (separable) type add_fresh_elt A which is A extended with a new element. We also assume that given a type B, a function f from A to B and an element b of B, extend $f\ b$ is a function which extends f and which takes the value b on the fresh element. Similarly, we assume that we can remove an element from a type. Given a in A, rem_one_elt a is the type of inhabitants of A which are different to a. The function restrict $a\ f$ is the restriction of f to rem_one_elt a. The functions add_fresh_elt, extend, rem_one_elt and restrict can actually be constructed in type theory.

Now we can stick to the specification of state considered in section 16.3.2. The definition of invoice is the same as previously. The operation add_order has a very simple definition thanks to add_fresh_elt and extend:

```
Definition add_order : state → ref → quant
→ state :=
 fun st r q ⇒
 (mkstate
   (stock st)
   (add_fresh_elt (orders st))
   (extend (ref_of_ord st) r)
   (extend (quant_of_ord st) q)
   (extend (status_of_ord st) pending) ).
```

We rely on the mathematical possibility to enrich a type with an additional abstract element. Note that it implies that the set of orders can become arbitrarily large. This deserves a discussion that we postpone to the refinement step.

An interesting point is that *the type discipline prevents us from defining* add_order *without asking what is the status of the new order*. Here, it is just impossible to reuse the old value of status_of_ord because the *type* of this function is not the same in the new state: its domain is add_fresh_elt (orders st) instead of orders st. And, as $A \rightarrow B$ is the type of *total* functions from A to B, we are obliged to declare what is the value returned by the function on the fresh element. Of course the best way to do this is to use a higher order function defined once for all, extend. This is yet another illustration of the interest of abstract (higher order) devices.

Question 13: What is the initial status of a new order?

Answer: We consider that the initial status is pending.

This is to be confirmed by the customer. The definition of cancel_order is in the same spirit.

Question 14: Can invoiced orders be canceled?

Answer: In real life, an order is usually invoiced only after the ordered product has been delivered, and the action, by a buyer, of giving back an ordered product and getting a refund is not called "canceling an order". So we decided that invoiced orders could not be canceled:

```
Definition cancel_order (st:state) (o: orders st) :
 status_of_ord st o = pending  →  state :=
 fun pre ⇒
 (mkstate
```

```
(stock st)
(rem_one_elt o)
(restrict (ref_of_ord st))
(restrict (quant_of_ord st))
(restrict (status_of_ord st)) ).
```

In the specification of add_in_stock, it is enough to consider that only one product is entered at a time:

```
Definition add_in_stock (st:state) (r:ref) : quant r
→ state :=
 fun q ⇒
 (mkstate
   (assign (stock st) (ref_of_ord st o) (stock st r + q))
   (orders st)
   (ref_of_ord st)
   (quant_of_ord st)
   (status_of_ord st) ).
```

16.4.2 Reference-dependent measure systems

In this section we show how to define measure systems and attach a measure system to each reference in stock, as suggested in section 16.2.3. Dependent types come naturally into the picture.

The first step is to define a structure for order relations[3]:

```
Section def_ord_rel.
 Variable A : Set.
 Record ord_rel : Type := mkord {
  Leq :> A → A → Prop ;
  refl : reflexive Leq ;
  antisym : antisymmetric Leq ;
  trans : transitive Leq       }.
End def_ord_rel.
```

Prop is the type of propositions. When a section is closed, all variables are abstracted: the type of ord_rel is Set →Type when def_ord_rel is closed. The symbol :> declares Leq as a coercion. Given a set A and an object R of type ord_rel A, R can be considered right away as a relation over A.

The above piece of specification shows how properties and distinguished elements can be attached to a mathematical structure inside a record-like object. In order to mimic usual mathematical practice ("let A be a set endowed with ...") the same name

[3]Logical implication between propositions is denoted by →. The same symbol is used for functional types. The reason is that proofs are considered as objects (see Footnote 2 and [COQ 04]). Similarly, we have seen that the typewriter notation for ∀s:A (P s) is forall s:A, P s.

is used for the underlying structure thanks to a coercion. Our notion of measure system is defined in the same way. It is a set endowed with an order relation, an addition, a subtraction and a neutral element:

```
Record measure : Type := mkmeas {
  base :> Set ;
  leq : ord_rel base ;
  add : base → base → base ;
  subtract : base → base → base ;
  zero : base;
  add_sub : ∀x,y:base, leq x y → add (subtract y x) x = y ;
  zero_min : ∀x:base, leq zero x ;
  neutral_r : ∀x:base, add x zero = x ;
  neutral_l : ∀x:base, add zero x = x          }.
```

Again, base is a coercion: an object with type measure can be seen as a Set.

It is important to check that we are building a consistent theory. Whenever we specify a mathematical structure, we should be able to find an inhabitant of this structure. This is straightforward here, using nat for base and $\leq$ for Leq.

We can now specify states and operations according to these dependent quantities. We declare a measure system for each reference:

```
Variable quant : ref → measure.
```

Now we adapt the definition of state introduced in section 16.3.2. We just have to provide the right argument for quant in function of adequate parameters:

```
Record state : Type := mkstate      {
  stock : ∀r:ref, quant r ;
  orders : Sep ;
  ref_of_ord : orders → ref ;
  quant_of_ord : ∀o:orders,  quant (ref_of_ord o) ;
  status_of_ord : orders → status  }.
```

Let us explain ∀r:ref, quant r; previously, stock had type ref→quant, meaning "to every reference, we associate a quantity". Here, the type means "to every reference, we associate a quantity in the measure system associated to this reference". The use of dependent types requires generalizing functions such as extend.

A quantity may be equal to zero. In the stock, this means that no product for the considered reference is available. But what does it mean for operations?

Question 15: Is it possible to order or add in stock a null quantity of a reference?

Answer: In real life this is usually not the case, but we have decided that it is.

The reason is that the specification is simpler that way, (there is no additional precondition for add_in_stock and add_order) but the final decision is up to the customer. It is a typical question that can hardly be seen on an informal specification, but arises during formalization.

```
Definition add_order : state → ∀r:ref, quant r → state :=
  fun st r q ⇒
  (mkstate
     (stock st)
     (add_fresh_elt (orders st))
     (extend (ref_of_ord st) r)
     (extend_q (quant_of_ord st) q)
     (extend (status_of_ord st) pending)      ).
```

16.5 Experimenting with the specification

16.5.1 Refining

The above specification, though very abstract, can be made executable. We consider it an important step from a methodological standpoint, as it helps us to see the behavior of our specification in particular cases, thus it may reveal errors in types definition, forgotten preconditions... and it often turns out very useful for providing scenarios to be discussed. The purpose of this section is to show how we can, to some extent, turn a specification into a prototype. Assumptions made in the sequel are not drawn from the text; they are our own, and are intended to serve as examples to be discussed with the customer. Refinement is based on case 2 with reference-dependent measure systems.

We need a system for naming orders: recall that in the above specification, the type of orders depends on the state. This proves useful in the specification, but naming instances of such orders becomes quite heavy. Moreover, orders are considered as an internal notion of the system. In real life, users handle orders using an identifier – let us call it a *key* – , and after all keys should not be confused with the orders they represent. Then, we will use a state-independent set of keys, in bijection with the state-dependent set of orders. A key is used to name an order: in operations, arguments of type order will then be replaced by arguments of type key. The actual type of keys should actually be decided with the customer. Our only requirement is that it is separable (two keys can be distinguished by computational means). We need to define the first key to be used and a way for computing a new key on request. Though it is quite easy to leave the type of keys as a parameter, there is little point in doing so and we readily implement keys by natural numbers. However, they are used in an abstract way in the sequel, using first_key, new_key and the function for testing equality on keys. The lemma eq_nat_dec, from the Coq library, states that nat is separable:

```
Definition key := mkSep eq_nat_dec.
Definition first_key : key := O.
```

Definition new_key : key→ key := S. (* successor *)

Then we define a type of states "able to communicate" (using keys) as an extension of states defined in section 16.4.2. Note that the new structure is constrained by predicates (they are invariants of the states we consider):

```
Record state_pub : Type := mksp{
  underlying_state :> state ;
  next_key : key ;
  key_of_ord : orders underlying_state → key ;
  ord_of_key : key → option (orders underlying_state) ;
  key_max : ∀o: orders underlying_state, key_of_ord o < next_key ;
  ord_key_ord : is_left_inverse  key_of_ord  ord_of_key }.
```

This state is "public": it offers a user interface thanks to the keys. Keys can be associated to orders, or to a special element not in orders: this is why ord_of_key is defined in option (orders underlying_state), instead of orders underlying_state. A key associated to this special element may thus be freely associated to an order.

The main invariant is key_of_ord. The predicate is_left_inverse means that key_of_ord and ord_of_key are inverse functions, i.e. key_of_ord is injective: one and only one key is associated to each order. We say that a key is good (predicate good_key) if an order is associated with it. Indeed, in the initial state where no order has been added, keys are associated to no order – no key is good; when adding a fresh order, a key associated to no order is chosen (using new_order) and becomes good; when an order is canceled, the key associated to it becomes not good – it is no longer associated to an order.

Operations are defined interactively: we show that we can construct an inhabitant of state_pub by applying (command apply in interactive proof mode) mksp, the state_pub type constructor to the result of the corresponding operations on states and to appropriate values for the key system, and by proving that invariants key_max and ord_key_ord are actually preserved. For instance, invoicing consists of applying invoice to the underlying state, leaving the set of keys unchanged.

```
Definition invoice_pub (sp:state_pub) (k:key) (g: good_key sp k),
    status_of_ord sp (retrieve g) = pending  →
    quant_of_ord sp (retrieve g) ≤ stock sp (ref_of_ord sp (retrieve g))
  → state_pub.
intros sp k g pre1 pre2.
apply (mksp  (invoice pre1 pre2) (next_key sp) (key_of_ord sp)
            (ord_of_key sp)).
  (* proofs of invariants... *)
Defined.
```

The functions cancel_order_pub and add_in_stock_pub are defined in the same way. The operation add_order_pub is slightly more complicated, because we want it to return the new state *with* the key of the new order (and a proof that this key is good). The type of the intended result is:

```
Record state_and_key : Type := mksk{
    sp_sk : state_pub ;
    k_sk :  key ;
    gk_sk : good_key sp_sk k_sk }.
```

Then we define the order-adding operation in two steps. First, we define add_order_pub_aux in the same way as other operations:

```
Definition add_order_pub_aux:
     state_pub → (r:ref)(quant r) → state_pub.
intros sp r q. apply (mksp (add_order sp q)
          (new_key (next_key sp))
          (extend (key_of_ord sp) (next_key sp))
          (refresh_add_new_opt (next_key sp) (ord_of_key sp)) ).
  (* proofs of invariants... *)
```

Then we define the three components of add_order_pub sp r q as, respectively, add_order_pub_aux sp q, next_key sp and a proof that the latter is a good key (to this effect, we provide the appropriate witnessing order; the remaining proof is found automatically):

```
Definition add_order_pub :
  state_pub → (r:ref)(quant r) → state_and_key.
  intros sp r q.
  exists (add_order_pub_aux sp q) (next_key sp).
  exists (fresh_elt (orders sp)); auto.
Defined.
```

As goodness is required on keys occurring as arguments of some operations, we also prove that each operation preserves the goodness of keys.

16.6 Running an example

Now we can produce various scenarios for the intended application. Our interface is the interactive Coq toplevel, which provides us with particular type-checking information and performs reductions (i.e. computations).

Consider a store selling a finite set Ref of products comprised of potatoes, oil and kiwis: each reference is associated to a unit of measure (respectively kilos, gallons and pieces); we use simply integers for them:

```
Definition quant (r: Ref) : measure :=
  Cases r of potatoes ⇒ kilos | oil ⇒ gallons | kiwis ⇒ pieces end.
```

Our initial state is empty:

```
Definition null (r: Ref) := zero (quant r).
Definition init_state_pub : state :=
```

```
(mkstate null empty_sep
        (f_empty ref) (f_empty_f quant (f_empty ref))(f_empty status) ).
Definition Init_state := init_state_pub quant.
```

We can now perform a transition, which adds an order for two gallons of oil:

```
Definition sk1 := add_order_pub Init_state (qt_of (2) oil).
Definition s1 := sp_sk sk1.
Definition ks1 := k_sk sk1.
```

The state sk1 has type state_and_key quant. The state we will consider afterwards is s1, the underlying state from sk1. The key of this order is ks1. We check that the goodness of keys is preserved:

```
Lemma~g1_1~: good_key s1 ks1.
```

We can perform reductions in order to check, interactively, the status of the order:

```
Coq < Eval compute in (Status_of_ord (retrieve g1_1)).
   = pending : status
```

16.7 Rephrasing the text

From our analysis and first attempt of specification, we can rephrase the text more precisely than the original one.

We are given orders, references to products and a notion of quantity for each reference. Quantities for the same reference can be added, subtracted and compared using an order relation, informally denoted by "less than or equal to". Quantities are also endowed with a zero, such that adding zero to any quantity yields the same quantity; zero is less than or equal to any quantity.

Orders have the following properties: each order has one and only one reference, one and only one quantity for this reference and one and only one status, which can be pending or invoiced.

We are also given a stock, which defines, for each reference, one and only one quantity. When this quantity is equal to zero, it means that no product is available for the considered reference in the physical stock.

We have to specify a system whose state is defined by the knowledge of the stock and of the set of orders. This state evolves through the following operations:

invoice: given an order whose status is pending and such that the ordered quantity is less than or equal to the quantity in stock, its status is changed to invoiced and the quantity in stock is updated in a way such that the total quantity remains invariant: adding the ordered quantity to the new quantity in stock yields the quantity in stock before invoicing.

add_order: given a reference r and a quantity q, a new order o is added; the reference corresponding to o is r, the quantity corresponding to o is q and the status of o is pending.

cancel_order: given an order whose status is pending, this order is discarded in the new state.
add_in_stock: given a reference and a quantity, the stock is updated by adding this quantity to the one in stock for that reference.

case 1: consider only invoice.
case 2: consider all operations.

16.8 Conclusion

The ability of Coq to describe new (and potentially arbitrarily complex) *ad hoc* theories proves useful, for instance, when formalizing abstract notions of quantities and of keys. Note also that the abstract view of orders developed here leads us to a clear separation between orders and their names, giving us the opportunity to ask questions about the space of possible orders.

Type theory has also specific interests. Some properties can be automatically checked in this way, e.g. existence and unicity of the status of a given order for relations such as status_of_ord. More surprisingly, type theory can force us to be complete in some sense: in section 16.4, we cannot escape the question of the initial value of the status of a new order.

We consider it important to state (and prove) theorems about the specification, in order to check that our specification has better chances of making sense. Here, we take care to ensure that specified objects do exist, at least from a mathematical point of view. This is illustrated in the proof that natural numbers satisfy the properties we require on abstract quantities.

A further tool for checking that a specification is the intended one is prototyping. The computational features of Coq can be used to this effect, to some extent. The next step in this direction would be to use program extraction as provided by Coq, yielding a program which is correct by construction.

As a last interesting methodological point, note that a preservation of matter principle helps us to express the pre- and post-conditions for invoice.

Bibliography

[ABR 96] Abrial J.-R. *The B-Book.* Cambridge University Press, 1996

[BER 04] Bertot I., Castéran P. *Interactive Theorem Proving and Program Development; Coq'Art: The Calculus of Inductive Constructions.* Texts in Theoretical Computer Science. An EATCS Series, XXV, 469 p., Springer Verlag, 2004, ISBN: 3-540-20854-2

[COQ 04] The Coq Development Team *The Coq Proof Assistant Reference Manual. Version 8.0.* INRIA, December 2004

[BID 91] Bidoit M., Kreowski H.-J., Lescanne P., Orejas F., Sanella D. (Eds.) *Algebraic System Specification and Development, a Survey and Annotated Bibliography.* Volume 501 of *LNCS*, Springer Verlag, 1991

[HEY 96] Heyd B., Crégut P. "A modular coding of Unity in Coq". In von Wright J., Grundy J., Harrison J (Eds.) *Theorem Proving in Higher Order Logic*. Volume 1125 of *LNCS*, Springer Verlag, 251–266, 1996

[HUE 04] Huet G., Kahn G., Paulin-Mohring C. The Coq Proof Assistant, a Tutorial, Version 8.0. Technical report, INRIA, http://coq.inria.fr/doc/tutorial.html, 2004